Collins

science

FOR AQA GCSE
ADDITIONAL
SCIENCE

Ken Gadd SERIES EDITOR
Mary Jones
Aleks Jedrosz
Emma Poole
Lesley Owen
Louise Petheram
Charles Golabek
Edmund Walsh

William Collins' dream of knowledge for all began with the publication of his first book in 1819. A self-educated mill worker, he not only enriched millions of lives, but also founded a flourishing publishing house. Today, staying true to this spirit, Collins books are packed with inspiration, innovation and a practical expertise. They place you at the centre of a world of possibility and give you exactly what you need to explore it.

Collins. Freedom to teach.

Published by Collins
An imprint of HarperCollinsPublishers
77–85 Fulham Palace Road
Hammersmith
London
W6 8JB

Browse the complete Collins catalogue at
www.collinseducation.com

British Library Cataloguing in Publication Data. A Catalogue record for this publication is available from the British Library.

Commissioned by Kate Haywood and Cassandra Birmingham; Publishing Manager: Michael Cotter; Project Editor: Penny Fowler; Page make-up and picture research by Hart McLeod, Cambridge; Page make-up by eMC Design; Edited by: Anita Clark and Rosie Parrish; Internal design by JPD; Cover design by John Fordham; Cover artwork by Bob Lea; Exam questions written by Dr Martin Barker, Lesley Owen and Karen Nicola Thomas; Glossary written by Gareth Price; Illustrations by Peters and Zabransky, Bob Lea, Peter Cornwell, Stephen Elford (Lemonade Illustration), Pete Smith (Beehive Illustration) and Roger Wade-Walker (Beehive Illustration); Production by Natasha Buckland; Printed and bound by Printing Express, Hong Kong

Acknowledgements

p.3 ©John Mitchell/SPL, ©Suthep Kritsanavarin/Ap/Empics, ©Stuart Westmorland/Corbis, ©Royalty Free/Corbis, ©Seymour/SPL; p.6 ©Robert Brocksmith/SP, ©Andrew Mcclenaghan/SPL, ©Dr Jeremy Burgess/SPL, Slawomir Fajer/Istock.com; p.7 ©Prof. K.Seddon & Dr. T.Evans, Queen's University Belfast/SPL, ©Sinclair Stammers/SPL, ©ISM/SPL, ©Frances Twitty/istock.com; p.8 ©Perttu Sironen/istock.com, ©istock.com, ©Oleg Prikhodko/istock.com; p.9 ©Dave Huss/istock.com, ©Jack Schiffer/istock.com, ©Luis Carlos Torres/istock.com, ©istock.com; p.10 ©Peter Galbraith/istock.com, ©istock.com; p.11 ©2006 Jupiterimages, ©istock.com, ©Mark Garlick/SPL, ©Seymour/SPL; p.14 1 ©Russell Kightley/SPL, 3 ©Biophoto Associates/SPL, 5 ©Eleanor Jones; p.15 8 ©Biophoto Associates, 9 ©Prof. P. Motta/Dept of Anatomy/University "La Sapienza", Rome/SPL; p.16 1 ©Steve Gschmeissner/SPL; p.17 7 ©Alfred Pasieka/SPL; p.18 1 ©John Mitchell/SPL; p.20 1 ©Photofusion Picture Library/Alamy; p.21 6 ©Steve Gschmeissner/SPL; p.22 1 ©Voisin/Phanie/Rex Features; p.24 1 ©Damien Lovegrove/SPL; p.26 1 ©Vera Bogaerts/istock.com; p.27 5 ©Angelafoto/istock.com; p.28 1 ©DK Limited/Corbis, 3 ©Eye of Science/SPL; p.29 7 ©Eleanor Jones; p.30 1 ©Holt Studios International Ltd/Alamy; p.31 4 ©blickwinkel/Alamy; p.34 1 ©Royalty-Free/Corbis; p.35 6 ©David R. Frazier Photolibrary, Inc./Alamy; p.36 1 ©Tim Graham/Alamy, 2 ©Peter Chadwick/SPL, 3 ©Naturfoto Honal/Corbis; p.37 5 ©Blackout Concepts/Alamy; p.38 1 ©Bruce Coleman Inc./Alamy; p.39 4 ©ImageState/Alamy, 5 ©blickwinkel/Alamy; p.40 1 ©Agripicture Images/Alamy, 2 ©Peter Hulme; Ecoscene/Corbis; p.41 3 ©Elder Neville/Corbis Sygma, 4 ©David R. Frazier Photolibrary, Inc./Alamy, 5 ©Mary Jones, 6 ©Cordelia Molloy/SPL; p.42 1 ©David Joel/Stone/Getty Images, 2 ©Andre Jenny/Alamy; p.43 3 ©Hawkeye/Alamy, 4 ©H. Schmid/zefa/Corbis, 5 ©Treps Jean-Jacques/Corbis Sygma, 6 ©Jack Fields/Corbis; p.44 1 ©Silkeborg Museum, Denmark/Munoz-Yague/SPL, 2 ©Author pic; p.45 4 ©Penny Tweedie/Corbis, 5 ©Carlos Davila/Alamy, 6 ©Rob Barker; p.46 1 ©Jean Schweitzer/istock.com, 2 ©Michael Blackburn/istock.com; p.47 6 ©Stephen Frink Collection/Alamy; p.48 1 ©NASA, ©Joy Prescott/istock.com; p.49 4 ©NASA, 5 ©Georgette Douwma/SPL; p.50 1 ©Micha Fleuren/istock.com; p.51 3 Picture of the

Montmorency forest, located North of Quebec City (CANADA) Natural Resources Canada, Canadian Forest Service, Laurentian Forestry Centre, Photographer: Sébastien Dagnault; p.52 ©2006, Jupiterimages; p.53 ©2006 Jupiterimages; p.60 ©Biophoto Associates/SPL; p.62 1 ©Ed Young/Agstock/SPL, 3 ©Cordelia Molloy/SPL; p.64 1 ©Face To Face/Bildagentur Gmbh/Alamy, 2 ©Ariel Skelley/Corbis, 3 ©Comstock Images/Alamy; p.65 ©C/B Productions/Corbis; p.66 1 ©Steve Starr/Corbis, 2 ©ISM/SPL; p.67 3 ©Dr Ray Clark & Mervyn Goff/SPL, 5 ©Steve Gschmeissner/SPL; p.68 ©George Hall/Corbis; p.69 5 ©Alexis Rosenfeld/SPL; p.70 ©Tom Mchugh/SPL; p.73 ©Suthep Kritsanavarin/Ap/Empics; p.74 ©Jaimie D. Travis/istock.com; p.75 ©Adam Booth/istock.com; p.76 ©Dr Mark J. Winter/SPL; p.77 4 ©SPL, 5 ©James King-Holmes/SPL; p.78 ©Eye Of Science/SPL; p.79 3-8 ©Dr Bernard Lunaud/SPL, 9 ©M I Walker/Wellcome Photo Library; p.80 ©CNRI/SPL; p.81 ©CNRI/SPL; P.82 1 ©Professor Miodrag Stojkovic/SPL, 2 ©Andrew Leonard/SPL; P.84 1 ©SPL, 3 ©Dr Tim Evans/SPL; 4 ©A. Barrington Brown/SPL; p.85 ©Peter Menzel/SPL; p.86 ©James King-Holmes/Science Photo; p.87 9 l ©J.C. Revy/SPL, r ©Darwin Dale/SPL; p.88 1 ©Alexis Rosenfeld/SPL, 2 ©L. Willatt, East Anglian Regional Genetics, Service/SPL; p.89 4 both ©Dave Watts/Alamy, 5 ©M.P. O'Neill/SPL; p.90 ©Alon Brik/istock.com; p.91 ©Will & Deni Mcintyre/SPL; p.92 1 ©Alec Jeffreys/Wellcome Photo Library, 2 ©Science Source/SPL; p.93 4 ©Wellcome Library, London, 7 ©Victor Habbick Visions/SPL; p.96 ©Betrand Collet/istock.com; p.97 ©David Parker/SPL; p.100/101 ©Laguna Design/SPL; p.102 ©Dr Erwin Mueller/SPL; p.103 4 ©SPL, 5 ©Dane Wirtzfeld/ istock.com; p.104 1 ©Rob Sylvan/ istock.com, 2 ©Thomas Mounsey/ istock.com; p.105 ©Martin Pernter/ istock.com; p.107 ©Martin Adams/istock.com; p.108 ©Andrew Robinson/ istock.com; p.110 1 ©Lori Sparkia/istock.com, 2 l ©2006, JupiterImages, 2 r ©Donald Gruener/istock.com; p.112 ©Matt Meadows/SPL; p.113 ©Claude Nuridsany & Marie Perennou/SPL; p.114 ©George Argyropoulos/ istock.com; p.115 ©Ann Triling/istock.com; p.116 1 ©Getty Images News, 2 ©Gregory Wright/istock.com, 3 ©Nick Byrne/istock.com; p.117 ©Olga Kolpakov/ istock.com; p.118 ©Los Alamos National Laboratory/SPL; p.119 4 ©Diane Miller/ istock.com, 8 ©Amy Seagram/ istock.com, 9 ©Richard Lloyd/istock.com; p.120 1 ©Chris Bishop/istock.com, 2 ©Andrew Lambert Photography/SPL; p.121 5 ©Randy Kruzan/istock.com, 7 ©George Bernard/SPL; p.124 1 ©Dr M. A. Ansary/SPL, 2 ©Charles D. Winters/SPL, 3 „istock.com; p.125 „Nicholas Sutcliffe/ istock.ccom; p.126 1 & 3 Alfred Pasieka/SPL, 3 ©Alfred Pasieka/SPL; p.127 4 ©2006, JupiterImages, 5 ©istock.com, 6 „Nick Mather/istock.com, 7 ©Kenn Wislander/istock.com; p.128 1 ©Stuart Westmorland/Corbis, 2 ©Tan Kian Khoon/istock.com; p.129 3 ©Cordelia Molloy/SPL; p.130 1 „Bojan Tezak/ istock.com; p.131 4 „Johanna Goodyear/ istock.com; p.132 1 „David Asch/ istock.com; p.133 „Peter Clark/ istock.com; p.134 1 „Charlotte Townsend/ istock.com, 3 ©Richard Gunion/istock.com, 4 „Terry Wilson/ istock.com; p.136 „Jeffrey Hochstrasser/ istock.com; p.137 ©AVTG/istock.com; p.138 1 ©Rob Barker; p.139 3 „ istock.com, 4 ©Andrew Lambert Photography/SPL, 5 ©Holt Studios International Ltd/Alamy; p.140 „Michael la-Cour/ istock.com; p.142 „David Broadway/ istock.com; p.144 ©Donald Gruener/istock.com, ©Michael la-Cour/istock.com; p.145 ©Randy Kruzan/istock.com; p.148/149 ©Alexis Rosenfeld/SPL; p.150 1 ©Shaun Lowe/istock.com, 2 ©Mark Bond/istock.com; p.152 1 ©Betina Richardt/istock.com, c l ©Lesley Owen; p.154 ©LaHeather/istock.com; p.156 ©Kenneth C. Zirkel/istock.com; p.157 ©Andrei Tchernov/istock.com; p.158 ©Martyn F. Chillmaid/SPL; p.160 1 ©2006, JupiterImages, 2 ©Lesley Owen; p.162 ©Baldur Tryggvason/istock.com; p.163 3 ©Stuart Blyth/istock.com, 4 ©Sabine Freyer/istock.com; p.164 1 ©Jacob Jenson/istock.com, 3 ©Juergen Sack/istock.com; p.165 6 ©iwka/istock.com; p.166 ©Lesley Owen; p.170 1 ©Nicola Stratford/istock.com, 2 ©Austrian Archives/Corbis; p.172 1 & 2 ©2006, JupiterImages; p.176 ©Damon Davison/istock.com; p.178 ©Lesley Owen; p.179 ©Lesley Owen; p.182 ©Donald Gruener/istock.com; p.184 ©2006, JupiterImages; p.186 ©istock.com; p.187 3 ©2006, JupiterImages, 4 ©Lesley Owen; p.189 ©Nicolas Metivier/istock.com; p.192/193 ©TRL Ltd/SPL; p.196 ©JupiterImages.com; p.198 ©2006, JupiterImages; p.200 ©Bradley Mason/istock.com; p.202 ©2006, 2006, JupiterImages; p.203 ©NASA/JPL/Cornell/Science Photo Library; p.204 ©2006, JupiterImages; p.206 ©AFP/GettyImages; p.207 ©Royalty Free/Corbis; p.208 1 ©2006, JupiterImages, 2 ©Luis Carlos Torres/istock.com; p.209 ©Joseph Sohm; ChromoSohm Inc./Corbis; p.210 ©Jeff Morgan/Alamy; p.211 3 ©Leigh Karchner/istock.com, 5 ©Jocelyn Lin/istock.com; p.212 ©T. Ranger/istock.com; p.213 3 ©Photo Dassault-Breguet/SPL, 4 ©Darren Bramley/istock.com; p.216 ©T A Crafts/istock.com; p.217 ©2006, JupiterImages; p.218 ©Joe Gough/istock.com; p.220 ©Tony Tremblay/istock.com; p.221 ©Popperfoto/Alamy; p.222 ©John Setzler/istock.com; p.223 4 ©Ayaaz Rattansi/istock.com, 6 ©Henning Dalhoff/Bonnier Publications/SPL; p.224 ©Alex Livesey/Getty Images; p.227 ©David Taylor/SPL; p.230 ©Mike Goldwater/Alamy; p.231 ©Roman Krochuk/istock.com; p.232 ©Hulton Archive/Getty Images; p.234 ©Giles Angel/istock.com; p.236 ©Steve Kaufman/istock.com; p.242 t l ©Volker Steger/SPL, b l ©Gusto/ SPL, t c ©Ton Kinsbergen/Scien SPL, b c ©Martyn F. Chillmaid/ SPL, t r ©Gusto/ SPL, b r ©Tek Image/ SPL; p.244 ©SPL; p.245 2 ©Martin Bond/ SPL, 3 l ©Lawrence Lawry/Sci SPL, r ©Susumu Nishinaga/ SPL, 3 ©Jerry Mason/ SPL; p.246 ©Sheila Terry/ SPL; p.248 ©Martin Bond/ SPL; p.249 6 ©Martyn F. Chillmaid/ SPL, 7 ©Andrew Lambert Photography/Sci SPL, 8 ©Kati Neudert/istock.com; p.250 ©Mike Bentley/istock.com; p.254 ©Sheila Terry/ SPL; p.255 ©Sheila Terry/ SPL; p.256 1, ©Gusto/ SPL, 3 ©Gusto/ SPL; p.257 ©Andrew Lambert Photography/ SPL; p.260 1 ©Martin Adams/istock.com, 2 ©Andrew Lambert Photography/ SPL; p.261 3 ©Sheila Terry/ SPL, 4 & 5 ©Sheila Terry/SPL; p.262 ©Andrew Lambert Photography/ SPL; p.264 © SPL; p.265 3 ©Tony Craddock/ SPL, 5 ©C. Powell, P. Fowler & D. Perkins/ SPL; p.266 ©Igor Kostin/Corbis; p.269 ©Martin Bond/SPL; p.270 © SPL; p.273 3 ©US Department of Energy/ SPL; p.276 1 ©2006, JupiterImages, 2 ©Seymour/ SPL; p.277 3 ©Mark Garlick/ SPL, 4 ©EFDA-JET/ SPL, 5 ©US Department of Energy/ SPL; p.278 ©Perry Kroll/istock.com, ©2006, JupiterImages; p.279 ©Peter Menzel/SPL; p.283 ©Anita Patterson/istock.com; p.285 ©Roger Harris/SPL; p.287 ©Tom Gillman/istock.com; Glossary pictures: ©George Ranalli/SPL, ©Dr Jeremy Burgess/SPL, ©Dr Kari Lounatmaa/SPL

Contents

PAGE 18

He smells out a mate.

PAGE 73

Quite a catch!

PAGE 128

Watch him glow!

PAGE 207

Is it a bird? Is it a plane?

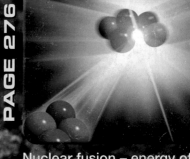

PAGE 276

Nuclear fusion – energy of the future?

Welcome to Collins GCSE Science!

This book aims to give you a fascinating insight into contemporary science that is relevant and useful to you, right now today. We have written it to convey the excitement of Biology, Chemistry and Physics, and hope it will help you to carry a knowledge and understanding of science and scientific thinking with you throughout life.

USING THIS BOOK

What you should know

Think back to what you have already learnt for GCSE Science. You need to remember and understand this work as your teacher will now develop it, explaining things in more detail. We've summarised what you should know for each main section: biology, chemistry and physics.

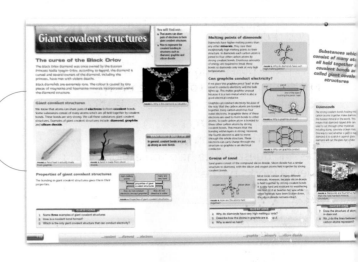

Unit opener

There are six units: two biology, two chemistry and two physics. Each begins with an image showing just some of the exciting science you will learn about. Also listed on this page are the spreads you will work through in the unit.

Main content

Each of the six units is made up of approximately 18 double page spreads. These tell you all you need to know. As you read through a spread you will start with some basic ideas and be guided to a more detailed understanding of the science. There are also questions for you to check your progress.

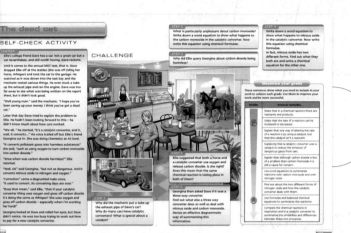

Mid-unit assessment

These give you opportunities to see how you are getting on. There are assessments for you to learn from. Each gives you a mini-case study to read, think about and then answer some questions.

Unit summary

Key facts and ideas, and the links between them, are summarised in spider diagrams. A really useful way of revising is to make your own concept maps. The diagrams are a good starting point for doing this. There is a quiz for you to try and an activity as well.

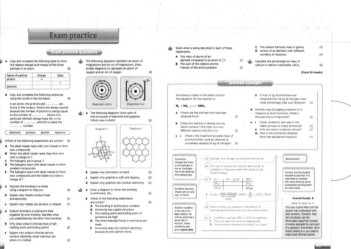

Exam practice

Once you've learned the science you have to show in an exam what you know and can do. Exam technique helps. It's important to be clear about what the examiner is looking for. It's also important to give your answer as clearly as possible. So we've provided you with some practice questions.

How Science Works

Scientists make observations and measurements. They try to make sense of these data and use them to develop scientific ideas. They design and carry out investigations. This section gives you some activities and questions to help you explore how science works further.

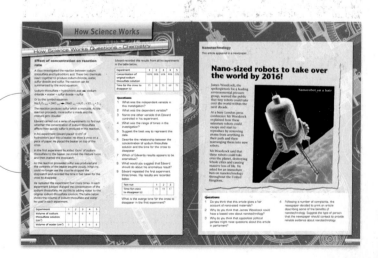

Cells

Animal cells and plant cells always have cytoplasm, a cell membrane and –usually – a nucleus. In addition, all plant cells have a cell wall and some plant cells 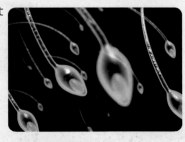 also have chloroplasts and a large vacuole containing cell sap. Each of these structures has a particular role to play in the activities of the cell.

Many of the cells in an animal or a plant are specialised to carry out particular functions. They have special structural features that help them to perform their roles.

1   What is the function of the nucleus in a cell?
2   What is the function of a sperm cell? How is a sperm cell adapted for its function?
3   What is the function of a root hair cell? How is a root hair cell adapted for its function?

Movement in and out of cells

Particles in a liquid or a gas are in constant motion, moving around randomly. Over time, they tend to move so that they are approximately evenly spread out  throughout the volume that they occupy. This is called diffusion.

Substances can enter and leave cells by diffusion through cell membranes. This is how cells get the oxygen they need for respiration, and lose the carbon dioxide that they produce.

4   Sugar is a solid. Do its particles move freely, or just vibrate on the spot, or not move at all? Do you think that sugar can diffuse?
5   When sugar dissolves in water, what happens to the sugar particles? Would the sugar particles be able to diffuse?

Photosynthesis

Plants make their own food by photosynthesis. They take carbon dioxide from the air and water from the soil. Energy in 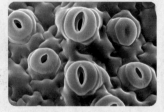 sunlight, captured by chlorophyll, is used to combine these two substances and form glucose. Oxygen is also formed, as a waste product.

Most photosynthesis happens in leaves. The cells in the palisade layer of the leaf are adapted for photosynthesis by having many chloroplasts containing a lot of chlorophyll. The whole leaf is also adapted for photosynthesis, by being very thin and having tiny air holes in its lower surface that let carbon dioxide and oxygen diffuse into and out of the leaf.

6   Write down the word equation for photosynthesis.
7   What is the approximate concentration of carbon dioxide in the air?

Food chains and cycles

Animals get their energy from the food that they eat. We can show how energy passes from one organism to another by drawing food chains, in which arrows show the direction of energy flow. Food chains always start with plants.

Whenever energy is transformed or transferred, some is lost to the environment.

Many of the molecules that make up the bodies of living organisms contain carbon. Plants take carbon dioxide from the air and use it to make carbohydrates and other substances. The carbon atoms are passed from one organism to another along a food chain. Some of them are released into the air as carbon dioxide, in respiration.

8   Write down a food chain with four links in it.
9   Write down the word equation for respiration.
10 Which kinds of living organisms respire?

Digestive enzymes and what they do

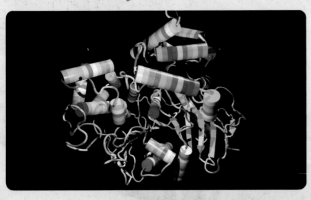

Digestive enzymes break down the food that we eat. Large molecules are broken down to smaller ones so that they can be absorbed into the blood system. We need food because it gives us energy as well as raw materials for growth and repair,

11 What job do digestive enzymes do?
12 Give three reasons why we need food.

Breathing and our lungs

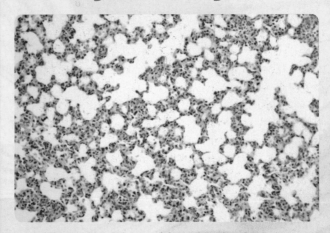

Our lungs are important in keeping us alive. Breathing in provides us with the oxygen we need so that energy can be released from food. Breathing out removes carbon dioxide and some water, which are waste products of respiration.

13 Why do we need oxygen?
14 What waste gas do we breathe out?

Getting energy from food

Aerobic respiration is the process that uses oxygen to release energy from the food we eat. The equation for respiration is:

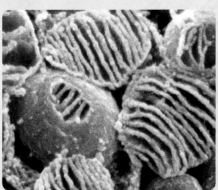

| glucose + oxygen | respiration → | carbon dioxide + water + energy |

We need the energy to do things.

15 What does *aerobic* mean?
16 What are the waste products of respiration?

Inheritance

Organisms show differences between them because of the features they have inherited as well as environmental factors. Sometimes the differences between individuals are great enough to place organisms into different groups – different species. Members of the same species are not all identical; these differences are called variation.

17 Think of a feature that could be used to put two organisms into different species.
18 List two features that show variation within a species.

Atoms

Elements are made of just one type of atom. There are only about one hundred different elements. In compounds the atoms of two (or more) elements are chemically combined. Atoms can join together to form compounds by giving, taking or sharing electrons to form chemical bonds. The properties of compounds are different from those of the elements from which they are made.

1   What is special about an element?
2   How can atoms join together to form compounds?

Metals

Metals have special properties which make them very useful materials. In fact, most machines are made from metals. They are hard and strong, and also good electrical and thermal conductors. Although a few metals like gold can be found as nuggets, most have to be extracted from their compounds which are called ores. Metals like iron, titanium and copper are extracted by chemical reactions; others like aluminium are extracted by electrolysis. Metals can be mixed together to form alloys.

3   How is aluminium extracted from its ore?
4   What is an alloy?

The periodic table

Elements can be represented by a unique one or two letter code called a symbol. For example, the metal magnesium has the symbol Mg. The elements are often displayed in the periodic table, with those elements with similar properties placed close to each other.

5   Which element has the symbol Cu?
6   What is the name of the element with the symbol K?

Equations

Chemical reactions can be summed up using word equations, which show the reactants used and the products formed. For example, when the element carbon is burnt, the compound carbon dioxide is formed:

carbon + oxygen → carbon dioxide.

The formula of a compound shows the type and ratio of the atoms in the compound. For example, calcium carbonate has the formula $CaCO_3$, which shows that it contains calcium, carbon and oxygen atoms in the ratio 1:1:3. Compounds always contain the same elements in the same proportions.

Symbol equations can also be used to sum up what happens in chemical reactions.

7   Carbon monoxide has the formula CO. What is the type and ratio of the atoms it contains?
8   Magnesium carbonate has the formula $MgCO_3$. What is the type and ratio of the atoms it contains?

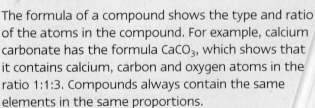

The pH scale

pH numbers indicate how acidic or alkaline a solution is. Neutral solutions like water have a pH of 7; acidic solutions have a pH below 7, and alkaline solutions have a pH above 7. Adding water to an acid or an alkali dilutes it and so makes it less hazardous. Universal indicator gives a range of colours in acidic and alkaline solutions, allowing comparison of the acidity and alkalinity of different solutions. Strong acids have a pH of 1 and weak acids have a pH above 1 but under 7; strong alkalis have a pH of 14 and weak alkalis have a pH below 14 but over 7. Strong acids and alkalis may be corrosive.

9 What is the pH of:
a) a strong acid; **b)** a strong alkali?

10 How could you make a spill of sulfuric acid safer?

Reactions of acids

Many different acids exist. There are strong acids like sulfuric and hydrochloric acid and weak acids like citric acid (in lemons) and ethanoic acid (in vinegar). These different acids react in similar ways with metals and metal oxides. When acids react with some metals they produce new substances, including hydrogen. Metals react in a similar way with acids, but some are more reactive than others: metals high in the reactivity series react vigorously with acids; low reactivity metals like gold and silver do not react with acids.

11 Name two acids with a pH of 1.

12 What gas is formed when metals react with acids and how could you test for it?

Ionic compounds

Atoms are neutral but when they form ionic compounds, metal atoms always lose electrons forming positive ions and non-metals always gain electrons forming negative ions. These oppositely charged ions form giant lattices with a regular structure – this is called ionic bonding. Ionic compounds have giant ionic structures or lattices with strong electrostatic forces holding the ions in fixed positions in the structure. When these substances are melted or dissolved in water, the ions are free to move and can then conduct electricity.

Copper is usually extracted by electrolysis and has properties that make it useful for electrical wiring and plumbing.

13 Describe ionic bonding.

14 Explain why solid ionic substances do not conduct electricity unless they are dissolved in water or melted.

Equilibrium reactions

In some chemical reactions, the products can react to produce the original reactants. These are called reversible reactions and can be represented by equations such as: A + B $\rightleftharpoons$ C + D. When this occurs in a closed system, a point of equilibrium is reached when the forward reaction (A and B reacting to make C and D) occurs at exactly the same rate as the reverse reaction (C and D reacting to make A and B). The relative amount of the substances present depends on the temperature and pressure conditions. One example is the Haber process which is used to make ammonia from nitrogen and hydrogen. This reaction is carried out at about 450°C and 200 atmospheres pressure in order to produce a reasonable yield of ammonia at a fairly good rate.

15 Write a word equation to show the Haber process.

16 What conditions are used in the Haber process and why?

Graphs of motion

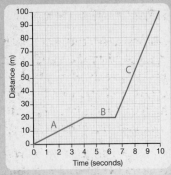

Distance-time graphs show us how something is moving. When the object is stationary its distance is not changing, so the graph is a straight, horizontal line. When the object is moving, its distance is changing so the graph is a slope. The steeper the slope, the faster the object is moving. We can work out the average speed from the graph, because the average speed is the total distance the object travels divided by the total time it takes.

1   List the sections A, B and C of the graph in order of the object's speed, starting with the slowest.

2   Calculate the average speed of the object. What would the graph look like if the object travelled at this speed for the whole journey?

Balanced and unbalanced forces

When the forces on an object are balanced, the object stays stationary, or stays moving in a straight line at a constant speed. If the forces are not balanced, the object speeds up, slows down or changes direction. There are two main forces on a hot air balloon, its weight acting downwards and an upthrust acting upwards. The driver of the balloon can heat the air in the balloon to make the upthrust bigger, or let it cool to make the upthrust smaller.

3   Can the driver of the balloon change the weight? If so, how?

4   What force or forces might make the balloon change direction?

5   How might the motion of the balloon change if the upthrust is bigger than the weight?

Energy

Everything that is moving has kinetic energy. More massive objects and faster objects have more kinetic energy. When we do work on an object to make it move, or to make it speed up, some of our energy is being transformed into the kinetic energy of the object. The bigger the force we use and the further it moves, the more work we do and the more energy the object gains. The person in the diagram is doing work against friction and work against gravity, and the object is gaining kinetic energy and potential energy.

6   How do you know that the object is gaining potential energy?

7   Use ideas of work and energy to explain why a smaller mass would be easier to push up the slope.

Static electricity

You know that all batteries have a positive terminal and a negative terminal, and often it is important to connect the batteries the correct way round in a circuit. All batteries (that are not flat) have a voltage. The voltage tells us that there is a difference in electrical charge between one side of the battery and the other, and the voltage makes a current (a flow of charged particles) flow round the circuit. Whenever we see a spark it means that some electricity (charged particles) are jumping from one place to another.

8   What is a spark?

9   What makes a current flow around a circuit?

10 What are the two types of electrical charge?

Resistance

For a resistor at a constant temperature, the current flowing is directly proportional to the p.d. (i.e. the resistance remains constant).

p.d. = current x resistance

However, not all components follow this rule. The resistance of a filament lamp increases as the filament heats up. A diode allows current to flow in one direction only. The resistance of a LDR decreases as light intensity increases. The resistance of a thermistor decreases as temperature increases.

The current through a component will depend on its resistance: the higher the resistance, the smaller the current.

11 What can you say about the resistance in a resistor at a constant temperature? Is this the same for all components?

12 Give two examples where the resistance does not remain constant. Explain how resistance changes.

Mains electricity

Domestic electricity in the UK is supplied at 230 V a.c. 50 Hz, which is potentially lethal. It is therefore important to know how to handle it safely and recognise dangerous practice.

Three-pin plugs must be wired correctly and fitted with the appropriate rated fuse. If a fault occurs, the fuse melts and the circuit is broken. Fuses are always connected in series with the live wire.

Earth wires are connected to all appliances with a metal casing. If a fault occurs and someone is in contact with the metal outer casing, current will flow safely to earth rather than through the person.

13 How does a fuse work and why is it so important to have the correct fuse fitted?

14 Explain why appliances with a metal outer casing must be earthed.

Radioactive substances

Isotopes are atoms of the same element with the same number of protons but different numbers of neutrons. They are unstable and disintegrate, releasing energy that is carried out of the atom by alpha and beta particles.

Rutherford and Marsden's scattering experiment involved firing alpha particles at gold leaf. Their findings were:

- Most particles passed straight through, indicating that the atom was mostly empty space.
- Some particles were deflected, indicating that the centre of the atom was positively charged.
- A few particles bounced straight back, indicating that the centre of the atom was small, heavy and dense.

15 What is an isotope and how does it lead to the release of radioactive particles?

16 State Rutherford's three observations and explain how he interpreted them.

Nuclear fission and nuclear fusion

Nuclear fission is the splitting up of large atoms like U-235. The atom breaks up into two smaller atoms and a huge amount of energy is released with three extra neutrons. If there is critical mass, a chain reaction takes place which results in an uncontrollable atomic explosion. It is possible to control the rate of the nuclear reaction to produce useable energy, i.e. in a nuclear power station.

Nuclear fusion is the joining of two small atoms, like hydrogen to form a larger atom, like helium and the release of huge amounts of energy. Nuclear fusion is the process by which stars are born and release their energy. At the moment, we do not have the technology to fully control a fusion reaction.

17 Describe nuclear fission and explain how such a reaction can get out of control.

18 In what way is nuclear fusion different to nuclear fission?

DISCOVER MARTIAN LIVING!

If we colonise Mars, we'll have to take plants with us.

The Martian atmosphere is too thin to be able to supply plants with enough carbon dioxide. We'll have to grow them in enclosed spaces with artificial atmospheres.

We'll need a way of getting rid of our wastes, and the dead plants. Maybe we'll have to take some decomposers with us, too.

The plants won't be able to grow in the red soil, because they won't have any nutrients.

There isn't as much light on Mars as on Earth, and it is much colder. The plants might therefore struggle to photosynthesise.

We'd need a source of water for ourselves and also the plants – there's no liquid water on Mars.

CONTENTS

Cells

You will find out:
- About the structure of animal cells and plant cells
- About what the different parts of a cell do

Hijacked

This cell has been attacked by viruses. Viruses are tiny particles of DNA and protein. They are not made from cells. They can't reproduce on their own. Instead, they invade cells and hijack them, making the cell produce multiple copies of the virus. The new viruses burst out of the cell, ready to find more cells to invade. Not surprisingly, the cell is killed by the viral attack.

FIGURE 1: Viruses are bursting out of this cell. Do you think it can survive?

Animal and plant cells

Your body contains more than 10 000 000 000 000 **cells**. Every one of those cells has been produced from the one single cell that began your life. It divided over and over and over again to make your body.

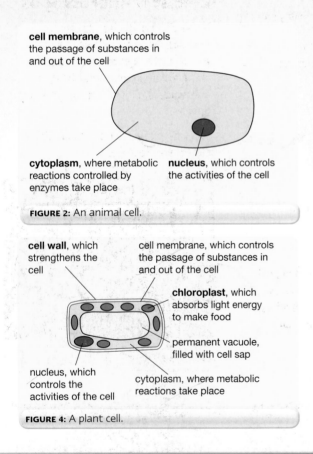

cell **membrane**, which controls the passage of substances in and out of the cell

cytoplasm, where metabolic reactions controlled by enzymes take place

nucleus, which controls the activities of the cell

FIGURE 2: An animal cell.

cytoplasm

cell membrane

nucleus

FIGURE 3: A photograph of human cheek cells seen through a microscope.

cell wall, which strengthens the cell

cell membrane, which controls the passage of substances in and out of the cell

chloroplast, which absorbs light energy to make food

permanent vacuole, filled with cell sap

nucleus, which controls the activities of the cell

cytoplasm, where metabolic reactions take place

FIGURE 4: A plant cell.

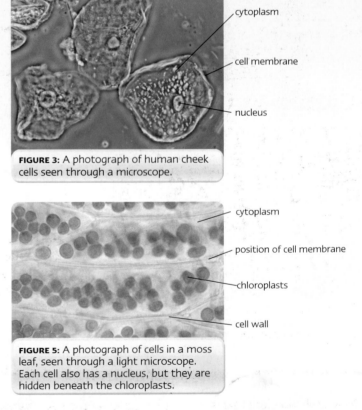

cytoplasm

position of cell membrane

chloroplasts

cell wall

FIGURE 5: A photograph of cells in a moss leaf, seen through a light microscope. Each cell also has a nucleus, but they are hidden beneath the chloroplasts.

❚❚ QUESTIONS ❚❚

1 List **three** structures that are found in animal cells and also in plant cells.
2 List **three** structures that are found in plant cells but not in animal cells.

...cell   ...cell membrane   ...cell wall   ...chloroplast

Cell organelles

The different parts of a cell are called organelles. Each organelle has a particular function.

With a really good microscope, we can see more detail in cells. These diagrams show some organelles that you can't usually see with the kind of microscope you use in school.

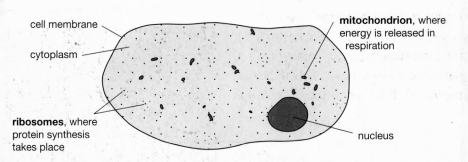

cell membrane

cytoplasm

mitochondrion, where energy is released in respiration

ribosomes, where protein synthesis takes place

nucleus

FIGURE 6: A more detailed look at an animal cell.

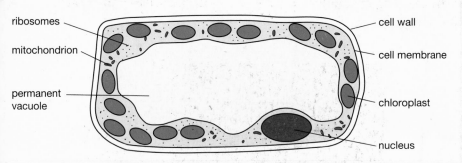

ribosomes

mitochondrion

permanent vacuole

cell wall

cell membrane

chloroplast

nucleus

FIGURE 7: A more detailed look at a plant cell.

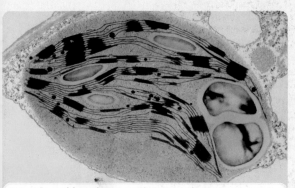

FIGURE 8: A chloroplast, seen using an electron microscope. Electron microscopes can show us much smaller structures than we can see with a light microscope.

Watch Out All cells have cell membranes. Only plant cells (and bacteria and fungi) have cell walls.

Electron microscopes

Research laboratories use electron microscopes. They send beams of electrons through the specimen. The electrons hit a screen or a sheet of photographic film where they make an image.

This image of a cell was made using an electron microscope.

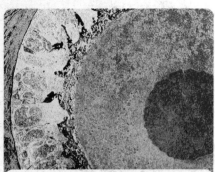

FIGURE 9: Part of a cell seen using an electron microscope.

QUESTIONS

3 Copy and complete this table. You will need to add several more rows.

Structure	Present in animal cell?	Present in plant cell?	Function
nucleus	yes	yes	controls the activity of the cell

QUESTIONS

4 Can you pick out any organelles in the electron micrograph? If you can, say what they are and how you recognised them.

Specialised cells

You will find out:
- That cells can be specialised for a particular function
- That cell structure is related to function

Life in a small world

These organisms are parameciums. They are very small – this picture has been magnified about 400 times. The paramecium is made of only one cell. It lives in ponds, in a world where most of what it experiences is too small for us to see. Parameciums feed on other organisms even smaller than themselves, such as bacteria.

FIGURE 1: How do you think these parameciums move through the water?

Different cells for different functions

In a paramecium, the single **cell** has to do everything. We've seen that your body contains millions of cells. They are not all the same. You have different cells to carry out different roles. The cells are **specialised** for particular **functions**.

Figure 2 is a sperm cell. The function of a sperm cell is to fertilise an egg. Notice the scale bar next to it. This is an especially small cell.

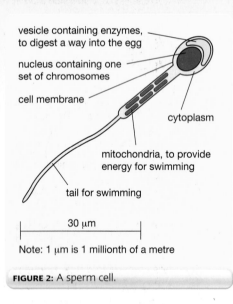

vesicle containing enzymes, to digest a way into the egg

nucleus containing one set of chromosomes

cell membrane

cytoplasm

mitochondria, to provide energy for swimming

tail for swimming

30 μm

Note: 1 μm is 1 millionth of a metre

FIGURE 2: A sperm cell.

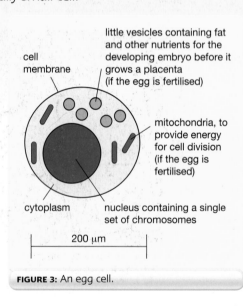

cell membrane

little vesicles containing fat and other nutrients for the developing embryo before it grows a placenta (if the egg is fertilised)

mitochondria, to provide energy for cell division (if the egg is fertilised)

cytoplasm

nucleus containing a single set of chromosomes

200 μm

FIGURE 3: An egg cell.

Figure 3 is an egg cell. The function of an egg cell is to be fertilised by a sperm, and then to form a zygote and an embryo. Again, look at the scale bar.

▥ QUESTIONS ▥

1. List **two** features of a sperm cell that are not found in most other animal cells. How do these features help the sperm cell to carry out its function?
2. List **two** features of an egg cell that are not found in most other animal cells. How do these features help the egg cell to carry out its function?
3. Which is larger – a sperm cell or an egg cell? How can you tell?

WANT TO KNOW MORE?

You can read about some other specialised cells on page 29.

...cell ...functions

A cell for every function

Here are some more examples of specialised cells that are found in the human body.

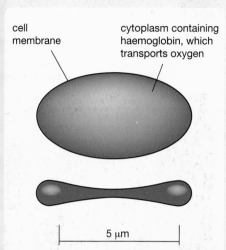

cell membrane

cytoplasm containing haemoglobin, which transports oxygen

5 µm

This is what the cell would look like if you cut it in half. This shape is good for quickly taking in and letting out oxygen.

Notice that the red blood cell does not have a nucleus.

FIGURE 4: A red blood cell.

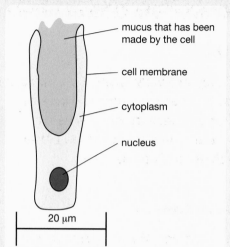

mucus that has been made by the cell

cell membrane

cytoplasm

nucleus

20 µm

Goblet cells are found in the lining of the alimentary canal, and in the tubes leading down to the lungs. They make mucus, which helps food to slide easily through the alimentary canal, and helps to stop bacteria getting down into your lungs.

FIGURE 5: A goblet cell.

Specialised plant cells

How does a single fertilised egg manage to produce so many different kinds of cells? We can actually see this happening if we use a microscope to look inside a plant root.

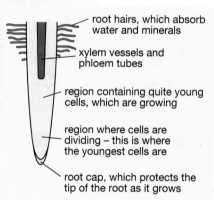

root hairs, which absorb water and minerals

xylem vessels and phloem tubes

region containing quite young cells, which are growing

region where cells are dividing – this is where the youngest cells are

root cap, which protects the tip of the root as it grows

FIGURE 8: The cells near the tip of a plant root.

New cells are produced near the tip of the root, so the cells above them are older cells. Some of these older cells turn into cells that are specialised for transporting materials within the plant.

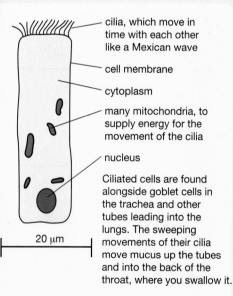

cilia, which move in time with each other like a Mexican wave

cell membrane

cytoplasm

many mitochondria, to supply energy for the movement of the cilia

nucleus

Ciliated cells are found alongside goblet cells in the trachea and other tubes leading into the lungs. The sweeping movements of their cilia move mucus up the tubes and into the back of the throat, where you swallow it.

20 µm

FIGURE 6: A ciliated cell.

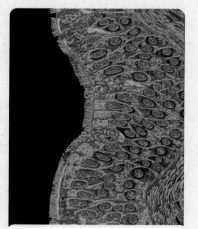

FIGURE 7: A photograph, taken through a microscope, of the cells lining the trachea.

QUESTIONS

6 None of the cells in a root have chloroplasts. Explain why.

7 What do root hair cells do? How are they adapted for this function?

QUESTIONS

4 State **two** features that all of the cells have in common.

5 Which cells stay in one place? Which move around? Suggest how their shapes are related to this.

Diffusion 1

You will find out:
- That diffusion is the spreading out of particles from a high concentration to a low concentration
- That diffusion can happen in gases and liquids, including solutions
- That diffusion happens faster at higher temperatures

How do moths detect smells?

This male moth's feathery antennae are the equivalent of your nose – but millions of times more sensitive. The antennae contain smell receptors, picking up scents that tell the moth there is a female around. Female moths emit scents called pheromones. A male can sense her if just five molecules of scent per second reach his antennae.

FIGURE 1: This Luna moth comes from North America.

Moving particles

Scents are substances that we can smell. A scent is made from molecules of gases that spread out in the air.

Molecules naturally spread out from a place where there are a lot of them into a place where there are fewer. They spread from a high **concentration** to a low concentration. This is called **diffusion**.

Any particles that can move around freely can diffuse. This includes particles in gases and liquids. We can define diffusion like this:

"Diffusion is the spreading of the particles of a gas, or of any substance in solution, from a region where they are of a higher concentration, into a region where they are in a lower concentration."

FIGURE 2: What molecules can the bee smell?

The particles in the ink drop in figure 3 spread out into the water. This happens even if we don't stir the water.

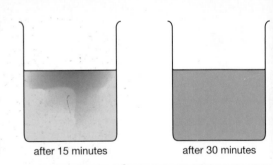

ink added to water   after 15 minutes   after 30 minutes

FIGURE 3: Does diffusion happen if the water is not stirred?

⬛ QUESTIONS ⬛

1 What is a scent? You should be able to write down **two** things.
2 How does a male moth know which way to fly when he smells the scent of a female moth?
3 Do you think particles in a solid can diffuse? Explain why you think this.

...concentration   ...diffusion

How diffusion happens

The diagram shows the particles in a sugar solution. The sugar is dissolved in the water. The sugar particles and the water molecules are moving around, bumping into each other and changing direction.

There are a lot of sugar molecules at the bottom of the beaker. The sugar solution here is concentrated.

There are fewer sugar molecules near the top of the beaker. The sugar solution here is dilute. As the sugar molecules move randomly around, some of them move from the bottom to the top while others move from the top to the bottom. On average, though, more will go from bottom to top than from top to bottom – simply because there were more of them at the bottom to start with. If we leave them for long enough, they will end up spread evenly through the water.

It's important to realise that the sugar molecules move all over the place, not just from the region where they are concentrated towards the region where they are less concentrated. We say that there is a **net movement** from the concentrated region to the less concentrated one. This means that, although they go both ways, on average more go towards the less concentrated region than in the other direction.

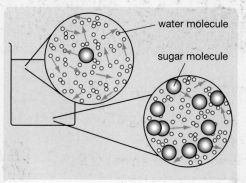

FIGURE 4: Diffusion in a beaker of sugar solution.

Diffusion and temperature

The faster particles move around, the faster they will diffuse. So diffusion tends to happen faster at high temperatures than at low temperatures.

Aromatherapists make use of this fact. They place scented oil in a container in a bowl of water and warm it over a candle or little spirit lamp. The warm water helps the scent to evaporate and spread out into the air.

FIGURE 5: How do aromatherapists use diffusion in their work?

A diffusion experiment

This diagram shows apparatus that can be used to measure the rate of diffusion.

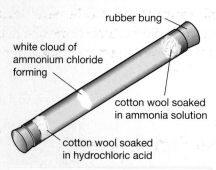

FIGURE 6: A diffusion experiment.

Ammonia is very smelly and unpleasant, so the experiment has to be done in a fume cupboard.

One piece of cotton wool is soaked in ammonia solution and another piece in hydrochloric acid. The pieces of cotton wool are placed at opposite ends of a tube and then rubber bungs are pushed in.

After a while, you can see a white cloud forming part way along the tube.

The cloud is ammonium chloride. It forms where the hydrochloric acid molecules and ammonia molecules come into contact with one another.

QUESTIONS

6 Explain how the ammonia molecules and hydrochloric acid molecules moved along the tube.

7 Which moved faster – the hydrochloric acid molecules or the ammonia molecules? How can you tell?

8 Explain how you could use this apparatus to investigate the effect of temperature on the rate of diffusion.

QUESTIONS

4 Explain what is meant by the net movement of a substance.

5 Do you think diffusion happens faster in a liquid or in a gas? Explain your answer.

Diffusion 2

You will find out:
- That oxygen for respiration passes through cell membranes by diffusion
- That the greater the difference in concentration, the faster the rate of diffusion

Fresh air for fish

This boat is bubbling air through a river, to try to make sure that the fish and other animals have plenty of oxygen. The animals depend on oxygen that has dissolved in the water. Oxygen diffuses into the water from the air. The bubbler mixes air into the water, which makes it easy for oxygen to get into the water, so the animals have plenty of oxygen for respiration.

FIGURE 1: This boat is bubbling air into the river.

Cells and diffusion

Cells need **oxygen** for **respiration**. This is the word equation for respiration:

glucose + oxygen ⟶ carbon dioxide + water

Figure 2 shows how the cell gets its oxygen.

Respiration happens inside the cell. Respiration uses up oxygen, so the concentration of oxygen inside the cell is low.

Outside the cell, the concentration of oxygen is higher. So oxygen **diffuses** into the cell, from the region where it is at a higher concentration to the region where it is at a lower concentration.

The cell membrane lets the oxygen go through easily. The cell membrane is said to be **permeable** to oxygen.

The faster the cell respires, the faster it uses up oxygen. This makes the concentration of oxygen inside the cell even lower than usual.

The greater the difference in concentration, the greater the rate of diffusion. So the faster the cell respires, the faster oxygen diffuses into the cell.

Figure 3 shows how oxygen gets into our blood in our lungs. Each lung contains millions of tiny air sacs, called **alveoli**. The diagram shows just one alveolus, and a blood capillary wrapped closely around it.

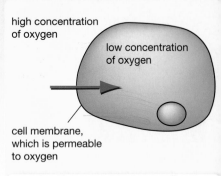

FIGURE 2: How oxygen enters a cell.

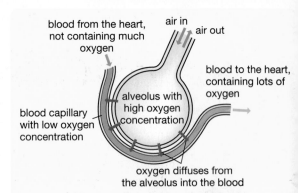

FIGURE 3: This diagram shows **gas exchange** in the lungs. Why does each lung have so many alveoli?

▮▮ QUESTIONS ▮▮

1 Copy and complete these sentences:
   Inside a respiring cell, carbon dioxide   oxygen .... is produced. This makes a
   .... concentration of carbon dioxide inside the cell. The
   concentration of carbon dioxide .... the cell is lower. So carbon
   dioxide .... out of the cell, through the cell membrane.

2 Make a copy of the alveolus diagram. Add some arrows showing the
   movement of carbon dioxide, and a sentence describing what it does.

...agar jelly ...alveoli ...antibiotic ...bacteria ...carbon dioxide ...diffuses

Diffusion in jelly

This diagram shows an experiment to find out how an **antibiotic** affects **bacteria**. The dish contains **agar jelly**, which bacteria can use to feed and grow. Jelly is not quite a solid and not quite a liquid. Particles can diffuse through agar jelly, though they do it much more slowly than they would in a 'real' liquid.

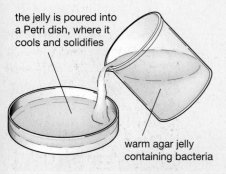
the jelly is poured into a Petri dish, where it cools and solidifies

warm agar jelly containing bacteria

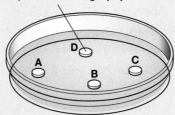
little discs of filter paper, each soaked in a different concentration of antibiotic and placed on the agar jelly

FIGURE 4: Setting up the antibiotic experiment.

The dish was kept in a warm place for two days. The bacteria grew on the agar jelly – but they could not grow right up to the little discs of antibiotics.

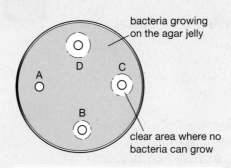
bacteria growing on the agar jelly

clear area where no bacteria can grow

FIGURE 5: This is what the dish looked like after two days.

The 'clear' areas, where no bacteria were growing, were measured. This table shows the results.

Disc	Concentration of antibiotic (arbitrary units)	Diameter of clear area / mm
A	0	0
B	1	4
C	5	6
D	10	9

TABLE 1: Effect of antibiotics on bacteria growth.

Speeding up diffusion

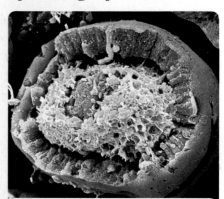

FIGURE 6: A cross-section of the small intestine.

This photograph shows the inside of the **small intestine**, also known as the ileum. You can see that it has millions of tiny pink folds. If you could run your hand over it, it would feel a bit like velvet. The little folds are called **villi**. Each villus is approximately 1 mm tall.

The food inside the small intestine (yellow) contains molecules such as glucose, which have been produced by digestion. If the concentration of glucose inside the small intestine is higher than the concentration inside the villi, then glucose diffuses into the villi.

Each villus contains tiny blood capillaries, and the glucose goes inside these and dissolves in the blood. The glucose is carried in the blood to cells all over the body.

Having so many villi helps diffusion to happen quickly, because there are more surfaces for the glucose to diffuse across. The greater the surface area, the faster the rate of diffusion.

░░░ QUESTIONS ░░░

3   How does disc A help us to interpret the results of this experiment?
4   Explain how the antibiotic spread out of the discs and into the agar jelly.
5   Explain why the clear area around disc C was wider than the clear area around disc B.

░░░ QUESTIONS ░░░

6   Describe how and why glucose would move from the blood and into a respiring cell.

Osmosis 1

You will find out:
- How a partially permeable membrane works
- What osmosis is
- That Visking tubing is an artificial partially permeable membrane

Kidney machine

This woman's kidneys have stopped working. Her blood is being cleaned in a kidney machine. The blood is running through tiny tubes made of a material like Visking tubing. It has microscopic holes in it. The tubes are immersed in a solution that is like blood without any waste products. The holes in the tubes let molecules of waste products diffuse out of the blood, but they won't let big molecules like proteins escape.

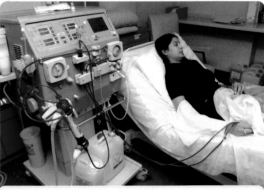

FIGURE 1: This woman would die if her blood were not cleaned in this machine.

Demonstrating osmosis

Visking tubing is a **partially permeable membrane**. This means it has holes in it that are big enough to let small molecules through, but not large molecules.

In the experiment in figure 2, the Visking tubing contains a solution with a lot of sugar molecules and also some water molecules. In the beaker, there is a solution with a lot of water molecules, and a few sugar molecules.

The water molecules **diffuse** from the dilute solution into the concentrated solution. They do this because the 'concentration' of water molecules is greater outside the tubing than inside.

The level of liquid gradually climbs up the glass tubing because of the water diffusing into the sugar solution. The diffusion of the water molecules is called **osmosis**.

Osmosis happens whenever a partially permeable membrane separates two solutions of different concentrations.

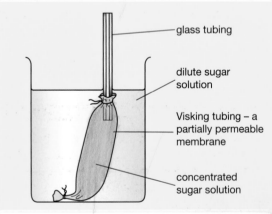

glass tubing

dilute sugar solution

Visking tubing – a partially permeable membrane

concentrated sugar solution

FIGURE 2: Using Visking tubing to demonstrate osmosis.

QUESTIONS

1 Copy and complete this sentence: Osmosis is the diffusion of .... from a .... solution to a .... solution, through a .... membrane.

2 Explain what is meant by 'partially permeable'.

3 In a dialysis machine, the solution surrounding the tubes in which the blood flows has to have the same concentration as the blood. Can you explain why?

...diffuse   ...osmosis

How osmosis happens

This diagram shows a concentrated sugar solution separated from a dilute sugar solution by a partially permeable membrane.

The sugar molecules and the water molecules are all moving around. They bump into each other and then bounce off in different directions. Sometimes, they bump into the membrane. Sometimes, they bump into a hole in the membrane.

If a sugar molecule bumps into a hole, it just bounces back, because it is too big to get through. But if a water molecule bumps into a hole, it shoots through to the other side.

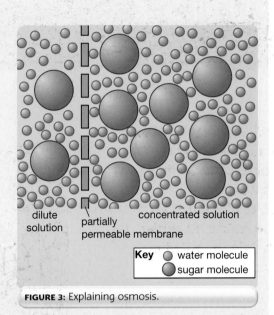

dilute solution   partially permeable membrane   concentrated solution

Key ○ water molecule   ● sugar molecule

FIGURE 3: Explaining osmosis.

What will happen if the two solutions are left like this for a while? The sugar all stays where it is. But some of the water molecules will move from one side of the membrane to the other.

There were more water molecules in the dilute sugar solution than in the concentrated sugar solution. So more water molecules will go from the dilute solution into the concentrated one than in the other direction. Water will diffuse from the dilute solution into the concentrated solution. After a while, there will be less water in the dilute solution, and more water in the concentrated solution.

QUESTIONS

4 An experiment was carried out to find out how concentration affects osmosis. Several sets of apparatus like the one on page 22 were set up. They were all identical, except that the concentration of the sugar solution in each one was different.

These are the results.

Concentration of sugar solution / grams per dm³	Height of liquid in the tube after five minutes / mm
0	0
5	6
10	14
15	20
20	25

a Draw a graph to show these results.

b Explain why the liquid went up the tube.

c What do the results indicate about the effect of solute concentration on the rate of osmosis?

A diffusion puzzle

This diagram shows an experiment to investigate diffusion.

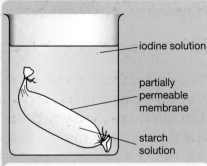

iodine solution

partially permeable membrane

starch solution

FIGURE 4: Are starch molecules large or small?

To understand what is happening, you need to think about each of the kinds of molecules in turn.

First, think about the starch molecules. Can they diffuse through the membrane?

Next, think about the iodine molecules. They are small enough to get through the holes in the membrane. Can they diffuse? What will happen to them after a while?

Next, think about the water molecules. The solutions on the two sides of the membrane are the same concentration. What will happen to the water molecules?

Lastly, you need to remember what happens when starch and iodine solution get together.

FIGURE 5: This diagram shows the experiment after 10 minutes.

QUESTIONS

5 Explain the results of this experiment.

6 Suggest **two** ways in which the experiment could be changed to get results more quickly.

Osmosis 2

You will find out:
- That all cells are surrounded by a partially permeable cell membrane
- How water can move into and out of cells by osmosis
- How animal cells and plant cells are affected differently when they lose or gain water by osmosis

Storage solutions

Sometimes, a person needs a blood transfusion because they don't have enough red blood cells. Some of the blood that people donate is stored as 'red cell concentrate'. The red blood cells are separated out of the blood, and then mixed with a solution containing salt and glucose. The solution has to be exactly the same concentration as the red blood cells, or the red blood cells would be killed.

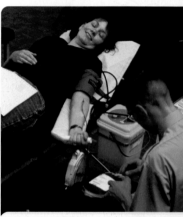

FIGURE 1: This woman is giving blood.

Osmosis and animal cells

Figure 2 shows an animal cell in distilled water. The **cytoplasm** in the cell is a fairly concentrated solution. The **cell membrane** is a **partially permeable membrane**.

Water goes into the cell by **osmosis**. The cell swells up with all the extra water. Eventually it bursts and dies (figure 3). Figure 4 shows an animal cell in a concentrated solution. Now the water goes *out* of the cell by osmosis. The cell shrivels up.

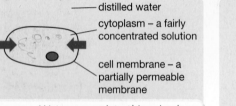

distilled water
cytoplasm – a fairly concentrated solution
cell membrane – a partially permeable membrane

FIGURE 2: Water moves into this animal cell by osmosis.

FIGURE 3: The cell swells, bursts and dies.

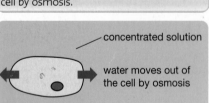

concentrated solution
water moves out of the cell by osmosis

FIGURE 4: Water moves out of this animal cell through the partially permeable cell membrane.

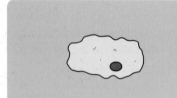

FIGURE 5: The animal cell shrinks and has wavy edges.

QUESTIONS

1   Copy and complete these sentences.

    If an animal cell is put into pure water, the water goes .... the cell by .... This happens because the cell .... of the animal cell is a partially .... membrane.

2   Explain why animal cells shrivel up if you put them into a concentrated solution.

3   Explain why it is important to keep red blood cells being kept for transfusions in a solution of salt and glucose, and not in pure water.

...cell membrane ...cell wall ...cytoplasm ...osmosis

Osmosis and plant cells

Figure 6 shows a plant cell in distilled water.

Like animal cells, plant cells have a partially permeable membrane. They also have a **cell wall**, which is fully permeable.

Water goes into the cell by osmosis. The cell swells up. But it does not burst, because it is surrounded by a strong cell wall.

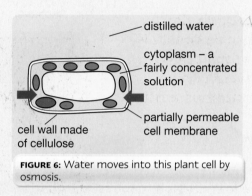

distilled water

cytoplasm – a fairly concentrated solution

partially permeable cell membrane

cell wall made of cellulose

FIGURE 6: Water moves into this plant cell by osmosis.

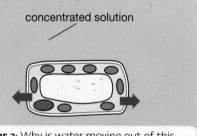

concentrated solution

FIGURE 7: Why is water moving out of this cell?

Figure 7 shows a plant cell in a concentrated solution. Water goes out of the cell by osmosis. The inside of the cell shrivels up.

But the cell wall is strong and doesn't collapse. So the inside of the cell pulls away from the cell wall. Sometimes, the cell membrane gets torn when this happens, and the cell dies. Sometimes, though, you can 'revive' the cell by putting it into water again (figure 8).

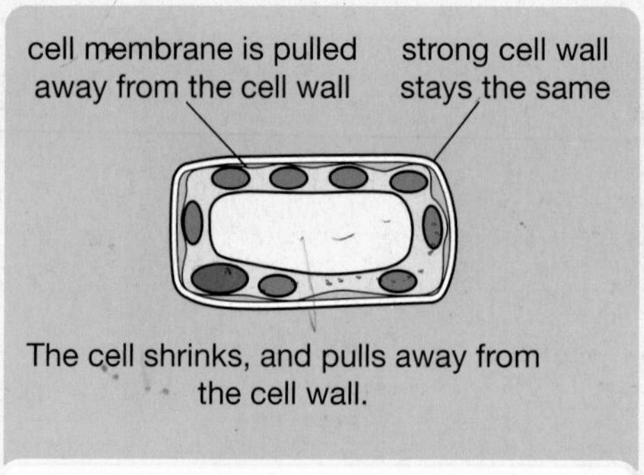

cell membrane is pulled away from the cell wall

strong cell wall stays the same

The cell shrinks, and pulls away from the cell wall.

FIGURE 8: How could you try to revive this cell?

QUESTIONS

4 Explain why animal cells burst if you put them into pure water, but plant cells don't.

5 Root hair cells are found near the tips of plant roots. They take up water from the soil. Explain how water moves into a root hair cell.

6 A student wrote: 'In plant cells, water moves in and out through the cell wall by osmosis.' What is misleading about this sentence?

Potato chips

A student investigated the effect of osmosis on potato cells. She cut three chips out of a raw potato, like this.

FIGURE 9: Why does the student measure each chip?

She measured the chips and recorded their lengths.

Then she put each chip into a sugar solution. One went into distilled water, one into a dilute solution and one into a concentrated solution.

She left the chips for 30 minutes and then measured them again. These are her results.

Solution	Change in length of chip / mm
Water	+6
Dilute sugar solution	+1
Concentrated solution	−4

QUESTIONS

7 Explain these results.

8 Suggest how the student could alter her experiment:

a to make her results more reliable,

b to find out the concentration of the cytoplasm in the potato cells.

Photosynthesis

You will find out:
- How carbon dioxide, water and light energy combine to form glucose and oxygen during photosynthesis

The food factory

This is a food factory. The plants are using the air, water and soil around them to make food. They don't make much fuss about it. They do it quietly and steadily, so we don't notice what they are doing. But if it were not for plants, there would be no animals in the world, because there would be nothing for animals to eat.

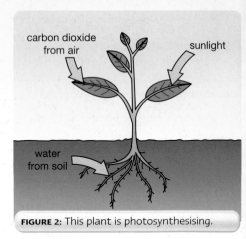

FIGURE 1: All these plants are making food.

Making food

Plants make food by **photosynthesis**. They take **carbon dioxide** from the air and water from the soil. In their leaves, they use energy from sunlight to make the carbon dioxide and water react together. The energy in the sunlight is absorbed by a green pigment (colouring) called **chlorophyll**.

This is the word equation for this reaction.

$$\text{carbon dioxide} + \text{water} \xrightarrow{\text{light energy}} \text{glucose} + \text{oxygen}$$

The first kind of food that the plant makes is **glucose**. Glucose is a **sugar**. It is a kind of **carbohydrate**. Later, the plant can use the glucose to make other kinds of food, such as **starch**, fats and proteins.

This is where all our food comes from. Everything that you eat can trace its history back to a plant. Millions of years ago, before there were any plants or microorganisms that could photosynthesise, there was hardly any oxygen in the air. Now more than 20 per cent of the air is oxygen.

carbon dioxide from air

sunlight

water from soil

FIGURE 2: This plant is photosynthesising.

FIGURE 3: Why are these people growing plants?

QUESTIONS

1. Write down the word equation for photosynthesis, without looking it up. Then check to see if you got it right.

2. Explain how plants are involved in making a hamburger.

...carbohydrate ...carbon dioxide ...chlorophyll ...energy ...glucose ...insoluble

Energy for living things

Photosynthesis uses light **energy**. This energy usually comes from the Sun, although some indoor plants use energy from artificial lighting.

In photosynthesis, light energy is transformed into chemical energy in glucose molecules.

This is where all of your energy comes from. You get your energy from the food that you eat. Somewhere – it might have been in Africa or just down the road from you – a plant transformed light energy into chemical energy. Some of the energy you are using today might have come from a sunbeam in Africa.

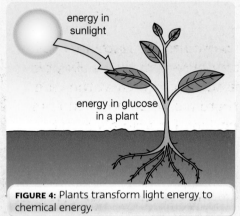
energy in sunlight

energy in glucose in a plant

FIGURE 4: Plants transform light energy to chemical energy.

Using the energy

All living things use energy. We get our energy when we break down glucose in **respiration**.

$$glucose + oxygen \longrightarrow carbon\ dioxide + water$$

This happens inside our cells, releasing energy that we can use for moving around, making new cells for growth, or for keeping us warm.

Respiration also happens inside plant cells. Plants use some of the glucose that they make in photosynthesis for respiration.

FIGURE 5: This plant uses energy to transport sugar from the leaves, where it is made, into the growing fruit.

<hr>

QUESTIONS

3   Your brain is using energy for thinking while you are reading this question. Draw an energy flow diagram showing where this energy came from.

4   Suggest why fruits like apples and oranges contain sugar.

Making other substances

Plants can make many different substances from the glucose that they make in photosynthesis. Here are some of them.

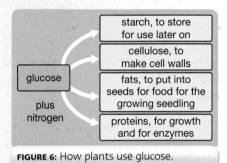
glucose plus nitrogen

starch, to store for use later on

cellulose, to make cell walls

fats, to put into seeds for food for the growing seedling

proteins, for growth and for enzymes

FIGURE 6: How plants use glucose.

Starch makes a good storage product because it is **insoluble**. It can be tucked away inside a cell and it just stays there – it doesn't dissolve in the watery fluids inside the cell.

This means that it won't get mixed up in the metabolic reactions that take place. Also, it will not cause extra water to be drawn in by osmosis.

Plants often store starch in their seeds. The starch provides food for the growing seedling, before it is big enough to photosynthesise for itself. Seeds often contain fats (oils) and proteins, too.

QUESTIONS

5   Suggest why fat makes a good storage product in a plant cell.

6   Find out which part of a plant these oils come from: sunflower oil, olive oil, corn oil. Why do these parts of the plant contain oil?

...oxygen ...photosynthesis ...respiration ...starch ...sugar

Leaves

You will find out:
- How leaves are adapted for photosynthesis
- How diffusion supplies a leaf with some of the raw materials for photosynthesis
- How different types of leaf cells are specialised for different purposes

Leaf eaters

This caterpillar is getting its energy from substances in the leaf, such as glucose and starch that have been made by photosynthesis. Unlike the caterpillar, we can't survive by eating just leaves because we can't digest the cellulose in their cell walls.

FIGURE 1: Why can't we live on leaves like this caterpillar?

Adaptations for photosynthesis

Most **photosynthesis** happens in leaves. This diagram shows how a **leaf** is **adapted** to help photosynthesis to happen.

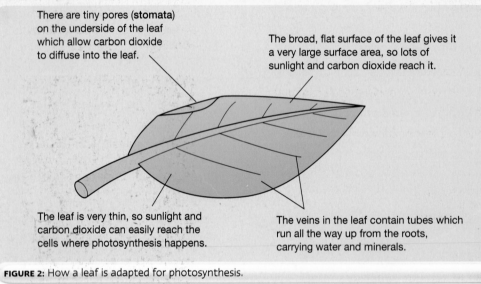

There are tiny pores (**stomata**) on the underside of the leaf which allow carbon dioxide to diffuse into the leaf.

The broad, flat surface of the leaf gives it a very large surface area, so lots of sunlight and carbon dioxide reach it.

The leaf is very thin, so sunlight and carbon dioxide can easily reach the cells where photosynthesis happens.

The veins in the leaf contain tubes which run all the way up from the roots, carrying water and minerals.

FIGURE 2: How a leaf is adapted for photosynthesis.

Inside the leaf, the cells are using up carbon dioxide in photosynthesis. This makes the concentration of carbon dioxide inside the leaf very low. The concentration of carbon dioxide outside the leaf is higher. So carbon dioxide **diffuses** into the leaf, through the stomata. Photosynthesis produces oxygen. This makes the concentration of oxygen inside the leaf higher than in the air outside. So oxygen diffuses out of the leaf, through the stomata.

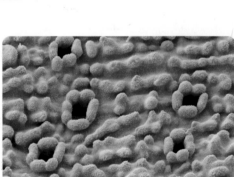

FIGURE 3: These holes are stomata on the underside of a leaf.

⬛ QUESTIONS ⬛

1. List **three** ways in which plant leaves are adapted for photosynthesis.
2. Leaves are usually green. Why is this?
3. At night, plants have to stop photosynthesising because they don't have any light. But they carry on respiring all through the night. What gas do you think diffuses into a leaf at night? Explain why it does this.

...*adapted* ...*diffuses* ...*leaf*

Specialised leaf cells

Figure 4 shows the cells inside a leaf.

The cells are arranged into groups, each group with a particular function. A group of similar cells, all carrying out the same function, is called a **tissue**. The labels on the right hand side of the diagram are the names of the tissues.

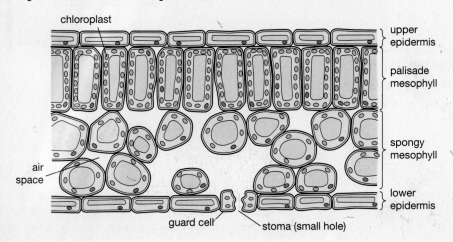

FIGURE 4: How many different tissues does this section of leaf contain?

Figure 5 shows a cell from the palisade mesophyll layer.

This cell is adapted for photosynthesis. It has many chloroplasts, each containing a lot of chlorophyll, to absorb energy from sunlight.

If the cell makes more glucose than it needs to use immediately, it can change some into starch and store it.

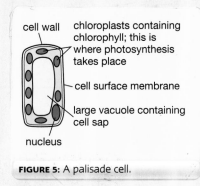

FIGURE 5: A palisade cell.

Unusual leaves

Most leaves are thin, flat, broad and green. But some plants have very unusual leaves.

This leaf belongs to a carnivorous plant, called a pitcher plant. The leaf is in the form of a deep tube with slippery slides. Insects go to the leaf because it produces a sugary nectar. They fall in and can't crawl out again. The plant digests the insects with enzymes. You can see the 'seam' where the leaf has curled around and its edges have grown together.

FIGURE 6: This pitcher is a modified leaf.

QUESTIONS

8   Pitcher plants get an element from the digestion of proteins in insects that they don't get in the glucose and starch they make in photosynthesis. Can you suggest what this element is?

9   Suggest how being carnivorous can help a plant to compete successfully with other plants, if they are growing in poor soil.

QUESTIONS

4   Look at the diagram of the tissues in a leaf. Why is it good for the palisade cells to be near to the upper surface of the leaf?

5   How do you think the air spaces inside the leaf might help with photosynthesis?

6   Look at the structure of the spongy mesophyll cells. What do you think they do?

7   Explain why it is useful for the leaf to be very thin.

Limiting factors

You will find out:
- How the rate of photosynthesis may be limited by:
  - temperature
  - light
  - carbon dioxide concentration

Extra care

Even though it is freezing outside, these plants are growing vigorously. Inside the glasshouse, they are given extra warmth and light to help them to photosynthesise. Outside, the plants are dormant, waiting for next spring to arrive.

FIGURE 1: A glasshouse can provide an ideal environment for photosynthesis.

Speeding up photosynthesis

How fast can a plant make food? It depends on how fast it can be supplied with the raw materials and how much light energy it is getting.

The following three factors affect the rate of photosynthesis.

Light intensity

The brighter the light, the more light energy the plant is receiving and the faster it can **photosynthesise**.

Carbon dioxide concentration

Carbon dioxide is one of the raw materials for photosynthesis. There isn't very much of it in the air. If you give a plant more carbon dioxide, it will probably be able to photosynthesise faster.

Temperature

Plants need to be warm to photosynthesise well. Most plants can't photosynthesise at all when it is really cold, such as on a cold winter's day. They photosynthesise faster in spring and summer, when the days are warmer.

QUESTIONS

1. List **three** factors that limit the rate of photosynthesis.
2. Some gardeners grow tomatoes in a glasshouse. Using what you know about photosynthesis, explain how this can help them to get a larger crop.
3. Some people think that talking or singing to their plants makes them grow faster. Using what you know about photosynthesis, do you think there could be any truth in this idea?

...carbon dioxide ...light intensity ...limiting

Light intensity

This graph shows how fast a plant photosynthesises at different light intensities.

When the **light intensity** is 0, there is no photosynthesis. As the light intensity increases, the rate of photosynthesis also increases.

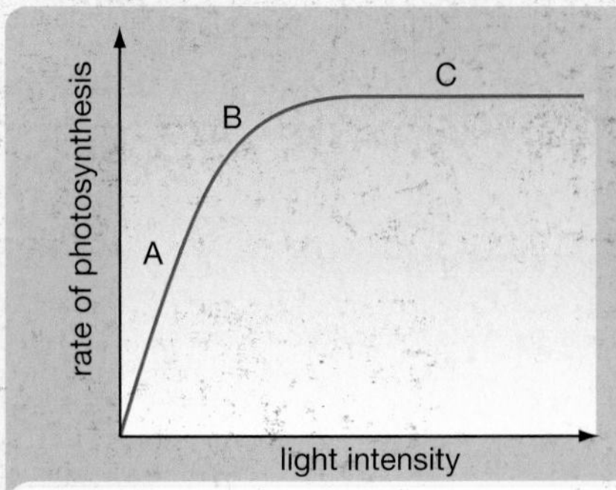

In region A of the graph, we can say that light intensity is **limiting** the rate of photosynthesis. We can tell this, because the graph shows that if we give the plant more light, then it can photosynthesise faster. We can say that light is a **limiting factor** for photosynthesis.

But there comes a point when the rate of photosynthesis does not increase any more, even when the plant is getting more light. This is because it is already photosynthesising as quickly as it can. Perhaps it hasn't got enough chlorophyll to absorb light any faster. Perhaps it hasn't got enough carbon dioxide.

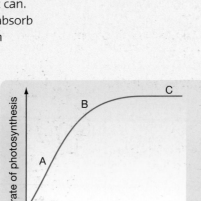

FIGURE 2: How light intensity affects the rate of photosynthesis.

Carbon dioxide concentration

This graph shows how fast a plant photosynthesises at different carbon dioxide concentrations.

FIGURE 3: How carbon dioxide concentration affects the rate of photosynthesis.

Glasshouses

Growing crops in a glasshouse gives the grower a lot of control over the conditions in which the plants live.

The grower needs to ensure that the costs of growing the plants are lower than the price they will get for the produce. For example, they may be able to produce more tomatoes more quickly if they heat the glasshouse but if the cost of the fuel outweighs the increase in the price they will get for selling the tomatoes, then it is not worth doing it.

Heating a glasshouse by burning a fuel such as paraffin benefits the plants in two ways. Firstly, it increases the temperature. Secondly, it produces carbon dioxide, which is often a limiting factor for photosynthesis.

FIGURE 4: Extra carbon dioxide can be provided in a glasshouse.

<hr>

QUESTIONS

4   Look at the graph showing the rate of photosynthesis at different light intensities.

   a What is the limiting factor in region A of the graph?

   b Suggest what could be the limiting factors in region C.

5   Look at the graph showing the rate of photosynthesis at different carbon dioxide concentrations.

   a What is the limiting factor in region A of the graph? How can you tell?

   b At what point on the graph does another limiting factor begin to take effect? How can you tell?

   c Can you suggest what this other limiting factor might be?

6   The concentration of carbon dioxide in the air is approximately 0.04 per cent. Using the information in the graph, suggest whether a gardener could make the plants in his glasshouse grow faster by giving them extra carbon dioxide. Explain your answer.

QUESTIONS

7   Despite the long distance they have to travel, imported strawberries are often sold more cheaply in supermarkets than homegrown ones in springtime. Can you suggest why this is?

8   Explain why tomatoes do not grow well in Britain in the winter, even if the glasshouses are heated.

A giant machine

SELF-CHECK ACTIVITY

Andy is 11. His class has a new Science teacher and she has some different ideas for the lessons. One lesson she gives each group of students a large sheet of paper and tells them she wants them to design a machine. They can talk about their ideas and draw what they think will work. She tells them what the machine has to be able to do and then puts the list on the board for them to refer to. Look at the board in the picture to see the list.

The class gets to work. This is what Andy's group comes up with.

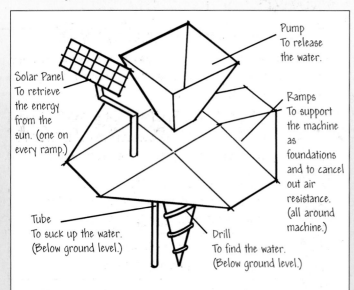

Pump
To release the water.

Solar Panel
To retrieve the energy from the sun. (one on every ramp.)

Ramps
To support the machine as foundations and to cancel out air resistance. (all around machine.)

Tube
To suck up the water. (Below ground level.)

Drill
To find the water. (Below ground level.)

After they have finished they put their drawings up on the walls and look at each other's work. There are some pretty weird ideas, but some of the features are quite similar.

"Now," says the teacher, "does anyone know what it is you've actually designed?"

There are lots of puzzled looks and a few muttered suggestions. Someone suggests it may be something to make life possible on another planet.

"Well," explains the teacher, "what you've just designed is a tree."

CHALLENGE

What does a tree do to get the water it needs? Why does a tree need water?

Your machine must be able to:
- Get water from under the ground – though it can't move from one place to another.
- Pump the water up high in the air. It doesn't need to store it there – it can just be released.
- Do this using solar power.
- Support itself and withstand fairly strong winds.

STEP 2

How does a tree get water to rise several metres (depending on the height of the tree)? Explain the energy transfers that take place in this process.

STEP 3

Look at the drawing that Andy's group produced. What are the similarities between their machine and a tree?

STEP 4

In fact a tree also carries out other functions that the machine doesn't. What are they?

STEP 5

The activity that Andy's teacher had set them was designed to get them thinking about why trees are like they are. Do you think it was a good way of doing this? Do you think the group would have a better idea why trees have their various features by the end of the lesson?

Maximise your grade

These sentences show what you need to include in your work to achieve each grade. Use them to improve your work and be more successful.

Grade	Answer includes...
F	Recognise that plants need a supply of water.
	Recognise that the word equation for photosynthesis applies to a tree.
	Relate the uptake of water to the word equation for photosynthesis.
	Describe how water moves through the tree.
C	Explain how energy is transferred to the water in transpiration.
	Recognise similarities and differences between the machine and a tree.
A	Use the machine to explain the form and function of various parts of the tree.
	Draw together several ideas to show how an activity such as the design of the machine can give insights into the form and function of a tree.

Healthy plants

You will find out:
- That plants absorb ions through their roots
- That nitrate ions are needed for making proteins, while magnesium ions are used for making chlorophyll

Giant pumpkin

Growing giant vegetables isn't everyone's idea of an exciting hobby, but some people spend most of their spare time trying to produce a record pumpkin – or at least one that can win a competition. They must get the growing conditions just right: warm and moist with plenty of all the different mineral salts that the pumpkin plants need.

FIGURE 1: It takes a lot of skill to grow a pumpkin this large.

Mineral salts

We've seen that plants need plenty of carbon dioxide, light and water for photosynthesis. With these, they can make glucose and other sugars, starch and cellulose.

Sugars, starch and cellulose are all **carbohydrates**. They contain three elements – carbon, hydrogen and oxygen.

Plants use the carbohydrates they have made to produce other substances. These include:

- **fats**   - **proteins**   - **chlorophyll**

This table shows the elements that are contained in some of the different kinds of substances that plants make.

substance	elements it contains				
	carbon	hydrogen	oxygen	nitrogen	magnesium
carbohydrate	✓	✓	✓		
fat	✓	✓	✓		
protein	✓	✓	✓	✓	
chlorophyll	✓	✓	✓	✓	✓

Plants get the extra elements that they need to make protein and chlorophyll in the form of **mineral salts**. They absorb the mineral salts from the soil, through their roots.

- Plants get **nitrogen** in the form of **nitrate ions**.
- Plants get **magnesium** in the form of **magnesium ions**.

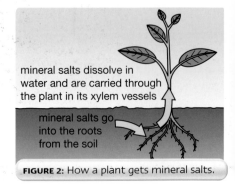

mineral salts dissolve in water and are carried through the plant in its xylem vessels

mineral salts go into the roots from the soil

FIGURE 2: How a plant gets mineral salts.

QUESTIONS

1. What element needs to be added to carbohydrates, in order to make proteins?
2. How do plants get this element?
3. What **two** elements need to be added to carbohydrates to make chlorophyll?
4. Do plants need any extra elements to make fats from carbohydrates? Explain your answer.

Deficiency symptoms

If plants don't get enough of the mineral salts that they need, they don't grow well.

This is a healthy potato plant. It has all the mineral salts that it needs.

FIGURE 3: This is a healthy potato plant.

This potato plant has not been given enough nitrate ions. It has not been able to make proteins. This has stopped it growing properly. It is small and stunted. It will not produce many potatoes.

FIGURE 4: This potato plant is short of nitrate ions.

This potato plant has not been given enough magnesium ions. It has grown quite large, but its leaves are yellow and unhealthy-looking.

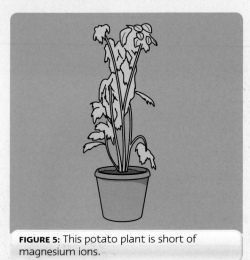

FIGURE 5: This potato plant is short of magnesium ions.

Fertilisers

Farmers can add mineral salts to the soil using **fertilisers**. They can add **organic** fertilisers such as cattle manure. Alternatively, they can use **inorganic** fertilisers, such as ammonium nitrate.

FIGURE 6: This farmer is spreading fertiliser.

Fertilisers are expensive, so farmers don't usually add more than necessary. They will test the soil to find out which mineral salts are lacking. They may be able to use global positioning satellites (GPS) and a computer in the tractor cab to map the precise mineral salt concentrations in different parts of the field. Different crops need different quantities of mineral salts. The farmer can use all this information to decide which mineral salts to add to which part of the field.

QUESTIONS

5 Using what you know about the way plants use nitrate ions, explain why the plant lacking nitrate ions is small and stunted.

6 Explain why the plant lacking magnesium ions has yellow leaves.

7 Will the plant lacking magnesium produce a good crop of potatoes? Explain your answer.

8 Do you think it would be possible to make these plants grow healthily? Explain your answer.

QUESTIONS

9 Suggest how adding organic fertilisers could benefit the soil more than adding inorganic fertilisers.

10 If a farmer wants to apply precise quantities of mineral salts to different parts of the field, would it be better for the farmer to use organic or inorganic fertiliser? Explain your answer.

11 Suggest how adding fertiliser to a field when it is raining could cause pollution.

Food chains

You will find out:
- That the Sun is the source of energy for most organisms
- That a food chain shows how energy is passed from one organism to another

Death in the sunshine

This lion has recently killed and eaten an antelope. All that is left are a few bones, some scraps of meat and its horns. The vultures are waiting their turn. Where do all of these animals get their energy? It all came from sunlight originally. The grass is like a huge power station, transforming energy from a form that our bodies cannot use into a form that we can use.

FIGURE 1: What are the vultures waiting for

Energy flow

You probably know that we can show how energy passes from one organism to another in a **food chain**, like this.

grass ⟶ antelope ⟶ lion

The arrows show how energy flows from one organism to the next. The energy is in the form of chemical energy in the food that the animals eat. Carbohydrates, fats and proteins all contain energy.

The grass in this food chain is a **producer**. It uses solar energy – from sunlight – to produce carbohydrates and other nutrients. All food chains begin with producers. The antelope and the lion are **consumers**. They consume food that has been made by plants.

FIGURE 2: Energy is flowing from the grass to the antelope.

- The antelope is a **primary consumer**, because it is the first consumer in the food chain. It is a **herbivore**. Herbivores eat plants.

- The lion is a **secondary consumer**, because it is the second consumer in the food chain. It is a **carnivore**. Carnivores eat other animals.

- The lion is also a **predator**. Predators kill and eat other animals for food. The animals that they kill are their **prey**.

FIGURE 3: This buzzard has killed a rabbit which it will eat.

QUESTIONS

1. Look at figure 3. Buzzards are eaten by eagle owls. Draw a food chain showing how energy from sunlight ends up as energy inside an eagle owl.

2. For each organism in the food chain you have drawn, say whether it is:
   - a producer
   - a consumer
   - a herbivore
   - a carnivore
   - a predator
   - prey

...carnivore ...chlorophyll ...consumers ...efficiency ...food chain ...food web ...herbivore

Food webs

A food chain shows just one pathway that energy can take as it passes from one organism to another. But things aren't really that simple. Usually, lots of food chains all interact with each other to form a **food web**.

For example, we can add the vultures to the grass ⟶ antelope ⟶ lion food chain.

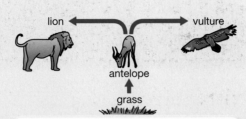

FIGURE 4: This food web shows that both vultures and lions feed on antelope.

Energy wastage

Figure 5 shows sunlight filtering through the leaves of a tree. The photographer was standing on the ground looking upwards.

Do the leaves catch all of the sunlight? Obviously not. We can see the sky through them, so some of the light is missing the leaves altogether, going straight down to the ground beneath the tree. And we can see *through* some of the leaves, so some light must be going right through them, and reaching our eyes.

Green plants capture only a small amount of the light energy that falls onto them. This is because:

- some light misses the leaves altogether
- some light hits the leaf and bounces back (reflects) from the leaf surface
- some light hits the leaf but goes all the way through without hitting any **chlorophyll**
- some light hits the chlorophyll, but isn't absorbed because it is of the wrong wavelength (colour).

FIGURE 5: Sunlight through leaves.

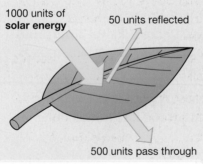

1000 units of **solar energy**

50 units reflected

500 units pass through

FIGURE 6: What happens to the solar energy that reaches a leaf?

Efficiency

Whenever energy is transferred or transformed, some of it is wasted.

We can calculate the efficiency of energy transfer like this:

$$\text{efficiency} = \frac{\text{useful energy transferred}}{\text{original amount of energy}} \times 100$$

For example, imagine that 200 units of solar energy hit a leaf, and the leaf uses 40 units of it in **photosynthesis**.

$$\text{efficiency} = \frac{40}{200} \times 100 = 20\%$$

Some of the energy that the plant does manage to capture is used to make carbohydrates and other substances. The energy is stored in these substances inside the cells of the plant and is therefore available to animals that eat the plant.

▦ QUESTIONS ▦

6 Calculate the efficiency of energy transfer in the leaf in figure 6.

7 Imagine that a plant is growing in conditions where the carbon dioxide concentration is very low. How would this affect the efficiency of energy transfer in photosynthesis? Explain your answer.

▦ QUESTIONS ▦

3 Look at figure 6 showing what happens to the sunlight that falls onto a leaf. Out of 1000 units of solar energy, how much can the plant use for photosynthesis?

4 Chlorophyll is green. What colours of light does it reflect?

5 What colour of light cannot be absorbed by chlorophyll?

Biomass

You will find out:
- That material and energy are lost along a food chain
- What a pyramid of biomass shows
- That energy is lost in organisms' waste material, and as heat

Gentle giant

This is a whale shark, the largest living species of fish. Whale sharks can be up to 20 m long. The largest one that has been caught had a mass of 40 tonnes. It is thought that whale sharks live for up to 60 years.

Despite their size, whale sharks feed on plankton, which are tiny organisms that float in the water. Millions of them go down into the whale shark's digestive system through its enormous mouth.

FIGURE 1: Why does this whale shark have such a large mouth?

Pyramids of biomass

Think back to this **food chain**:

grass ⟶ antelope ⟶ lion

How many antelope do you think are needed to support one lion? Probably several hundred in its lifetime. And how much grass do you think is needed to support one antelope? It will be much more than the antelope's own body mass.

If we could measure the mass of all the grass needed to supply the antelope and the mass of all the antelopes needed to support the lion, we might find something like figure 2.

The mass of living material is called **biomass**. Figure 2 shows a **pyramid of biomass**. It depicts the biomass at each step in a food chain. At each step in a food chain, there is less biomass than in the step before.

Consider why this happens. Firstly, the antelope don't eat all the grass. For example, the roots of the grass are under the ground, so not all the grass biomass is eaten by the antelope.

Secondly, not all the antelope are killed and eaten by lions. And even if the lion does kill an antelope, it doesn't eat absolutely all of it. So not all the antelope biomass is passed on to lions.

mass of lion

mass of antelope

mass of grass

FIGURE 2: A pyramid of biomass.

▪ QUESTIONS ▪

1   Suggest **one** other reason why not all the grass biomass is passed on to antelopes.
2   Which parts of an antelope are not eaten by lions?
3   Draw a pyramid of biomass that has a whale shark at the top of it. (You will have to come to an amazing conclusion about the mass of plankton in the sea!)

...biomass ...food chain ...homeotherm

Energy losses

Whenever energy is transferred or transformed, some is wasted. This happens in food chains. At each step of the chain, energy is lost.

This is why biomass gets less as we move along a food chain. At each step, there is less energy available for the organisms to use. Less energy means less biomass.

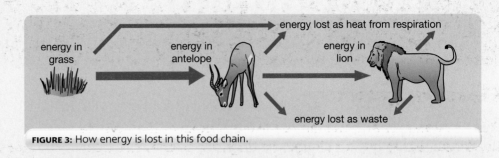

FIGURE 3: How energy is lost in this food chain.

Homeotherms

A **homeotherm** is an animal that maintains a constant body temperature. You can read about how humans do this on pages 74 to 75.

Mammals and birds are homeotherms. Extra **respiration** in their cells uses glucose to provide heat energy to keep their body temperatures high, even when the temperature of their surroundings is low.

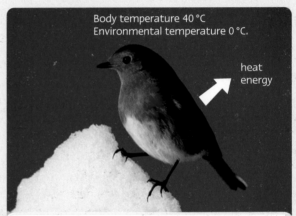

Body temperature 40 °C
Environmental temperature 0 °C.

heat energy

FIGURE 4: How does this robin keep its body temperature constant?

FIGURE 5: This snake is using solar energy to heat its body.

This means that energy losses from birds and mammals are even greater than energy losses from other organisms in a food chain. Other animals, such as snakes, frogs and fish, don't use respiration to keep their bodies warm. They just stay the same temperature as their environment.

▥▥▥ QUESTIONS ▥▥▥

4   Explain why biomass gets less as you move along a food chain.

5   Suggest why many mammals and birds need to eat more in the winter than in the summer.

6   Explain why snakes need to eat only about once a month, whereas most mammals and birds need to eat much more regularly.

7   Write down **two** food chains, one containing at least one mammal and one containing at least one reptile, fish or amphibian. Using what you know about losses of energy from different kinds of animals, sketch pyramids of biomass for these two food chains to show how their shapes would differ.

...pyramid of biomass   ...respiration

Food production

You will find out:
- How the efficiency of food production can be improved by keeping food chains short
- How keeping animals warm and stopping them moving around saves energy

Feeding cattle

These cattle are eating silage made from maize. The maize plants grew in a field through the summer, and were harvested in the autumn, before being processed to produce food for the cattle. Is this a good way to make use of the maize? Would it be better if we ate it ourselves, rather than feeding it to cattle and then eating them or drinking the milk they produce?

FIGURE 1: Would it be more efficient for us to eat this maize rather than feeding it to these cows?

Short food chains

We've seen that **energy** is lost along **food chains**. This is why biomass gets less and less as you go along the chain. Some people think it would be good if we were all vegetarians. This would mean we would always be at the end of a short food chain, like this:

maize plants ——→ humans

If we eat meat or drink milk, the food chain is longer:

maize plants ——→ cattle ——→ humans

If we reduce the number of steps in the food chain when we produce food, the **efficiency** of **food production** is increased. In theory, more people could be supported on a given area of land.

Fish food

Farmed salmon are fed on meal that is made from other fish that have been caught in the sea. Those fish ate smaller fish, which ate plankton (tiny floating plants and animals).

This is a very long food chain. By the time we eat the farmed salmon, we are a long way along the chain. A lot of energy has been lost along the way. Eating farmed salmon is not very efficient.

FIGURE 2: Feeding salmon at a fish farm.

▥ QUESTIONS ▥

1. Explain why it is more energy efficient to eat plants rather than animals.
2. Cows eat grass. Would it be better if we ate the grass rather than drank the milk the cows produce? Explain your answer.

...efficiency ...energy

Reducing energy losses

Farmers think hard about how to reduce energy losses along the food chains involved in producing their crops and animals.

We've seen that mammals and birds use up a lot of energy to keep their bodies at a constant temperature. If the farmer keeps animals warm, they don't need so much food, because they don't have to generate as much heat. This is more comfortable for the animals, too.

FIGURE 3: These turkeys are housed in a heated barn.

FIGURE 4: Why are these pigs prevented from moving around?

However, another way of reducing energy losses is not so animal-friendly. Animals use up a lot of energy by moving around. If they are kept in a small area where they can't move very much, then more of the energy in their food can go into making more muscle or milk. Less of the energy in the food gets wasted.

Why keep animals?

In many parts of the world, even where people are poor, keeping animals is important for reasons other than just eating them.

- Pigs can eat up scraps and food waste that are inedible for humans. Then the humans can eat the pigs.
- Cattle and yaks can pull ploughs to cultivate the soil, as well as providing milk, meat and skins.

FIGURE 5: These yaks are being used to plough land ready to plant crops.

Food for the world

There have been many ideas about how to produce food for all the people in the world who do not get enough to eat.

Some scientists have looked into growing microorganisms for food. This could be done in huge vats, rather than using up land. For example, in the UK a food called Quorn is made from fungi. The fungi grow in huge steel containers, called fermenters, that are 40 m high. They are fed on glucose syrup or other plant products.

FIGURE 6: Quorn is made from a fungus.

QUESTIONS

6   When milk is used to make cheese, the watery part of the milk, called whey, is a waste product. Some of the whey is used to provide food for yeast, which is grown in a large vat and made into food for cattle.

Draw a food chain using this information. What is odd about it? Do you think this is an energy-efficient system of producing food?

QUESTIONS

3   Find out if anyone in your class is a vegetarian. Why have they decided not to eat meat?

4   In some parts of the world, people are subsistence farmers. This means that they grow most of their own food. Why might it be better for them to be vegetarians?

5   Think of some more reasons why subsistence farmers might keep animals, other than the two listed above.

The cost of good food

You will find out:
- That managing food production can have positive and negative effects
- That solutions to food production and distribution may require compromise between competing priorities

Transport costs

It is estimated that the cost of transporting food in the United Kingdom is as much as £9 billion each year. Food transport accounts for one-quarter of all the miles covered by lorries. This produces 19 million tonnes of carbon dioxide.

Food miles

Since 1974, the quantity of food transported by lorries in the UK has doubled. This is partly because we now buy much more food from supermarkets than we used to. Supermarkets have central distribution points. All the food they buy goes to the central distribution point and is then collected by lorries and taken out to the supermarkets.

In the past, people bought more food from local shops. Now many people are starting to try to do this again. They like to buy locally produced food.

FIGURE 1: A supermarket central distribution point.

Animal welfare

Being able to buy cheap food can mean that the animals it was produced from were kept cheaply. They may not have been given space to move around. They may not have been fed on good-quality food themselves.

In Britain, we have minimum welfare standards that all farmers must meet when they are keeping animals. These standards are often not so high in other countries. This is one reason why food from other countries is often cheaper than food that is produced here.

FIGURE 2: All the food sold at this farmers' market is produced locally.

▪ QUESTIONS ▪

1 Explain what is meant by saying that food miles represent a cost to the environment.
2 Suggest why many people shopping in supermarkets do not look to see where the food has come from.

...barn hens ...battery hens

Egg production

There are three different ways in which eggs are produced.

Battery hens are kept in small cages, indoors, in a heated building. There are up to five hens in each cage. They are fed and provided with water by automated systems. There are regulations about how battery hens may be kept. The EU wants to phase out battery cages by 2012.

In 2005, 60 per cent of the eggs sold in Britain were produced from battery hens.

FIGURE 3: Battery hens.

FIGURE 4: Barn hens.

Barn hens are kept indoors, in a heated building. They are free to walk around and are provided with perches.

In 2005, 6 per cent of the eggs sold in Britain were produced from barn hens.

Free-range hens spend the night indoors, but are free to leave the building and walk around in a large, outside area during the daytime. The area is usually fenced.

In 2005, 34 per cent of eggs sold in Britain were produced from free-range hens.

FIGURE 5: Free-range hens.

QUESTIONS

3 Using what you know about energy uses by animals, suggest why farmers keep hens in battery cages.

4 Suggest why barn eggs and free-range eggs are more expensive than eggs from battery hens.

5 Draw a table to compare the welfare standards for battery hens, barn hens and free-range hens. You could include: space to move, ability to preen, perches provided, provision of warmth, danger from predators, and any other factors that you think of.

Importing food

More than 55 per cent of the food that we eat in the UK is grown in another country. Sometimes, the reason for this is obvious. We cannot grow bananas or oranges here, for example. But quite often food is imported that we *could* produce in our country. Each year we import over 170 million litres of milk, even though we can produce milk really well here.

FIGURE 6: why can't we grow bananas in the UK?

There are many reasons for importing food. For example:

■ We may want to buy food at times of the year when it can't grow here, for example strawberries in March.

■ It may cost less to buy food that has been produced overseas where wages are low, rather then here in the UK where production costs are much higher.

■ It may help the economy of developing countries if we buy food from them.

QUESTIONS

6 Do you think Britain should be self-sufficient in food production? Put forward arguments to support your answer.

7 Discuss how decisions about the best ways to produce and sell food often involve compromises between animal welfare, damage to the environment and the cost of food in the shops.

...food miles ...free-range hens

Death and decay

You will find out:
- That materials decay because they are broken down by microorganisms
- That microorganisms digests things faster in warm, moist conditions
- That many microorganisms are more active when there is plenty of oxygen

Bog body

This body is about 2000 years old. It was found in a peat bog in Cheshire. It is a man who died during Roman times. He had been hit on the head with great force, before having his throat slit. His stomach contained the remains of his last meal – some bread. The body is so well preserved that his clothing, skin, hair and internal organs are all still there.

FIGURE 1: This man died 2000 years ago.

Decay

What happens when something **decays**? Why didn't the body in the bog decay?

FIGURE 2: The blue mould is breaking down the lemon using enzymes.

Decay happens when **microorganisms** feed on a dead body, or waste material from animals and plants, or food. The microorganisms include bacteria and fungi. The microorganisms produce enzymes that digest the food material. It gradually breaks down and dissolves.

Most of these microorganisms need oxygen. They use oxygen for **aerobic respiration**. If they don't have oxygen, then they can't cause decay.

Peat bogs are very wet. There is so much water in them that microorganisms cannot get enough oxygen for respiration. This is why bodies can be preserved in a peat bog. Once the body is buried in the peat, it will decay only very slowly.

⊞ QUESTIONS ⊞

1. What happens when something decays?
2. Think of **three** substances that can decay, and **three** that cannot decay.
3. Explain why the body in the bog did not decay.

...aerobic   ...aerobic respiration   ...decay

Speeding or slowing decay

We have seen that decay is caused by microorganisms. Anything that affects the microorganisms can affect the rate of decay.

Temperature

Microorganisms function most rapidly at warm temperatures.

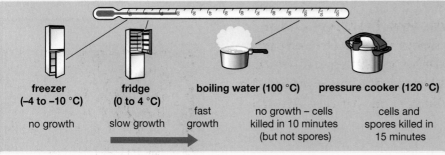

freezer (−4 to −10 °C)	fridge (0 to 4 °C)	boiling water (100 °C)	pressure cooker (120 °C)
no growth	slow growth	fast growth	no growth – cells killed in 10 minutes (but not spores)	cells and spores killed in 15 minutes

FIGURE 3: How temperature affects the activities of microorganisms.

This happens because enzymes catalyse their metabolic reactions, just like ours. Decay will happen fastest at the optimum temperature for their enzymes. Different microorganisms have different optimum temperatures, but for most of them this is somewhere between 25 °C and 45 °C. If we heat them up a lot, they will be killed. However, some microorganisms produce **spores**, which can survive at very high temperatures.

Moisture

Microorganisms need moisture in order to breed and feed. Some kinds can survive when it is very dry, but they won't do anything until some water is available.

FIGURE 4: There is no water in this dried food, so microorganisms cannot grow.

FIGURE 5: This food has been vacuum-packed. All the air has been sucked out, so microorganisms cannot grow.

Oxygen

Many microorganisms are **aerobic**. This means that they need oxygen for respiration. So they are more active when oxygen is available.

Preventing decay

If we don't want food to decay, we can do things to it that slow down or stop the activity of microorganisms.

This photo shows some examples of food that has been treated to stop or slow down decay.

FIGURE 6: Jam, pickled onions and tinned fish have all been treated in different ways to slow down decay.

QUESTIONS

7   The jam is made of fruit that has been cooked with a lot of sugar. Using what you know about osmosis, explain how the high concentration of sugar could stop microorganisms growing in the jam.

8   The onions have been cooked and then put into vinegar. Using what you know about enzymes, explain how this stops microorganisms growing.

9   The fish has been put into a can, heated to a very high temperature and then sealed. Explain how this preserves the fish.

QUESTIONS

4   A fridge is usually kept at about 4 °C. A freezer is usually kept at about −10 °C. Explain why food can be kept for longer in a freezer than in a fridge.

5   What do you think would happen to some frozen food if it is thawed and left in a warm kitchen for a while?

6   Using what you know about microorganisms, temperature and decay, explain why previously frozen food should not be put back into the freezer once it has thawed.

Cycles

You will find out:
- That materials are constantly cycled between the organisms in a community
- That in a stable community, the processes that remove materials are balanced by processes that return materials

Cow-pats

Cow dung contains undigested material from the food that the cows ate. One cow produces more than a cubic metre of dung each day. We are not knee-deep in cow-pats because microorganisms and other small organisms, such as dung beetles, break down and digest the material in the cow-pats.

FIGURE 1: Cow dung is cleared up by microorganisms.

What if...

...there were no **microorganisms** or other animals to cause **decay**? Every dead body or piece of body waste (such as a cow pat) would stay just as it was. None of the substances locked up in the body or the waste would be released. Decay releases substances that plants need to grow. With no decay, plants would not get so many nutrients so they would not grow well.

Recycling

But this isn't what happens. Living organisms take materials from the environment. When they die or produce waste, the material returns to the environment. Some animals such as earthworms, eat dead bodies and waste material and are called **detritus feeders**. Microorganisms also help to make the material decay, releasing the substance back into the environment again.

FIGURE 2: Why do you think the grass near these gravestones is growing so well?

All the organisms that live in one place – a **community** of organisms – are constantly reusing materials that have been part of other organisms. If the community is stable, then there is a balance between the processes that remove materials from the environment, and the processes that return materials to the environment.

Gardeners often make compost heaps of fallen leaves, weeds, unwanted plants – as well as waste food. Inside the heap, microorganisms digest the materials in the plants. After a while, it is broken down into a crumbly brown substance. This compost can be put onto the garden, to provide materials that help the plants to grow.

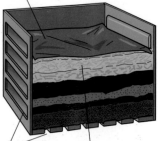

waterproof covering

slats so air can get in

layers of garden waste: the newest is on the top, while the oldest – at the bottom – has been changed into compost

FIGURE 3: Why do you think the compost heap has slats to let the air in?

▪▪ QUESTIONS ▪▪

1. How can decaying waste help plant growth?
2. Explain why it is good for a compost heap to be warm and moist inside.
3. Suggest how having a compost heap in the garden can help the environment.

...biomass   ...community   ...decay   ...detritus feeders

Recycling and food chains

When we have looked at **food chains** and food webs, we haven't thought about microorganisms. This food web shows how they fit into a simple food chain.

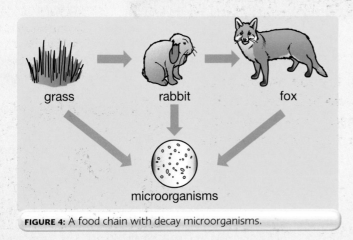

grass　　　rabbit　　　fox

microorganisms

FIGURE 4: A food chain with decay microorganisms.

You can see that these decay microorganisms feed on every organism in the chain. They will break down most of the waste material that the plants and animals produce, and then finally their bodies when they die.

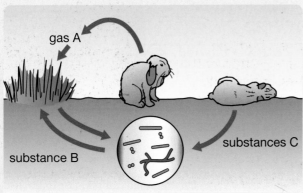

gas A

substance B　　substances C

FIGURE 5: This diagram shows how materials are recycled in an ecosystem.

QUESTIONS

4　Suggest why we don't usually include decay microorganisms when we draw food webs.

5　Are these decay microorganisms producers or consumers? Explain your answer.

6　Think back to what you know about pyramids of **biomass**. Suggest how the biomass of the decay microorganisms might compare with the biomass of the animals in the food chain. Explain your answer.

7　Look at figure 5. What might gas A be? Explain your answer.

8　Think about what plants take up from the soil into their roots. What might substance B be?

9　Think about the substances found in an animal that could be digested. What kind of substances might make up substances C?

Dead whales

If a whale dies at sea, its body will probably sink to the bottom.

Here, there is no light, so nothing photosynthesises. But whole communities of organisms use the whale carcass as food.

FIGURE 6: What happens to a dead whale?

Many different animals, including crabs, worms and fish, eat the whale's body. Microorganisms gradually decay the whale's tissues. The bones are the last to be decayed. The whole process can take decades.

QUESTIONS

10　Draw a food web that includes all the organisms involved with the dead whale. You will need to think about what the producers must have been.

11　Suggest how the nutrients released from the dead whale by the decay microorganisms could eventually get back to the producers.

12　Bodies of whales that die on beaches usually decay much more quickly than those that die at sea. Using what you know about microorganisms and decay, suggest why this is so.

The carbon cycle 1

You will find out:
- That photosynthesis removes carbon dioxide from the atmosphere
- That respiration returns carbon dioxide to the atmosphere
- That carbon is contained in carbohydrates, proteins and fats in plants and animals

Plants on Mars

This is a computer graphic, produced by NASA, showing what greenhouses might look like on Mars. Plants wouldn't be able to grow in the Martian atmosphere, which is much thinner than ours, even though it is mostly carbon dioxide. On Mars, they would need to be kept at a higher pressure than the atmosphere outside them, so that they could get enough carbon dioxide for photosynthesis.

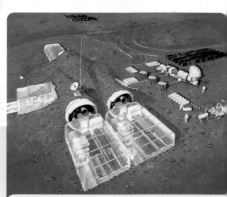

FIGURE 1: Why wouldn't plants be able to grow in the Martian atmosphere?

The importance of carbon

Many of the different substances that make up your body contain carbon. They include carbohydrates, fats and proteins.

The carbon in your body was originally part of a **carbon dioxide** molecule in the air. Somewhere in the world, a plant absorbed some of this carbon dioxide, and used it to make carbohydrates, by **photosynthesis**.

carbon dioxide + water ⟶ glucose (a carbohydrate) + oxygen

The plant also made fats and proteins, all containing some of the carbon atoms it had taken from the air.

You ate food made from that plant, or made from an animal that ate it. That food contained carbon, in carbohydrates, fats or proteins.

FIGURE 2: These peas contain carbohydrates and proteins that the plant made, which will now become food for humans.

Plants use some of these carbohydrates for themselves. They release energy from them, by **respiration**.

glucose + oxygen ⟶ carbon dioxide + water

You are doing the same. In your cells, respiration is happening. The carbon atoms in glucose molecules are becoming part of carbon dioxide molecules.

When you breathe out, you return this carbon dioxide to the air.

This constant cycling of carbon is called the **carbon cycle**.

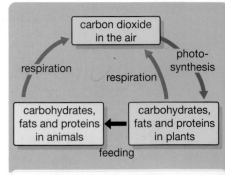

FIGURE 3: A simple carbon cycle.

▌▌ QUESTIONS ▌▌

1. Explain why living organisms need carbon.
2. Where does a plant get its carbon from?
3. Where does your body get its carbon from?
4. Name the process that happens in plants and animals, which returns carbon dioxide to the air.

...carbon cycle ...carbon dioxide ...oxygen

A Martian greenhouse

If people ever live on Mars, they will probably spend most of their time inside a building where the composition of the atmosphere and the temperature are controlled.

NASA is carrying out experiments to find out how they could grow plants on Mars. The plants would need light, so they would grow inside transparent buildings. They would take carbon dioxide out of the air and put oxygen into it, which would help the atmosphere to stay breathable for humans.

On Earth, we rely on plants to keep taking carbon dioxide out of the atmosphere. Overall, the quantity of carbon dioxide that plants take out by photosynthesis approximately equals the quantity that is put back in by respiration.

FIGURE 4: This dome is part of an experiment into how plants could be grown on Mars.

An oxygen-free Earth

Long ago, there was no oxygen on Earth. All the first organisms must have been able to live anaerobically – without oxygen.

Then photosynthesis evolved. It is thought that the first photosynthetic organisms were a kind of bacteria called cyanobacteria. We know this because fossils of weird structures made by these bacteria, called stromatolites, have been found that date back to more than 3 billion years ago. Bacteria like these still live in Shark Bay in Western Australia.

FIGURE 5: Stromatolites in Shark Bay.

These photosynthetic bacteria made so much oxygen that they completely changed the Earth's atmosphere. Now aerobic organisms could begin to evolve.

QUESTIONS

5   The diagram shows an experiment that was set up to investigate the effect of plants and animals on the carbon dioxide content of the air.

The concentration of carbon dioxide in each box was measured. Boxes A, B and C were left in a light place. Box D was put into a dark cupboard. After one week, the concentration of carbon dioxide in each box was measured again.

The table shows the results for boxes A, B and C.

Box	A	B	C
concentration of carbon dioxide at start	0.04%	0.04%	0.04%
concentration of carbon dioxide after 1 week	0.02%	0.04%	0.10%

a   Copy and complete this table to show which process or processes were happening inside each box.

Box	A	B	C	D
respiration	✓			
photosynthesis	✓			

b   Using your answer to question **a** above, explain, for each box in turn, the results for boxes A, B and C.

c   Suggest the result for box D. Give an explanation for your suggestion.

QUESTIONS

6   Imagine you are an anaerobic organism living on Earth 3.5 billion years ago. You are worried that these up-and-coming stromatolites are polluting the Earth's atmosphere. Write a newspaper article (to be read by anaerobic readers) highlighting the problem and suggesting what can be done about it.

The carbon cycle 2

You will find out:
- That when plants and animals die, animals and microorganisms feed on their bodies
- That respiration by the microorganisms returns carbon dioxide to the atmosphere

Deadly beauty

Most of this fly agaric **fungus** is under the ground. Its body is a mass of tiny threads, growing amongst tree roots and dead leaves. The threads secrete enzymes which digest waste materials from the plants and animals in the community. Fly agarics produce toadstools above the ground in the autumn. The toadstools make spores, which can be spread into new areas where they will grow into new fly agarics. Fly agarics are very poisonous.

FIGURE 1: Fly agaric fungus.

The carbon cycle

So far, we have thought mostly about how plants and animals are involved in the **carbon cycle**. But what about the **decomposers**?

Figure 2 shows how animals, plants and decomposers all interact with each other in the carbon cycle.

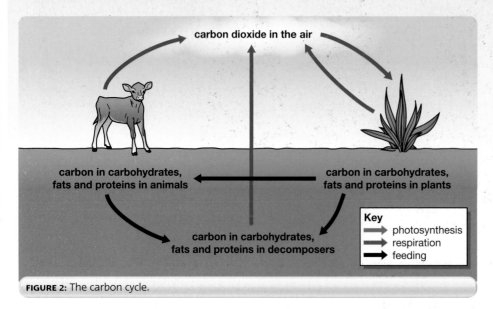

carbon dioxide in the air

carbon in carbohydrates, fats and proteins in animals

carbon in carbohydrates, fats and proteins in plants

carbon in carbohydrates, fats and proteins in decomposers

Key
→ photosynthesis
→ respiration
→ feeding

FIGURE 2: The carbon cycle.

⬛ QUESTIONS ⬛

1   How does this diagram of the carbon cycle differ from the one on page 48?
2   Use the diagram to describe, in your own words, how decomposers help in the carbon cycle.

...carbon cycle ...decay ...decomposers ...fungus

Do trees store carbon?

The concentration of carbon dioxide in the air is slowly increasing. One way that we might be able to take some of this carbon dioxide out of the atmosphere could be to plant more trees. Trees take carbon out of the air when they **photosynthesise**, and some of this carbon is locked up inside their trunks, roots and leaves.

FIGURE 3: *Montmorency forest.*

Researchers in Canada have looked carefully at what happens to carbon in a forest called Montmorency, near Quebec. Figure 4 shows what they found.

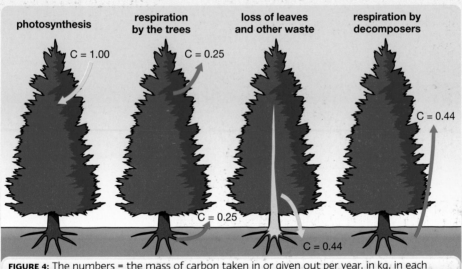

photosynthesis   C = 1.00

respiration by the trees   C = 0.25   C = 0.25

loss of leaves and other waste   C = 0.44

respiration by decomposers   C = 0.44

FIGURE 4: The numbers = the mass of carbon taken in or given out per year, in kg, in each square metre of Montmorency forest.

QUESTIONS

3   How much carbon do the trees use in photosynthesis?

4   How much carbon do the trees give out in respiration?

5   How much carbon do the trees lose in dead leaves and other waste?

6   What happens to this carbon?

7   Use your answers to questions **3**, **4** and **5** to work out how much carbon the trees in the forest store each year.

8   If the trees were cut down and burnt, what would happen to this store of carbon?

9   Which group of organisms has been left out from this study? Suggest how they might affect what happens to the carbon in the forest.

Unit summary

Concept map

Cells all have a cell membrane, a nucleus and cytoplasm.

Plant cells also have a cell wall and vacuole, and sometimes have chloroplasts.

Cells are the basic unit of living organisms.

Cells

Chemical reactions in cells are controlled by enzymes.

Cells can be specialised for particular functions.

Substances enter and leave cells through their partially permeable cell membrane.

Water enters and leaves cells by osmosis, which is a special kind of diffusion.

Substances diffuse from a high concentration to a low concentration.

Photosynthesis happens inside chloroplasts, which contain chlorophyll that absorbs sunlight.

The glucose can be changed into starch for storage, or used in respiration.

Plants use carbon dioxide, water and sunlight to make glucose and oxygen.

Photosynthesis

With the addition of nitrates and magnesium absorbed from the soil, plants can also make proteins and chlorophyll.

The rate of photosynthesis is affected by light, temperature and levels of carbon dioxide.

These can be limiting factors for photosynthesis.

If a plant is short of these mineral salts, it can show deficiency symptoms.

Carbon is removed from the air by photosynthesis and returned to it by respiration.

A pyramid of biomass shows there is less biomass at each level in a food chain.

Decay happens faster when conditions are warm and moist with plenty of oxygen.

Energy passes between organisms along food chains, but some energy is lost at each transfer.

Food webs and cycles

Decomposers feed on all the organisms in a food web.

The shorter the food chain, the more efficient the energy transfer.

Decomposers release carbon dioxide into the air when they respire.

Unit quiz

1 List **three** structures that are found in plant cells but never in animal cells.

2 List **two** ways in which a sperm cell is adapted for its function.

3 Where does diffusion happen fastest – in gases, solids, or liquids?

4 Explain why animal cells burst in pure water, but plant cells do not.

5 Write down the equation for photosynthesis.

6 In what form do plants store the carbohydrates they make during photosynthesis?

7 List **three** factors that can limit the rate of photosynthesis.

8 Explain why plants need nitrate ions.

9 Why are pyramids of biomass pyramid-shaped?

10 Why are eggs from battery hens cheaper than eggs from free-range hens?

11 Name the process that takes carbon from the atmosphere in the carbon cycle.

12 How do decomposers help in the carbon cycle?

Literacy activity

Coral bleaching

Coral reefs are made by colonies of tiny animals, related to jellyfish and sea anemones. The corals make hard skeletons out of calcium carbonate. They feed by catching tiny organisms with their tentacles, which they hold out into the water ready to grab anything that floats by.

The coral animals have a very close relationship with some even smaller, single-celled plant-like organisms. These are called zooxanthellae, and they live *inside* the cells of the coral animals. The zooxanthellae have chloroplasts and can photosynthesise. The coral animals and the zooxanthellae share nutrients with each other.

Coral reefs can only form in shallow water, because there must be enough light for the zooxanthellae to be able to photosynthesise. As global warming happens, it is likely that sea levels will rise, and there will also be a rise in sea temperatures. This could destroy many coral reefs. The first sign that this is happening is when the corals 'bleach' – they lose their bright colours because the zooxanthellae are dying.

QUESTIONS

1 Suggest **two** ways in which the cells of the coral animals and the zooxanthellae differ from one another.

2 What gas, produced by the coral animals, might help the zooxanthellae to photosynthesise?

3 Explain why some coral reefs may not survive if sea levels rise.

4 Many fish graze on corals. Construct a simple food chain for a coral reef.

Exam practice questions

1 The diagram shows an osmosis experiment, using cylinders of potato (cut with a cork borer). Before the experiment started, each cylinder was placed in water for 30 minutes.

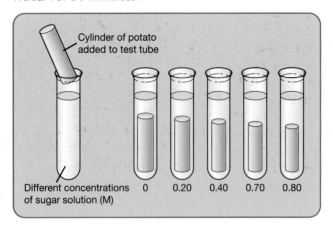

Each cylinder was blotted dry, weighed, then placed in one of the different tubes for 30 minutes. Finally, the potato cylinders were again blotted dry and weighed. The table shows the results of this experiment.

Concentration of sugar solution (M)	0	0.13	0.26	0.45	0.53
Average mass lost (g)	0	0.20	0.40	0.70	0.80

a Copy the grid below and draw a line graph of these results [3]

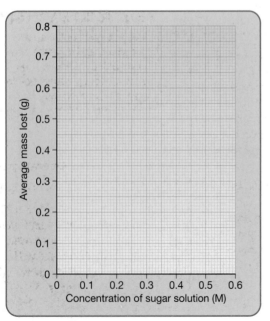

b Use your graph to find:
  i the average mass lost (g) from potato cylinders in 0.3 M sugar solution.
  ii what concentration of sugar solution (M) will result in a loss of mass of 0.17g.

c **i** What happens to the mass of potato cylinders as the concentration of sugar solution increases?
  ii Briefly explain why this happens.

2 The diagram below shows a variegated leaf, used in an experiment on photosynthesis. Only the parts labelled in the diagram contained chlorophyll.

Black card was placed over both sides of the leaf, in the position shown. The plant was placed in the dark for 48 hours. The plant was then exposed to light for several days.

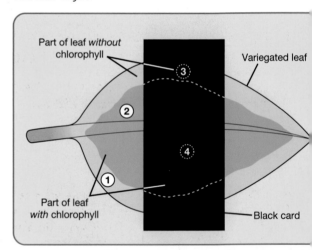

Finally, the card was removed and disks were cut from the leaf in the positions one to four (disks three and four had been **under** the card). The disks were then tested for the presence of starch.

a **i** Which disk/disks was/were likely to contain starch?
  ii What does this experiment tell us about **two** conditions needed for photosynthesis?

b Explain why the plant was placed in the dark for several days.

(Total 13 marks)

Read the passage below about the use of resources in meat production.

The world's meat production has been increasing faster than the rate at which the world's human population has increased. During the period 1950 to 1994, the rate of meat production increased from 18 to 35.4 kg per person. The total weight of the world's 15 billion farm animals is one and a half times greater than the total weight of humans in the world. Populations of humans and farm animals all require resources from the environment. These resources include food, water, space to live, and transportation. However, over-use of these resources is having a detrimental impact on the environment. For example, the land area required for meat-production (1.6 hectares per person) is greater than for non-meat production (0.2 hectares).

This difference is because farm animals do not convert plant protein to animal protein very efficiently. Farm animals, like all animals, 'waste' energy that is therefore not passed along the food chain to humans. The actual production of meat also requires energy. It is estimated that meat production, processing and packaging requires 10 to 20 times more energy per edible tonne than is used for grain production.

a Explain why 'The world's meat production has been increasing faster than the rate at which the world's human population increased.' [2]

b Explain what is meant by 'over-use of these resources is having a detrimental impact on the environment.' [2]

c Explain what is meant by 'farm animals 'waste' energy that is therefore not passed along the food chain.' [2]

This answer is incomplete, because it doesn't account for the difference in rates of meat consumption in relation to the human population. The average consumption **per individual** must also have increased.

a The world's meat production has been going up because more people are eating meat, because the human population has gone up.

b Over-use of resources means using up resources. This happens because some resources are used more quickly than they are replaced. Some resources cannot be replaced, such as forests cut down to make land to graze cattle on for meat production. I think this is wrong, people shouldn't do it.

The main part of the answer is correct, and contains two good points. However, you should avoid personal opinion unless it is asked for.

c Energy is only passed from one feeding level to the next by food, the parts of the farm animal that are actually eaten. Farm animals waste energy by moving about, by keeping their temperature up and by excreting and digesting. This energy does not go to humans, the next animal in the food chain.

This is a good answer. It shows an understanding of principles involved in energy transfer within ecosystems.

Overall grade: B

How to get an A

Read the question carefully. Then, read your answer carefully! Have you fully answered the question?

Biology 2b

DISCOVER DNA!

Chromosomes are found in the nucleus of cells. They are made of DNA. DNA stores information as a code: the Genetic Code. Each section of the DNA is a gene. Each gene codes for the production of a different protein.

A cell.

Its nucleus.

The double helix of DNA showing the code.

The DNA molecule is highly coiled in the nucleus.

CONTENTS

Enzymes – biological catalysts

You will find out:
- How enzymes work
- That temperature and pH can affect enzymes
- That enzymes are involved in chemical processes, such as respiration and photosynthesis

Acid indigestion

Hannah was having a great day. She got an 'A' in maths and the boy she likes had said "hi". For lunch she had a beefburger with cheese, peppers, and lots of onions washed down with a fizzy drink. That afternoon, in science, she felt a burning sensation in the back of her throat. Her stomach started to hurt too. Hannah had a mean case of ... acid indigestion!

Speeding up chemical reactions

There are hundreds of different chemical reactions going on in our cells all the time. These reactions are necessary for life. **Enzymes** are **biological catalysts**. They speed up reactions that would otherwise be too slow. All enzymes have the same characteristics:

- they are **protein molecules**
- they are affected by **temperature**
- they are affected by **pH**
- they control one specific chemical reaction
- they make the reaction happen quickly
- they are not used up (the enzyme can be reused).

Enzymes are made of long chains of **amino acids**. These are folded to give the enzyme a special shape. This is very important as it allows another chemical molecule to fit into the shape of the enzyme. It's a bit like your hand and a glove. The glove is the enzyme and your hand is the molecule. Your hand will fit into the glove just like the other chemical will fit into the enzyme.

The chemical that an enzyme works on is called a **substrate**. The part of an enzyme molecule that reacts with its substrate is called the **active site**.

High temperatures change the shape of the enzyme molecule. If the shape is altered then the chemical on which the enzyme works will not fit. This means that the enzyme stops working. Different enzymes work best at different pHs.

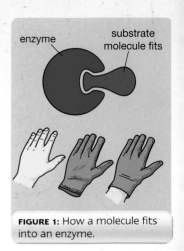

enzyme   substrate molecule fits

FIGURE 1: How a molecule fits into an enzyme.

Name of enzyme	Where it is found	Its optimum (ideal) pH
salivary amylase	mouth	6.5 – 7.5
pepsin (a protease)	stomach	2.0
lipase (from the pancreas)	small intestine	7.0

TABLE 1: Digestive enzymes.

Some chemical reactions

Enzymes make the following chemical reactions happen:

- **respiration** in plant and animal cell
- **protein synthesis** in plant and animal cells
- **photosynthesis** in plant leaf cells.

▣▣ QUESTIONS ▣▣

1. What are enzymes and what do they do?
2. Why does an enzyme have to be a special shape?
3. Why does an enzyme stop working when it is heated up too much?
4. Name an enzyme that has an ideal pH of 2. Where is this enzyme found?

...active site   ...amino acid   ...biological catalysts   ...denatured   ...enzymes ...pH

More about enzymes

There are two main groups of enzymes:

Group 1: These enzymes break down large molecules into smaller molecules. Digestive enzymes belong to this group.

Group 2: These enzymes takes smaller molecules and builds them up into larger ones. Enzymes involved in making proteins from amino acids belong to this group.

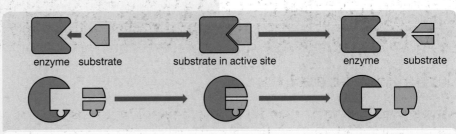

FIGURE 2: The enzyme above breaks things down, the enzyme below builds things up.

enzyme substrate   substrate in active site   enzyme   substrate

What happens when enzymes are heated up?

Most of the enzymes in our body work best at about 37 °C. This is normal body heat and is called the optimum temperature. Optimum means *best*. At temperatures below the optimum (below 37 °C) enzymes work more slowly. At very low temperatures they are inactivated. However, if you warm it up again the enzyme starts working. At temperatures above the optimum the enzyme is permanently changed. Its active site is no longer the right shape and so the substrate no longer fits. When the enzyme is permanently changed like this it is said to have **denatured**.

a normal enzyme   a denatured enzyme

FIGURE 3: The enzyme on the right has been denatured. Will its substrate now fit?

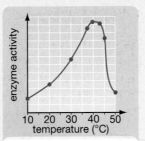

FIGURE 4: Graph showing the effect of temperature on enzyme action.

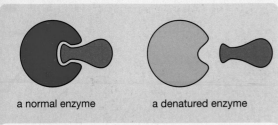

optimum pH of pepsin   optimum pH of amylase

FIGURE 5: Graph showing the effect of pH on enzyme activity.

What happens when the pH is changed?

Enzymes are also sensitive to pH, which is how much acid or alkali is present. Different enzymes have different optimum pHs, see Table 1. If the pH is wrong then the enzyme denatures.

Hotter is faster!

Chemical reactions go faster if they are heated up. Scientists have discovered that, at temperatures below their optimum, enzymes double their rate of reaction for every 10 °C increase in temperature.

Catalase is an enzyme that catalyses the break down of hydrogen peroxide. Hydrogen peroxide is a poisonous by-product of the metabolism of some plant and animal cells, including those found in peas, potatoes and the liver.

Here is the equation:

hydrogen peroxide $\xrightarrow{\text{catalase}}$ water + oxygen

In an experiment, some raw potato was liquidised and put into eight separate test tubes. Each was kept at a different temperature. Equal volumes of hydrogen peroxide were poured into each test tube and the oxygen released was collected. Here are the volumes collected:

Temp. °C	0	10	20	30	37	50	60	70
Volume of oxygen produced in 1 min (cm³)	2	4	9	17	32	15	1	0

TABLE 2: Oxygen produced at different temperatures in 1 min (cm³).

QUESTIONS

5 What is the optimum temperature for our body's enzymes?

6 What happens to an enzyme when it is denatured? Suggest something that can cause this.

7 Look at figure 4; describe what happens to the reaction as the temperature increases.

8 Now look at figure 5, describe how the pepsin curve is different from the amylase curve.

QUESTIONS

9 Draw a graph of these results.

10 Do these results support the idea that the rate of reaction doubles for each increase of 10 °C?

11 What happens to the rate of reaction at temperatures above 37 °C? Explain why.

Enzymes and digestion

You will find out:
- That some enzymes work inside cells and others work outside
- That there are three main groups of digestive enzymes
- About the conditions that allow these enzymes to work most effectively

Barium meal

Barium sulfate shows up in X-rays. Doctors will give you a drink of barium sulfate so that they can look at your stomach and intestines without operating on you. This picture shows the stomach (in yellow) full of barium sulfate. This technique can be used to show up problems like ulcers and cancer. The stomach in this picture is healthy.

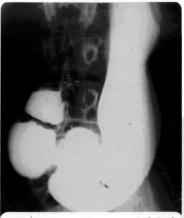

FIGURE 1: X-ray of a stomach full of barium sulfate.

Digestive enzymes

Digestive enzymes break down large, insoluble molecules into smaller, soluble ones. These can then be absorbed into the blood system. Digestive enzymes are like scissors. They cut large food molecules into smaller bits. The blood transports the smaller bits to where they are needed. Specialised cells in glands make digestive enzymes. The enzymes pass out of the gland cells and into the gut. Here they come in contact with the food we eat. They then start to digest it.

There are three main groups of digestive enzymes. Each type digests a different food group.

- **Amylase** enzymes (figure 2) – these break down starch into sugars in the mouth and small intestine.

- **Protease** enzymes (figure 3) – these break down **proteins** into **amino acids** in the stomach and small intestine.

- **Lipase** enzymes (figure 4) – These break down **fats** and **oils** into **fatty acids** and **glycerol** in the small intestine.

Enzyme producing **glands** are found in different parts of the gut (see figure 5).

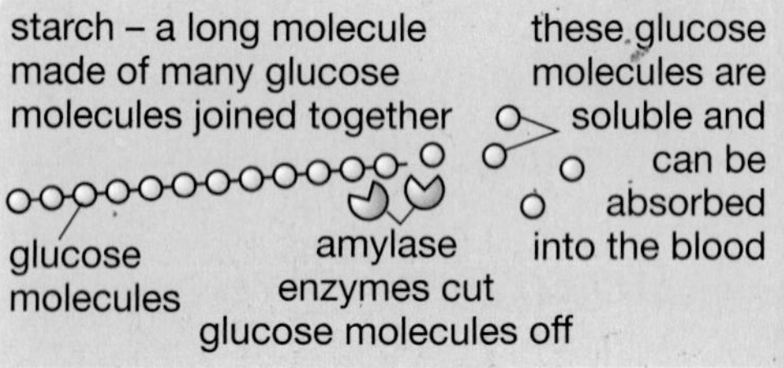

starch – a long molecule made of many glucose molecules joined together

these glucose molecules are soluble and can be absorbed into the blood

glucose molecules

amylase enzymes cut glucose molecules off

FIGURE 2: How starch is digested.

protein molecule - made of many amino acid molecules joined together

amino acid molecules are soluble - they can be absorbed into the blood

protease enzymes cut amino acid molecules off

FIGURE 3: How protein is digested.

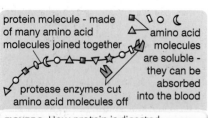

glycerol

fatty acid
fatty acid
fatty acid

lipid

lipase enzymes cut the glycerol from the fatty acids - they can absorbed into the blood

FIGURE 4: How fat and oil is digested.

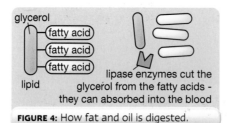

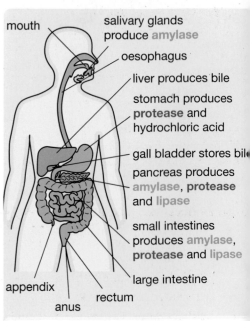

mouth

salivary glands produce amylase

oesophagus

liver produces bile

stomach produces **protease** and hydrochloric acid

gall bladder stores bile

pancreas produces amylase, **protease** and lipase

small intestines produces amylase, **protease** and lipase

large intestine

appendix

rectum

anus

FIGURE 5: The human digestive system.

QUESTIONS

1 What do digestive enzymes do?
2 What are the **three** different types of digestive enzymes?

amino acids ...amylase ...bile ...digestive enzymes ...fat ...fatty acids ...gall bladde

Why is there acid in the stomach?

As well as producing protease, (it's actually called **pepsin**) the stomach also produces hydrochloric acid. It does this for several reasons:

- it kills many of the bacteria that we eat with our food (so it's an important part of our defences)
- it changes the shape of the proteins we eat (denatures them), which makes them easier to digest
- it activates the stomach enzymes which can only work in acid conditions.

When pepsin is first made it is *inactive*. This is just as well because it could start digesting our own stomach! The hydrochloric acid *activates* the enzyme so that it can digest the proteins we eat.

What does bile do?

The **liver** produces **bile**, which is stored in the **gall bladder**. Bile is a strong alkali. It **neutralises** the acid from the stomach when it passes into the small intestine. The enzymes in the small intestine need an alkaline pH to work most effectively.

It also emulsifies the fats that we eat. This means that it breaks large drops of fat or oil into much smaller ones. This increases the surface area for the lipase enzymes to work on.

As well as producing different enzymes to digest our food, the small intestine also absorbs digested food. It is specially adapted to do this by having millions of finger-like villi (the singular is villus).

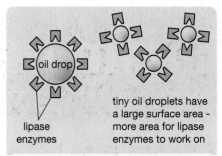

tiny oil droplets have a large surface area - more area for lipase enzymes to work on

lipase enzymes

oil drop

FIGURE 6: Why are tiny fat droplets digested faster?

Stapled stomach

The human digestive system is between six and seven metres long. It starts with your mouth and ends at your anus. Food takes up to about 48 hours to pass through. As it moves from one part of the alimentary canal to the next it is digested. Some people are obese. In an attempt to lose weight they have part of their stomach stapled together. As a result of this the stomach is effectively made smaller.

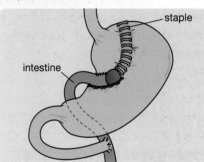

staple

intestine

FIGURE 8: How does a stapled stomach help weight loss?

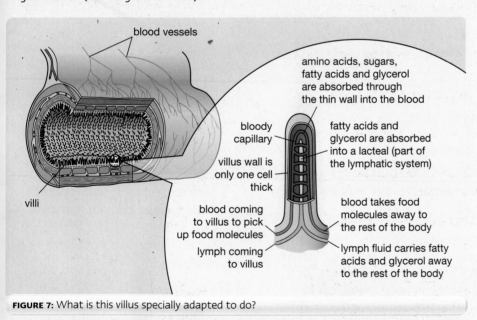

blood vessels

amino acids, sugars, fatty acids and glycerol are absorbed through the thin wall into the blood

bloody capillary

fatty acids and glycerol are absorbed into a lacteal (part of the lymphatic system)

villus wall is only one cell thick

villi

blood coming to villus to pick up food molecules

blood takes food molecules away to the rest of the body

lymph coming to villus

lymph fluid carries fatty acids and glycerol away to the rest of the body

FIGURE 7: What is this villus specially adapted to do?

QUESTIONS

3 Use the word 'optimum' to explain why the stomach produces hydrochloric acid.

4 Why is it important for pepsin to be inactive when it is first made?

5 What **two** jobs does bile do?

6 Describe how villi are adapted to absorb digested food.

QUESTIONS

7 Why is the human digestive system so long?

8 Why does food remain in it for such a long time?

9 How would stapling someone's stomach affect his or her eating habits?

10 Some people feel that stomach stapling should be freely available. Others argue that it should only be available privately i.e. patients should pay for it (the procedure is very expensive). In your group discuss both of these points of view. List as many reasons as you can for each side of the argument.

Enzymes at home

You will find out:
- That enzymes are useful to us in the home
- That biological detergents contain enzymes that digest stains on clothes

Grapes, yeast and alcohol

People have been making wine for about 8000 years. The process involves fermentation. No one knows how it was first discovered. Perhaps some grapes got squashed and were left for a few days. Then maybe someone tasted the juice and liked it! Grapes have a white 'bloom' on their skin, which is a type of yeast. This makes an enzyme that changes the sugar in grape juice into alcohol.

FIGURE 1: Grapes with yeast on their skins

At home with enzymes and food

Enzymes are very useful to us. Not only do they help us digest the food we eat, they also help to make some of the food we eat. **Microorganisms** produce many of these enzymes. They make enzymes that pass out of their cells. We can use the microorganisms to make certain foods. Most of these useful enzymes are carbohydrases. They help to break down sugars (carbohydrates).

Figure 2 shows some foods and drinks we make with the help of enzymes from microorganisms. The foods and drinks in the left hand group are made using yeast, while those in the right-hand group are made using bacteria.

FIGURE 2: These are made with the help of enzymes

Biological detergents

These are washing powders that contain two important enzymes:

- **proteases** (protein digesting)
- **lipases** (fat digesting).

Many different chemicals stain our clothes. These include proteins (such as blood and egg) and lipids (such as butter and oil).

When proteins get onto clothes, they dry and leave a stain. The proteins cling onto the fibres of the clothes and are very difficult to remove. Non-biological washing powders (they don't have enzymes) have to be heated up to almost boiling point to remove these stains. This can shrink clothes or make the colours run. Biological washing powders work at lower temperatures, about 35–40°C.

Lots of people use **biological detergents**, but not everyone can. Some people are allergic to them. They come out in rashes or even blisters.

FIGURE 3: Biological versus non-biological washing powders: which is best?

> ## QUESTIONS
>
> 1. Which microorganisms can we use to make foods?
> 2. What is the difference between biological and non-biological detergents?
> 3. Why do some manufacturers suggest not to heat up their biological washing powders too much?
> 4. What can happen to clothes if they are heated up too much?

...biological detergents ...enzymes ...lipases

How biological detergents work

Some stains will dissolve in water. They can be washed out quite easily. However, many stains are insoluble. This means that they have to be changed, they have to be made soluble.

Protein stains

Protein molecules are made of long chains of amino acids. Blood is a common stain. Haemoglobin in blood is a protein and contains 574 amino acids.

Protease enzymes do two things:

- they digest the protein 'glue' that binds the stain to the fabric
- they digest the protein stain directly.

Once the stain has been detached from the fabric, it can be rinsed away in the water.

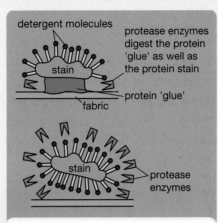

FIGURE 4: Removing a protein stain.

Fat stains

Fats are insoluble in water. So to remove them, like proteins, their molecules have to be changed. Detergents are long molecules that have a 'head end' that is attracted to water and a long 'tail' that is repelled from water. Figure 6 shows how a fat stain is dealt with.

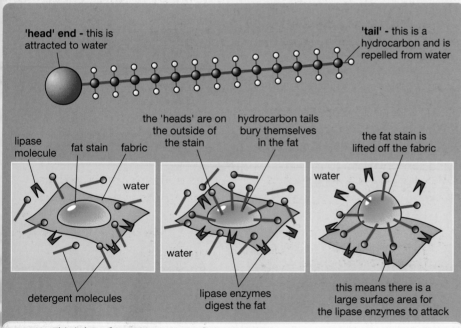

FIGURE 5: This is how fat stains are removed.

┅┅┅ **QUESTIONS** ┅┅┅

5   Why are protein and fat stains difficult to remove using non-biological detergents?

6   Describe how protein stains are removed from fabric.

7   Draw a flow chart that shows how fat stains are removed.

Enzyme toothpaste

FIGURE 6: Lack of saliva can be a big problem.

Normally we produce enough saliva to keep the inside of our mouths wet and to start digesting the food we eat. Some people suffer from a condition known as 'xerostomia' or dry mouth. Their salivary glands do not produce enough liquid. Doctors suggest the following 'dos' and 'don'ts':

Do

- sip liquids regularly, especially with meals
- eat meals with gravy or sauces
- take small mouthfuls and eat slowly

Don't

- eat spicy, acidic or very salty food
- drink alcohol or fizzy drinks
- use mouthwashes containing alcohol

A manufacturer has produced a special toothpaste that claims to combat xerostomia.

┅┅┅ **QUESTIONS** ┅┅┅

8   Imagine you are a doctor. A patient comes to you complaining of a very dry mouth. What questions would you ask them to help you decide if they had xerostomia?

9   Now imagine you are a research scientist. Design an experiment to see if this special toothpaste really works.

Enzymes and industry

You will find out:
- That some microorganisms produce useful enzymes
- That enzymes are used in the preparation of baby foods
- The advantages and disadvantages of using enzymes in industry

Would you eat old boots?

Some meat is tender; some is tough as old boots! One way to make tough meat tender is to beat it with a meat mallet. Why does this work? The mallet smashes up the cells in the meat and releases the enzymes inside them. The proteases start to digest the tough fibrous proteins. This makes the meat tender and easier to eat.

FIGURE 1: Why would a chef use a meat mallet?

More uses of enzymes

Enzymes are biological catalysts. They break down large molecules into smaller ones. They help to digest our food (see pages 60–61) as well as being used in the home (see pages 62–63).

Enzymes are also used to make:

- baby foods
- sugar syrup
- slimming foods.

Baby foods

When babies are born, their digestive systems are not fully developed. Some baby-food manufacturers add **proteases** (protein digesting enzymes) to their products. By '**pre-digesting**' the proteins, they make it easier for the baby to digest the food.

FIGURE 2: Lots of people buy specially produced baby foods – but do they know what's in them?

Sugar syrup

When a solution of **starch** or **sugar** is *saturated* it is called a **syrup**. **Carbohydrases** are enzymes used to convert starch syrup into sugar syrup. Potatoes and corn starch are commonly used. Starch syrup is cheaper to make than sugar syrup. It can then be changed into sugar syrup by adding carbohydrase to it. Sugar syrups are ingredients of sports drinks. We drink these to give us energy.

Slimming foods

Lots of people try to lose weight. Some just eat less. Others eat special slimming foods. These foods contain a sugar called **fructose**. Fructose is much sweeter than **glucose**. This means that slimming food manufacturers can use less of it. Glucose can be changed into fructose by an enzyme called **isomerase**.

$$glucose \xrightarrow{\text{isomerase}} fructose$$

FIGURE 3: A strenuous workout means you use a lot of energy.

QUESTIONS

1. What are proteases?
2. Why are they added to some manufactured baby foods?
3. Why do sports drink manufacturers use carbohydrases?
4. Explain why slimming foods might contain fructose instead of glucose.

...carbohydrases ...enzymes ...fructose ...glucose ...isomerase

How fast is that?

Enzymes break down large molecules very quickly. When an enzyme molecule catalyses a reaction the enzyme is not used up, it is recycled. It can be reused. Some enzyme molecules can catalyse over 10 million reactions per second. This means that you only need a very little enzyme to do a lot of reactions.

The biochemistry of baby foods

Baby foods contain all the basic food groups including carbohydrates, proteins and fats. A baby cannot digest everything it eats so baby food manufacturers add proteases to their foods. These enzymes break down large protein molecules. When the baby eats this pre-digested food it can absorb the amino acids and so grow and be healthy. As the baby grows, its own digestive system develops and produces all the enzymes it needs. Babies grow out of needing pre-digested foods as they can digest all they need for themselves.

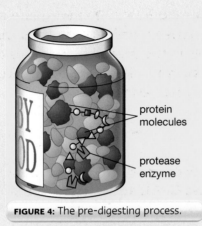

protein molecules

protease enzyme

FIGURE 4: The pre-digesting process.

Do slimming foods work?

The amount of food you need each day depends on a range of factors including your:

- age
- sex/gender
- level of activity.

Age	Energy used each day (kJ)
14–15 year old girl	9700
14–15 year old boy	12 500

TABLE 1: Typical daily energy requirements.

If you eat more food than you need the chances are you will put on weight. Slimming foods often contain less fat and sugars. Fats and sugars are responsible for most people gaining weight.

Advantages and disadvantages

You have now read about the various uses of enzymes. Clearly there are advantages to using enzymes in the home (see pages 62–63) and in industry. But can you think of any disadvantages?

(see pages 62–63)

see pages 62–63

Those soft-centred chocolates were hard once!

FIGURE 5: What makes these chocolates soft-centred?

Soft-centred chocolates are made with the help of enzymes.

This is how they are made:

- a mixture of sucrose, fruit flavouring, colouring and a little water are mixed together
- a very small amount of sucrase is added
- the mixture is moulded into appropriate shapes
- they set
- liquid chocolate is poured over them and left to set
- they are warmed up to 37 °C (chocolate melts at a higher temperature).

The following chemical reaction happens inside the chocolate case:

$$sucrose \xrightarrow{sucrase} glucose + fructose$$

Glucose and fructose are much more soluble than sucrose. Very little water is needed for them to dissolve. When you eat the chocolates the centres are soft and runny.

QUESTIONS

5. Why do manufacturers only have to add very small quantities of enzymes to the foods they produce?

6. Suggest why baby foods have to be 'pre-digested'.

7. What might happen to a 15-year-old boy if he eats food that provides 18 000 kJ each day?

8. Why do slimming foods often contain reduced amounts of fats or sugars?

QUESTIONS

9. Which ingredient should be left out if you wanted the centres to be hard?

10. Why does the recipe use sucrose?

11. Why do the chocolates have to be warmed up to 37 °C?

12. Why do the centres become runny?

...pre-digesting ...protease ...starch ...sugar ...syrup

Respiration and energy

You will find out:
- What aerobic respiration is
- What the formula for respiration is
- That most respiration happens in cell organelles called mitochondria
- About some of the uses of energy from respiration

C is for cyanide; D is for death

Over 1,000 different plants produce cyanide. But even low concentrations of cyanide are very toxic. Cyanide poisons us by stopping a particular enzyme from working. This enzyme is involved in releasing energy from glucose. It is found in every cell of our body. Without energy we die.

FIGURE 1: Cyanide – a deadly poison.

Where does energy come from?

We get the **energy** we need from food. Carbohydrates are an important source of energy. When they are digested we get sugars. A vital sugar is **glucose**. Because it is soluble, glucose is absorbed into the blood and transported to active cells. The blood also takes **oxygen** to these cells. Glucose and oxygen react and release energy. This reaction is called **aerobic respiration**. It's called *aerobic* because it uses oxygen. Respiration that does not use oxygen to release energy is called *anaerobic respiration*. Aerobic respiration can be summarised by this equation:

glucose + oxygen ⟶ carbon dioxide + water + energy

This reaction happens in special organelles called **mitochondria** (the singular is mitochondrion).

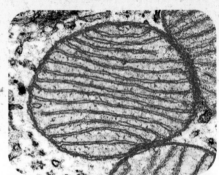

Where does the energy go?

All living things need energy to do things. Here is a list of some of the things animals use energy for:

- to build large molecules from small ones
- to make proteins from amino acids
- to make muscles contract for movement
- birds and mammals (including us) use energy to maintain a steady body temperature in colder surroundings.

We also use energy:
- to sleep
- to think! (do *you* use a lot of energy for this?)

Plants use energy:
- to make sugars
- to make proteins from nitrates and other nutrients.

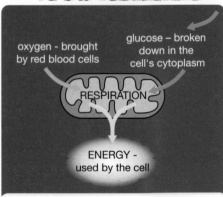

FIGURE 2: A mitochondrion – where aerobic respiration happens.

QUESTIONS

1. What is aerobic respiration?
2. Where does it happen?
3. List **two** things that animals need energy for.
4. What do plants need energy for?

...aerobic respiration ...energy ...glucose ...mitochondria

How animals use energy

When glucose reacts with oxygen in the mitochondria, energy is released. This energy is used for various things.

Energy and muscles

Muscles need energy to contract. This lets us move from one place to another. Energy is also needed to move food through our digestive system.

Energy and heat

Birds and mammals are *warm-blooded*. This means that their temperature is higher than that of their surroundings. Our body temperature is normally around 37 °C. Most mammals and birds have a temperature of between 36 °C and 40 °C. Releasing energy as heat allows these animals to live in places that are too cold for many other, cold-blooded animals.

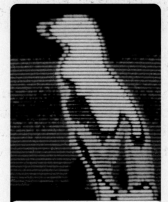

FIGURE 3: On this thermogram of a penguin the white and pale blue areas are warm and the dark blue areas are cold.

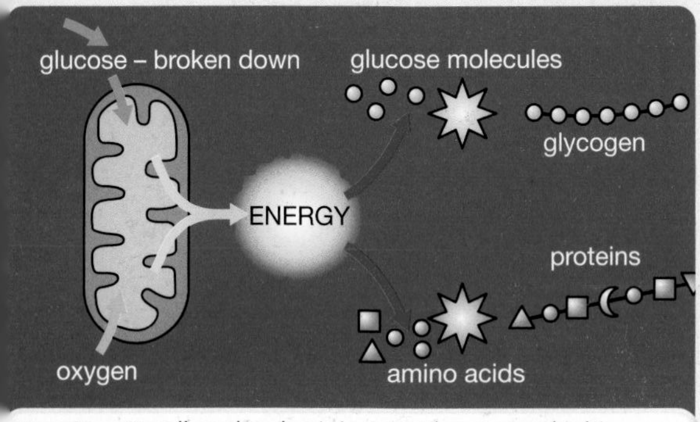

FIGURE 4: Small molecules join together to make big ones.

Building big molecules

Energy is needed to make large molecules from smaller ones. So when glucose molecules are linked together to make glycogen, energy is needed. Glycogen is useful because it is insoluble and so can be stored for future use. When a cell needs energy it can break the glycogen down into glucose molecules again. The glucose is then respired to release energy for the cell. Amino acids are joined together to make enzymes and other proteins.

How plants use energy

Plants photosynthesise. They use light energy to convert carbon dioxide and water into sugars and oxygen.

The sugars can be either stored as starch or used by mitochondria and respired. The plants can then use this energy. Glucose can be altered by combining it with **nitrates** and other **nutrients** (which are absorbed by the roots). This is used to make amino acids, which can be built into proteins.

Sperms – do they have the energy?

When sperms are released at the top of a woman's vagina they still have a long way to travel. A human sperm will have to cover between 10–15 cm before it gets to the egg. Each sperm is about 40 microns long (there are a million microns in a metre). About 200 000 000 sperms are released during sexual intercourse of which only a few hundred get anywhere close to the egg. As they move along the oviduct they often stop for short periods. Most sperms die on the way either in the uterus or in the oviduct. Though sperms have lots of mitochondria they have no food reserves for respiration

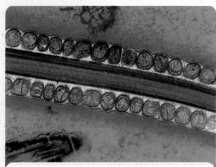

FIGURE 5: This photomicrograph shows a section of a sperm tail (the line across the centre of the picture) between tightly packed rows of mitochondria.

QUESTIONS

9 Why do sperms have so many mitochondria?

10 Where do they get the sugars and oxygen they need for respiration?

11 Suggest a reason why sperms stop on the way to the egg.

QUESTIONS

5 Why do muscles need energy?

6 What advantage do *warm-blooded* animals have over *cold-blooded* animals?

7 Where do plants get the nitrogen they need to make amino acids?

8 Why is it so important for plants and animals to build proteins?

...nitrates ...nutrients ...oxygen

Removing waste: lungs

You will find out:
- That carbon dioxide is made as a by-product of respiration
- That this carbon dioxide has to be removed from the body
- How the lungs remove carbon dioxide

Lungs can cause dehydration

A common problem when you fly in a plane is dehydration. The air in the cabin is not always properly humidified. As you breathe out you lose water from your lungs. As a result, you can also suffer from a dry mouth and nose. To prevent dehydration, drink water regularly throughout the flight, especially if it's a long one. But your lungs are designed for another, very important purpose – gas exchange. Without gas exchange we would die.

FIGURE 1: Drink water on flights to prevent dehydration.

The lungs – a waste disposal unit

When we **respire** we make **carbon dioxide**. This is a waste substance and has to be excreted. Carbon dioxide is produced by our cells and is transported to the lungs by blood's plasma. In the **lungs** it **diffuses** out from the blood into the air sacs (alveoli). Then, when we breathe out, it is removed from our bodies.

Breathing in and out – ventilation

Breathing in is called **inspiration** and breathing out is called **expiration**. We have muscles that help us do this. They are:

- two sets of **intercostal muscles** – found between our ribs
- the **diaphragm** – found at the bottom of the thorax (chest).

If you sit quietly and put your hands on your chest you will feel it go up and down. Going up is breathing in and going down is breathing out.

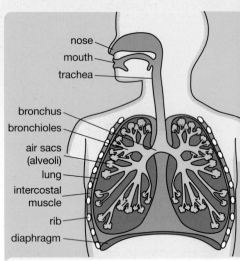

FIGURE 2: How do our lungs get rid of carbon dioxide?

nose
mouth
trachea
bronchus
bronchioles
air sacs (alveoli)
lung
intercostal muscle
rib
diaphragm

INSPIRATION	EXPIRATION
diaphragm muscle contracts and moves down	diaphragm muscle relaxes and returns to its original position
one set of intercostal muscles contract and move the ribs up	the other set of intercostal muscles contract and move the ribs back down
the air pressure in the lungs decreases and air is sucked in	this causes the air pressure in the lungs to increase and so air is blown out
the volume of the chest cavity increases	the volume of the chest cavity decreases

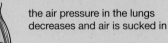

FIGURE 3: How does the diaphragm help us to breathe?

QUESTIONS

1. What **two** substances do we make during respiration?
2. Look at the picture of the lungs in the chest in figure 2. Starting with the nose, list the parts, in order, through which air passes to get to the alveoli.
3. What is the difference between inspiration and expiration?
4. Describe how the diaphragm moves during breathing.

Watch Out The lungs inflate because of the movements of the diaphragm and one set of intercostal muscles. They deflate because these muscles return to their original positions. It's not the other way round.

...carbon dioxide ...diaphragm ...diffuses ...expiration

Carbon dioxide out and oxygen in

In order to remove all the carbon dioxide we make (and to get the oxygen we need) we have specially adapted lungs.

They have the following features:

- thin walls so that the gases can diffuse quickly
- a very large surface area so that enough of the two gases can pass through
- a rich blood supply to transport the gases.

Somebody once worked out that the surface area of the lungs was about the size of a tennis court!

Carbon dioxide diffuses out of the blood and into the alveoli (singular is alveolus) down a concentration gradient. At the same time oxygen moves in the opposite direction. Table 1 shows the percentages of the main gases in the air.

Name of gas	In inhaled air (approximate %)	In exhaled air (approximate %)
carbon dioxide	0.04	4
oxygen	21	16
nitrogen	79	79
water vapour	Variable	high

TABLE 1: Percentages of gases in inhaled and exhaled air.

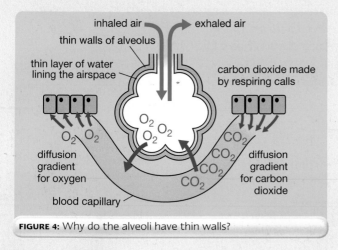

FIGURE 4: Why do the alveoli have thin walls?

Control of breathing

Normally we do not have to think about breathing. Our brain takes care of everything, it is automatic. If carbon dioxide levels in our blood get too high then the brain sends extra nerve impulses to the diaphragm and the intercostal muscles. This makes us breathe more deeply and faster and so excrete more carbon dioxide.

SCUBA diving

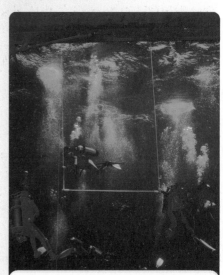

FIGURE 5: These divers are decompressing under their boat after a dive.

Self-contained underwater breathing apparatus (SCUBA) allows you to swim underwater. The gas tank contains compressed air, which is in the same proportions as ordinary air, (see Table 1). As you dive, gases from the tank are absorbed into your blood. You need the oxygen, but not the nitrogen. The deeper you dive the more nitrogen is absorbed. If you then come to the surface too quickly some of the nitrogen will come out of solution and form bubbles in your blood stream. This is called having the 'bends' and can be very painful and dangerous.

QUESTIONS

5   Why do our lungs have to have such a large surface area?

6   Explain why there is so much more carbon dioxide in the air we breathe out than in the air we breathe in.

7   Explain why there has to be a concentration gradient for the carbon dioxide to be excreted.

8   What happens when there is too much dissolved carbon dioxide in our blood?

QUESTIONS

9   What is 'the bends'?

10 What effect does enriching the air have on a diver's ability to dive?

11 Design a leaflet or poster about the possible dangers associated with diving.

Removing waste: liver and kidneys

You will find out:
- That the body produces waste products that have to be removed
- How urea from protein digestion is removed
- How the liver and kidneys remove waste substances

FIGURE 1: This kangaroo rat lives in one of the hottest places on Earth – and does not drink!

All mammals make urea

Some mammals have very efficient kidneys. The kangaroo rat can produce urine that is 17 times more concentrated than its blood. The best we can do is four times as concentrated. Kangaroo rats survive without drinking water. They manage on the water content of their food and the water produced by respiration. We like to think we are highly advanced. So why don't we have kidneys as efficient as this?

What happens to excess proteins?

A balanced diet must include **proteins**. When these are digested they are broken down into **amino acids**. Amino acids contain nitrogen. Some amino acids are used to build proteins that we need. Others have to be removed. They are converted into **urea** in the **liver**. Urea is taken to our **kidneys** by the blood. The kidneys then filter the blood and remove waste substances, including urea. This liquid is called **urine** and is temporarily stored in the **bladder**.

What does urine contain?

Table 1 compares what is in urine with what is found in solution in blood plasma.

Substance	Found in blood plasma %	Found in urine %
water	92	95
amino acids	0.05	0
proteins	8	0
glucose	0.1	0
salt	0.37	0.6
urea	0.03	2

TABLE 1: Composition of urine and blood plasma.

The liver

food in the small intestines

amino acids used to make proteins

proteins digested here

waste amino acids converted into urea

amino acids transported by the blood

urea transported to the kidneys in solution in blood plasma

kidney

urine passes down this tube – the ureter – to be stored in the bladder

blood is filtered here and urea is removed

FIGURE 2: How our bodies remove urea.

■■ QUESTIONS ■■

1 What happens to the amino acids that we do not need?
2 Where is urea made?
3 What is urine?
4 Name two things that are found in blood plasma but not in urine.

...*amino acids* ...*bladder* ...*filtrate* ...*kidneys* ...*liver*

The liver

The liver is the largest organ in our bodies and weighs about 1.5 kg. It does about 450 jobs and produces over 1 000 different enzymes. These control all the chemical reactions that go on in the liver.

The liver converts un-needed amino acids into urea. Figure 3 shows how.

How the kidneys work

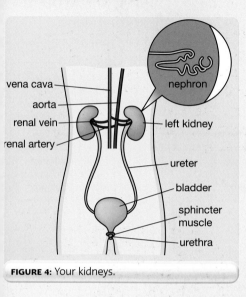

FIGURE 4: Your kidneys.

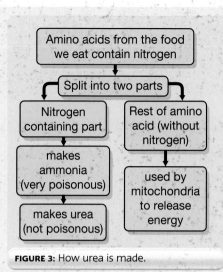

FIGURE 3: How urea is made.

We have two kidneys and they are at the back of the abdomen, one on each side of our backbone.

Each kidney contains about one million tiny filters called **nephrons**. These nephrons filter about 1700 litres of blood each day. Figure 5 shows how the kidneys work.

Nephrons filter about 1700 litres of blood each day

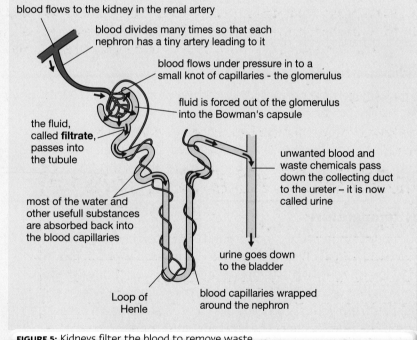

FIGURE 5: Kidneys filter the blood to remove waste.

▓▓▓ QUESTIONS ▓▓▓

5   What happens to un-needed amino acids in the liver?

6   What happens to the blood in the glomerulus?

7   What happens to the filtrate as it passes through the tubule and Loop of Henle?

8   What does urine contain?

...nephrons ...proteins ...urea ...urine

Homeostasis

You will find out:
- That the human body's internal conditions have to be carefully controlled
- That these internal conditions include water content, ion content, temperature and sugar levels

Keeping it constant

The National Botanic Garden of Wales has a greenhouse. It is so big it can be seen from the moon! Plants compete for your attention. Every few seconds you can hear a very quiet 'buzzing'. Computerised sensors are constantly monitoring the internal temperature and humidity of the greenhouse. Little electric motors are automatically opening or closing various windows. We, too, have an internal monitoring system – only better. There's no buzzing!

What is homeostasis?

Homeostasis literally means *staying the same*. Your body depends on maintaining steady **internal conditions**. Many of your organs are constantly adjusting your **temperature** and the contents of tissue fluid so that things are optimum. This is important for the efficient working of our cells.

You will survive only if certain things are kept constant (see figure 1). These include:

- blood sugar levels
- temperature
- water content
- ions and minerals.

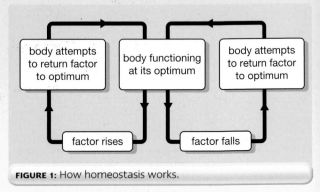

FIGURE 1: How homeostasis works.

Blood sugar levels

Blood sugar levels are normally about 90mg of glucose per 100cm^3 of blood. Insulin, produced by the pancreas, controls glucose concentration. If your glucose level is too high it could kill you. Insulin allows cells to absorb glucose from the blood. It can then be converted into glycogen for storage. You can learn more about this on pages 76–77.

Body temperature

If your body temperature is not around 37 °C then enzymes will not work properly. This could make you very ill. It could even kill you. Your brain is able to control the temperature so that your body can work properly. When you are hot you **sweat**. The water you sweat evaporates from your skin to the air. This cools you down because evaporation removes heat. There is more information about controlling your body's temperature on pages 74–75.

Minerals and water

Minerals and ions enter your body in the food you eat. Their concentration in your body has to be correct. If it is not then too much water could enter your cells and they will be damaged. They could even swell and burst

FIGURE 2: On cold days we sweat very little but urinate lots, on hot days we sweat a lot (to keep us cool) and produce little urine.

⬛ QUESTIONS ⬛

1. What does homeostasis mean?
2. Why is it important to keep your temperature at approximately 37 °C?
3. Explain why you do not sweat on a very cold day.
4. Why do we urinate more on cold days?

...blood sugar levels   ...homeostasis   ...internal conditions

Water in – water out

You have a problem! You are constantly losing water from your body. If you are to avoid serious dehydration then this water has to be replaced. Figure 4 shows how daily water loss can be balanced by water gain.

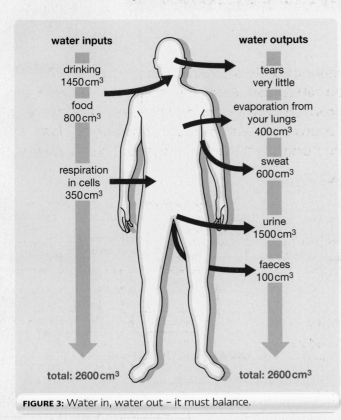

water inputs

drinking
1450 cm³

food
800 cm³

respiration
in cells
350 cm³

total: 2600 cm³

water outputs

tears
very little

evaporation from
your lungs
400 cm³

sweat
600 cm³

urine
1500 cm³

faeces
100 cm³

total: 2600 cm³

FIGURE 3: Water in, water out – it must balance.

Urine production

A scientist did a survey. She asked a group of people to measure how much urine they produced during five, hot summer days. They did the same for five, cold winter days. During both parts of the survey people's diets and levels of activity were the same. Table 1 shows the mean results.

	Day 1	Day 2	Day 3	Day 4	Day 5
Mean summer daily urine production/cm³	995	1000	975	1005	990
Mean winter daily urine production/cm³	1325	1295	1310	1300	1305

TABLE 1: Is there a difference between summer and winter?

QUESTIONS

5 List **three** ways in which our bodies can gain water.

6 Which are the **two** most important ways that our bodies lose water?

7 Look at table 1. What do you notice about the volumes of urine in the summer in comparison to the winter? Explain your answer.

8 Why was it important to keep the diets and the levels of activity the same during the five days in summer and the five days in winter?

Water balance in a freshwater fish

You would think that fish would not have a problem with water. Not true!

The facts:

- their body fluids are more concentrated than the water in which they live
- their outer covering of scales and mucus is impermeable to water and mineral salts
- their kidneys produce very large quantities of dilute urine
- their gills are permeable to oxygen; carbon dioxide and water
- their gills have special cells which can absorb mineral salts from the water
- fish constantly absorb water through their gills
- fish constantly lose minerals through their gills.

So why don't the fish die? Clearly, some sort of homeostatic mechanism must exist to keep them alive.

FIGURE 4: This freshwater fish had water problems!

QUESTIONS

9 Use the ideas of osmosis and diffusion to explain why freshwater fish do not die.

10 Seawater fish live in water that is more concentrated than their own tissue fluids. What homeostatic mechanisms must these fish have to prevent them from dying?

11 What would you expect to happen if you put a freshwater fish into seawater? Explain your answer.

Keeping warm, staying cool

You will find out:
- How our body temperature is monitored and controlled
- What happens when we get too hot
- What happens when we get too cold

We sweat, dogs pant!

A sweltering dog breathes through its mouth rather than its nose. Its breath is hot and damp. Nice! With each breath, cool air enters its lungs. The cool air becomes hot and moist. Hot blood flows through the dog's wet tongue. As the dog exhales, its breath makes the water on its tongue evaporate. This cools the dog. Fortunately we are able to control our body temperature in other ways.

FIGURE 1: Panting – a dog's cooling system.

It's nice to be warm

Our body temperature is normally between 35.5 and 37.5°C. This is called the **core body temperature**. If our bodies get too hot, or too cold, then our enzymes stop working properly. This can make us extremely ill so it is very important to keep a constant core body temperature.

Keeping close to 37 °C

Your **brain** has a temperature regulation centre. It's called the **thermoregulatory centre**. As blood flows through this control centre its temperature is constantly monitored by special **temperature receptors**. There are also temperature receptors in your **skin**, which send impulses to the thermoregulatory centre.

The thermoregulatory centre can detect the slightest changes in temperature. In response it will send other nerve impulses to different parts of the body. These instruct the body to do various things to return the temperature to normal.

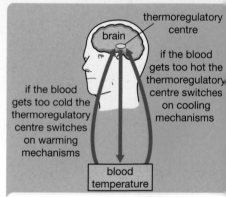

FIGURE 2: Temperature control is a homeostatic mechanism.

Body temperature in °C	What happens to you
38–40	you have a fever (a temperature)
37	normal body temperature
36	goose bumps on your skin
35	you shiver
32	you lose feeling
30	you fall into a coma
27	you stop breathing
25	you die

Sometimes things go wrong

If your body temperature falls below 35 °C you suffer from hypothermia. The big problem with hypothermia is that your thermoregulatory centre stops working. As a result your body temperature continues to fall. You do not realise that you are getting colder and colder. The table shows what happens to you at different temperatures, although these temperatures will vary slightly from person to person. Old people and young children are particularly susceptible to hypothermia.

QUESTIONS

1. What is the core body temperature?
2. Why is it important to keep your core body temperature constant?
3. Describe how the thermoregulatory centre works.
4. Suggest why the elderly and young children are susceptible to hypothermia.

...blood capillaries ...brain ...core body temperature ...shiver

How do we warm up?

If our core temperature falls below 37 °C we need to warm up. The brain's thermoregulatory centre makes three important things happen:

- we **shiver**
- we do not sweat
- less blood flows through our capillaries.

When we shiver our muscles contract and relax repeatedly. This needs energy from respiration and produces heat. Shivering can produce five times more heat than we produce when we are quietly resting. By not sweating we do not loose heat. Figure 3 shows what happens to the **blood capillaries** in our skin. We can also choose to do things to warm us up, like put on warm clothes.

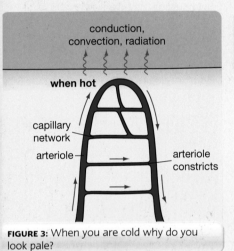

FIGURE 3: When you are cold why do you look pale?

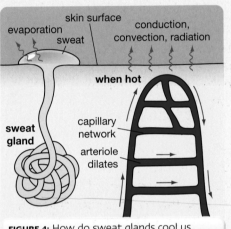

FIGURE 4: How do sweat glands cool us down?

How do we cool down?

If our core temperature exceeds 37 °C we need to cool down. Now the thermoregulatory centre makes different things happen:

- more blood flows through capillaries
- we sweat
- we do not shiver.

Figure 4 shows what happens in our skin. Here again, we can choose to do things that will cool us down, like take clothes off!

 Watch Out Capillaries cannot dilate. It's the arterioles that lead to them that can.

QUESTIONS

5 Explain how shivering, not sweating and restricting blood flow to the capillaries in the skin warms you up.

6 Now explain how sweating, not shivering and letting more blood pass through the skin capillaries cools you down.

7 List as many things as you can think off that you can choose to do to warm you up and cool you down.

Shivering can produce five times more heat than we produce when we are resting

The Komodo dragon

These giant lizards live on the Indonesian island of Komodo, about 500km east of Bali. They are reptiles and can grow up to 3 m long. They are vicious carnivores, though they also eat carrion. Their sense of smell is extraordinary. Using their yellow, forked tongue, they can detect food up to 11 km away. Unlike us, they are cold-blooded. They control their body temperature by basking in the sun to warm up and looking for shade when they are too hot. When their bodies are at their optimum temperature Komodo dragons can run at about 24 km/h. They are an endangered species.

FIGURE 5: : It's a reptile: a cold-blooded killer (literally!)

QUESTIONS

8 As Komodo dragons are an endangered species what should be done to conserve, and increase their numbers?

9 Design an investigation, which would establish the range of temperatures over which these reptiles are most active.

...skin ...sweat gland ...temperature receptors ...thermoregulatory centre

Treating diabetes

You will find out:
- That blood glucose levels are controlled by the hormone insulin
- That diabetes is a disease where blood glucose levels rise too high
- That diabetes can be treated by careful diet and insulin injections

Diabetes worldwide

There are 177 million people worldwide who suffer from **diabetes**. This is expected to double by 2030. The countries with the highest numbers of sufferers are: India; China; USA; Indonesia and Russia. Most of the increase is expected in developed countries. This is largely due to unhealthy diets, obesity and sedentary, *couch-potato* lifestyles. Are you going to be part of these statistics? [Data taken from The World Health Organisation (WHO)]

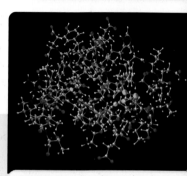

FIGURE 1: Insulin: the molecule that saves lives.

Supply and demand – the glucose balance

When carbohydrates are digested we get **glucose**. Glucose is absorbed into the blood from the small intestines. Normally you will have about 90 mg of glucose per 100 cm^3 of blood. After a meal this could rise to over 150 mg per 100 cm^3 of blood. If blood glucose concentrations get too high it can be very dangerous; you could even die. Fortunately your **pancreas** controls the concentration by producing a **hormone** called **insulin**.

Insulin affects the membranes of our cells. It makes them absorb glucose from the blood. Once in the cells, the glucose is converted into glycogen. Glycogen can be stored, especially in muscle cells and liver cells.

No insulin – big problem!

Some people suffer from **diabetes**. This is when your pancreas does not produce enough, or any, insulin. Blood glucose levels rise, eventually reaching dangerously high concentrations. Some of the symptoms of diabetes are:

- going to the toilet a lot (to urinate)
- feeling very thirsty
- being tired all the time
- glucose in the urine
- losing weight
- having blurry vision.

Diabetes can be controlled by injecting insulin. But it is not easy to get the dose right.

Diabetes cannot be cured, but in the 1920's, two Canadian scientists discovered that if you injected chemical extracts from a healthy pancreas into someone who suffered from diabetes, the illness could be controlled.

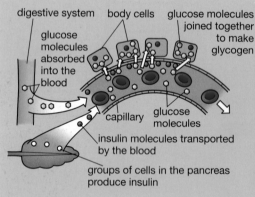

FIGURE 2: Blood glucose, insulin and cell membranes.

digestive system   body cells   glucose molecules joined together to make glycogen

glucose molecules absorbed into the blood

capillary   glucose molecules

insulin molecules transported by the blood

groups of cells in the pancreas produce insulin

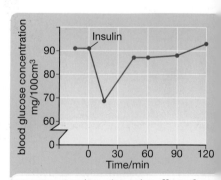

FIGURE 3: Graph to show the effect of an insulin injection on blood glucose levels.

QUESTIONS

1. What happens to carbohydrates when they have been digested?
2. Where in the body is insulin made?
3. What is diabetes and what are its symptoms?
4. Explain how insulin works.

...diabetes ...glucose ...hormone

Early ideas about diabetes

Two thousand years ago, the Greeks thought that faulty kidneys caused diabetes. It wasn't until about 1788, that the Englishman, Thomas Cawley, identified the pancreas as the problem. But we still didn't know about insulin. In 1869, the German scientist Paul Langerhans discovered special groups of cells in the pancreas. However, many scientists were not convinced that a faulty pancreas caused diabetes. All this set the scene for the final discovery, which proved that the pancreas and insulin were involved in diabetes.

The experiments of Dr. Banting and Dr. Best

In 1921, Dr. Banting and Dr. Best did experiments on dogs in their laboratory in Canada. Banting's idea was that the special cells, which were first spotted by Langerhans, produced something to prevent diabetes. An extract could be made from these cells and injected into diabetic dogs. If his idea was right then this would relieve the symptoms of diabetes.

The way Banting planned the experiment was that he would remove the pancreas from some dogs to make them diabetic. The dog's blood glucose levels would become very high. Best would then do blood glucose tests on the dogs. They would then inject the diabetic dogs with extract from a healthy dog's pancreas.

The dogs survived and their diabetes was controlled. Banting and Best then injected the same extract into a 14-year-old diabetic boy called Leonard Thompson. He was dying of diabetes but after the injections his diabetes was also controlled.

There is some evidence that Banting and Best were not the first to treat diabetics with insulin. Nevertheless their work and experiments are now recognised as establishing the treatment of diabetics.

FIGURE 4: Charles Best, Sir Frederick Banting and the first diabetic dog to be kept alive with insulin injections.

Treating diabetes

The treatment of diabetes usually involves the patient injecting himself or herself with insulin. In recent years teams of scientists have been working on developing an 'artificial pancreas'.

This does two things:

- it measures blood glucose concentrations
- it automatically injects just the right amount of insulin when it is needed.

FIGURE 5: Working at The City University, London, Dr Havorka has developed an artificial pancreas.

Other teams have been experimenting with the idea of transplanting the special groups of cells that Langerhans discovered all those years ago. Early results from these experiments show that when these cells are injected into the blood of a diabetic they move to the liver (rather than the pancreas) where they produce their insulin.

QUESTIONS

5 Why did the Greeks think that faulty kidneys caused diabetes?

6 Why did Banting and Best remove the pancreas from dogs?

7 Why did Best test a dog's blood for glucose after its pancreas had been removed?

8 Why did the dogs survive after the injections?

QUESTIONS

9 How is diabetes treated?

10 The development of new ways of treating diabetes is very expensive. In your group, justify this expense.

11 An elderly relative has developed diabetes. Write them a letter explaining what diabetes is and what the options are for its control.

Keep it clean

SELF-CHECK ACTIVITY

CONTEXT

Will is doing some work on enzymes as part of his GCSE Science course. The teacher has told them that they are going to design their own washing powder and that, in order to do this, they have to understand how stains work. She explains that what often makes stains stick to clothes is protein acting as a kind of glue. The washing process has to break down the protein to loosen the stain and get the clothes clean.

Will and his group discuss how the stain might look if magnified to show the protein glue and draw a diagram to explain their ideas. They are keen to make a start on the practical work and confidently expect to be presented with a pile of dirty washing to try out the washing powders. Will is surprised to see boiling tubes appear – and no cloth.

The teacher explains that they are going to use photographic film that has been used and processed. The film is clear plastic and the image consists of silver halide crystals attached by gelatine. Because gelatine is a protein, if the washing powder can break down proteins it will wash the film clean and produce a piece of clear plastic.

Will uses the basic enzyme-free washing powder, while a couple of others in the group add different enzymes to their powders. Each student is going to test their powder at a number of temperatures: room temperature, 30 ^{0}C, 40 ^{0}C, 60 ^{0}C and 100 ^{0}C. They have to predict what effect this will have. Will thinks his non-enzyme powder will work better the higher the temperature, but he isn't sure if the enzyme ones will. He rather thinks that they will do best at 40 ^{0}C as this is close to body temperature.

They cut the old photographic film into strips and put them into the boiling tubes with solutions of the washing powders. They time them to see which solution at which temperature cleared the image from the film.

CHALLENGE

STEP 1

What kind of drawing do you think Will's group might have come up with to show how protein glue sticks a stain to a piece of clothing? Draw a labelled sketch to show your ideas.

STEP 2

Why do you think Will predicted that his non-enzyme washing powder would work better the higher the temperature? Why might a washing powder that only works well at high temperatures be of limited use? Why do you think he predicted that enzyme-based powders might work best at body temperature?

STEP 3

The class used photographic film instead of stained clothes. How do you think this helped with the reliability of the experiment? How do you think it might have affected the validity of the experiment?

Maximise your grade

These sentences show what you need to include in your work to achieve each grade. Use them to improve your work and be more successful.

Grade	Answer includes...
F	Have some idea about what the students did in the experiment.
	Describe what the students did in the experiment.
	Explain the purpose of some of the stages in the experiment.
	Explain the purpose of all of the stages in the experiment.
C	Sketch graphs to show predictions of effectiveness of enzyme and non-enzyme washing powders.
	Draw diagrams to explain how enzyme-based washing powders work.
A	Use both diagram and ideas about enzymes to predict the outcome of the experiment.
	Use diagrams, graphs and ideas about enzymes to predict the outcome of the experiment.

STEP 4

Will's group decided they would display their results as a scatter graph and that they wouldn't run any of the tests for more than 20 minutes (if it takes that long, they reasoned, it's not going to be much good). Discuss and decide what you think their graph might look like. Use your knowledge of enzymes and the effects of temperature on solubility to help you.

Cell division – mitosis

It's happening all the time

As you are reading this paragraph, millions of cells all over your body are dividing. But not all cells divide at the same pace. Those lining your small intestine are the fastest – once every two to three days. By contrast, the cells of your nervous system never divide. Between these two extremes are the cells of the rest of your body, for example, skin cells divide every week or so.

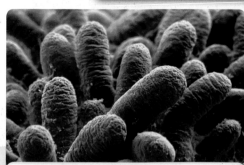

FIGURE 1: Villi in the small intestines – how often are worn out cells replaced?

Why do cells need to divide?

We are made of cells. Billions and billions of them. When we grow two things happen:

- existing cells get bigger
- we get more cells.

There is a limit to how large our cells can grow and stay alive. If cells get too big then they cannot respire properly.

Normal body cells have two sets of **chromosomes**. These consist of long chains of genes, which contain instructions for inherited features. Ordinary body cells divide by **mitosis**.

Mitosis is very important because it provides us with cells for three reasons:

- for **growth**
- to **replace** worn out cells
- to replace dead cells.

When a cell divides by mitosis it makes two new cells. Both new cells are identical. Each will have two sets of chromosomes.

How mitosis makes cells

Figure 2 shows the main stages of mitosis.

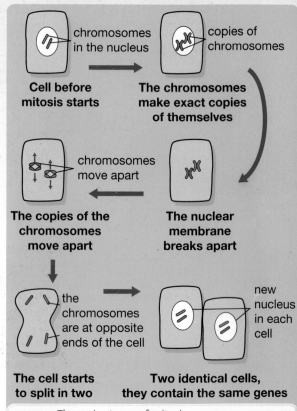

chromosomes in the nucleus

copies of chromosomes

Cell before mitosis starts

The chromosomes make exact copies of themselves

chromosomes move apart

The copies of the chromosomes move apart

The nuclear membrane breaks apart

the chromosomes are at opposite ends of the cell

new nucleus in each cell

The cell starts to split in two

Two identical cells, they contain the same genes

FIGURE 2: The main stages of mitosis.

QUESTIONS

1. What **two** things happen when we grow?
2. What is mitosis?
3. Why is mitosis important?
4. What would happen if mitosis didn't take place?

...carcinogen   ...chromosomes   ...growth

Stages of Mitosis

Here is a series of photomicrographs (photographs taken down a microscope) that show the stages of mitosis.

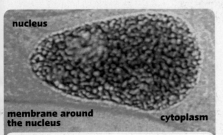
nucleus

membrane around the nucleus
cytoplasm

FIGURE 3: The cell just before the nucleus starts to divide.

FIGURE 4: The membrane around the nucleus disappears and the chromosomes make copies of themselves.

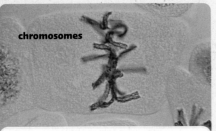
chromosomes

FIGURE 5: The chromosomes arrange themselves in the middle of the cell.

FIGURE 6: The chromosomes move to opposite ends of the cell.

FIGURE 7: The chromosomes now form into two nuclei.

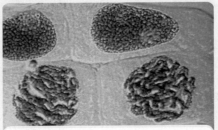

FIGURE 8: New cell membranes form and two new cells are made.

Asexual reproduction

Some organisms reproduce asexually. Cells of the offspring are made by mitosis. These cells contain the same genes as each other, and the original cell.

Many unicellular organisms can reproduce like this.

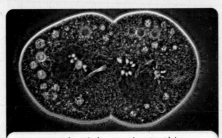

FIGURE 9: What is happening to this paramecium?

What is cancer?

Cancer results when a cell divides out of control. Special genes control cell division (mitosis):

- proto-oncogenes tell a cell when to divide
- tumour suppressor genes tell a cell when not to divide
- suicide genes cause a cell to 'self destruct' when something goes wrong
- DNA is constantly being damaged, DNA-repair genes repair the damage.

A **mutation** is a change in the structure of a gene that is likely to alter how it works. A **mutagen** is anything that causes a mutation. If the mutagen causes cancer then it's called a **carcinogen**. We are constantly exposed to carcinogens, for example:

- 23 of the chemicals found in cigarette smoke (there are over 4000 in total!)
- UV light from the sun
- X-rays in hospitals and dental surgeries.

QUESTIONS

7   What is a mutation?

8   What would happen if proto-oncogenes or suicide genes mutated?

9   People should not be allowed to smoke in public places such as cinemas, restaurants and bars. Discuss this statement in your group.

10 Do you think there should be health-warning signs at the seaside telling people of the dangers of UV light?

QUESTIONS

5   Carefully look at the pictures of mitosis. Write a paragraph that describes what happens in each one.

6   Suggest **one** advantage and **one** disadvantage of asexual reproduction.

...mitosis   ...mutation   ...mutagen   ...replace

81

Cell division – meiosis

You will find out:

● Where sex cells, gametes, are made
● That sex cells are made by a special cell division called meiosis
● What happens during fertilisation
● How sexual reproduction leads to variation

Early ideas about sperms

The Dutchman Antonie van Leeuwenhoek lived between 1632 and 1723. A very keen amateur scientist, he built his own microscopes. He was the first person to look at human sperms. He suggested that each sperm contained a little person, which would grow into maturity after fertilisation. He got that wrong then, didn't he?!

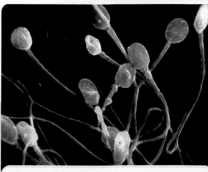

FIGURE 1: Sperm cells.

Another type of cell division

Ordinary body cells are made by **mitosis**. In humans, **gametes** are made by **meiosis**. They are made in the **ovaries** and **testes**.

During meiosis the following things happen:

■ the chromosomes are copied
■ the cell divides twice – so four cells (gametes) are made
■ the number of chromosomes is reduced by half

Each gamete therefore only contains one set of chromosomes.

What happens during fertilisation?

Fertilisation is when an egg joins with a sperm. As a result we get one new cell. This contains two sets of chromosomes, one from the sperm and a second from the egg. This new cell will develop into the new offspring. It divides by mitosis. This means that each cell in the new individual will contain two sets of chromosomes.

In humans, sperms and eggs contain 23 chromosomes each, that's one set each. The fertilised egg, which will develop into a baby, contains 46 chromosomes (two sets).

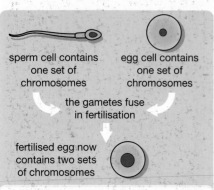

FIGURE 3: Fertilisation – one set of chromosomes plus another set gives us two sets.

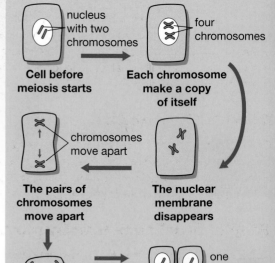

FIGURE 2: The main stages of meiosis.

(In figure: nucleus with two chromosomes — four chromosomes — Cell before meiosis starts — Each chromosome make a copy of itself — chromosomes move apart — The nuclear membrane disappears — The pairs of chromosomes move apart — four chromosmes move apart — A chromosome from each pair is now separate. The cell starts to split into four — one chromosome in each cell — Four new cells (gametes) made)

(In figure 3: sperm cell contains one set of chromosomes — egg cell contains one set of chromosomes — the gametes fuse in fertilisation — fertilised egg now contains two sets of chromosomes)

▌▌ QUESTIONS ▌▌

1 Name **two** places where meiosis happens.
2 How many sets of chromosomes are there in a sperm cell?
3 How many sets of chromosomes are there in a fertilised egg?
4 How many chromosomes are there in
  a an egg cell **b** a sperm cell **c** a fertilised egg cell **d** a normal body cell?

Why are there two types of cell division?

There are important differences between mitosis and meiosis. Table 1 summarises these:

Mitosis	Meiosis
Two cells are made	Four cells are made
Cells made can go on and divide again	Cells made cannot divide
All cells have the same number of chromosomes	Cells made have half the number of chromosomes
Cells made have two sets of chromosomes	Cells made have one set of chromosomes
Body cells are made	Gametes made

TABLE 1: Differences between meiosis and mitosis.

Things can go wrong

Sometimes cells end up with:

- too many chromosomes
- too few chromosomes
- bits of chromosomes missing
- extra bits of chromosomes.

Cri du Chat Syndrome

Very occasionally a baby is born whose cry sounds like a kitten. This is because its vocal chords do not work properly. The baby also has a rounded face, a large head and is severely mentally disabled. Part of one of its chromosomes is missing.

Down's Syndrome

Children born with this syndrome have an extra chromosome. An abnormal meiosis means that there is an extra chromosome in one of the gametes. The child will have physical and mental problems.

Why is fertilisation so important?

Fertilisation results in **variation**. The alleles in sperm cells will be different to the alleles in the egg cells. When the gametes fuse (join) the alleles come together and form pairs again. Each pair controls a different feature. This means that the fertilised egg contains alleles from both parents. As a result, the offspring will have features from both parents and will be different from both parents.

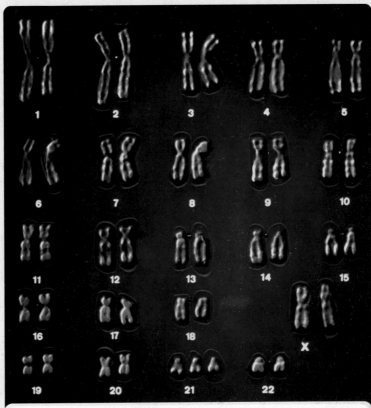

FIGURE 4: Down's syndrome chromosomes. Where is the extra chromosome?

QUESTIONS

5 Look at figure 2. Now write a paragraph that describes meiosis.

6 List **three** differences between mitosis and meiosis.

7 What can go wrong during cell division?

8 Explain why fertilisation is important.

Stem cells

You will find out:
- What stem cells are
- Where stem cells are found
- What happens to stem cells in plants and animals
- How stem cells are used in medical research and treatments

Transplant an organ or some stem cells?

Donated organs and tissues are often used to replace ill or damaged tissue. Unfortunately, the need for transplant tissues and organs far outweighs their availability. Stem cells might offer the possibility of a renewable source of replacement cells and tissues. They could be used to treat Parkinson's disease, Alzheimer's disease, spinal cord injuries, strokes, burns, heart disease and diabetes.

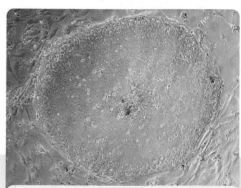

FIGURE 1: Stem cell – it doesn't look special – but it is!

Specialised cells

Most cells in your body are specialised. This means they are **differentiated** to do a particular job. Animal cells differentiate soon after they are made. Plant cells can differentiate at any time during their lives. From the time a cell has differentiated it can only do one job. For example, a heart cell is specialised to contract and help the heart to beat. It cannot change and do the job of a brain cell. **Stem cells** are quite different. They are **unspecialised** and so could turn into any type of cell. Stem cells divide by mitosis. The new cells can stay as stem cells or become differentiated into another type of cell.

Where are stem cells found?

There are two types of stem cells:
- adult stem cells
- **embryo** stem cells.

Adult stem cells are found in many of our tissues and organs including **bone marrow**. Scientists now think that it is possible to use stem cells as a 'maintenance kit'. They can be used to repair damaged parts of your body and paralysis.

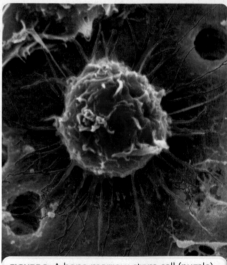

FIGURE 2: A bone marrow stem cell (purple).

◖ QUESTIONS ◗

1. What does it mean if a cell is differentiated?
2. What is the difference between an ordinary cell and a stem cell?
3. Where are stem cells found?
4. Scientists think that stem cells can be used as a 'maintenance kit'. What does this mean?

...bone marrow   ...cell growth medium   ...differentiated

Adult stem cells

These are found in many of our organs and tissues. These include:

- bone marrow ▪ blood vessels ▪ muscle ▪ skin ▪ liver ▪ brain.

Stem cells from these tissues are undifferentiated, but they are likely to develop into whatever tissue they came from.

Bone marrow stem cells

There are two types of bone marrow stem cells. One type can develop into red blood cells or white blood cells. The other type can make: bone cells, cartilage cells, tendons and fat cells.

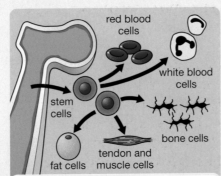

FIGURE 3: Scientists have known about bone marrow stem cells for over 30 years.

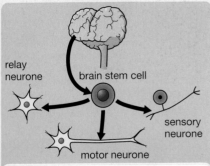

FIGURE 4: Brain stem cells can make nerve cells.

Brain stem cells

These were first seen in rats about 40 years ago, but it wasn't until the 1990's that scientists agreed that adult human brains contain stem cells. They can differentiate into three different types of nerve cell.

Embryo stem cells

Embryo stem cells come from embryos where the egg was fertilised in vitro (in a test tube). They are not taken from pregnant women. Stem cells are taken from 4–5 day old embryos. At this stage the embryo is a hollow ball of cells. The cells are put into **cell growth medium**. This contains all the nutrients the stem cells need to grow. The cells can be kept like this for months without letting them differentiate. Cells are then treated in different ways to make them differentiate into different cells. The treatment involves adding special proteins to the cells. This has the effect of turning different genes on or off. As a result the stem cells differentiate.

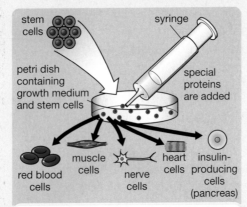

FIGURE 5: Embryo stem cells can do all this.

QUESTIONS

5   Name **three** places in your body where stem cells are found.

6   What does cell growth medium contain?

7   What can bone marrow stem cells differentiate into?

8   Is it right to use stem cells from embryos? Explain your answer.

Stem cells and the treatment of Parkinson's disease

In Britain about 2% of people over 65 will develop Parkinson's disease. It is a very serious disease of the nervous system. Special neurones fail to produce the vital chemical dopamine.

Sufferers can show the following symptoms:

- their hands will shake
- they will not be able to move about easily.

Experiments have been done on laboratory rats that have a form of Parkinson's disease. When stem cells were transplanted into their brains they showed greatly improved ability to move. If it works for rats could it work for humans? Scientists are now using stem cells to make neurones that secrete dopamine. This could mean the end of Parkinson's disease? But research of this type raises lots of questions.

QUESTIONS

In your group discuss the following issues:

- should rats, or other animals, be used in laboratory experiments?
- should embryonic stem cells be used in research that could benefit us?

Now do the following:

9   Draw up a table of the pros and cons of animal experimentation.

10 Your local newspaper has started a debate about embryonic stem cell research. Join the debate by writing a letter to the editor either in favour, or against, embryonic stem cell research.

...embryo   ...stem cells   ...unspecialised

Chromosomes, genes and DNA

You will find out:
- What DNA stands for
- What DNA is
- What genes and chromosomes are
- How proteins are made

Rosalind Franklin – the Nobel Prize winner that never was

Rosalind Franklin was born in 1920 and, sadly, died of cancer when she was 37. She worked on DNA. Her discoveries allowed Crick, Watson and Wilkins to go on and suggest a structure for DNA and how it could make copies of itself. Undoubtedly, had she lived, she would have been given a Nobel Prize.

FIGURE 1: Rosalind Franklin worked at King's College, London.

What are chromosomes made of?

Our body cells normally contain two sets of **chromosomes**. We have 46 chromosomes, 23 pairs. They are found in the **nucleus**. Each chromosome is made of a very long molecule of **deoxyribonucleic acid** (**DNA** for short). Chromosomes are divided into sections called **genes**. There are lots of genes on each chromosome.

What genes do

Genes store information as a type of code, called the **genetic code**. It's a bit like a 'blue-print', or 'instruction manual'. The genetic code organises which **amino acids** are joined together to make a specific **protein**. Some of these proteins are enzymes. They control all the chemical reactions that go on in the cytoplasm of our cells. Each enzyme controls a different chemical reaction. There are thousands of different chemical reactions that go on in our cells, so we need thousands of different enzymes. Each gene code is for a different enzyme. This explains why we need thousands of genes.

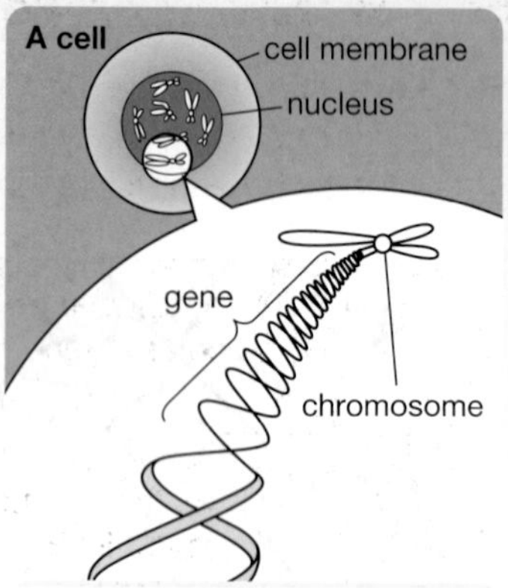

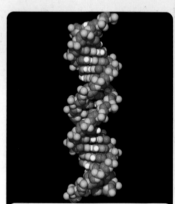

FIGURE 2: Where most DNA is found.

FIGURE 3: This model shows a short length of DNA.

Discovering the structure of DNA

In 1962 Maurice Wilkins, Francis Crick and James Watson shared a Nobel Prize. They had discovered the structure of DNA. The newspapers said that they had discovered the 'secret of life'. DNA carries the genetic code of all cells and many viruses.

FIGURE 4: Crick and Watson in front of their model of DNA.

QUESTIONS

1. What chemical are chromosomes made from?
2. Write a sentence that shows you understand the meanings of the following words: chromosome, gene and DNA.
3. What is the genetic code?
4. Why do we need thousands of genes?

...amino acids ...bases ...chromosomes ...complementary ...deoxyribonucleic acid

How DNA is copied

DNA molecules have two strands. These are twisted around each other; the shape is called a **double helix**. The two strands are held together by sub-units called **bases**. There are four different nucleotide bases: A, T, C and G. The bases on one strand pair up with the bases on the other strand. The two strands of the DNA molecule are **complementary**. A always pairs up with T and G always pairs up with C. For a cell to divide the DNA has to be copied.

This is what happens:

- the two strands of DNA 'un-zip'
- the bases of the two strands are temporarily 'un-paired'
- each strand attracts complementary bases
- these attach themselves to the two single strands
- each strand is now a double strand
- mitosis can now proceed (see pages 78–79)
- new cells are made – each one will have an exact copy of the DNA it needs.

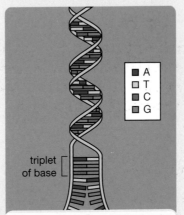

A
T
C
G

triplet of base

FIGURE 5: Part of a DNA molecule – triplets of bases are the genetic code for amino acids.

Making proteins – the process of protein synthesis

Cells use enzymes all the time. To make an enzyme molecule the genetic code has to be decoded. Three bases along a strand of DNA is the code for one amino acid. Three bases – one amino acid: that's why it's sometimes called the **triplet code**. There are 20 different amino acids commonly found in proteins. Each one has a different code. So each gene codes for a particular combination of amino acids which makes a specific protein.

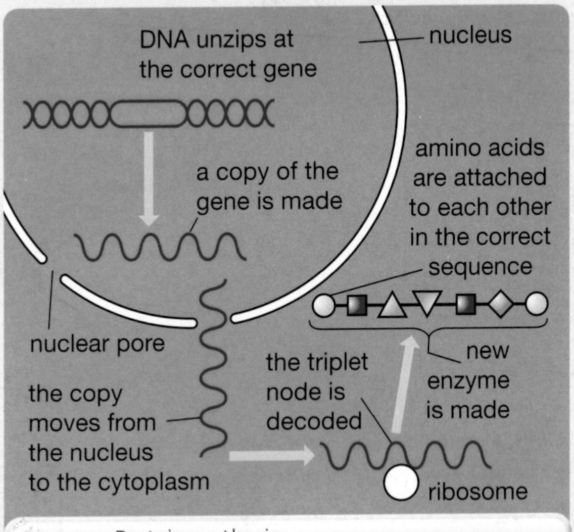

40% of our genes are also found in bananas

DNA unzips at the correct gene

nucleus

a copy of the gene is made

amino acids are attached to each other in the correct sequence

nuclear pore

the copy moves from the nucleus to the cytoplasm

the triplet node is decoded

new enzyme is made

ribosome

FIGURE 6: Protein synthesis.

QUESTIONS

5 Why is DNA called a 'double helix'?

6 The two strands of DNA are said to be complementary. What does this mean?

7 What is the triplet code?

8 Why do we constantly need to make proteins?

Who owns your genes?

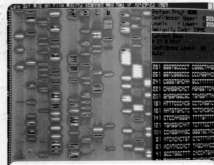

FIGURE 7: Computer display of DNA sequencing of the human genome.

The *Human Genome Project* was set up to discover the sequence of all the bases in our chromosomes. There are millions of these bases in the human genome. We now know that there are about 31 000 different genes in humans. That's fewer than was originally estimated. But many of these genes are not unique to us! We share over 99% of our genes with another species – the chimpanzee. 40% of our genes are also found in bananas.

An issue now arises: who owns specific genes? Pharmaceutical companies produce different medicines. Some of these are used to treat genetically based diseases, diseases that are inherited. These companies want to copyright genes. This would prevent other companies from making their own versions of medicines for the same diseases.

QUESTIONS

9 Draw up a list of **three** or **four** different living things that we might share many of our genes with. Explain your choices.

10 Now think of **three** or **four** other living things that we might share few of our genes with. Explain your choices.

11 In your group discuss whether it is right for a pharmaceutical company, or anyone else for that matter, to copyright genes.

Inheritance

You will find out:
- About Mendel's contribution to the study of inheritance
- That different forms of genes are called alleles
- How some alleles are dominant and others are recessive
- How to construct and interpret genetic diagrams

Prayers and peas

Gregor Johann **Mendel** was an Austrian monk. He was born in 1822 and died in 1884 and was a very keen gardener. In 1856 he started doing a few experiments on inheritance in pea plants. By the time he did his last experiment, in 1868, he had recorded over 20 000 results! Mendel presented his findings to the local natural history society in 1865, but sadly they were forgotten until they were rediscovered by an English scientist called William Bateson in 1900.

FIGURE 1: This was Mendel's garden, it still exists but the peas have long gone!

Mendel's experiments

Mendel noticed that some of the pea plants growing in his monastery garden had red flowers, others had white flowers. This got him thinking. There were no 'in-betweens', no pink flowers. He decided to set up an experiment that involved **crossing** different pea plants – getting them to breed together.

This is what he did:

1. he pollinated red flowers with pollen from red flowers – he crossed them
2. white flowers were crossed with white flowers
3. the seeds were collected and planted
4. if they grew into plants that looked like their parents they were **pure breeding**.

We now know that a pair of **genes** controls each **characteristic**. These are inherited through sex cells, one from each parent.

Each gene has different forms, called **alleles**. In Mendel's pea plants the gene for flower colour has two alleles, one is for red flowers and the other for white flowers. The red allele is **dominant**. This is because a plant only needs one of these alleles to have red flowers. The white allele is **recessive**. For pea plants to have white flowers both of its flower colour genes must be white. The allele for red flowers is given the letter R (big R) and the one for white flowers is r (little r).

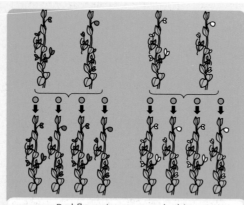

FIGURE 2: Red flowering peas and white flowering peas. What did Mendel get?

He then:

5. pollinated pure breeding white flowering plants with pollen from pure breeding red flowering plants (he called these plants the Parental generation or P generation)
6. collected the seeds that were produced and planted them.

He found that this first generation of offspring plants (the F1 generation) had red flowers (see figures 4 and 5).

Even though each seed had a white allele, because red is dominant to white, the seeds grew into plants with red flowers.

He continued his experiment:

7. he let all the first generation red flowering plants pollinate each other
8. again he collected the seeds and planted them.

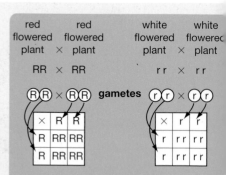

FIGURE 3: This is a **Punnett square**. It shows how the genes in this cross are inherited.

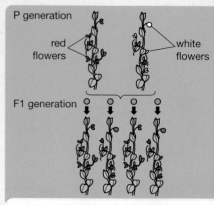

FIGURE 4: Why did all the seeds grow into red flowering plants?

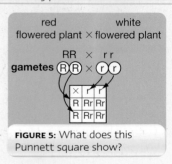

FIGURE 5: What does this Punnett square show?

...alleles ...characteristic ...crossing ...dominant ...genes ...genetics ...heterozygous

When these grew he found that most plants had red flowers, just a few had white flowers. These are called the F2 generation. He counted the plants and found that for every three red flowering plants he got one plant with white flowers.

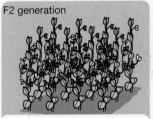
FIGURE 6: Mostly red flowers; some white flowers. Why?

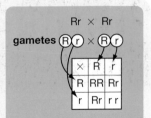
FIGURE 7: This Punnett square explains why!

Plants from seeds which contain at least one red allele (RR and Rr) have red flowers. Plants with rr have white flowers. When the alleles are the same they are called **homozygous** (e.g. RR and rr). If they are different (Rr) they are called **heterozygous**.

Whilst doing this experiment Mendel noticed that pea plants showed other features. Figure 8 shows a list of all the features Mendel eventually studied.

None of these features show 'in-betweens'.

Mendel repeated his experiment with each of these features. No wonder it took him 12 years to complete!

He wondered how these features were **inherited**. He came up with three conclusions:

- Each feature is controlled by 'units' or 'factors' (*genes*).
- An individual will inherit one of these 'units' from each parent.
- A character might not show up in a plant but it can still be passed on to the next generation.

Though Mendel's research was on plants, the basic ideas that he discovered are now known to apply to animals and humans as well. The basic mechanisms of inheritance are the same.

TRAIT	dominant		recessive	
seed shape		smooth		wrinkled
seed colour		yellow		green
seed coat colour		grey		white
pod shape		inflated		constricted
pod colour		green		yellow
flower position		at sides		at tips
stem height		tall 2.0m		short 0.3m

FIGURE 8: This is what the features look like.

QUESTIONS

1 What does 'pure breeding' mean?

2 What is the difference between 'gene' and 'allele'?

3 What colour of flower will seeds produce if they have the following allele: RR, Rr and rr?

4 Why are pea plants only ever tall or short?

5 When Mendel investigated how the height of pea plants was inherited he crossed two heterozygous plants and collected 750 seeds that grew into tall plants and 250 seeds that produced small plants. How can you tell from these results which feature is dominant?

6 Write a paragraph describing how Mendel did his pea height experiment.

Genetics of the fruit fly – *Drosophila melanogaster* (H)

These little flies are commonly seen buzzing around rotting fruit. Their short life cycle and easy to identify features make them attractive to scientists studying **genetics**. Crosses can be set up and results recorded within about three weeks. At best Mendel got two generations of pea plants per year.

In the fruit fly the gene for wings comes in different alleles. Normal wings are dominant over vestigial wings. Flies with vestigial wings cannot fly!

Kate, a geneticist, crossed a pure breeding normal winged fly with a pure breeding vestigial winged fly. She then crossed the F1 generation amongst themselves. From the F2 generation she collected 1500 flies of which 375 had vestigial wings.

FIGURE 9: The fly on the left is a mutant: it has 'vestigial' wings. The fly on the right has 'normal' wings.

QUESTIONS

7 Draw genetic diagrams to explain the normal wing/vestigial wing cross described above.

8 Fruit flies normally have red eyes, however some have recessive white eyes. Kate set up a cross between a pure breeding red-eyed fly and a pure breeding white-eyed fly. Draw genetic diagrams to help her predict the results she would get in the F2 generation.

How is sex inherited?

You will find out:
- There are 23 pairs of chromosomes in normal human body cells
- One pair carries genes which determine sex
- In females the sex chromosomes are the same (XX)
- In males the sex chromosomes are different (XY)

Male or female?

A hermaphrodite has both male and female sex organs. Earthworms are hermaphrodites. Some fish can change sex. The Tiger grouper lives in the warm seas of the Caribbean. It starts life as a female and then changes to become a male. As they continue to grow, large individuals are all males. Our sex is determined by the chromosomes we inherit.

FIGURE 1: This male Tiger grouper started life as a female.

Boys will be boys; girls will be girls!

The nucleus of each body cell (skin cells; liver cells; brain cells; etc) contains 23 pairs of chromosomes. One pair of these is called the **sex chromosomes**. The other 22 pairs are called **autosomes**.

Sex cells (eggs and sperms) contain 23 chromosomes: 22 autosomes and a single sex chromosome.

Sex chromosomes are of two types:

- **X chromosomes**
- **Y chromosomes**.

When an egg from your mother is fertilised by a sperm cell from your father the chromosomes combine. Each cell in the embryo that develops has 44 autosomes and two sex chromosomes.

So will you be a girl or a boy?

It all depends on which sex chromosomes you inherit. If an embryo has two X chromosomes (one from the egg and the other from the sperm) then you're a girl. But if the embryo gets one of each, an X from the egg and a Y from the sperm, then you're a boy. We say that sex is **determined** by the sex chromosomes that are inherited.

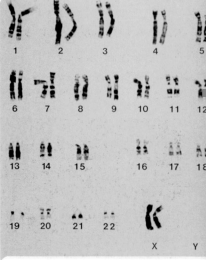

FIGURE 2: This is a picture of someone's chromosomes. Are they a boy or a girl?

Sex chromosome in egg	Sex chromosome in sperm	Sex chromosomes in embryo	Sex of embryo
X	X	XX	Female
X	Y	XY	Male

TABLE 1: How sex is determined.

░░ QUESTIONS ░░

1. How many chromosomes do the following human cells have:
   a liver cell   b egg cell   c white blood cell   d neurone   e sperm cell?
2. How many sex chromosomes does each of these cells have?
3. How many different sex chromosomes are there and what are they?
4. What sex chromosomes does a a boy and b a girl, have?

Some fish can change sex!

...autosomes ...determined ...sex chromosomes

Sex determination

Figure 3 shows how sex is inherited in humans.

Sex ratio

Figure 3 shows that we would expect to get a 50:50 ratio of males to females. Men produce about 200 000 000 sperms each day. That's over 2300 per second! Half of these sperms will contain an X chromosome and the other half will contain a Y chromosome. All of a woman's eggs will contain X chromosomes only. During fertilisation one sperm combines with one egg so it is the male that determines the sex of the offspring. Not that men can choose the type of sperm to fertilise the egg. It's down to chance. For a person to be male they must have a Y chromosome. For a person to be female they must NOT have a Y chromosome. However, worldwide, there are more women than men.

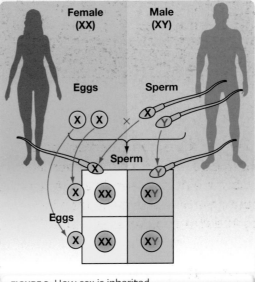

FIGURE 3: How sex is inherited.

Why is meiosis important?

We learned about meiosis on pages 80–81. It is important to halve the number of sex chromosomes (as well as the autosomes) so that when fertilisation occurs sex determination can happen properly.

A very unusual set of sex chromosomes

The duck billed platypus lives in rivers in Australia. It has no fewer than ten sex chromosomes!

Males are YX; YX; YX; YX; YX and females are XX; XX; XX; XX; XX.

FIGURE 4: The one on the left is female, or is it the other way round? Counting chromosomes would tell us.

WOW FACTOR!

The duck-billed platypus has 10 sex chromosomes.

Temperature-dependent Sex Determination (TSD)

FIGURE 5: Here are newly hatched sea turtles – but are they males or females?

Until recently, scientists thought that all vertebrates had sex chromosomes. Now we know that the environment controls the sex of many reptiles. The temperature at which their eggs are incubated determines their sex. This discovery has great conservation implications as many endangered species have TSD. These species include: sea turtles, Galapagos tortoises and some species of crocodile and alligator. In sea turtles, females hatch out if the incubation temperature is 30°C or higher. If it's below 28 °C we get males. Incubating the eggs at 28 °C we get both. Many conservation programs worldwide collect their eggs and incubate them artificially. This prevents them being eaten by predators. The problem is that such interventions result in more males than females being released into the wild.

QUESTIONS

7   Design an experiment that could determine if a newly discovered species of sea turtle showed TSD.

8   What advice would you give to turtle conservation groups?

QUESTIONS

5   Why is the sex of a baby down to the father?

6   Suggest why population surveys show that there are more women than men.

...X chromosomes   ...Y chromosomes

Inherited disorders

You will find out:
- That some diseases are inherited
- That Huntington's disease is inherited from just one parent
- That cystic fibrosis is inherited from both parents
- That unborn embryos can be tested for genetic disorders

Cats inherit diseases too

In the year 2000 there were an estimated 250 million cats kept as pets worldwide. Cat breeders met at an international conference on inherited diseases in cats. "Purebred cats are at risk from inherited diseases," said one delegate. "We are eager to improve the health of our cats," said another. It would be possible to keep breeding records for cats, but is it possible to track the inheritance of diseases in people?

FIGURE 1: How could breeding records be kept?

You can't catch it but you can suffer from it

Sometimes not all the genes that we inherit from our parents are good for us. Body cells normally contain 22 pairs of chromosomes and one pair of sex chromosomes. All these carry the genes that make our bodies grow and function. Some people inherit **genetic disorders** from their parents. A person who has an inherited disorder will have it for the whole of their life.

Cystic fibrosis

Cystic fibrosis is a disorder of cell membranes. It is caused by a **recessive allele**. This means that you have to inherit the allele from both of your parents. You would then have two alleles for cystic fibrosis. Some people carry one cystic fibrosis allele. These people do not have cystic fibrosis, they just **carry** the allele. They are called **carriers**. Most people do not have the allele.

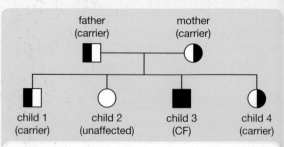

FIGURE 2: What are the chances of two carrier parents having a child with cystic fibrosis?

Huntington's disease

This is a disease that affects the nervous system. It is caused by a **dominant** allele. This means that you only need one allele to suffer from the condition. In spite of this, **Huntington's disease** is very rare. About one person in every 13 000 has it.

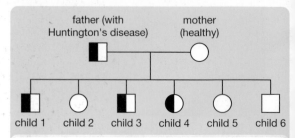

FIGURE 3: What are the chances of one parent with Huntington's disease having children with the same condition?

QUESTIONS

1. How is cystic fibrosis inherited?
2. What does it mean to be a 'carrier' of cystic fibrosis?
3. How is Huntington's disease inherited?
4. Why can you not be a 'carrier' of Huntington's disease?

...carriers ...carry ...cystic fibrosis ...dominant

True story about cystic fibrosis

One day Sophie met James. They fell madly in love. After a year they married and decided to start a family. They tried to have children but after three years – nothing! Then Sophie realised that her period was late. Her doctor tested her and, yes, she was pregnant. Sophie and James were delighted and after nine months Sophie gave birth to a little girl.

Sadly tests showed that the baby had cystic fibrosis. A year later Sophie became pregnant again and gave birth to a boy. He also had cystic fibrosis. Even though Sophie and James were quite healthy and did not have the disease, both of their children had it.

Why?

Further tests showed that though Sophie and James were healthy they were carriers. They each had one allele for cystic fibrosis. By chance they passed on cystic fibrosis carrying gametes to their children. Their children ended up with two alleles for the disease. People with cystic fibrosis can suffer from the following symptoms, which affect the lungs and the gut:

- they cannot digest their food properly
- excess, sticky mucus accumulates in their airways
- they get chest infections, including pneumonia
- they have fertility problems
- they have shorter life expectancies – typically sufferers die by the age of 40–50.

There is no cure for cystic fibrosis, but the symptoms can be treated:

- by enzyme tablets
- by chest physiotherapy
- by the use of antibiotics to treat infections.

Pregnant mothers can have their embryos **screened** for these and other genetic disorders.

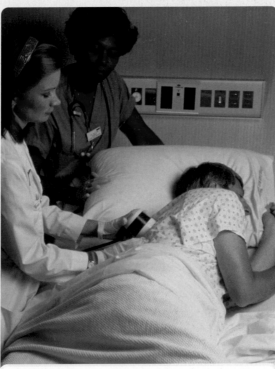

FIGURE 4: Sophie and James's son has physiotherapy to help him cough up the extra mucus his body produces.

Screening for inherited diseases

Scientists are now able to locate the gene for cystic fibrosis (on chromosome 7) and the gene for Huntington's disease (on chromosome 4). They can tell parents whether their unborn child will have either condition. Genetic counselling is commonly available. Some of the symptoms of cystic fibrosis are given above and those for Huntington's disease are listed below.

Huntington's symptoms

These may only become apparent in middle age. Death often occurs within 15–20 years of the onset of the symptoms.

They include:

- jerking, uncontrollable movements
- rapid up and down eye movements
- poor memory and forgetfulness
- slower thinking
- depression
- loss of appetite
- uncontrollable anger and even violence
- dementia.

QUESTIONS

9   You're a genetic counsellor.

   a Write a letter inviting a couple to come to a consultation with you to discuss the possibility that they might have a child with cystic fibrosis.

   b Write notes on how you would conduct this consultation

10 Design a leaflet which could be used at a doctor's surgery describing how Huntington's disease is inherited and its symptoms

QUESTIONS

5   Why did Sophie and James's children have cystic fibrosis?

6   Could Sophie and James have had children who did not have cystic fibrosis? Explain your answer.

7   Why do people with cystic fibrosis take enzyme tablets?

8   What effect does chest physiotherapy have?

DNA fingerprinting

You will find out:
- That every one has unique DNA (except identical twins)
- That this can be used to identify individuals
- That this is called DNA fingerprinting

It's a biological bar code (only much, much better)

The year: 1987 – police do a mass screening by genetic fingerprinting. They collect over 5000 DNA samples. This helps to eliminate innocent people. But it also convicts a murderer. Today, anyone arrested by the police, for any reason, will have a sample of their DNA taken and kept on file. DNA fingerprinting is routinely used by forensic scientists to help solve crimes.

What is a DNA fingerprint?

Everyone has their own, exclusive, set of fingerprints. In the same way, each of us has **DNA** that is **unique**. Everybody's DNA is slightly different, unless you are an **identical twin**. Identical twins have the same DNA because they originally came from the same fertilised egg. Because of this we can all be identified from a sample of our DNA. That's why it is called a **DNA fingerprint** or **DNA profile**. But, whereas your fingerprints could be removed from your fingers by chemicals or changed by surgery, you can't change your DNA. Your DNA stays with you all of your life, and beyond! Unlike ordinary fingerprints, DNA fingerprints can tell you if people are related.

Samples of DNA can be found in:
- hairs
- saliva
- blood (even if it's dried up)
- semen.

We can even get DNA from bones and teeth. Sometimes that's all a forensic scientist (scientists who study objects related to crimes) will have to be able to identify someone. To get an image of a genetic fingerprint, like the one in figure 1, scientists have to treat the DNA with special enzymes and radioactive chemicals.

So you want to be a burglar?

Well forget it! We leave DNA clues behind us everywhere we go. The police just need to find a few cells and that's it!

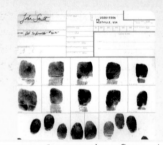

FIGURE 1: Is this genetic fingerprint unique?

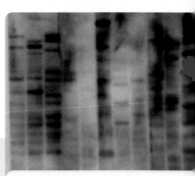

FIGURE 2: Compare these fingerprints to the genetic fingerprint in figure 1.

If I hadn't dropped one of my 50 million million cells I would have got away with it

Dna try that again!

FIGURE 3: You don't have to be filmed on CCTV or leave fingerprints to get caught!

QUESTIONS

1. What have ordinary fingerprints and genetic fingerprints got in common?
2. Why do identical twins have the same DNA fingerprints?
3. List **two** places where DNA samples can be found.
4. What is a forensic scientist?

Your DNA stays with you all of your life, and beyond!

...DNA   ...DNA fingerprint   ...DNA profile

How to make a DNA fingerprint

After many years of research Professor Sir Alec Jeffries from Leicester University discovered how to produce DNA fingerprints.

This is how it's done.

1 Obtain a DNA sample.

2 Cut it up into different lengths with special enzymes.

3 Separate the bits out using a technique called 'electrophoresis' (a bit like chromatography).

4 Treat the sample with a radioactive chemical.

5 Expose it to X-ray film.

6 Develop the film – this is a picture of the DNA fingerprint (like the one in figure 1).

FIGURE 4: Professor Alec Jeffries working on a DNA fingerprint.

DNA fingerprinting

DNA fingerprints can be used in a range of situations including solving:

■ crimes ■ paternity disputes ■ immigration issues.

DNA fingerprints and crime

Forensic scientists collect DNA from the crime scene and from suspects and compare the DNA profiles. If they match up then they come from the same person. If they don't they must be from someone else.

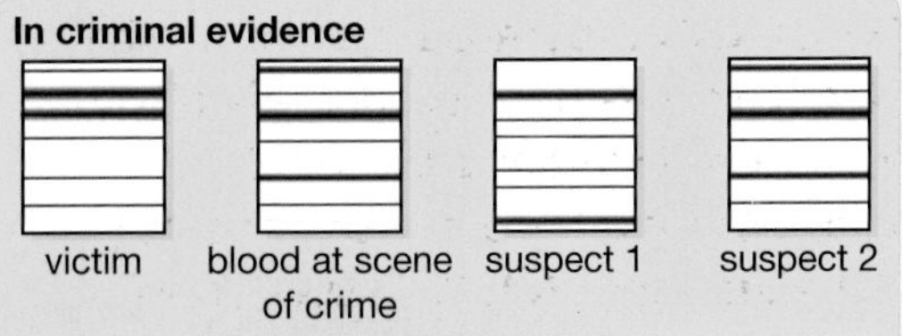

In criminal evidence

victim | blood at scene of crime | suspect 1 | suspect 2

FIGURE 5: Who is the criminal?

Proving paternity

Children have genes from both parents. This means that a child's DNA profile will have some features of the mother as well as some from the father. Sometimes people have to prove that they are the biological parents of children. This technique is also used in immigration issues.

In paternity cases

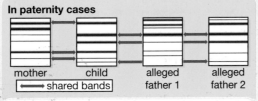

mother | child | alleged father 1 | alleged father 2

← shared bands

FIGURE 6: Compare these DNA fingerprints – who is the father?

Other uses for DNA fingerprints

DNA profiling can also be used on plants and animals. The technique proved that Dolly the sheep was a true clone. The RSPB (Royal Society for the Protection of Birds) has used DNA evidence against people who claim to have reared endangered species from chicks bred in captivity. DNA fingerprints have shown that the birds were caught in the wild.

QUESTIONS

5 Explain how a DNA fingerprint can help convict a criminal.

6 How can a DNA fingerprint prove who the father of a child is?

7 Explain how DNA fingerprints helped to prove that Dolly the Sheep was a clone.

8 Why do forensic scientists have to be very careful of DNA contamination?

Who are you?

FIGURE 7: What information about you could an ID card store?

Citizens of many countries around the World have ID cards. In Britain some politicians want to enforce them too. Some people are in favour of ID cards, as they believe they would make our society safer. Others believe that ID cards are an infringement of our civil liberties. With micro-electronics it would be possible to store vast amounts of data about an individual on their ID card including:

■ name

■ blood group

■ medical records

■ bank details.

What else?

Each of us has unique DNA so could ID cards incorporate a person's DNA information?

QUESTIONS

9 In your group draw up a list of information that an ID card could contain.

10 Parliament is about to hold the big ID card debate. Write a letter to your PM explaining either why you believe ID cards are a good idea or why you believe they are a bad idea. Whichever letter you choose to write make sure you explain your point of view clearly and fully.

Unit summary

Concept map

Enzymes
What are they and what do they do?

They are involved in respiration, photosynthesis, protein synthesis and digestion.

There are three main groups of digestive enzymes: carbohydrases, lipases and proteases.

Enzymes are used in industry in food production and in the home in biological detergents.

Homeostasis
How does our body keep internal conditions constant?

Our body temperature is kept constant at about 37°C.

Sweating is important in maintaining a steady body temperature.

Blood sugar levels are controlled by insulin produced by the pancreas.

Inheritance
How are different features inherited?

Cells divide by mitosis or meiosis.

Living organisms, including ourselves, inherit characteristics, including certain diseases.

Sex is determined by the inheritance of the X and Y sex chromosomes.

Stem cells have great importance in medical research.

Genetic fingerprints are used in solving questions of family relationships and solving crimes.

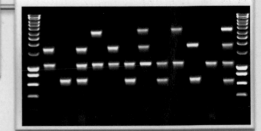

Unit quiz

1 Why are enzymes called *biological catalysts*?

2 List the **three** main groups of digestive enzymes.

3 What is the equation for respiration?

4 What happens to the excess proteins that we eat?

5 What does *homeostasis* mean?

6 Why is our core body temperature about 37°C?

7 How does insulin control blood sugar levels?

8 Explain why mitosis is important for growth.

9 What are the main differences between mitosis and meiosis?

10 What are stem cells and why are they important to us?

11 Describe how proteins are made in our cells.

12 Explain how sex is inherited.

13 Explain how the inheritance of cystic fibrosis is different from the inheritance of Huntington's disease.

14 Explain how genetic fingerprints help police to solve crimes.

Literacy activity

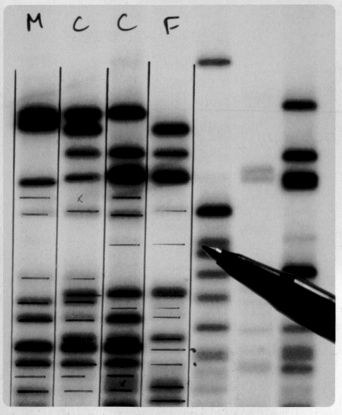

The fingerprints of history

In 1902, in Paris, the great French detective Alfonse Bertillon solved a horrible murder. He used a piece of new technology, which struck fear into the heart of the criminal community. Eighty-three years later two young girls were killed near the Leicestershire village of Narborough. Again, the murderer was found through a technical advance, although the machinery involved would have baffled Bertillon. These events link the earliest and the latest developments in human genetics.

[taken from: *"The language of genes"* by Steve Jones, published by Flamingo]

QUESTIONS
1 What was the new technology that Bertillon used that struck fear into the hearts of criminals in 1902?

2 What was the technical advance that helped solve the Narborourgh murders?

3 Why would the technology employed in the Narborourgh murders have baffled Bertillon?

4 What is the link between the two technologies mentioned in this passage?

Exam practice

Exam practice questions

1 The diagram shows the carbon cycle.

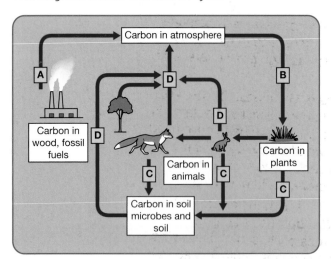

a What process is occurring in each of the parts of the carbon cycle labelled A to D? [4]

b In what form does carbon mainly occur in the atmosphere? [1]

2 The diagram shows a nephron.

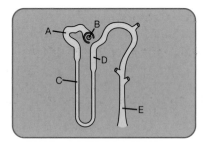

a Which organ in the human body contains nephrons? [1]

b Copy the table below and complete it to show which labels on the diagram show these parts of nephron.

Part of nephron	Letter on diagram
loop of Henlé	
glomerulus	
first convoluted tubule	
collecting duct	
second convoluted tubule	

[3]

c The content of the blood changes as it passes through the nephron.

Copy the table below and put ticks or crosses in the boxes to show whether each substance is present in these fluids in a healthy person's kidneys.

Substance	Blood in renal artery	Blood in renal vein	Urine
protein			
glucose			
water			
urea			

3 The diagram illustrates part of the process of sexual reproduction. A, B and C are cells.

Sexual reprodution

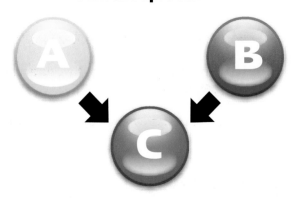

a If cell **A** is a sperm, what type of cell is **B**?

b If cell **C** is a zygote, what is the name given to the process by which it is formed from cell **A** an cell **B**?

c If the diagram represents sexual reproduction in humans, what is the usual number of chromosomes in each of the cells?

(Total 16 mark

Read the passage below, which is about genetically modified crops.

Genetically modified (GM) crops are plants that have had additional 'foreign' genes inserted into their chromosomes. These genes can give the GM crop new characteristics, such as high growth rate, and resistance to pests.

There has been a massive rise in the use of GM crops. The area of land planted for GM crops has increased from 1.5 million hectares in 1996, to 33 million hectares in 1999. GM crops have been developed to help solve the problem of feeding the world's growing human population while reducing the human impact on the environment. Supporters of GM crops argue that GM crops could end hunger.

However, critics believe that the human impact on the environment could actually be increased by using GM crops. For example, opponents argue that pollen from GM crops could contaminate other species, possibly resulting in undesirable changes in other species. For reasons such as these, in Britain only 2% of the public in a recent survey agreed with the use of GM crops.

a Explain how 'These genes can give the GM crop new characteristics'. [2]

b By how many times did the land area used for GM crops increase during the period 1996 to 1999? [1]

c Explain what is meant by 'pollen from GM crops could contaminate other species'. [2]

This is correct. The answer includes the basic idea of gene ➡ protein ➡ characteristic.

a Genes control which proteins are made in cells. So, new genes can make new proteins. These new proteins control new characteristics, e.g. growth rate.

This is correct. It is a good idea to show your working.

b The land area increased by 33 ÷ 1.5 = 22 times

This is a reasonable answer, but it does not refer to the fact that **modified genetic material** is carried within the pollen grains.

c Pollen from the GM plant's flower is carried by wind or insects to the stigma of a plant that is not GM. This would contaminate the other flower.

Overall grade: A

How to get an A
Read the question carefully and make sure that your answer answers it fully.

DISCOVER BUCKMINSTERFULLERENE!

Buckminsterfullerene can be dissolved in some solvents to form vivid purple solutions.

Each buckminsterfullerene molecule has a relative formula mass of 720 and consists of 60 carbon atoms.

The carbon atoms are held together by strong covalent bonds.

Buckminsterfullerene is just one of the exciting new substances that scientists have recently discovered. It consists of the element carbon. The carbon atoms are joined together in pentagons and hexagons to form a perfect sphere. Scientists hope to use buckminsterfullerene in cancer treatments and to target bacteria that have become resistant to antibiotics.

Buckminsterfullerene is the smallest and most stable fullerene but others including C_{70} also exist.

Buckminsterfullerene, diamond and graphite are all allotropes of carbon.

Buckminsterfullerene molecules are sometimes affectionately referred to as 'bucky balls'.

Atomic structure

The field-ion microscope

Since the 5th century BC, some people have believed that atoms exist. However, it wasn't until scientists developed a microscope powerful enough to see images smaller than the wavelength of light that we could actually see atoms. The field-ion microscope uses a beam of ions to show the positions of individual atoms. Atoms are shown by bright spots.

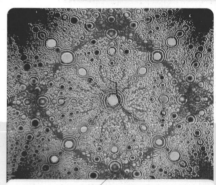

FIGURE 1: Here is an image of a platinum crystal. The bright spots show the positions of individual atoms.

What's inside an atom?

Although scientists originally thought that **atoms** could not be split into anything smaller, we now know that each atom actually consists of even tinier **particles**. These are called **protons**, **neutrons** and **electrons**.

At the centre of an atom is its **nucleus**. This consists of protons and neutrons. The nucleus is surrounded by a shell of electrons. We call the protons, neutrons and electrons **sub-atomic** particles.

Sub-atomic particles

This table shows the **relative masses** and **relative charges** of protons, neutrons and electrons.

Particle	Relative mass	Relative charge
Proton	1	+1
Neutron	1	0
Electron	Very small	−1

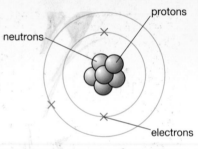

FIGURE 2: The structure of an atom.

Mass number

In the periodic table each **element** is represented by a **symbol** and two numbers. Here we can see the information for the element sodium.

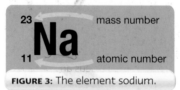

FIGURE 3: The element sodium.

The mass number tells us the total number of protons plus the number of neutrons in an atom.

The atomic number tells us the number of protons in an atom. This is the same as the number of electrons. In the modern periodic table the elements are arranged in order of increasing atomic number.

QUESTIONS

1. Name the **three** sub-atomic particles.
2. Which particles are found in the nucleus of an atom?
3. What is the charge of an electron?
4. What is an element?

...atoms   ...electrons   ...element   ...neutrons   ...nucleus   ...particles

How ideas about atoms have changed

Thousands of years ago the Greek scientist Demokritos believed that everything consisted of tiny particles that could not be broken down into anything smaller. He called these particles 'atoms' from the Greek word meaning indivisible.

The atomic theory was not generally accepted until the early 19th century. At this time Dalton described his ideas about the properties of atoms:

- All matter consists of atoms which cannot be divided up.
- Atoms of the same element are similar but are different from atoms of different elements.
- Matter cannot be created or destroyed.
- Atoms can be joined together to form molecules.

Since then our knowledge of atoms has rapidly increased:

- 1895: Electrons were discovered.
- Around 1900: Scientists found that atoms could be split into smaller particles.
- 1911: Rutherford discovered the nucleus.
- 1919: Rutherford discovered protons.
- 1932: Neutrons were discovered.

Even today we do not know the whole story and scientists continue to study atoms to find out more about them.

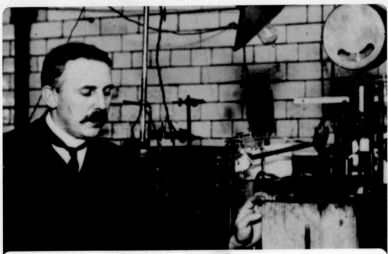

FIGURE 4: Rutherford discovered the nucleus and protons.

Why ideas about atoms have changed

Our ideas about atoms have changed over time as technology improves. Today we routinely use instruments that give us detailed, accurate data about materials. This allows us to refine our ideas in the light of each new piece of information.

Nuclear reactions

During chemical reactions, the elements remain the same and just the outer electrons are rearranged. However, during nuclear reactions the nucleus of an atom changes and new substances are produced. These substances include new elements. Nuclear reactions also release a lot of energy.

FIGURE 5: During nuclear reactions atoms of different elements are made.

QUESTIONS

5   Why were atoms named using the Greek word for indivisible?

6   Why do scientific ideas change over time?

7   If an atom has seven protons, is it an atom of oxygen?

QUESTIONS

8   What is the difference between a chemical reaction and a nuclear reaction?

...protons   ...relative charge   ...relative mass   ...sub-atomic   ...symbol

Electronic structure

You will find out:
● How to represent the electronic structure of the first 20 elements
● How electrons occupy shells or levels

Glowing with energy

These glow sticks don't have batteries so how do they give off light? It's all to do with the way the electrons in the atoms inside the glow sticks are arranged. When the glow stick is bent, the chemicals inside mix together and a reaction takes place. This reaction releases energy. The energy is used to promote electrons from their ground state (the energy level where they are normally found) to an excited state (a higher energy level). However, this is unstable and, as the electrons fall back down, energy in the form of light is released.

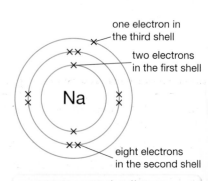

FIGURE 1: Why do glow sticks give off light?

What is an atom?

The magnet in figure 2 is made from the **element** iron. Elements are made from only one type of **atom**. This iron magnet is made entirely from iron atoms.

What is in an atom?

We know that inside atoms there are even tinier particles called sub-atomic units: **protons**, **neutrons** and **electrons**. The **nucleus** of the atom consists of neutrons and protons. The electrons are found in **shells** around the nucleus.

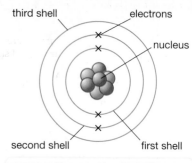

FIGURE 2: What are these magnets made from?

The way that an atom reacts is largely dependent on the number of electrons that the atom has and on the way that these electrons are arranged.

How are the electrons arranged?

Figure 3 shows how we name the electron shells of an atom. The shell closest to the nucleus is called the first shell. The next shell out is called the second shell and the next the third. In our model, the first shell can hold up to two electrons, while the remaining shells can hold up to eight electrons. The electrons fill the shells in order, starting with the shell closest to the nucleus.

The number of electrons in the atom's outermost shell is important. It shows us which group of the periodic table that element belongs to.

Atoms of the element sodium have one electron in their outer shell. So sodium belongs to Group 1 of the periodic table.

third shell electrons
nucleus
second shell first shell

FIGURE 3: How are the electrons arranged in an atom?

one electron in the third shell
two electrons in the first shell
Na
eight electrons in the second shell

FIGURE 4: How are the electrons arranged in a sodium atom?

▥ QUESTIONS ▥

1. What is special about elements?
2. Name the sub-atomic units.
3. What is the central part of an atom called?
4. Draw an atom. Label the nucleus and the first three electron shells.

...atom ...electron notation ...electrons ...element

Magnesium

Magnesium is a reactive metal used to make flares. Atoms of magnesium have 12 electrons. We can use our model to work out how the electrons are arranged:

- The first two electrons are used to fill the first shell.
- The next eight electrons fill the second shell.
- The two remaining electrons go into the third shell.

This electron arrangement can be shown using the **electron notation** 2, 8, 2. The first number shows the number of electrons in the first shell, the second shows the number of electrons in the second shell and the third shows electrons in the outermost shell.

We can use this information to calculate that magnesium has two electrons in its outer shell so must belong to Group 2 of the periodic table.

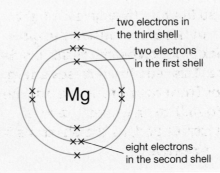

two electrons in the third shell

two electrons in the first shell

eight electrons in the second shell

FIGURE 5: How are the electrons arranged in a magnesium atom?

Calcium

Calcium is an essential component of bones and teeth. Atoms of calcium have 20 electrons. We can use our model to work out how the electrons are arranged:

- The first two electrons are used to fill the first shell.
- The next eight electrons fill the second shell.
- The next eight electrons fill the third shell
- The two remaining electrons go into the fourth shell.

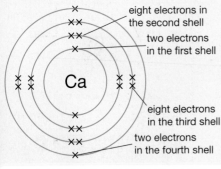

eight electrons in the second shell

two electrons in the first shell

eight electrons in the third shell

two electrons in the fourth shell

FIGURE 6: How are the electrons arranged in a calcium atom?

This electron arrangement can be shown using the electron notation 2, 8, 8, 2. We can use this information to calculate that calcium has two electrons in its outer shell so must belong to Group 2 of the periodic table.

> **EXAM HINTS AND TIPS**
>
> Electrons fill the electron shells in order, starting with the shell closest to the nucleus.

Dolomite

FIGURE 7: Dolomite rocks

The similarity in the electron structures of magnesium atoms and calcium atoms means that these Group 2 metals have very similar properties. They are both soft, white metals and are good thermal and electrical conductors. They also react in similar ways.

Both metals are normally extracted from carbonate rocks. Magnesium can be obtained from the mineral magnesite which consists of magnesium carbonate. Calcium can be extracted from the mineral calcite which is found in rocks such as limestone and consists of calcium carbonate.

Another carbonate mineral called dolomite shows just how similar atoms of these two metals really are. Dolomite consists of calcium magnesium carbonate. The mineral is formed from calcite and occurs when some magnesium ions exchange for calcium ions in the original mineral. This substitution is only possible because atoms of these two metals are so similar.

QUESTIONS

5 An atom of an element has 14 electrons. How are these electrons arranged?

6 An atom has 19 electrons. Which group does the atom belong to?

7 Atoms of which element have the electron arrangement 2, 8, 3?

8 Sketch the electron arrangement for an atom which has nine electrons.

QUESTIONS

9 Describe how the electron arrangement in a magnesium atom and a calcium atom are similar to each other.

…neutrons …nucleus …protons …shells

Mass number and isotopes

You will find out:

- The total number of protons and neutrons in an atom is its mass number
- Isotopes are atoms of the same element which have different numbers of neutrons

Dating the round table

According to legend, in the early 6th century King Arthur ruled Camelot. He built a round table around which he and his trusted knights could sit to discuss affairs of state. A round table can be seen in Winchester castle. But could it really be King Arthur's?

The mystery was solved by scientists who examined the ratio of different forms (or isotopes) of carbon in the wood of the table. They were able to date the table as being made around 1270, many centuries after King Arthur and Camelot.

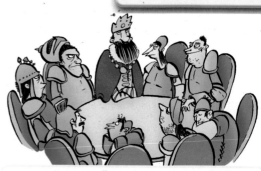

FIGURE 1: Isotopes allow scientists to age objects accurately

Why are elements special?

So far we have discovered around one hundred different **elements**, including oxygen, nitrogen and carbon. Elements are special because they only contain one type of **atom**. Atoms of the same element always have the same number of **protons**.

We know that oxygen is an element so it only consists of oxygen atoms. Every oxygen atom has eight protons. We often display the elements in the periodic table.

Group I	II											Group III	IV	V	VI	VII	0
			$^{1}_{1}$H hydrogen														$^{4}_{2}$He helium
$^{7}_{3}$Li lithium	$^{9}_{4}$Be beryllium											$^{11}_{5}$B boron	$^{12}_{6}$C carbon	$^{14}_{7}$N nitrogen	$^{16}_{8}$O oxygen	$^{19}_{9}$F flourine	$^{20}_{10}$Ne neon
$^{23}_{11}$Na sodium	$^{24}_{12}$Mg magnesium											$^{27}_{13}$Al aluminium	$^{28}_{14}$Si silicon	$^{31}_{15}$P phosphorus	$^{32}_{16}$S sulfur	$^{35}_{17}$Cl chlorine	$^{40}_{18}$Ar argon
$^{39}_{19}$K potassium	$^{40}_{20}$Ca calcium	$^{45}_{21}$Sc scandium	$^{48}_{22}$Ti titanium	$^{51}_{23}$V vanadium	$^{52}_{24}$Cr chromium	$^{55}_{25}$Mn manganese	$^{56}_{26}$Fe iron	$^{59}_{27}$Co cobalt	$^{59}_{28}$Ni nickel	$^{64}_{29}$Cu copper	$^{65}_{30}$Zn zinc	$^{70}_{31}$Ga gallium	$^{73}_{32}$Ge germanium	$^{75}_{33}$As arsenic	$^{79}_{34}$Se selenium	$^{80}_{35}$Br bromine	$^{84}_{36}$Kr krypton
$^{85}_{37}$Rb rubidium	$^{88}_{38}$Sr strontium	$^{89}_{39}$Y yttrium	$^{91}_{40}$Zr zirconium	$^{93}_{41}$Nb niobium	$^{96}_{42}$Mo molybdenum	$^{99}_{43}$Tc technetium	$^{101}_{44}$Ru ruthenium	$^{103}_{45}$Rh rhodium	$^{106}_{46}$Pd palladium	$^{108}_{47}$Ag silver	$^{112}_{48}$Cd cadmium	$^{115}_{49}$In indium	$^{119}_{50}$Sn tin	$^{122}_{51}$Sb antimony	$^{128}_{52}$Te tellurium	$^{127}_{53}$I iodine	$^{131}_{54}$Xe xenon
$^{133}_{55}$Cs caesium	$^{137}_{56}$Ba barium	$^{139}_{57}$La lanthanum	$^{178}_{72}$Hf hafnium	$^{181}_{73}$Ta tantalum	$^{184}_{74}$W tungsten	$^{186}_{75}$Re rhenium	$^{190}_{76}$Os osmium	$^{192}_{77}$Ir iridium	$^{195}_{78}$Pt platinum	$^{197}_{79}$Au gold	$^{201}_{80}$Hg mercury	$^{204}_{81}$Tl thallium	$^{207}_{82}$Pb lead	$^{209}_{83}$Bi bismuth	$^{210}_{84}$Po polonium	$^{210}_{85}$At astatine	$^{222}_{86}$Rn radon
$^{223}_{87}$Fr francium	$^{226}_{88}$Ra radium	$^{227}_{89}$Ac actinium															

FIGURE 2: The periodic table.

What are isotopes?

Isotopes are atoms of the same element which have different numbers of **neutrons**. Hydrogen has three isotopes.

All of the isotopes of an element are found at the same place in the periodic table. Isotope means 'at the same place'.

$^{1}_{1}$H This isotope of hydrogen has 1 proton and no neutrons

$^{2}_{1}$H This isotope of hydrogen has 1 proton and 1 neutron

$^{3}_{1}$H This isotope of hydrogen has 1 proton and 2 neutrons

FIGURE 3: Hydrogen has three isotopes.

QUESTIONS

1 An atom has three protons and two neutrons.
  a What element is it? **b** What is the atomic number of the atom?
  c What is the mass number of the element?

2 An atom has three protons and three neutrons.
  a What element is it? **b** What is the atomic number of the atom?
  c What is the mass number of the element?

...atom ...element ...isotopes ...mass number

Relative atomic mass

Sometimes an element has more than one isotope. The **relative atomic mass** of an element is an average value taking into account all the isotopes of an element. We measure this on a scale where 12 g of carbon–12 is equal to 12. Relative atomic mass is represented by the symbol A_r.

The mass number

We can use the **mass number** and atomic number to work out the number of protons, neutrons and electrons present in an atom.

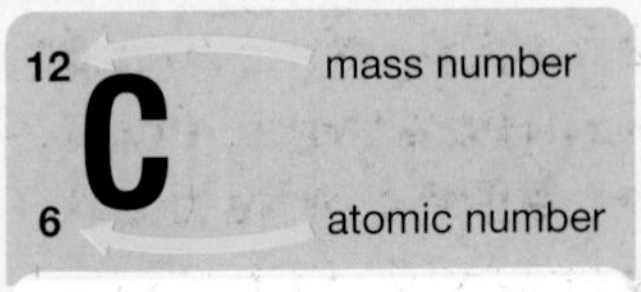

The atomic number of this atom is 6. So this atom has six protons. This is true for all atoms of carbon. All carbon atoms will also have six electrons. Subtracting the atomic number from the mass number gives us the number of neutrons. Here 12 – 6 = 6, so this atom of carbon has six neutrons.

12 **C** mass number
6 atomic number

FIGURE 4: This carbon atom has a mass number of 12 and an atomic number of 6.

How are isotopes similar?

All the isotopes of an element are similar to each other. We know that isotopes of the same element have the same number of protons, so they must also have the same number of electrons and an identical electronic structure. This means that isotopes of the same element will react chemically in the same way.

How are isotopes different?

Although isotopes of the same element are chemically identical they do have different physical properties. This means that different isotopes will have different melting points, boiling points and densities.

Chlorine

The element chlorine has two common isotopes. 25% of chlorine atoms have a mass of 37 and the remaining 75% of chlorine atoms have a mass of 35. The relative atomic mass is the average value for both isotopes. Chlorine therefore has a relative atomic mass of 35.5.

$$
\begin{aligned}
25 \times 37 &= 925 \\
75 \times 35 &= 2625
\end{aligned} +
$$
$$
\underline{3550}
$$
$$
3550 \div 100
$$
$$
= \underline{35.5}
$$

FIGURE 5: Working out the relative atomic mass of chlorine.

Dating the Earth

Today, scientists believe the Earth was made 4.5 billion years ago. They base this calculation on the use of isotopes. They discovered that radioactive isotopes of some elements are not stable and decay over time to form atoms of new elements. If we know the decay rate of an isotope we can date the age of a specimen by working out the proportion of remaining radioactive isotopes to decay products. In particular, scientists study the ratio of isotopes of uranium and lead.

After studying minerals from the Earth, rocks brought back from the Moon and meteorites, scientists have found the age of the Earth and the rest of the Solar System. This use of isotopes has revolutionised our views about evolution.

FIGURE 6: Isotopes have allowed scientists to calculate the age of the Earth.

▦▦▦ QUESTIONS ▦▦▦

3 Why do isotopes of the same element react in the same way?

4 An atom of magnesium can be represented by:
   a How many protons are present in one atom?
   b How many electrons are present in one atom?
   c How many neutrons are present in one atom?

   24
   12 **Mg**

5 An atom of phosphorous can be represented by:
   a How many protons are present in one atom?
   b How many electrons are present in one atom?
   c How many neutrons are present in one atom?

   31
   15 **P**

▦▦▦ QUESTIONS ▦▦▦

6 The relative atomic mass of bromine is 80. Bromine has two isotopes. One has a mass number of 81 and a relative abundance of 50%. What is the mass and abundance of the other isotope of bromine?

Ionic bonding

Where do atoms come from?

Scientists believe our Universe was created by the 'Big Bang'. Immediately after the Big Bang only atoms of the elements hydrogen, helium and lithium existed. However, if you look at the modern periodic table you will see we have identified over 100 different elements. Atoms of heavier elements are believed to be made in stars.

FIGURE 1: When old stars explode they release stardust.

What is an ion?

All **atoms** have equal numbers of **protons** and **electrons** so they have no overall **charge**. An **ion** is an atom which has gained or lost electrons and so has become charged.

When metal atoms form ions they lose electrons. Metal ions always have a **positive** charge. When non-metal atoms form ions they gain electrons. Non-metal ions always have a **negative** charge. The strong attraction between these oppositely charged ions is called an **ionic bond** and holds the compound together.

Sodium and chlorine

When sodium metal is heated in chlorine gas, a chemical reaction takes place which produces the ionic compound sodium chloride. Figures 2 and 4 show how the electrons are arranged in sodium and chlorine atoms. When sodium atoms react they lose an electron to form a sodium ion (figure 4). The sodium ion has a 1+ charge. This ion has a full outer shell of electrons, just like a **noble gas** .

During the reaction, an electron is transferred from the outer shell of the sodium atom to the outer shell of the chlorine atom.

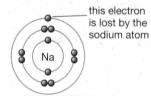

FIGURE 2: The electron arrangement in a sodium atom is 2, 8, 1.

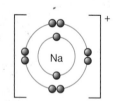

FIGURE 3: The electron arrangement in a sodium ion is 2, 8.

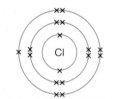

FIGURE 4: The electron arrangement in a chlorine atom is 2, 8, 7.

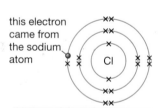

FIGURE 5: The electron arrangement in a chlorine ion is 2, 8, 8.

The ion that is formed is called a chloride ion and has a 1− charge. This ion also has a full outer shell of electrons (figure 5).

QUESTIONS

1. Why do metal atoms form positive ions?
2. Why do non-metal atoms form negative ions?
3. What is an ionic bond?
4. Why do atoms gain or lose electrons?

...atoms ...charge ...electrons ...ion ...ionic bond

Magnesium and oxygen

When we burn magnesium metal it reacts with the oxygen in the air to form the ionic compound magnesium oxide. During the reaction, magnesium atoms lose two electrons to form magnesium ions. These ions carry a 2+ charge and have an electron configuration of 2, 8 which is the same as the noble gas neon.

The oxygen atoms gain two electrons to form oxide ions. These oxide ions carry a 2– charge and also have an electron configuration of 2, 8.

The compound magnesium oxide is held together by strong forces of attraction between these oppositely charged ions.

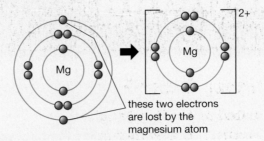

these two electrons are lost by the magnesium atom

FIGURE 6: When a magnesium atom reacts it loses two electrons to form an ion with a 2+ charge.

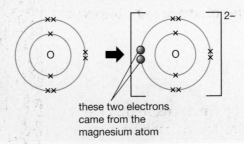

these two electrons came from the magnesium atom

FIGURE 7: When an oxygen atom reacts it gains two electrons to form an ion with a 2– charge.

Calcium and chlorine

When calcium is heated in chlorine the ionic compound calcium chloride is formed. During the reaction the calcium atoms lose their two outer electrons to form calcium ions which have a 2+ charge. These ions have the electron configuration 2, 8, 8 which is the same as the noble gas argon.

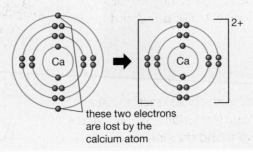

these two electrons are lost by the calcium atom

FIGURE 8: When a calcium atom reacts it loses two electrons to form an ion with a 2+ charge.

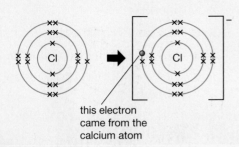

this electron came from the calcium atom

FIGURE 9: Each chlorine atom gains one electron to form a chloride ion with a 1– charge.

Two chlorine atoms both gain one electron each to form chloride ions. Each chloride ion has a 1– charge. These ions also have the same electron configuration as a noble gas.

The compound is held together by the strong forces of attraction between calcium ions and chloride ions.

Conducting electricity

Here is a battery connected to a lamp. If an electric current is passed through the circuit the bulb lights up. If the wire between the battery and the lamp is broken and the two ends placed in a beaker of distilled water, electric current cannot flow and the bulb does not light.

However, if some sodium chloride salt is added to the water, the bulb relights. The bulb relights because an electric current can flow. When the sodium chloride is dissolved in water the sodium ions and chloride ions are free to move. The charged sodium and chloride ions carry the charge through the salty water.

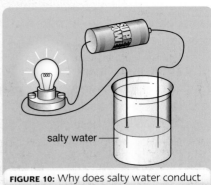

salty water

FIGURE 10: Why does salty water conduct electricity?

QUESTIONS

5 Explain why magnesium oxide has the formula MgO.

6 Explain why calcium chloride has the formula $CaCl_2$.

7 Predict the formula of the ionic compound magnesium chloride.

QUESTIONS

8 Would you expect a solution of calcium chloride to conduct electricity? Why?

...negative ...noble gas ...positive ...protons

Ionic compounds

You will find out:
- That ionic substances consist of giant structures of ions
- That ionic compounds are held together by strong electrostatic forces between oppositely charged ions called ionic bonds

Salty foods

Human blood contains low levels of sodium chloride, essential for good health. However, an adult only requires around two and a half teaspoons of salt each day. Most people eat too much salt because it is 'hidden' in foods such as crisps and bread. Too much salt is linked to raised blood pressure and a higher incidence of heart disease and strokes.

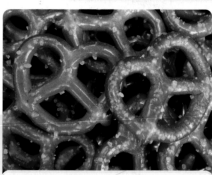

FIGURE 1: Too much salt can be bad for us.

Common ionic compounds

We use many ionic compounds in everyday life. Examples include sodium chloride which is added to food, sodium hydroxide which can be used to unblock sinks and magnesium sulfate which is in plaster of paris and is used to set broken bones.

FIGURE 2: Ionic compounds can be very useful.

What is the structure of ionic compounds?

Ionic compounds consist of **metal** and **non-metal ions**. Ions are formed when atoms gain or lose electrons. Metal atoms lose electrons to become positively charged, while non-metal atoms will gain electrons to become negatively charged.

Ionic compounds consist of very many ions which form a **giant structure** in which the **positive** ions and **negative** ions are placed alternately. Strong **forces of attraction** act in all directions to hold all the ions together. We call these electrostatic forces of attraction between the oppositely charged particles ionic bonds.

Properties of ionic compounds

What are the properties of ionic compounds?

- They have high melting points.
- They have high boiling points.
- They conduct electricity when **molten**.
- They conduct electricity when **dissolved**.
- They do not conduct electricity when solid.

█ QUESTIONS █

1 In which state are ionic compounds at room temperature?
2 What is an ionic bond?
3 What sort of ions do metal atoms form?
4 What sort of ions do non-metal ions form?

...dissolved ...forces of attraction   ...giant structure   ...ionic   ...ions

Melting and boiling points

We know that ionic compounds form giant ionic structures. In these structures there are lots of strong ionic bonds. A great deal of energy is required to overcome the forces of attraction between the ions so ionic compounds will only melt and boil at high temperatures. In fact most ionic compounds will only melt at temperatures above 500 °C.

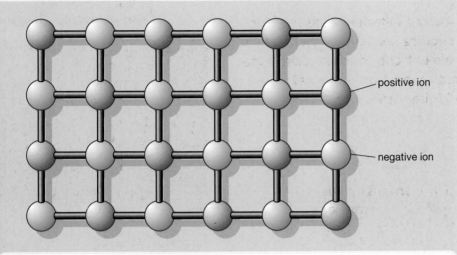

FIGURE 3: Ionic compounds contain lots of strong bonds.

positive ion

negative ion

Why do ionic substances conduct electricity when molten?

If an ionic compound is heated up until it melts, the ions are free to move. As the positive and negative ions move, they carry charge around the circuit. Therefore molten ionic compounds conduct electricity.

Why do solutions of ionic substances conduct electricity?

Many ionic compounds will dissolve in water to form solutions. When the compound dissolves in water the ions are free to move. As they move around the circuit they carry charge. Therefore solutions of ionic compounds conduct electricity.

Electroplating

A solution of the ionic compound copper sulfate can be used to cover a metal paper clip with copper. The paper clip is connected to the negative terminal of the power pack and the copper strip is connected to the positive terminal. Both metals are then placed into the solution of copper sulfate. The solution of copper sulfate contains positive metal ions and negative sulfate ions. When the power pack is turned on, the positive copper ions move towards the negative electrode. Here they receive electrons to form copper atoms which are deposited on the paper clip. This is called electroplating. It works because when ionic compounds are dissolved, the ions are free to move.

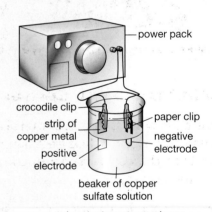

power pack

crocodile clip

strip of copper metal

positive electrode

paper clip

negative electrode

beaker of copper sulfate solution

FIGURE 4: When ionic compounds are molten or dissolved they can conduct electricity.

QUESTIONS

5 Predict the state of calcium chloride at room temperature.

6 Does a solution of sodium hydroxide conduct electricity? Why?

7 Does solid magnesium oxide conduct electricity? Why?

8 Would molten sodium chloride conduct electricity? Why?

QUESTIONS

9 If the ionic compound magnesium bromide is heated up it will melt. Why does magnesium bromide have a high melting point?

10 Would you expect molten magnesium bromide to conduct electricity? Why?

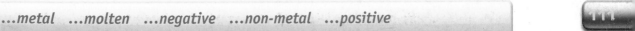

Covalent bonding

You will find out:
- That when atoms share pairs of electrons they form covalent bonds
- That some covalently bonded substances consist of simple molecules
- How to represent the covalent bonding in some simple molecules

Dry ice

Dry ice fog is a special effect used in many scary films. In fact, dry ice is not ice at all but frozen carbon dioxide, a covalently bonded compound. It is special because it changes from a solid straight to a gas, without forming a liquid. This is called sublimation. If chunks of dry ice are dropped into a container of water they quickly sublime to form a gas and a mysterious fog flows out.

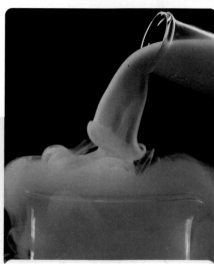

FIGURE 1: Why is dry ice fog used in films?

Non-metal atoms

When non-metal atoms react, both atoms need to gain **electrons** to get a full outer shell. They can only get this structure by **sharing** outer electrons.

Covalent bonding

A **covalent bond** is formed when two atoms share electrons. This shared pair of electrons holds the atoms together. Covalent bonds are very strong.

Representing covalent bonds

Covalent bonding occurs in **simple molecules** and in **giant covalent structures**. Simple molecules are small groups of atoms held together by strong covalent bonds. Examples of simple molecules include: hydrogen, chlorine, oxygen, water, ammonia, hydrogen chloride and methane.

The element hydrogen exists as diatomic (two atom) molecules. These molecules are formed when two hydrogen atoms share a pair of electrons to form a covalent bond. We can represent the bonding in hydrogen using diagrams (figure 2).

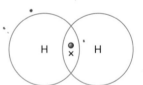

FIGURE 2: The atoms in a hydrogen molecule are held together by a covalent bond.

The covalent bonding in a hydrogen molecule can also be represented by a line drawn between the two hydrogen atoms as in figure 3.

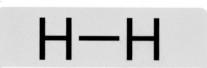

FIGURE 3: What does the line between the two hydrogen atoms represent?

⁞⁞ QUESTIONS ⁞⁞

1 Why do non-metal atoms form covalent bonds when they react together?
2 What is a covalent bond?
3 Describe the bonding in a hydrogen molecule.

EXAM HINTS AND TIPS

A covalent bond is a shared pair of electrons.

...*covalent bond* ...*electrons* ...*giant covalent structure*

Chlorine and oxygen

Chlorine, Cl_2 molecules consist of two chlorine atoms held together by a strong covalent bond. Chlorine atoms have seven electrons in their outer shell, so they need one more electron for a full shell. If two chlorine atoms share a pair of electrons, both atoms are able to gain a full, stable outer shell of electrons

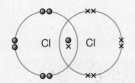

FIGURE 4: In molecules of chlorine two chlorine atoms are held together by a strong covalent bond.

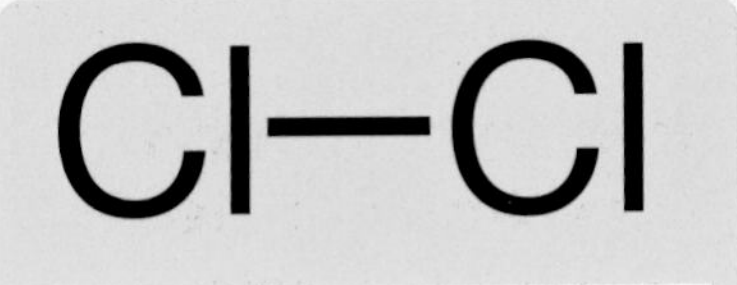

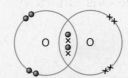

FIGURE 5: Another way of representing the covalent bond in chlorine molecules.

Oxygen, O_2 molecules consist of two oxygen atoms. Oxygen atoms have six electrons in their outer shell, so they need two more electrons for a full shell. If two oxygen atoms share two pairs of electrons, both atoms are able to gain a full, stable outer shell of electrons. As two pairs of electrons are shared by the oxygen atoms this is called a double covalent bond.

A double covalent bond can be represented by two lines drawn between the two oxygen atoms.

FIGURE 6: In molecules of oxygen two oxygen atoms are held together by a double covalent bond.

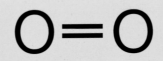

FIGURE 7: We can use two lines to represent a double covalent bond.

Water and ammonia

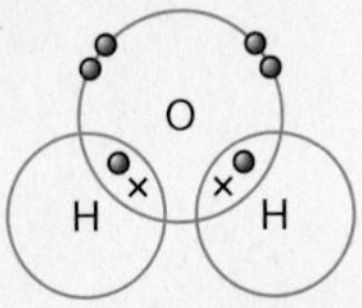

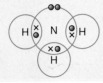

FIGURE 8: In molecules of water the atoms are held together by a strong covalent bond.

FIGURE 9: In molecules of ammonia the atoms are held together by strong covalent bonds.

Water, H_2O molecules consist of two hydrogen atoms and one oxygen atom held together by strong covalent bonds. Oxygen atoms have six electrons in their outer shell, so they need two more electrons for a full shell. If each oxygen atom shares a pair of electrons with two hydrogen atoms, all the atoms are able to gain a full, stable outer shell of electrons.

Ammonia, NH_3 molecules consist of one nitrogen atom and three hydrogen atoms held together by strong covalent bonds. Nitrogen atoms have five electrons in their outer shell, so they need three more electrons for a full shell. If each nitrogen atom shares a pair of electrons with three hydrogen atoms, all the atoms are able to gain a full, stable outer shell of electrons.

> ## A covalent bond is formed when two atoms share electrons

Sublimation

Iodine, I_2 molecules consist of two atoms of iodine held together by strong covalent bonds.

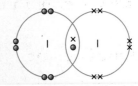

FIGURE 10: The bonding in an iodine molecule.

Although the bonding within the covalently bonded iodine molecules is very strong, the bonding between molecules is much weaker. This means that the forces of attraction between molecules can be easily overcome.

At room temperature iodine is a dark grey solid but at just 30 °C solid iodine sublimes into a purple vapour.

In fact, many covalently bonded molecules are gases at room temperature.

FIGURE 11: At room temperature iodine is a solid. When heated gently, iodine forms a purple vapour.

▦▦▦ QUESTIONS ▦▦▦

4 What is the difference between a single covalent bond and a double covalent bond?

5 Explain the bonding in water, H_2O.

6 Draw the bonding in hydrogen chloride, HCl.

7 Draw the bonding in methane, CH_4.

▦▦▦ QUESTIONS ▦▦▦

8 Would you expect chlorine to be a gas at room temperature? Why?

Simple molecules

You will find out:
- That substances that consist of simple molecules have low melting and boiling points
- That in molecular substances there are only weak forces of attraction between molecules

Hydrogen

Scientists have found evidence that hydrogen is present in the Sun and in most stars. It derives its name from 'hydro genes' because it reacts with oxygen to make water.

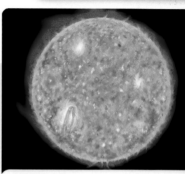

FIGURE 1: The element hydrogen is present in the Sun and most stars.

Molecules of elements

A **molecule** is formed when a group of atoms is joined together by shared pairs of **electrons** called **covalent bonds**. Many elements such as hydrogen and oxygen consist of molecules.

Hydrogen, H_2 molecules consist of two hydrogen atoms joined together by one shared pair of electrons called a covalent bond (figure 2).

Oxygen, O_2 molecules consist of two oxygen atoms joined together by two shared pairs of electrons called a double covalent bond (figure 3).

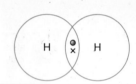

FIGURE 2: The bonding in a hydrogen molecule.

Molecules of compounds

Molecules of **compounds** are formed when two or more different types of atom are joined together by shared pairs of electrons.

Water, H_2O molecules consist of two hydrogen atoms and one oxygen atom joined together by covalent bonds (figure 4).

Ammonia, NH_3 molecules consist of one nitrogen atom and three hydrogen atoms joined together by covalent bonds (figure 5).

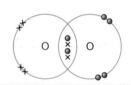

FIGURE 3: The bonding in an oxygen molecule.

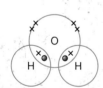

FIGURE 4: The bonding in a water molecule.

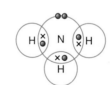

FIGURE 5: The bonding in an ammonia molecule.

Simple molecules

Simple molecules contain only a few atoms held together by strong covalent bonds. Their properties are:

- They do not **conduct** electricity.
- They have low melting and boiling points and are often liquids or gases at room temperature.
- Solid molecules are often soft or waxy.
- Solid molecules are brittle.
- They are usually insoluble in water but may dissolve in other liquids.

▤ QUESTIONS ▤

1 What does a covalent bond consist of?
2 How are molecules of hydrogen formed?
3 Would you expect oxygen gas to conduct electricity?
4 Give **three** common properties of molecular solids.

Melting and boiling points

Although many simple molecular substances are liquids or gases at room temperature, we know that a few, like sulfur, are solids with low melting points.

Solid simple molecules have a regular crystalline structure. Although there are strong forces of **attraction** within each molecule there are only weak forces of attraction between molecules.

Sulfur

Sulfur molecules consist of eight sulfur atoms joined together by strong covalent bonds in a ring-like structure.

Although the forces of attraction between the sulfur atoms within each molecule are strong, the forces of attraction between molecules are much weaker.

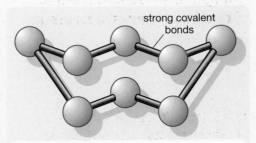

FIGURE 6: There are strong bonds between the sulfur atoms in each molecule.

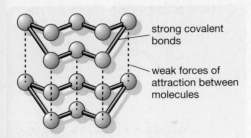

FIGURE 7: There are much weaker forces of attraction between sulfur molecules.

Little energy is required to overcome these weak forces of attraction between molecules so sulfur melts at just 119 °C.

Conducting electricity

Simple molecules do not conduct electricity even when molten or dissolved. This is because there are no charged particles in simple molecules to carry the charge around the circuit.

> A molecule is formed when a group of atoms is joined together by shared pairs of electrons called covalent bonds

Alcohol in perfumes

Perfumes consist of alcohol and essential oils. Plant oils such as magnolia, violet and almond, together with oils from animals such as musk deer and sperm whales are used. Each type of perfume has a slightly different blend of oils and a slightly different fragrance. These oils are mixed with alcohols such as ethanol. Ethanol consists of molecules so it has a low boiling point and evaporates easily from the skin. As it evaporates it carries the oils so that we are able to smell the perfume even at a distance.

FIGURE 8: Many perfumes contain alcohol.

QUESTIONS

8   Some fragrances contain more ethanol than others. Would a perfume that contains more ethanol last a longer or shorter time on the skin?

QUESTIONS

5   How many atoms of nitrogen are present in a molecule of N_2?

6   Explain why oxygen is a gas at room temperature.

7   Explain why ice melts at such a low temperature.

...covalent bond ...electrons ...molecule

Giant covalent structures

You will find out:
- That atoms can share pairs of electrons to form giant covalent structures
- How to represent the covalent bonding in structures such as diamond, graphite and silicon dioxide

The curse of the Black Orlov

The Black Orlov diamond was once owned by the Russian Princess Nadia Vyegin-Orlov. According to legend, the diamond is cursed and several owners of the diamond, including the princess, have met with violent deaths.

Black diamonds are extremely rare. The colour is caused by tiny pieces of magnetite and haematite minerals incorporated within the diamond structure.

FIGURE 1: Why is this diamond so valuable?

Giant covalent structures

We know that atoms can share pairs of **electrons** to form **covalent** bonds. Some substances consist of many atoms which are all held together by covalent bonds. These bonds are very strong. We call these substances giant covalent structures. Examples of giant covalent structures include: **diamond**, **graphite** and **silicon dioxide**.

FIGURE 2: Pencil lead is actually made from graphite.

FIGURE 3: Sand is made from silicon dioxide.

Properties of giant covalent structures

The bonding in giant covalent structures gives them their properties.

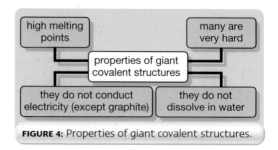

high melting points

many are very hard

properties of giant covalent structures

they do not conduct electricity (except graphite)

they do not dissolve in water

FIGURE 4: Properties of giant covalent structures.

QUESTIONS

1 Name **three** examples of giant covalent structures
2 How is a covalent bond formed?
3 Which is the only giant covalent structure that can conduct electricity?

...covalent ...diamond ...electrons

Melting points of diamonds

Diamonds have higher melting points than any other **minerals**. They owe their exceptionally high melting points to their structure. In diamonds each carbon atom is joined to four other carbon atoms by strong covalent bonds. Enormous amounts of energy are required to break these bonds so diamonds only melt at very high temperatures.

FIGURE 5: Why do diamonds have such high melting points?

Can graphite conduct electricity?

If we place this graphite pencil 'lead' in the circuit it conducts electricity and the bulb lights up. This makes graphite unusual because it is a non-metal which is also a good electrical conductor.

Graphite can conduct electricity because of the way that the carbon atoms are bonded together. Every carbon atom has four outer electrons. In graphite three of these electrons are used to form bonds to other atoms. So each carbon atom is bonded to three other carbon atoms by strong covalent bonds. This means that the bonding within layers is strong. However, the fourth electron is able to move through the whole structure. These electrons can carry charge through the structure so graphite is an electrical conductor.

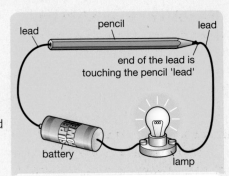

FIGURE 6: Why is graphite unusual?

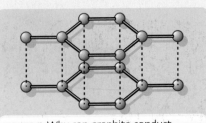

FIGURE 7: Why can graphite conduct electricity?

Substances which consist of many atoms all held together by covalent bonds are called giant covalent structures

Diamonds

The strong covalent bonds holding the carbon atoms together make diamond the hardest mineral in the world. This means that diamond-tipped drills can be used to cut through other materials including stone, concrete or even metals. One way to test whether a gem is really a diamond is to scratch it against glass. A diamond will cut the glass but a fake will not.

FIGURE 9: Diamonds are four times harder than the next hardest mineral, corundum.

Grains of sand

Sand grains consist of the compound silicon dioxide. Silicon dioxide has a similar structure to diamond, with the silicon and oxygen atoms held together by strong covalent bonds.

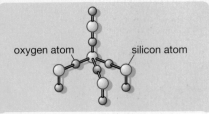

oxygen atom   silicon atom

FIGURE 8: How are the atoms held together?

Most rocks consist of many different minerals. However, because silicon dioxide is held together by strong covalent bonds it is very hard and resistant to weathering. We find sand at beaches because while other minerals have been broken down, the silicon dioxide remains intact.

QUESTIONS

4 Why do diamonds have very high melting points?
5 Describe how the atoms in graphite are arranged.
6 Why is sand so hard?

QUESTIONS

7 Draw the structure of atoms in diamond.
8 What do the lines between carbon atoms represent?

…graphite   …minerals   …silicon dioxide

Metals

You will find out:
- That metals consist of giant structures of atoms
- How atoms in a metal are arranged in a regular way
- That electrons in the outer shell of metal atoms are delocalised

Uranium – uses and dangers

Uranium is a metal used in nuclear reactors to generate electricity on a massive scale. It was also used in the first atomic bomb.

Uranium is a very dense, naturally radioactive material. When one of the isotopes of uranium, ^{235}U, is bombarded with neutrons, it decays to form two smaller nuclei releasing some neutrons and a great deal of energy. If the neutrons released by the decaying uranium atoms are absorbed by neighbouring ^{235}U atoms, a chain reaction occurs. The first atomic bomb dropped on Hiroshima in 1945 worked in this way.

FIGURE 1: What were the consequences of dropping this atomic bomb on Hiroshima?

Properties of metals

Metals are incredibly important in modern life. They have a range of **properties** that make them useful to us (see figure 2). In fact, most of our machines are made from metals.

The way the atoms are bonded together gives metals their special properties.

Atoms in metals

Figure 3 shows an atom of the element magnesium.

Magnesium atoms have two electrons in their outer shell. In magnesium metal these outer, negatively charged **electrons** are released by the magnesium atoms and become shared throughout the metal structure. We say that these electrons are delocalised. Once the magnesium atoms have lost electrons they become positive magnesium ions.

In fact, all metal atoms have a small number of electrons in their outer shells and behave in a similar way to produce metal ions and **delocalised** electrons.

The **electrostatic attraction** between these positive metal ions and the negatively charged electrons is called **metallic bonding**. This bonding gives metals their special properties.

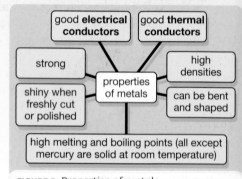

FIGURE 2: Properties of metals.

good **electrical conductors** | good **thermal conductors** | strong | shiny when freshly cut or polished | **properties of metals** | high densities | can be bent and shaped | high melting and boiling points (all except mercury are solid at room temperature)

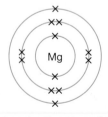

FIGURE 3: An atom of the element magnesium.

QUESTIONS

1 Barium is a metal. What state do you predict it to be at room temperature?
2 Why is copper used in electrical wiring?
3 Why is steel used to make bridges?
4 Why are metal ions attracted to delocalised electrons?

...delocalised   ...electrical conductors   ...electrons   ...electrostatic attraction

Conducting electricity

Copper is used in the electrical wiring in our homes. We use metals in this way because they are good electrical conductors. To find out why they conduct electricity we need to understand more about their structure.

An electric current is a flow of charge. Metals are good electrical conductors because their outer electrons are delocalised and not bound to individual atoms. When a potential difference is placed across a piece of metal these delocalised electrons are free to move and carry the charge through the structure.

FIGURE 4: Why is this wire made from metal?

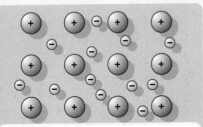

delocalised electrons move through the metal

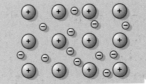

FIGURE 5: Why can the delocalised electrons in a metal move?

Thermal conduction

Below we can see the arrangement of metal ions and the delocalised electrons inside a metal.

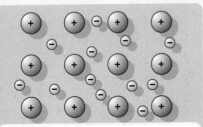

FIGURE 6: Only the outer electrons become delocalised.

If one end of this piece of metal is heated, the electrons start to move faster and their kinetic energy increases. The delocalised electrons are free to move and so this energy is quickly transmitted through the whole structure making metals very good conductors of heat.

Shaping metals

Figure 7 shows what happens when metals are stressed. The metal is held together by the attraction between the positive metal ions and the negative delocalised electrons. This means metals can change shape without fracturing.

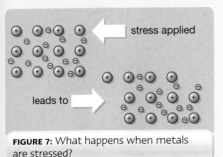

stress applied

leads to

FIGURE 7: What happens when metals are stressed?

FIGURE 8: Why are these gates made from metal?

Nichrome

Nichrome is an alloy of nickel, iron and chromium metals. It has a much higher electrical resistance than most metals. Even a short length of the wire will get hot very quickly when an electrical current passes through it.

Nichrome has a higher resistance than other metals such as copper because it is made from a mixture of different metal atoms. The atoms of the different elements are different sizes and cannot arrange themselves in a very regular way. This means that electrons cannot pass smoothly through a nichrome wire and it has a higher resistance.

FIGURE 9: Why is a nichrome element used in a toaster?

QUESTIONS

8   Draw the structure of a piece of the element silver.
9   Would you expect silver to have a high or a low resistance? Why?

QUESTIONS

5   Explain why metals are good electrical conductors.
6   Do all the electrons move when a metal conducts electricity?
7   Why are saucepans made from metals?

Alkali metals

You will find out:
- That the elements in Group 1 of the periodic table are called the alkali metals
- That all the elements in Group 1 have similar chemical properties
- That elements in Group 1 react with non-metals to form ionic compounds

Street lights

Street lights are a common sight in urban areas. These lamps contain sodium metal together with small amounts of neon and argon. When the lamps are first turned on they glow pink as the sodium metal is warmed. After a short while the sodium metal vaporises and a current is passed through the gaseous atoms. The bright orange light is caused by the collision between electrons and sodium atoms. This produces excited sodium atoms which then emit light.

FIGURE 1: The Group 1 metal sodium is used in street lights.

Where is Group 1?

Group 1 is on the far left of the periodic table. The elements of **Group 1** are sometimes called the **alkali metals**.

Group 1 elements

The alkali metals are a family of very **reactive** metal elements. The group includes lithium, sodium and potassium. These are silver-coloured metals which are less dense than water. These metals are stored under oil so that they do not react with air or moisture. The metals react rapidly with water, releasing hydrogen gas and producing metal hydroxide solutions. Rubidium, caesium and francium also belong to the group. These metals are denser than water and react so violently that they can only be safely used with special equipment.

FIGURE 3: The alkali metals react vigorously with water.

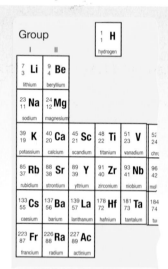

FIGURE 2: The Group 1 elements are found on the far left of the periodic table.

How alkali metals react

The alkali metals react readily with non-metals to form **salts** which are **ionic compounds**. The alkali metal atoms react to form ions which have a 1+ charge.

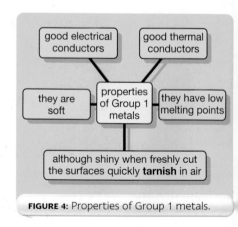

FIGURE 4: Properties of Group 1 metals.

> good electrical conductors — good thermal conductors — they are soft — properties of Group 1 metals — they have low melting points — although shiny when freshly cut the surfaces quickly **tarnish** in air

▌▌ QUESTIONS ▌▌

1 Which of the properties of Group 1 metals are typical for metals?
2 Which of the properties of Group 1 metals are unusual for metals?
3 Why does sodium float on top of water?
4 What is the charge on a sodium ion in the compound sodium chloride?

...alkali metals   ...Group 1   ...ionic compounds

Alkali metals react in a similar way

All the Group 1 elements react in a similar way because they all have a similar electron structure. Group 1 elements all have just one electron in their outer shell. Here we can see the equation for the reaction between potassium metal and chlorine gas. The ionic compound potassium chloride is formed.

Potassium + chlorine ⟶ potassium chloride

FIGURE 5: Fertilisers help plants to grow. Many contain potassium chloride.

Alkali metals form ions with a 1+ charge

Alkali metal atoms form ions by losing one electron to get a full outer shell, like a noble gas. This means that all Group 1 atoms form ions which have a 1+ charge.

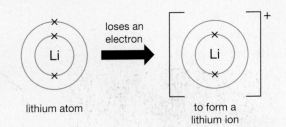

lithium atom   loses an electron   to form a lithium ion

FIGURE 6: Why do lithium atoms lose just one electron when they react?

Differences in reactions

Although all alkali metals react in a similar way, there are differences between them. The larger the alkali metal atom, the more easily it can lose an electron to form an ion. This is because in larger atoms the outer electron is further from the nucleus, so there is less attraction between the nucleus and outer electron.

In addition, larger atoms have more shells of electrons between the nucleus and the outer electron. These shells of electrons shield the outer electron from the nucleus, making it easier for the outer electron to be lost.

This means that the alkali metals get more reactive down the group.

QUESTIONS

5 Predict the number of electrons in the outer shell of caesium.

6 Which is the least reactive alkali metal?

7 Give a word equation for the reaction between potassium and bromine.

8 Predict the charge of a rubidium ion.

Discovering alkali metals

Alkali metals are never found as pure metals in nature, they are always combined with other elements in compounds.

Some metals, like copper, have been known and used since prehistoric times. However, sodium and potassium, which are the sixth and seventh most abundant elements in the Earth's crust, were only discovered around two hundred years ago by the English scientist Sir Humphry Davy.

FIGURE 7: Sir Humphry Davy.

Many metals, like copper, can be extracted from their compounds by heating the compound with hydrogen or carbon. However, alkali metals are so reactive that they form very stable compounds. This makes it difficult to extract the metal from the compound. Alkali metals could therefore only be extracted from their compounds when a process called electrolysis was developed.

QUESTIONS

The element caesium belongs to the alkali metal family.

9 Predict the properties of caesium.

10 Why is the reaction between caesium and chlorine more vigorous than the reaction between sodium and chlorine?

...reactive ...salts ...tarnish

Chemical structures

SELF-CHECK ACTIVITY

CHALLENGE

CONTEXT

Andy likes science; he is part of a team of pupils that visit classes of younger pupils to work with them to develop their understanding of science. He likes using models and analogies to explain ideas and thinks he has come up with a good one to explain why conductors conduct electricity and insulators don't.

The model goes like this. All materials are made of atoms; sometimes the atoms are joined up to make molecules. Atoms have a nucleus that consists of protons and neutrons, and they also have electrons. The number of electrons has to be the same as the number of protons in order to make the atom neutral. It's the electrons that are really crucial in this model.

Andy then sets out a number of plastic Petri dishes in a row. He says that each of these represents an atom. The atom needs exactly the right number of electrons. If it has too many the extra ones will be repelled. If it doesn't have enough it will attract more until it does.

He then gets some marbles and puts some in each dish. To fill the dish, without any being stacked up on top of others, takes exactly thirteen. The marbles represent the electrons in the atom.

Andy then says that in order for a current to flow along this wire, extra electrons have to arrive at one end, displace electrons from the first dish to the second, from the second dish to the third, and so on. This is conduction.

He now gets the Petri dish lids and puts them on the dishes, enclosing the marbles. Now if more marbles are supplied at one end, the others can't move along. In this model, electrons can't be transferred. This is insulation.

STEP 1

Draw a diagram of the row of Petri dishes set up to model conduction and label it to show what the object represent.

STEP 2

Now draw the model and label it as it is set up to model insulation.

Do you think Andy has come up with a good model?
- Explain how it explains conduction and insulation well.
- Now explain the shortcomings of the model.

One of Andy's friends comes up with some other features that the model might be able to show. Explain, perhaps using diagrams, how you could use or develop the model to show that:
- wires are not just one atom wide
- atoms of different materials have different numbers of electrons
- atoms also have protons and neutrons (though they don't flow)
- some materials are better conductors than others.

Maximise your grade

These sentences show what you need to include in your work to achieve each grade. Use them to improve your work and be more successful.

Grade	Answer includes...
F	State that atoms have electrons.
	Know that in some cases electrons can move from one atom to another.
	Know that this can be used to explain the difference between conduction and insulation.
	Understand how Andy's model shows this difference.
C	Explain using the model why some materials conduct and others don't.
	Suggest ways in which Andy's model is not like the atomic structure of a real material.
A	Take two of the features in Step 4 and modify the model to show them.
	Take all of the features in Step 4 and modify the model to show them.

Halogens

You will find out:
- That elements in Group 7 of the periodic table are called the halogens
- That all the elements in Group 7 have similar chemical properties

Iodine deficiency

Iodine deficiency affects more than 10 per cent of the world's population and can lead to serious health problems including goitres and mental retardation.

Scientists are working to eliminate iodine deficiency diseases by adding tiny amounts of iodine to salt. Salt is eaten in small quantities on a regular basis and it costs just a few pence a year to produce enough iodised salt to protect people from these diseases.

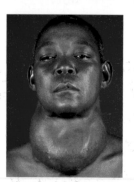

FIGURE 1: This person has a goitre. Most goitres are caused by a lack of iodine in the diet.

Where is Group 7?

Group 7 is on the right of the periodic table. The elements of Group 7 are sometimes called the **halogens**.

Group 7 elements

The halogens are a family of reactive **non-metal** elements which includes:

- **fluorine** – a pale yellow, poisonous gas
- **chlorine** – a green, poisonous gas; the most common halogen
- **bromine** – a dark red poisonous liquid
- **iodine** – a dark grey crystalline solid which sublimes to form a purple vapour when heated
- **astatine** – has no uses because it is extremely radioactive.

All the halogens form molecules which consist of two atoms joined together by a shared pair of electrons called a covalent bond.

FIGURE 2: Halogens are highly reactive non-metals.

How halogens react

The halogens react readily with alkali metals to form **salts** which are **ionic compounds**. In fact, the word 'halogen' comes from the Greek for salt-bringers.

FIGURE 3: Chlorine is used to kill bacteria in drinking water and in swimming pools.

QUESTIONS

1. Which halogen is a liquid at room temperature?
2. Which halogen is a solid at room temperature?
3. Which halogen is radioactive?
4. What is formed when a halogen reacts with a Group 1 metal?

...astatine   ...bromine   ...chlorine   ...fluorine   ...Group 7   ...halide

Halogens react in a similar way

All the Group 7 elements react in a similar way because they have a similar electron structure. Group 7 elements have seven electrons in their outer shell. Figure 2 shows the reaction when sodium metal is burnt in chlorine gas. The ionic compound sodium chloride is formed (figure 4).

Sodium + chlorine ⟶ sodium chloride

Other halogens react in a similar way to form similar ionic compounds.

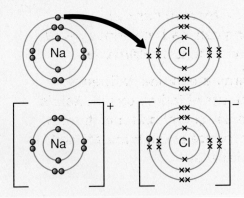

FIGURE 4: When chlorine atoms react they gain an electron to form a chloride ion which has a 1− charge.

Halogens form ions with a 1− charge

Non-metal atoms form ions by gaining electrons to get a full outer shell, like a noble gas. We know that all halogen atoms have seven electrons in their outer shell so they can get a full outer shell by gaining a single electron. This means that all atoms of Group 7 elements form ions which have a 1− charge. We call halogen ions **halide** ions.

Reactivity of fluorine

Although all the halogens react in a similar way, there are clear differences between them and this is due mainly to the size of the atoms. The smaller the halogen atom the more strongly it attracts an electron to form a halide ion. This makes fluorine more reactive than other halogens.

FIGURE 5: This mineral contains the compound calcium fluoride.

The halogens react readily with alkali metals to form salts which are ionic compounds

Displacement reactions

The halogens can be placed into an order of reactivity. The halogens become increasingly less reactive down the group.

A more reactive halogen can displace a less reactive halogen from its compound.

This order of reactivity is shown by the reaction between chlorine and potassium bromide. When chlorine gas is bubbled through a solution of potassium bromide, the chlorine displaces the bromide from the solution producing potassium chloride and bromine gas.

Chlorine + potassium bromide ⟶ bromine + potassium chloride

The more reactive halogen, chlorine, displaces the less reactive halogen, bromine, from the solution of potassium bromide.

▮▮▮▮ QUESTIONS ▮▮▮▮

Astatine is a radioactive element which belongs to the halogen family.

9 Predict the state of astatine at room temperature.

10 Explain what would happen if astatine was reacted with sodium metal.

▮▮▮▮ QUESTIONS ▮▮▮▮

5 Predict the number of electrons in the outer shell of a group 6 element.

6 Which is the second most reactive halogen?

7 Give a word equation for the reaction between sodium and bromine.

8 Predict the charge of an iodide ion.

...halogens ...iodine ...ionic compounds ...non-metal ...salts

Nanoparticles

You will find out:
- That nanoparticles have properties which are different from the properties of the same materials in bulk quantities
- How nanoparticles are being used and might be used in the future to improve people's lives

Smallest test tubes in the world

Scientists at Oxford and Nottingham Universities have carried out experiments in the smallest test tubes in the world. These test tubes are made from cylinders of carbon atoms and have a diameter thousands of times smaller than the width of a human hair.

Carrying out experiments in extremely confined spaces allows scientists to influence the products of reactions carried out. The products made in these test tubes form linear molecules. In the future scientists hope to apply this idea to produce higher quality polymers.

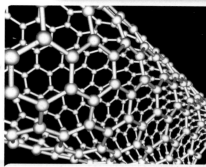

FIGURE 1: Scientists have carried out experiments inside test tubes like these.

What is nanoscience?

Nanoscience is an exciting new area of science concerned with extremely small pieces of materials. These materials consist of just a few hundred atoms and are called **nanoparticles**. Nanoparticles are between one and one hundred **nanometres** in size.

1 nanometre

FIGURE 2: What is the diameter of a hydrogen atom?

How big is a nanometre?

A nanometre is almost unimaginably small. One human hair has a width of about 100 000 nanometres. Incredibly, atoms are even smaller. A line of 10 hydrogen atoms side by side would measure about 1 nanometre.

Qualities of nanoparticles

Nanoparticles have a unique structure due to the precise way the particles are arranged. Nanoparticles are so small that they have extremely high **surface area** to **volume** ratios. Scientists have found that materials behave differently on a small scale; for example, nanosized particles of the element gold have a red colour.

Scientists are discovering that nanoparticles can make valuable contributions to real world applications, including computers, **catalysts**, sensors, coatings and lighter **constructive** materials.

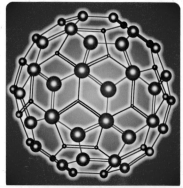

FIGURE 3: Nanoparticles like this buckyball have high surface area to volume ratios.

▪ QUESTIONS ▪

1 How big are nanoparticles?
2 Roughly how many atoms are in a nanoparticle?
3 Why do nanoparticles have unique structures?
4 Suggest some different applications for nanoparticles.

...catalysts ...constructive ...nanometres ...nanoparticles

Better constructive materials

Nanoscience offers us the opportunity to produce unique structures in which the atoms are precisely arranged. Scientists are working to produce ultra-lightweight materials that are harder and stronger than any that have previously existed. In the future we could see bridges and planes built from nanoparticles.

FIGURE 4: Lighter, stronger sportswear could help athletes to perform better.

Improved biosensors

FIGURE 5: Nanoparticles could be used as biosensors to protect people from chemical or biological attacks.

Scientists working for the military are particularly interested in using nanoparticles as biosensors. These tiny particles could be used to detect very low levels of chemical or biological agents and warn soldiers to seek protection.

Other uses of nanoparticles

Other exciting real-life applications of nanoparticles include the development of new coatings.

FIGURE 6: Sunscreens which contain nanoparticles could help to protect sun-bathers in the future.

FIGURE 7: Safety goggles coated with nanoparticles could be more scratch-resistant.

Nanomaterials could be used to develop a new generation of cheap computers that would process information millions of times faster than today. In the future computers made from nanoparticles could be the size of a wrist watch.

Nanoparticles have a large surface area to volume ratio. Scientists are keen to exploit this feature of nanoparticles in a new generation of catalysts. Reactions occur at the surface of catalysts. This makes nanoparticles excellent catalysts which will increase the speed of manufacturing processes.

> *A nanometre is almost unimaginably small. One human hair has a width of about 100 000 nanometres.*

Safety concerns

There has been a lot of interest in the media about the safety of nanoparticles. Stories warn that they could escape and start to reproduce, perhaps becoming new weapons of mass destruction or even taking over the planet.

While most nanoparticles pose no risks, there are some concerns. Substances previously thought to be safe may cause problems in nano-sized amounts as they may be able to pass into the body. Clearly a mature debate is needed.

▦▦▦ QUESTIONS ▦▦▦

8   Should scientists continue to develop applications for nanoparticles? Write a newspaper article explaining the advantages and disadvantages of these tiny particles.

▦▦▦ QUESTIONS ▦▦▦

5   Why can nanoparticles be used to build stronger and lighter materials?
6   How can nanoparticles be used to protect soldiers from war gases?
7   Why do nanoparticles make excellent catalysts?

Smart materials

Bioluminescence

Some living organisms have developed very unusual features which help them to survive. Most deep-sea creatures can convert chemical energy to light energy in a process known as bioluminescence. Most of these creatures produce light in the blue and green regions of the visible spectrum as this is most efficient at penetrating water. Today, scientists are developing a range of new materials that have dramatic and unusual properties.

FIGURE 1: Why does this creature produce light?

What are smart materials?

Have you ever seen glasses that change colour when placed in bright light? These very useful glasses have **photochromic** lenses. If worn outside on a sunny day they quickly get darker, then lighten again when back inside. This is more convenient than having to have both normal glasses and sunglasses.

Photochromic lenses are an example of a **smart material**. Smart materials have at least one **property**, such as colour or size, which can be dramatically altered by changes in the **environment**. These alterations are **reversible** so the smart material goes back to normal once the trigger for the change is removed.

A variety of smart materials already exist, including shape memory alloys, photochromic materials, electroluminescent materials, and thermochromic materials.

FIGURE 2: Why are photochromic lenses so useful?

QUESTIONS

1. Why are smart materials special?
2. The changes in the properties of smart materials are reversible. What does this mean?
3. Name **four** types of smart material.

...*electroluminescent* ...*environment* ...*photochromic* ...*property*

Changes affecting smart materials

We know that some smart materials **respond** to changes in light intensity. Some respond to other changes in the environment, including changes in temperature, changes in moisture levels, electric fields and magnetic fields.

Thermochromatic materials

Thermochromatic materials respond to changes in temperature by changing colour. The colour change is reversible so once the material returns to its original temperature it also returns to its original colour. The temperature at which the colour change occurs can be adjusted depending upon the particular application that the smart material is being used for.

Cups that change colour or reveal new designs when hot liquid is poured into them and T-shirts that change colour as the temperature of the wearer changes are both popular applications of this technology.

FIGURE 3: Why does this mug change colour?

Smart materials have at least one property which can be dramatically altered by changes in the environment

Electroluminescent materials

Electroluminescent materials respond to an AC current by emitting light of different colours. These materials produce a cold light source and are often flexible. They are used in advertising signs and Christmas decorations.

Applications of smart materials

Scientists are working to develop even more smart materials and to find new and exciting applications for the ones we already have. In particular, scientists hope to use them in medical and military applications.

QUESTIONS

4   What factors can affect smart materials?
5   What is a thermochromatic material?
6   Write a short explanation, to be placed on the side of a thermochromatic cup, to explain to people what a smart material is.

QUESTIONS

7   Photochromic glass can be used to make smart windows in offices. How would these smart windows help to improve conditions for people working in these offices?

...respond   ...reversible   ...smart material   ...thermochromatic

Compounds

Polytetrafluoroethene

Polytetrafluoroethene, or PTFE, is better known by its trademark name of Teflon. It is an amazing compound made from carbon and fluorine atoms and was discovered by accident by scientists working to produce new refrigerant gases. They found that the compound has some unusual, useful properties. It is biologically inert and surfaces coated with PTFE have low friction. It has many uses including non-stick saucepans and replacement heart valves.

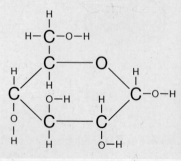

FIGURE 1: PTFE is an extremely useful compound.

What is a compound?

We know that **elements** contain just one type of **atom**. Scientists have found about 100 different types of element and everything in the world is made from atoms of these different elements. When atoms of two or more elements are **chemically combined**, a new substance called a compound is formed.

Glucose **molecules** have the chemical **formula** $C_6H_{12}O_6$. This formula shows us the type and number of the atoms in a molecule of glucose. Each glucose molecule has 6 carbon atoms, 12 hydrogen atoms and 6 oxygen atoms (see figure 2).

Glucose is a single substance made from atoms of three different elements. Some compounds consist of giant structures, for example salt consists of unimaginably large numbers of sodium and chloride ions. The formula for sodium chloride is NaCl. Figure 3 shows us the type and ratio of the elements involved. Here the sodium and chloride ions are present in the ratio 1:1.

FIGURE 2: This shows the way that atoms are arranged in one molecule of glucose. The lines between the atoms represent chemical bonds.

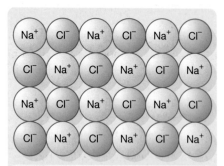

FIGURE 3: Each grain of salt contains a huge number of sodium and chloride ions.

QUESTIONS

1 What is special about an element?

2 What is special about a compound?

3 A molecule of methane has the formula CH_4. How many atoms of carbon and hydrogen are present?

4 Are atoms created or destroyed during chemical reactions?

...atom ...chemically combined   ...elements   ...formula

Writing balanced equations

During respiration, glucose from the food we eat reacts with oxygen in a chemical reaction. This chemical reaction produces new substances and releases energy. We can sum up what happens in a **word equation**:

Glucose + oxygen ⟶ carbon dioxide + water

Sometimes we might want to write a **symbol equation** to sum up what happens:

$C_6H_{12}O_6 + 6O_2 \longrightarrow 6CO_2 + 6H_2O$

During any chemical reaction the atoms are rearranged. So there must always be the same number of each type of atom at the beginning and end of the reaction. In the above equation we can see that at the start of the reaction there are 6 carbon atoms, 12 hydrogen atoms and 18 oxygen atoms. At the end of the reaction we still have 6 carbon atoms, 12 hydrogen atoms and 18 oxygen atoms; they are just arranged in a different way.

Mixtures and compounds

In a compound, atoms of different elements are chemically combined to form a pure new substance. Compounds have a formula which shows the type and ratio of the atoms involved. However, many objects are mixtures of different substances. A cup of tea containing water, milk and sugar is a mixture of several different substances.

FIGURE 4: Mixtures contain more than one substance mixed together but not chemically combined.

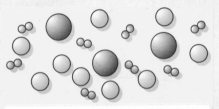

FIGURE 5: In a mixture different substances are mixed together but not chemically combined.

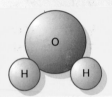

FIGURE 6: In a compound, atoms of different elements are chemically combined. Here atoms of hydrogen are chemically joined to an atom of oxygen.

Why balance equations?

Here we can see the word equation to sum up the reaction between hydrogen and oxygen to produce water.

Hydrogen + oxygen ⟶ water

If we substitute chemical formulae for the names we get:

$H_2 + O_2 \longrightarrow H_2O$

However, there is clearly something wrong with our equation. We started with two atoms of oxygen but here the reaction only produces one atom of oxygen and the other atom of oxygen seems to have disappeared. Of course, this cannot happen. We simply need to balance the equation.

$2H_2 + O_2 \longrightarrow 2H_2O$

Now the equation balances and sums up the whole reaction.

Balancing equations

Being able to balance equations is an important skill in science. A balanced equation allows us to calculate the amount of material that we should use to produce a particular amount of the product. This is especially important in industrial processes.

QUESTIONS

5   What is the difference between a mixture and a compound?

6   Is air a compound or a mixture?

QUESTIONS

7   Balance the following equations.

 a $Mg + O_2 \longrightarrow MgO$

 b $Na + Cl_2 \longrightarrow NaCl$

 c $Fe_2O_3 + CO \longrightarrow Fe + CO_2$

 d $CH_4 + O_2 \longrightarrow CO_2 + H_2O$

...*molecules* ...*symbol equation* ...*word equation*

Percentage composition

You will find out:
- How to calculate the relative formula mass of a compound
- How to calculate the percentage of an element in a compound

Potassium nitrate

Potassium nitrate, KNO_3 is an oxidising agent. This means that it releases oxygen which allows other substances to burn better. Traditionally, potassium nitrate has been mixed with sulfur and charcoal to form gunpowder. This mixture burns rapidly and can be used to propel missiles like bullets. Today potassium nitrate is sometimes used in fireworks.

FIGURE 1: Why is potassium nitrate used in fireworks?

Potassium in potassium nitrate

Potassium nitrate is a fertiliser with the **formula** KNO_3. We add potassium nitrate to the soil to increase the amount of crop that we can grow. We can work out the **relative formula mass** of potassium nitrate by adding together the relative atomic mass of each of the **atoms**, in the **ratio** shown in the formula, KNO_3, as shown here.

$$K \quad N \quad O_3$$
$$39 \quad + \quad 14 \quad + \quad (3 \times 16)$$
$$= 101$$

We can use the relative formula mass of potassium nitrate to calculate the percentage of potassium by mass in potassium nitrate.

$$\text{\% mass of an element in a compound} = \frac{\text{relative atomic mass of the element} \times \text{number of atoms of element in the formula}}{\text{relative formula mass}} \times 100$$

$$\text{\% mass of potassium in potassium nitrate} = \frac{39 \times 1}{101} \times 100$$
$$= 38.6\%$$

The percentage of potassium in potassium nitrate is:

QUESTIONS

Nitrogen has a relative atomic mass of 14.

Hydrogen has a relative atomic mass of 1.

Oxygen has a relative atomic mass of 16.

1. What is the formula mass of ammonia, NH_3?
2. What is the formula mass of nitrogen dioxide, NO_2?
3. What is the formula mass of nitric acid, HNO_3?

...atoms ...formula ...percentage

Phosphorus in ammonium phosphate

Ammonium phosphate is a fertiliser with the formula $(NH_4)_3 PO_4$. We can use this formula to work out the relative formula mass (M_r) of ammonium phosphate.

$$(NH_4)_3 \ PO_4$$

$$(14 + (4 \times 1)) \times 3 \ + \ 31 + (4 \times 16)$$

$$= 149$$

The percentage of phosphorus in ammonium phosphate is:

$$\text{\% mass of phosphorus in ammonium phosphate} = \frac{31 \times 1}{149} \times 100$$

$$= 20.8\%$$

Nitrogen in ammonium nitrate

Ammonium nitrate is a fertiliser with the formula, NH_4NO_3.

We can use this formula to work out the relative formula mass of the compound.

$$NH_4 \ NO_3$$

$$14 + (4 \times 1) \ + \ 14 + (3 \times 16)$$

$$= 80$$

The percentage of nitrogen in ammonium nitrate is:

$$\text{\% mass of nitrogen in ammonium nitrate} = \frac{14 \times 2}{80} \times 100$$

$$= 35\%$$

Fertilisers

Plants need relatively large amounts of nitrogen, phosphorus and potassium. Without sufficient nitrogen, plants do not grow well and their leaves turn yellow. Without enough phosphorus, plants do not grow or mature properly and without sufficient potassium, the plants will not flower well.

When farmers grow crops, they remove nutrients from the soil. If the farmer wishes to continue producing high yields, these nutrients must be replaced. The soil is tested and a fertiliser is applied, which replaces the elements in which the soil is deficient.

FIGURE 2: Why do farmers add fertiliser to the land?

...ratio   ...relative formula mass

Moles

You will find out:
- That the relative formula mass of a substance, in grams, is known as one mole of that substance
- That the masses of reactants and products can be calculated from the balanced symbol equation for a reaction

The mole

Scientists have found that the number of particles in one mole of a substance is:

$$6 \times 10^{23}$$

One mole of any substance contains the same number of particles. This is a fantastically large number. If we could count 1 million atoms every second it would take about 20 billion years to count the atoms in one mole of an element.

FIGURE 1: How many atoms does one mole of gold contain?

What is a mole?

We know that **atoms** of different **elements** have different masses and that atoms are so tiny that we cannot measure them individually. However, we can measure one **mole** of a substance. One mole of any substance contains the same number of particles. The **relative formula mass**, in **grams**, of a substance is known as the mass of one mole of the substance. Water has the formula H_2O. The relative formula mass of water is 18 (see figure 2).

Water can be produced when hydrogen is burnt. This reaction can be summed up by the word equation:

Hydrogen + oxygen ⟶ water

... or by the **balanced symbol equation**:

$$2H_2 + O_2 \longrightarrow 2H_2O$$

From this equation we can see that two moles of hydrogen react with one mole of oxygen to make two moles of water.

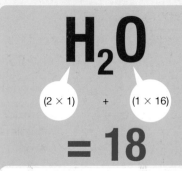

H_2O

(2 × 1)   +   (1 × 16)

= 18

FIGURE 2: The mass of one mole of water is 18 g.

FIGURE 3: Imagine how many moles of water there are in here.

FIGURE 4: Sulfur has a relative atomic mass of 32. What is the mass of one mole of sulfur?

QUESTIONS

1. Why don't we measure the mass of individual atoms?
2. What is a mole?
3. What is the mass of one mole of hydrogen molecules, H_2?
4. What is the mass of one mole of oxygen molecules, O_2?
5. What is the mass of one mole of hydrogen peroxide, H_2O_2?

EXAM HINTS AND TIPS

You need to know how to calculate the number of moles present in a given sample.

...atoms ...balanced symbol equation ...elements

Magnesium oxide

When magnesium metal is burnt in air it reacts with oxygen to form the compound magnesium oxide. This reaction can be summed up by the balanced equation:

$$2Mg + O_2 \longrightarrow 2MgO$$

This equation shows that two moles of magnesium react with one mole of oxygen molecules to produce two moles of the compound magnesium oxide. Magnesium has a relative atomic mass of 24. One mole of magnesium has a mass of 24 g.

To calculate the number of moles present in 12 g of magnesium, we divide the mass of magnesium we have by the mass of one mole of magnesium

$$\text{number of moles in magnesium} = \frac{\text{mass of magnesium}}{\text{mass of one mole of magnesium}}$$

$$= \frac{12}{24}$$

$$= 0.5 \text{ moles}$$

We know that two moles of magnesium should produce two moles of magnesium oxide, so 0.5 moles of magnesium should produce 0.5 moles of magnesium oxide.

The relative formula mass of magnesium oxide is 40. The mass of one mole of magnesium oxide is 40 g. We can now work out the mass of 0.5 moles of magnesium oxide.

$$\underset{24}{Mg} \underset{16}{O} = 40$$

$$\text{mass of magnesium oxide} = \text{number of moles of magnesium oxide} \times \text{relative formula mass of magnesium oxide}$$

$$= 0.5 \times 40$$

$$= 20g$$

Burning 12 g of magnesium should produce 20 g of magnesium oxide.

Carbon dioxide

When carbon is burnt in a good supply of air it reacts with oxygen to form the compound carbon dioxide. This reaction can be summed up by the balanced equation:

$$C + O_2 \longrightarrow CO_2$$

This equation shows that one mole of carbon reacts with one mole of oxygen molecules to produce one mole of the compound carbon dioxide.

$$\underset{12}{C} \underset{(2 \times 16)}{O_2} = 44$$

Carbon dioxide has a relative formula mass of 44. One mole of carbon dioxide has a mass of 44 g. To calculate the number of moles present in 11 g of carbon dioxide, divide the mass of carbon dioxide we have by the mass of one mole of carbon dioxide.

$$\text{number of moles of carbon dioxide} = \frac{\text{mass of carbon dioxide}}{\text{mass of one mole of carbon dioxide}}$$

$$= \frac{11}{44}$$

$$= 0.25 \text{ moles}$$

We know that one mole of carbon should produce one mole of carbon dioxide, so 0.25 moles of carbon dioxide should be made from 0.25 moles of carbon.

The relative atomic mass of carbon is 12. The mass of one mole of carbon is 12 g. We can now work out the mass of 0.25 moles of carbon

$$\text{mass of carbon} = \text{number of moles of carbon} \times \text{relative atomic mass of carbon}$$

$$= 0.25 \times 12$$

$$= 3g$$

To produce 11 g of carbon dioxide we should burn 3 g of carbon.

Why are moles useful?

Mole calculations are extremely useful. They allow scientists to calculate the amount of product that a chemical reaction can produce even though the particles involved might have different masses.

QUESTIONS

6 What mass of magnesium oxide is produced when 24 g of magnesium is burnt?

7 What mass of magnesium oxide is produced when 6 g of magnesium is burnt?

8 What mass of carbon should be burnt completely to produce 5.5 g of carbon dioxide?

9 What mass of carbon should be burnt completely to produce 22 g of carbon dioxide?

QUESTIONS

10 When carbon is burnt, why might the amount of carbon dioxide produced be less than might be expected?

Percentage yield

You will find out:
- That the amount of product obtained in a reaction is called the yield
- How to calculate the percentage yield for a particular reaction
- That reactions that have a high percentage yield have a high atom economy

Sweet air

Candyfloss is made from sugar, air and colouring. Candyfloss machines heat the mixture until the sugar melts, then spin the liquid sugar in a drum. This is forced through small holes to form thin strands which cool and solidify when they hit the air, forming a web of sugar strands.

However, not all of the ingredients end up as candyfloss. Some sugar remains stuck to the sides of the machine, so the amount of candyfloss actually made is less than you might expect.

FIGURE 1: Why might the amount of candyfloss made be less than you might expect?

The yield of a reaction

We call the amount of **product** made during a chemical **reaction** the **yield**. One way of judging the success of a reaction is to calculate its **percentage yield**. This is a way of comparing the amount of product actually made during the reaction (the actual yield) with the maximum amount of product calculated mathematically (the **theoretical yield**). To do this we use this equation:

$$\text{percentage yield} = \frac{\text{actual yield}}{\text{theoretical yield}} \times 100$$

If a reaction has an actual yield of 3.2 g and a theoretical yield of 4.0 g, the percentage yield of the reaction is calculated as:

$$\text{percentage yield} = \frac{\text{actual yield}}{\text{theoretical yield}} \times 100$$

$$\text{percentage yield} = \frac{3.2}{4.0} \times 100$$

$$= 80\%$$

Reactions like this one which have a high percentage yield also have a high **atom economy**. Most of the starting materials end up as useful products.

QUESTIONS

1 What is the yield of a reaction?
2 What is the percentage yield of a reaction?
3 If a reaction has a percentage yield of 7%, what can you say about the atom economy of the reaction?

EXAM HINTS AND TIPS

If a reaction has a high percentage yield it has a high atom economy.

...atom economy   ...percentage yield   ...product   ...reaction

Actual and theoretical yields

There may be many reasons why the yield of a reaction is less than we might have predicted by simply using maths:

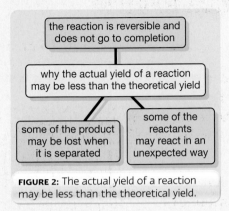

the reaction is reversible and does not go to completion

why the actual yield of a reaction may be less than the theoretical yield

some of the product may be lost when it is separated

some of the reactants may react in an unexpected way

FIGURE 2: The actual yield of a reaction may be less than the theoretical yield.

High atom economy

We know reactions that have a high percentage yield have a high atom economy. This is attractive financially because a high proportion of the reactant materials end up as useful products. It is also important for **sustainable development** as these reactions do not waste large amounts of material making undesirable products.

FIGURE 3: The efficiency of this power station depends on the percentage yield of its reactions.

One way we can judge how successful a reaction is, is to calculate the percentage yield

Percentage yield

Knowing the percentage yield of a reaction is very important for scientists because it allows them to calculate exactly how much of each reactant they should use to make the desired amount of a particular product.

QUESTIONS

4 A reaction has an actual yield of 1.3 g and a theoretical yield of 2.3 g. What is the percentage yield of this reaction?

5 Could you have a percentage yield greater than 100%?

6 A reaction has an actual yield of 2.2 g and a percentage yield of 60%. What is the theoretical yield for this reaction?

7 A reaction has a theoretical yield of 3.0 g and a percentage yield of 80%. How much product is actually made?

QUESTIONS

8 A reaction between magnesium and oxygen has a percentage yield of 75%. 1.0 g of magnesium has a theoretical yield of 1.67 g. How much magnesium should be burnt to produce 1.0 g of magnesium oxide?

Reversible reactions

You will find out:
- What reversible reactions are
- How to represent reversible reactions using equations

Esters

Scientists make esters using a reversible reaction between carboxylic acids and alcohols. Many esters have sweet fruity or floral fragrances. They also taste pleasant and can be used to flavour foods such as sweets, ice cream and cakes.

FIGURE 1: The pleasant fruity taste of pear drops is caused by esters.

Heating ammonium chloride

You may have seen the **chemical reaction** which takes place when ammonium chloride is heated. Ammonium chloride is a white solid which, when heated, breaks down to form two colourless gases: ammonia and hydrogen chloride. However, when the gases cool down they react together to re-form ammonium chloride. These reactions can be summed up by the word equation:

Ammonium chloride ⇌ ammonia + hydrogen chloride

The ⇌ is used to show that this is a reversible reaction.

When ammonium chloride is heated, it breaks down to form ammonia and hydrogen chloride. On cooling, ammonia and hydrogen chloride react together to form ammonium chloride (figure 2).

What is a reversible reaction?

A **reversible reaction** is a chemical reaction that can proceed in both directions. In the **forward** reaction, the **reactants** can react together to form new materials called **products**. In the **backwards** reaction, the products can react to form the original starting materials called the reactants. This means that the reaction may not actually go to completion.

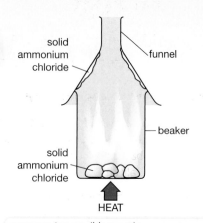

solid ammonium chloride — funnel

beaker

solid ammonium chloride

HEAT

FIGURE 2: A reversible reaction.

A reversible reaction is a chemical reaction that can proceed in both directions

▦ QUESTIONS ▦

1   What new substances are produced when ammonium chloride is heated?
2   What is the sign used to show that a reaction is reversible?
3   Explain why heating ammonium chloride is a reversible reaction.

...backwards ...chemical reaction ...forward ...products

Heating copper sulfate

We know that copper sulfate crystals have a pretty blue colour. In fact, these crystals are really hydrated copper sulfate crystals and have the chemical formula $CuSO_4.5H_2O$. The second half of the formula shows us that this salt contains five molecules of water for each copper sulfate unit. These water molecules are known as the **water of crystallisation**.

If we heat up hydrated copper sulfate crystals, the water molecules change colour from blue to white as the water of crystallisation is lost and anhydrous copper sulfate is formed. However, if we add water to anhydrous copper sulfate, the water reacts with the white anhydrous copper sulfate to form blue hydrated copper sulfate. These two reactions can be summed up by this word equation:

Hydrated copper sulfate $\rightleftharpoons$ anhydrous copper sulfate + water

FIGURE 3: What happens when hydrated copper sulfate is heated?

FIGURE 4: What happens when water is added to anhydrous copper sulfate?

Cobalt chloride paper

We can use cobalt chloride paper to test for the presence of water. Cobalt chloride paper is blue. If it turns pink it shows that water is present. This is because anhydrous cobalt chloride is blue and if water is present the water reacts with the anhydrous cobalt chloride to produce hydrated cobalt chloride which is pink.

However, if the paper is left out of its container for a while it can react with the moisture in air and turn pink, but we don't have to throw the paper away. If this paper is placed in a warm oven, the hydrated cobalt chloride loses water to form anhydrous cobalt chloride and changes colour from pink to blue. This can be summed up by the word equation:

Hydrated cobalt chloride $\rightleftharpoons$ anhydrous cobalt chloride + water

Usefulness in industry

Many useful new materials like ammonia are made during reversible reactions.

In industry, we want to make as much useful product as possible. By knowing about what happens during reversible reactions, scientists can adjust the conditions to make their process as profitable as possible.

FIGURE 5: Ammonia is made by a reversible reaction. Ammonia can be used to make fertilisers.

QUESTIONS

4. Why should blue copper sulfate really be called hydrated copper sulfate?
5. What colour is anhydrous copper sulfate?
6. How could you make anhydrous copper sulfate from hydrated copper sulfate?
7. How could you make hydrated copper sulfate from anhydrous copper sulfate?

QUESTIONS

8. Hydrated cobalt chloride has the formula $CoCl_2.6H_2O$. Give the word and symbol equation for the reversible reaction between anhydrous cobalt chloride and water.

...reactants ...reversible reaction ...water of crystallisation

Equilibrium

You will find out:
- That when a reversible reaction is carried out inside a closed system, eventually equilibrium will be reached
- At equilibrium the rate of the forward reaction is the same as the rate of the backward reaction

Red blood cells

The red blood cells found in people and other animals contain the chemical haemoglobin. It is an important molecule that transports oxygen around the body.

In the lungs where the concentration of oxygen is high, each haemoglobin molecule binds with four oxygen molecules to form oxyhaemoglobin. In fact, this is a **reversible reaction**. The oxyhaemoglobin is carried around the body to other cells where the concentration of oxygen is lower. Here the oxyhaemoglobin molecules release oxygen re-forming haemoglobin.

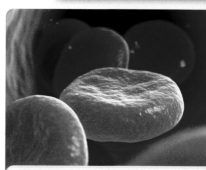

FIGURE 1: Haemoglobin joins with oxygen to form oxyhaemoglobin in a reversible reaction.

Reversible reactions

We can use this general equation to represent what happens during a reversible reaction:

$$A + B \rightleftharpoons C + D$$

A and B represent **reactants** and C and D represent **products**. In the **forward** reaction A and B react together to form C and D. In the **reverse** reaction C and D can react to form A and B. Of course, in some reactions there could be different numbers of reactants and products. For example, in the reaction between nitrogen and hydrogen to make ammonia there is only one type of product made:

$$\text{Nitrogen + hydrogen} \rightleftharpoons \text{ammonia}$$

If we carry out a reversible reaction in a **closed system** where nothing can enter or leave, eventually we will reach a balance point called **equilibrium**. At equilibrium all four chemicals (A, B, C and D) are present and the overall amount of each of the four chemicals no longer changes.

However, if we change the conditions, for example by changing the temperature, we can change the balance point of the reaction and so change the amount of each chemical present.

EXAM HINTS AND TIPS

You need to know how changing the temperature or the pressure can affect the position of equilibrium.

▣ QUESTIONS ▣

1 What is special about a reversible reaction?
2 What does a closed system mean?
3 What is equilibrium?

...*closed system* ...*dynamic* ...*equilibrium* ...*forward*

What is a dynamic equilibrium?

We know that, if a reaction is carried out in a closed system, equilibrium will be reached. At equilibrium the overall amount of each chemical present stays the same. There is no net change but the forwards and backwards reactions do not stop; chemical reactions are still taking place but the rates of the forwards and backwards reactions are now equal. This is known as a **dynamic** equilibrium.

Reaction conditions

We know that at equilibrium the overall concentration of the reactants and products stays the same but the relative amounts of each chemical present at equilibrium depends on the reaction conditions. If we change the conditions, we can change the position of equilibrium to favour either the forward or the reverse reaction. If we favour the forward reaction then at equilibrium more of the product will be present. If we favour the reverse reaction then more of the reactants will be present at equilibrium.

If the forward reaction is exothermic (gives out energy), as the temperature increases the yield of the product decreases. If the forward reaction is endothermic (takes in energy), as the temperature increases the yield of the product also increases.

The reaction between hydrogen and chlorine to produce hydrogen chloride is exothermic and can be summed up by the equation:

$$H_{2(g)} + Cl_{2(g)} \rightleftharpoons 2HCl_{(g)}$$

By reducing the temperature, we can increase the yield of hydrogen chloride.

Some reactions involve products or reactants that are gases. In these reactions changing the pressure may change the yield of the product at equilibrium. Increasing the pressure favours the side with fewer gaseous molecules. Decreasing the pressure favours the side with more gaseous molecules.

You may remember the thermal decomposition of limestone. The reaction can be summed up by this equation:

$$CaCO_{3(s)} \rightleftharpoons CaO_{(s)} + CO_{2(g)}$$

By reducing the pressure we can favour the forward reaction. Industrially this reaction is carried out in well-ventilated kilns to increase the amount of calcium oxide produced.

Catalysts

Catalysts affect the rate of reaction but not the position of equilibrium. Adding a catalyst will not affect the yield of product; it will just mean that we reach the equilibrium position more quickly.

> If we carry out a reversible reaction in a closed system, eventually we will reach a balance point called equilibrium

Changing conditions in industry

Sulfuric acid is used to make a wide range of products including fertilisers, paints and plastics.

Most sulfuric acid is produced by the contact process. In this process sulfur is reacted with oxygen to form sulfur dioxide. The sulfur dioxide is then reacted with more oxygen to produce sulfur trioxide. The sulfur trioxide is then dissolved in concentrated sulfuric acid before being carefully diluted down to the desired concentration.

The reaction between sulfur dioxide and oxygen is exothermic and reversible. It can be summed up by the symbol equation:

$$2SO_{2(g)} + O_{2(g)} \rightleftharpoons 2SO_{3(g)}$$

The reaction is carried out at a temperature of 450 °C with a vanadium (V) oxide catalyst.

QUESTIONS

7 Why is a catalyst used?
8 How would increasing the pressure affect the yield of sulfur trioxide produced?
9 How would increasing the temperature affect the yield of sulfur trioxide produced?
10 How would increasing the temperature affect the rate of reaction?

QUESTIONS

4 What does dynamic mean?
5 In the reaction between hydrogen and chlorine, how does increasing the temperature affect the yield of hydrogen chloride? Why?
6 In the reaction between hydrogen and chlorine, how does increasing the pressure affect the yield of hydrogen chloride?

Haber process

You will find out:
- That the Haber process is used to produce ammonia
- The raw materials for the Haber process and where they come from
- That the Haber process is a reversible reaction
- About the conditions used in the Haber process

Life on Mars

Scientists working with the European Space Agency's Mars Express probe have found trace amounts of the gas ammonia in the atmosphere of Mars. They believe that the gas may be evidence of life on Mars. Ammonia gas is not stable in a Martian atmosphere and would break down in hours. Its presence shows that a continuous supply is being formed. The ammonia could be formed by living microbes or volcanoes. Despite extensive searches, scientists have identified no active volcanoes. In the future they hope to work out exactly where the ammonia comes from.

FIGURE 1: Is the presence of ammonia evidence that there is life on Mars?

Why is ammonia important?

Nitrogen is an important element that plants need to grow. We know that some plants, like peas, can take nitrogen directly from the air but most can only absorb nitrogen from compounds in the soil. **Ammonia** is important because it contains nitrogen and can be used to make fertilisers which help plants to grow. This allows farmers to grow more crops and gives us a better supply of cheap food.

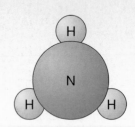

FIGURE 2: An ammonia molecule contains three hydrogen atoms and one nitrogen atom.

The Haber process

Most of the ammonia produced today is made by the **Haber process**. This was developed by **Fritz Haber** who won a Nobel prize for chemistry for his work.

In the Haber process, nitrogen from the air is reacted with **hydrogen** (which can be extracted from natural gas) to produce ammonia. The process is **reversible** and some ammonia will break down to form nitrogen and hydrogen. These reactions can be summed up by the equation:

Nitrogen + hydrogen $\rightleftharpoons$ ammonia

The production of ammonia is a continuous process. Ammonia is removed by cooling the reaction mixture down. The ammonia **liquefies** and is removed, while any unreacted nitrogen and hydrogen are recycled to help reduce costs.

Conditions

The conditions used in the Haber process are:
- an iron catalyst
- a temperature of about 450 °C
- a pressure of about 200 atmospheres.

▦ QUESTIONS ▦

1. How is ammonia used?
2. Name the scientist who developed the process of making ammonia from nitrogen and hydrogen.
3. List the conditions used in this process.

...ammonia   ...exothermic   ...Fritz Haber   ...Haber process   ...hydrogen

Increasing the pressure

We can sum up the reaction between nitrogen and hydrogen to produce ammonia using a symbol equation:

$$N_2(g) + 3H_2(g) \rightleftharpoons 2NH_3(g)$$

The (g) symbol shows us that the nitrogen, hydrogen and ammonia molecules are all gases. On the reactant side of the equation we can see that there is one nitrogen and three hydrogen molecules. This gives a total of four gaseous molecules. On the product side of the equation there are just two gaseous molecules.

By increasing the pressure we encourage more nitrogen and hydrogen molecules to join together to form ammonia molecules. This increases the **yield** of ammonia. Increasing the pressure also means that the gaseous molecules will collide more often and this will increase the rate of reaction.

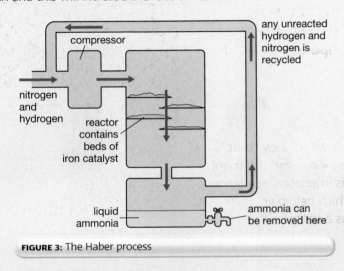

compressor

any unreacted hydrogen and nitrogen is recycled

nitrogen and hydrogen

reactor contains beds of iron catalyst

liquid ammonia

ammonia can be removed here

FIGURE 3: The Haber process

Increasing the temperature

The reaction between nitrogen and hydrogen to produce ammonia is **exothermic** (it gives out energy). If we increase the temperature, the gaseous molecules move faster. This means they collide more often and with more energy. So there are more collisions and more of these collisions are successful. Increasing the temperature increases the rate of reaction.

However, increasing the temperature also affects the yield of ammonia produced. As we increase the temperature we decrease the yield of ammonia.

Why is a catalyst used?

We use a catalyst in the Haber process to increase the rate of reaction between nitrogen and hydrogen. A catalyst has no effect on the yield of ammonia.

Conditions (H)

Why are these conditions chosen?

- A high pressure is used to increase the yield of ammonia formed.
- A catalyst is used to speed up the rate of reaction.
- A compromise temperature of 450 °C is used because it gives a reasonable yield of ammonia reasonably quickly.

QUESTIONS

4 What does the $\rightleftharpoons$ sign mean?

5 Describe the forwards reaction in the Haber process.

6 Describe the backwards reaction in the Haber process.

7 Why does increasing the temperature of the reaction increase the rate of reaction? If a reaction is exothermic how does increasing the temperature of the reaction affect the yield of the product made?

QUESTIONS

8 Describe the conditions in the Haber process and explain why we use these conditions.

...liquefies ...nitrogen ...reversible ...yield

Unit summary

Concept map

An element's mass number tells us the total number of protons plus the total number of neutrons in an atom.

Sub-atomic particles

Atoms consist of sub-atomic particles called protons, neutrons and electrons.

Isotopes are atoms which have the same number of protons but a different number of neutrons.

An element's atomic number tells us the number of protons in an atom.

Ionic bonding is the attraction between oppositely charged ions.

Structure, properties and uses

Non-metal atoms can share pairs of electrons to form covalent bonds.

Ionic substances have high melting and boiling points and conduct electricity when molten or when dissolved.

Nanoparticles are very small structures which have special properties due to the precise way in which the atoms are arranged.

A balanced equation allows us to calculate the amount of material we should use to make a particular amount of a given product.

How much can we make, how much should we use?

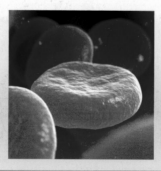

Reversible reactions are chemical reactions which can proceed in both directions.

Percentage yield can be used to compare the actual yield with the theoretical yield.

If we carry out a reversible reaction in a closed system, eventually equilibrium will be reached.

Unit quiz

1 What is the mass of a proton?

    0   1   2   −1

2 An atom has 10 electrons. What is its electron configuration?

    8, 2   10   2, 8   2, 2, 6

3 An atom has a mass number of 31 and an atomic number of 15. How many neutrons does it have?

    16   15.5   15   31

4 Sodium reacts with chlorine to form the ionic compound sodium chloride. What is the charge on a sodium ion?

    1−   2−   1+   2+

5 Which of these substances is not an example of a simple molecule?

    hydrogen   **ammonia**
    water   **graphite**

6 Molecules of hydrogen chloride have the formula HCl. Which of these properties do you predict hydrogen chloride to have?

    high melting point
    high boiling point
    hard
    will not conduct electricity

7 Which of these materials does not have a giant covalent structure?

    silicon dioxide
    graphite
    diamond
    oxygen

8 What is the charge on a halide ion?

    1−   2−   1+   2+

9 What is the width of a human hair in nanometres?

    100 000   100   1000   10 000

10 What is the percentage of calcium in the compound calcium carbonate, $CaCO_3$?

    100%   120%   40%   33%

11 A reaction has a theoretical yield of 12 g and an actual yield of 10 g. What is the percentage yield of the reaction?

    83.3%   120%   100%   10%

12 Ammonia is produced in the Haber process. What is the formula of an ammonia molecule?

    NH N_3H NH_3 N_3H_3

Literacy activity

Ammonia is made in a reversible reaction between nitrogen and hydrogen in the Haber process. This table shows the percentage of ammonia in the reaction mixture at equilibrium at different temperatures.

Temperature (°C)	Percentage of ammonia in the reaction mixture at equilibrium (%)
200	90
300	65
400	40
500	20
600	12
700	5

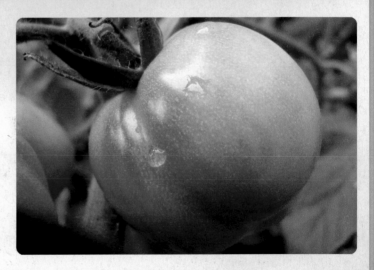

QUESTIONS

1 Draw a line graph to show the results.

2 At what temperature is the highest percentage of ammonia produced?

3 Compare the percentage of ammonia at equilibrium at 500 °C and 700 °C.

Exam practice

1 a Copy and complete the following table to show the relative charges and masses of the three particles in an atom. [3]

Name of particle	Charge	Mass
proton	+1	
		1
electron		

b Copy and complete the following sentences using the words in the list below. [4]

In an atom, the protons and .... are found in the nucleus. Atoms are always neutral because the number of protons is always equal to the number of .... Atoms of a particular element always have the same number of .... and this is called the .... number.

| electrons | protons | atomic | neutrons |

2 Which of the following statements are correct? [5]

A The alkali metals react with non-metals to form ionic compounds.

B When the alkali metals react they form ions with a charge of 1^-.

C The halogens are in group 7.

D The halogens react with alkali metals to form covalent compounds.

E The halogens react with alkali metals to form ionic compounds and the halide ions have a charge of 1^-.

3 a Describe the bonding in a metal using a diagram to help you. [4]

b Explain why metals conduct heat and electricity. [1]

c Explain why metals can be bent or shaped. [1]

4 a Sodium chloride is a solid and is held together by ionic bonding. Describe what you understand by the term 'ionic bonding'. [2]

b Why does sodium chloride have a high melting point and boiling point? [2]

c Explain why sodium chloride cannot conduct electricity when solid but can when it is melted. [2]

5 The following diagrams represent an atom of magnesium and an ion of magnesium. Draw similar diagrams to represent an atom of oxygen and an ion of oxygen.

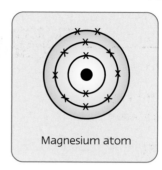

Magnesium atom

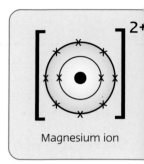

Magnesium ion

6 a The following diagrams show part of the structures of diamond and graphite. Which one is which?

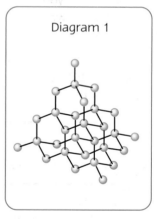

Diagram 1

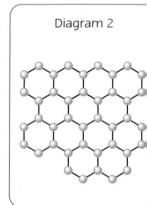

Diagram 2

b Explain why diamond is so hard. [

c Explain why graphite is soft and slippery. [

d Explain why graphite can conduct electricity. [

7 a Draw a diagram to show the bonding in ammonia, NH_3. [

b Which of the following statements are correct? [

A The bonding in ammonia is covalent.

B Ammonia has a giant structure.

C The melting point and boiling point of ammonia are high.

D The intermolecular forces in ammonia are weak.

E Ammonia does not conduct electricity because its ions cannot move.

3 State what is being described in each of these statements.

A The mass of atoms of an element compared to an atom of $^{12}_{6}C$. [1]

B The sum of the relative atomic masses of the atoms present. [1]

C The relative formula mass in grams. [1]

D Atoms of an element with different numbers of neutrons. [1]

9 Calculate the percentage by mass of calcium in calcium carbonate, $CaCO_3$. [2]

(Total 49 marks)

Worked example

Ammonia is made in the Haber process. The equation for the reaction is:

$$N_2 + 3H_2 \rightleftharpoons 2NH_3$$

a Where are the nitrogen and hydrogen obtained from? [2]

b When this reaction is carried out you cannot achieve 100% yield. Give two different reasons why this is so. [2]

c i What is the maximum possible mass of ammonia that could be obtained by completely reacting 56 kg of nitrogen? [3]

ii If only 22 kg of ammonia was obtained from 56 kg of nitrogen then what percentage yield was obtained? [2]

d Another way of judging a reaction is to measure its atom economy. What is this and why is it important? [2]

e i What conditions are used in the Haber process to make ammonia? [3]

ii Why are these conditions chosen? [2]

iii How is the ammonia obtained from the equilibrium mixture? [1]

Correct for nitrogen but there is no hydrogen in the air. Hydrogen has to be obtained from natural gas.

a Hydrogen and nitrogen are obtained from the air.

Good answer.

b This may be because the reaction does not go to completion or because some other products are formed instead.

Correct, but the student needed to add that 'it is important to consider this when thinking about sustainable development' for both marks.

Excellent answers. Clearly set out and easy to follow.

c i

N_2 +	$3H_2$ $\rightleftharpoons$	$2NH_3$
28 g		34 g
56 kg		68 kg

ii % yield = $\frac{mass\ obtained}{max.\ possible\ mass}$ x 100% = $\frac{22}{68}$ x 100% = 32.4%

Another condition is the use of an **iron** catalyst. As well as achieving a good rate of reaction, these conditions also give a **good yield**.

d Atom economy is a measure of the amount of starting material that ends up in the useful product.

e i Conditions used are: 450 °C, 200 atmospheres.

ii This is to make the ammonia really quickly.

iii The ammonia is removed by turning it to a liquid.

Overall Grade: B

How to get an A

This was a good effort and the student was methodical with their answers. However, they did not always use the information about the number of marks available for each part of a question. Remember, three marks means that you need to make three different points.

DISCOVER
ELECTROLYSIS!

The picture shows a child's iron death mask recovered during an archaeological dig. Chemists had to provide a solution to help preserve it and to remove the rust from it without damaging it further.

Chemists thought of reacting the rust (iron oxide) with acid but were worried that the acid might react with the metal itself as well as the oxide, causing damage to the mask.

They used electrolysis to remove the rust. It was held in a tank of very dilute hydrochloric acid and attached to the negative electrode of a D.C power supply. The other electrode was made of iron.

The rate of the chemical reaction was kept low by keeping the acid's temperature and concentration low.

CONTENTS

Rates of reactions

You will find out:
- That chemical reactions occur at different rates
- How to find the rate of a chemical reaction
- The factors that affect the speed of a chemical reaction

Fast and slow reactions

Industrial chemists are very clever people! They know exactly how to control the conditions in a reaction to make them happen at just the right speed. If a reaction happens too quickly, it could become dangerous but if it happens too slowly the company would never make any money.

FIGURE 1: The chemicals in these fireworks are reacting very quickly.

FIGURE 2: Not all reactions happen so quickly. This car is rusting very slowly.

How can we speed up reactions?

Figure 3 shows a test tube with a piece of magnesium ribbon reacting with some hydrochloric acid. As the magnesium reacts, it forms hydrogen gas and the magnesium dissolves making magnesium chloride.

We can see how quickly it reacts by timing how long the magnesium takes to dissolve or how quickly bubbles of hydrogen gas are formed.

FIGURE 3: Magnesium + hydrochloric acid ⟶ magnesium chloride + hydrogen

Make the acid hotter

Make the acid more concentrated

How could we speed up this reaction?

Grind the metal to a powder

Use a catalyst

QUESTIONS

1   How could you prove the gas formed when magnesium reacts with acid is hydrogen?

2   When magnesium burns in air, is this a fast or a slow reaction?

3   When concrete sets, is this a fast or a slow reaction?

4   Give **four** ways of making a reaction go faster.

...catalyst ...concentration ...mole ...pressure

Measuring the rate of a reaction

The **rate of reaction** tells you how fast a reaction is occurring. To find the speed you walked to school, you would need to measure two things: the distance you travelled and the time it took. You would then do this calculation:

$$\text{Speed} = \frac{\text{distance walked (m)}}{\text{time taken (s)}}$$

The speed would be in metres per second or m/s.

The rate of a chemical reaction can be measured by seeing how fast a **reactant** is used up. You would need to measure the amount of reactant used up and the time taken.

$$\text{Rate of reaction} = \frac{\text{amount of reactant used up}}{\text{time}}$$

Or you can see how quickly a **product** is formed. You would need to measure the amount of product formed and the time this takes.

$$\text{Rate of reaction} = \frac{\text{amount of product formed}}{\text{time}}$$

Measuring rate of reaction between magnesium and acid

We could measure the volume of hydrogen gas formed (in cm^3) and the time it takes to form it (in seconds). We could do this with the apparatus shown here.

As the magnesium reacts, the hydrogen goes into the gas syringe. The faster the reaction, the faster the gas is made and the faster the plunger is pushed out.

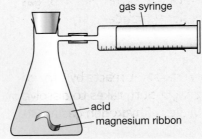

FIGURE 4: Measuring the gas formed with a gas syringe.

gas syringe

acid

magnesium ribbon

Reactions involving gases

If the reaction involves a gas, the rate of reaction can be speeded up by increasing the **pressure** of the gas. This makes the particles come closer together and increases the frequency with which they collide. And they need to collide to react!

What is concentration?

The **concentration** of solutions are given in **moles** per cubic decimetre (mol/dm^3). The mole is the unit used by chemists to measure the amount of a substance.

A dm^3 is the same as $1000\ cm^3$ which is the same as 1 litre. So concentration tells us the amount of substance dissolved in $1\ dm^3$.

What is a catalyst?

A **catalyst** can speed up a chemical reaction but it is not used up itself.

QUESTIONS

5 If rate of reaction = $\dfrac{\text{volume of gas }(cm^3)}{\text{time (s)}}$ then what would the units rate of reaction be?

6 Why does using magnesium powder make the reaction go faster?

7 If a graph of volume against time is plotted for the reaction above, it looks like this. What volume of gas is made in the first 50 seconds of the reaction?

8 What is the **rate** of reaction in the first 50 seconds?

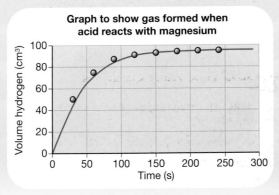

Graph to show gas formed when acid reacts with magnesium

QUESTIONS

9 If I have $2000\ cm^3$ of water, how many dm^3 would this be?

10 If there is 0.5 of a mole of solute in $500\ cm^3$ of a solution, what is the concentration of the solution?

11 If I had $100\ cm^3$ of hydrochloric acid which had a concentration of $1\ mol/dm^3$, what would be the new concentration if I added a further $100\ cm^3$ of water to it?

12 What **two** things would you need to prove to show that a substance acts as a catalyst for a reaction?

...*product* ...*rate of reaction* ...*reactant*

Following the rate of reaction

You will find out:
- Different ways you can follow a reaction
- How to choose the most appropriate way of following a reaction
- That some methods are more accurate than others

Measuring reaction rates

To measure how fast something happens, you need to time it. But what exactly will you time? This depends on the particular reaction you are trying to measure the rate of. Does the reaction make a gas? Is there a solid that disappears? Are there any other changes that can be measured?

FIGURE 1: How can I measure the rate of this reaction?

The speed of a reaction

In the reaction between magnesium ribbon and hydrochloric acid, the magnesium ribbon dissolves making magnesium chloride and hydrogen gas is given off.

How can we follow this reaction?

Method A
Measure how quickly it makes the gas

Method B
It will get lighter so measure how quickly it loses mass

Method C
Measure how long the magnesium takes to dissolve

QUESTIONS

1. Copy and complete this WORD equation:

   magnesium + hydrochloric acid ⟶ .... + ...

2. Which method to follow the rate of reaction between magnesium and acid needs a balance throughout the experiment?

3. Which method to follow the rate of reaction between magnesium and acid only needs a beaker, the acid and magnesium and a stopwatch?

4. Could you use Method C to measure how quickly some iron is rusting?

WHAT IS A PRECIPITATE?

If two solutions are added together and a solid is formed, the solid is called a **precipitate**.

...data logger ...displace

Measure the volume of gas

These first four methods only work if the reaction actually makes a gas!

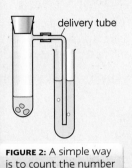

FIGURE 2: A simple way is to count the number of bubbles formed.

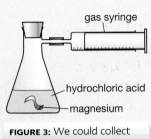

FIGURE 3: We could collect the gas with a gas syringe.

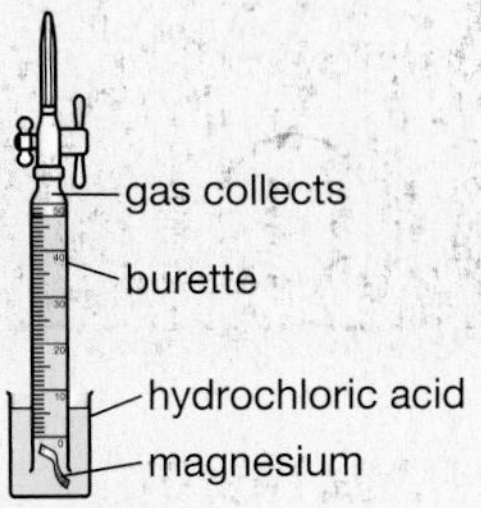

FIGURE 4: We could collect the gas in an upturned burette.

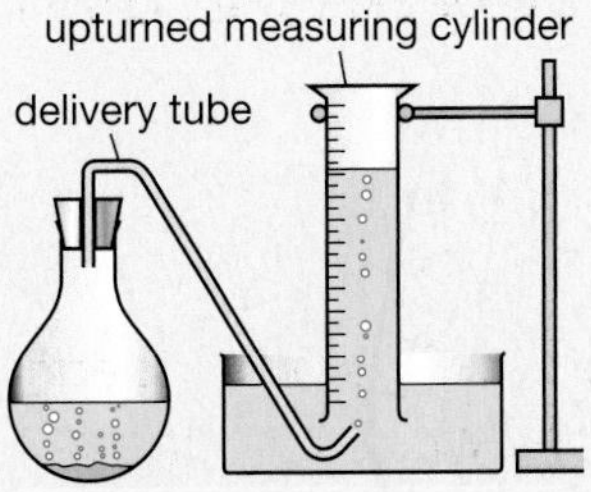

- gas collects
- burette
- hydrochloric acid
- magnesium

- gas syringe
- hydrochloric acid
- magnesium

FIGURE 5: We could collect the gas in an upturned measuring cylinder.

- upturned measuring cylinder
- delivery tube

Time how quickly a solid dissolves

This method does not give much information. We cannot follow the reaction as it progresses and this only gives us a single time measurement. Also, this method is only any good if the reaction happens fairly (but not too) quickly.

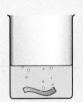

FIGURE 6: It could be a long wait for a slow reaction!

Measure the mass loss if a gas forms

21.05 g

FIGURE 7: The mass goes down as the gas escapes from the beaker.

See how quickly a solution goes cloudy

This works if two solutions react together to make a solid. You can time how long a cross placed below the beaker takes to disappear. This can be used to follow the reaction between sodium thiosulfate and hydrochloric acid.

$$Na_2S_2O_{3(aq)} + 2HCl_{(aq)} \longrightarrow SO_{2(g)} + S_{(s)} + 2NaCl_{(aq)} + H_2O_{(l)}$$

You could use a **datalogger** with a light sensor to measure how much light passes through the solution.

QUESTIONS

5   When would it be better to use the method in figure 4 than that in figure 5?

6   What is the name of the precipitate formed in the above reaction?

7   Draw a diagram of the apparatus you could use to do the experiment with sodium thiosulfate.

8   If you used a light sensor to measure the amount of light passing through the solution, what would happen to the reading as the experiment progressed?

Some pitfalls

Counting bubbles. This is only a good idea if the gas is fairly **insoluble** and it is forming relatively slowly. Even then it is not very accurate.

Collecting a gas by displacing water. If you look at the reaction between sodium thiosulfate and hydrochloric acid, you can see that the equation shows a gas forming. If you tried to collect this gas you would be unlucky – it is very soluble in water and much of it dissolves in the solution in the flask.

Measuring mass loss. If a gas forms, be careful that the gas does not cause a spray of liquid that also leaves the flask.

Watching a solid dissolve. This is inappropriate if it takes too long to dissolve. It is also a fairly tedious experiment!

QUESTIONS

9   Name a gas that is very soluble in water and could not be collected by displacing it.

10 How could the problem of wanting gas to escape from the flask, but not any liquid, be resolved?

11 Name a metal that reacts quickly with acid so it would be possible to watch the solid dissolve to measure the rate of reaction.

12 Give **four** ways of following the reaction between calcium carbonate and acid.

$$CaCO_{3(s)} + 2HCl_{(aq)} \longrightarrow CaCl_{2(aq)} + H_2O_{(l)} + CO_{2(g)}$$

Collision theory

You will find out:
- That particles must collide in order to react
- That particles must collide with enough energy for a reaction to occur
- Different ways of getting more successful collisions and faster rates of reaction

You have to crack the egg to make the omelette

To break the egg, the hammer has to collide with it! If the egg is tapped gently it does not crack. The hammer must hit the egg with enough energy to break it.

Chemical reactions are similar. Particles must collide with enough energy if a reaction is going to happen.

FIGURE 1: That seems to have been enough energy!

Making more collisions successful

Collisions are more frequent if we:

- Increase the **concentration** of solutions. This is like having lots of eggs.
- Increase the **pressure** of gases. This is also like increasing the number of eggs.
- Increase the **temperature**. This is like hitting the eggs much harder.
- Increase the **surface area** of solids. This is like having lots of little eggs.
- Use a **catalyst** so the reaction requires less energy to happen. The eggs would be easier to smash lying on their sides rather than upright.

BIOLOGICAL CATALYSTS

Enzymes are biological catalysts needed in biological processes like digestion. They work best in warm conditions.

EXAM HINTS AND TIPS

When talking about acids you should use the word concentration to describe how much acid is in the solution.

QUESTIONS

1. Give **four** ways to speed up the reaction between magnesium and hydrochloric acid.
2. Give **three** ways to speed up the reaction between nitrogen and hydrogen.
3. If you crack five eggs in 10 seconds, at what rate are you cracking the eggs? Give your answer in eggs per second.
4. If the number of eggs on the table was doubled, how many eggs per second would you expect to crack?

...*activation energy*   ...*catalyst*   ...*concentration*   ...*frequency*   ...*kinetic energy*

Increase the concentration of solutions

If you increase the concentration of one (or both) of the reactants, collisions are more likely. By doubling the concentration of a reactant you would expect to double the chance of a collision. Check figure 2 to see if this has happened.

Increasing the concentration increases the number of particles in a given volume so the **frequency** of collisions (how often they collide) is increased. This increases the chances of a **successful collision** (one that leads to a reaction).

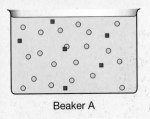 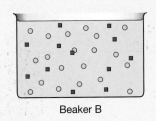 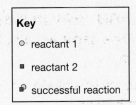

Beaker A · Beaker B

Key
○ reactant 1
■ reactant 2
⬢ successful reaction

FIGURE 2: The concentration of reactant 2 (■) has been doubled in Beaker B.

Increase the pressure of gases

This is the same as increasing the concentration of a solution and has just the same effect.

Increase the temperature

This increases the **kinetic energy** of the particles so they collide more often and with more energy. There is more chance of a collision being successful.

Increase the surface area of solids

When a solid reacts, collisions can only occur at its surface. Making lumps into a powder increases the surface area where collisions can occur.

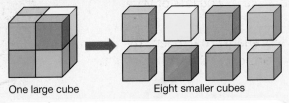

One large cube · Eight smaller cubes

FIGURE 3: If the cube is divided into eight, the surface area doubles.

Use a catalyst

Catalysts work by finding an easier way for the reaction to occur. There may be an alternative pathway for the reaction or it may weaken bonds in the reactants so they are easier to break.

QUESTIONS

5 If you double the concentration of a reactant, what would you expect to happen to the rate of the reaction?

6 If the cube in figure 4 had a side of 2 cm, what would be the:
   a area of one face?   b total area of all six faces?

7 If the cube in figure 4 is broken into eight smaller cubes, what would be the:
   a area of one face of the new smaller cube?
   b total surface area of the six faces of each new cube?
   c total surface area of the eight new cubes?

Activation energy

The minimum amount of energy needed for a successful collision is called the **activation energy**. Methane from a laboratory gas tap does not burn without a match. The burning match provides heat energy to start the reaction.

Activation energy is used to break bonds in the reactants. We can draw energy level diagrams to show this.

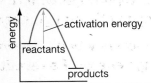

FIGURE 4: Energy level diagram.

This shows that when reactants change to products they must climb over an energy barrier. The energy needed is the activation energy.

How catalysts work

Catalysts lower the activation energy of a reaction. The reactant molecules are adsorbed on to the catalyst surface. This weakens their bonds, making them easier to break.

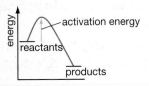

FIGURE 5: The catalyst lowers the activation energy.

Choosing a catalyst

Different reactions need different catalysts. Transition metals and their compounds make good catalysts.

QUESTIONS

8 Catalysts are usually made in the form of a mesh or gauze. Explain why.

9 Why are catalysts important in industry?

10 How does a catalyst work?

11 Once gas is lit with a match you do not have to keep lighting it. Explain why.

Heating things up

You will find out:
- How to carry out experiments to see the effect of changing the temperature on rate of reaction
- How to interpret graphs showing rates of reaction
- What effect an increase of 10 °C has on the rate of reaction

Keeping it cool

Food keeps longer in a refrigerator. This works because the chemical reactions that cause food to decompose can only act very slowly at low temperatures.

Usually we want to make reactions go faster. Increasing the temperature is one way to do this.

FIGURE 1: "It's cold in here. I think that is so chemical reactions are slowed down".

The reaction between sodium thiosulfate and hydrochloric acid

$$Na_2S_2O_{3(aq)} + 2HCl_{(aq)} \longrightarrow SO_{2(g)} + S_{(s)} + 2NaCl_{(aq)} + H_2O_{(l)}$$

As this reaction produces solid sulfur, it can be followed by seeing how quickly the solution becomes opaque. The reaction is carried out in a flask placed over an **✗** on a piece of paper (figure 2).

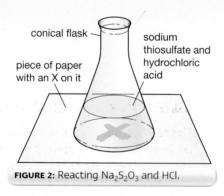

conical flask

sodium thiosulfate and hydrochloric acid

piece of paper with an X on it

FIGURE 2: Reacting $Na_2S_2O_3$ and HCl.

A graph of the results is shown in figure 3. At 20 °C the reaction took 500 seconds but at 50 °C it only took about 60 seconds.

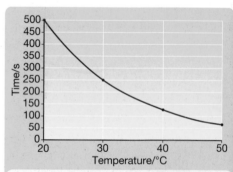

FIGURE 3: Graph to show the time for a cross to disappear at different temperatures when $Na_2S_2O_3$ and HCl react.

QUESTIONS

Use the graph in figure 3 to answer the following questions.

1 How long does the reaction take at 30 °C?
2 How long does the reaction take at 40 °C?
3 What is the effect of an increase of 10 °C on the time this reaction takes?
4 At what temperature does the reaction take 200 seconds?

WOW FACTOR!

Thio means some oxygen has been replaced by sulfur in a compound so sodium thiosulfate is sodium sulfur-sulfate!

...factors ...fair

Planning the experiment

When planning an experiment to see how temperature changes affect rate of reaction, you would first do a **trial experiment**. This would enable you to choose the volumes and concentrations of the two solutions you would use to make the reaction last for a sensible amount of time. You would also need to think about keeping the experiment **fair** by ensuring all other **factors** remain the same.

Procedure for the experiment

- Make a cross on a piece of paper and put the flask over the cross.
- Measure out 50 cm^3 of 0.02 mol/dm^3 sodium thiosulfate and place it in the flask.
- Measure out 5 cm^3 of 2.0 mol/dm^3 hydrochloric acid in a separate measuring cylinder.
- As you add the acid to the flask and swirl it to mix the reactants, start the timer.
- Take the temperature at the beginning of the experiment.
- View from a set distance (about 10 cm) above the flask. Time how long the cross takes to disappear.
- Repeat the experiment but this time warm the hydrochloric acid to about 30 °C before adding it. Do the experiment at a minimum of five different temperatures, keeping all the volumes the same.
- Plot a graph of time taken for the cross to disappear against temperature.

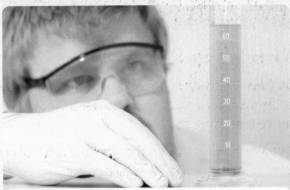

FIGURE 4: For a fair test I will need to pour some away. I need 50 cm^3.

Watch Out Concentrations of solutions are given in mol/dm^3. The hydrochloric acid has 2 moles of HCl dissolved in every dm^3 of solution.

What else does the graph tell us?

Figure 3 shows the results from such an experiment. We can draw the following conclusions from the graph:

- As the temperature increases, the time taken decreases. The reaction takes longer at 20 °C than it does at 50 °C.
- An increase of 10 °C halves the time taken for the cross to disappear.
- Changing the temperature from 20 °C to 30 °C has more effect on the rate of the reaction than changing it from 30 °C to 40 °C.
- The points plotted all lie on a perfect curve so the experiment must have been perfect! (If you do this experiment you may not get all of the points to plot exactly on the line.)

Can you explain the results?

The reaction goes faster at higher temperatures because the particles in the solution have more energy so they are moving about faster. This means they will collide with more energy and more frequently. More collisions will be successful.

If the time is halved when the temperature rises by 10 °C, it must mean the number of effective collisions is doubling with this change in temperature.

QUESTIONS

5   Why does the cross disappear in this experiment?

6   It is difficult to get such a perfect graph as this. What do you think the experimenter did to make his results so good?

7   Why do you need separate measuring cylinders for the two solutions?

8   How long do you think the experiment would take at 60 °C?

Grind it up, speed it up

You will find out:
- How particle size affects reaction rate
- How to carry out experiments to see the effect of changing the surface area on rate of reaction
- How to interpret graphs showing rates of reaction

Danger ... bread ingredients!

We don't think of the ingredients for making bread as being dangerous but on December 27th 2003, Pakistan reported at least five people were dead in a flour mill explosion. In 1998 in Wichita, USA, 10 people died in a similar explosion.

Fine particles can react much more quickly than large particles because they have a greater **surface area**.

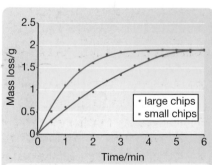

FIGURE 1: Don't try this at home! This is what happens when a small amount of flour dust is ignited.

The reaction between marble chips and acid

$$CaCO_{3(s)} + 2HCl_{(aq)} \longrightarrow CaCl_{2(aq)} + CO_{2(g)} + H_2O_{(l)}$$

How could you follow the **rate** of this reaction? Carbon dioxide gas (CO_2) is being made so we can measure how fast the gas is produced. You could do this by measuring either the volume of carbon dioxide produced or the loss in mass of the reaction mixture as carbon dioxide is released.

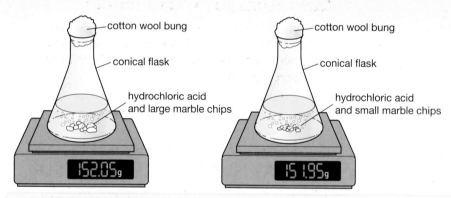

cotton wool bung
conical flask
hydrochloric acid and large marble chips
152.05 g

cotton wool bung
conical flask
hydrochloric acid and small marble chips
151.95 g

FIGURE 2: Finding the loss in mass when marble chips of two different sizes react with acid.

As gas is lost the flask gets lighter. The mass is measured every 30 seconds and the results put on a graph (figure 3).

WOW FACTOR!

Custard powder and mustard powder can also cause explosions if they come into contact with a spark.

FIGURE 3: Graph to show the mass of carbon dioxide gas lost when acid reacts with marble chips of two different sizes.

QUESTIONS

1 Why does the flask on the balance lose mass?
2 Do large or small chips make the most gas in the first minute?
3 Which size of chips reacts the fastest?
4 Which size of chips gives the steepest curve?

...rate ...particles

Planning the experiment

When designing an experiment to find the effect of **particle** size on the rate of reaction, you should first do a trial experiment to find a good mass of marble chips and a good volume and concentration of hydrochloric acid to use. As you will carry out the experiment several times to verify your results, it should last no more than 10 minutes.

You will also need to work out which factors must be kept the same. In this case you want to change particle size, so you must keep the volume, concentration and temperature of the acid the same throughout. You must also keep the same mass of marble chips in each experiment.

Procedure for the experiment

- Measure out 5 g of large marble chips onto a piece of paper.
- Measure out 20 cm^3 of 2.0 mol/dm^3 hydrochloric acid into a flask.
- Place the flask, the paper with marble chips and the cotton wool bung onto the balance.
- Set the reading on the balance to zero.
- Start the timer when you add the marble chips to the flask.
- Measure the mass of the flask and contents every 30 seconds for 10 minutes.
- Repeat the experiment keeping everything the same but replacing 5 g of large chips with 5 g of small chips.
- For both sizes of marble chips, plot a graph of mass lost against time.

What else does the graph tell us?

Figure 3 shows the results from such an experiment. We can see that the small chips react faster than the large chips. But what else can we tell from this graph?

- If we measure the mass of gas formed in the first minute for each experiment, we find that the large chips make 0.6 g of gas and the small chips make 1.1 g. From this we can calculate the rate of reaction.
- The total amount of gas formed in both experiments is the same.
- The slope of the graph is steepest at the beginning of both experiments. This tells us the rate of reaction is greatest at the start of the reaction. As the reaction proceeds the slope gets less steep. This tells us the rate of reaction decreases as the reaction proceeds.

$$\text{Rate of reaction} = \frac{\text{amount of product formed}}{\text{time}}$$

Can you explain the results?

- The reaction can only occur at the surface of the marble chips, so having more surface area increases the number of collisions. The number of successful collisions rises, increasing the rate of reaction.
- The total amount of gas is the same in both experiments because the amount of each reactant is the same.
- The reaction is fastest at the beginning of the experiment because the acid concentration is highest then. As the reaction proceeds the acid is used up so the rate of reaction decreases until all of the acid is gone.

▮▮▮▮ QUESTIONS ▮▮▮▮

5   From the graph, calculate the rate of reaction in the first minute for both the small and large chips.

6   How do the reaction rates compare? What does this suggest about the surface area of the different chips?

7   What is the purpose of the cotton wool bung in figure 2?

8   If one reactant is in excess, it makes sure the other reactant is used up completely. What observation would tell you that the marble chips were in excess in the experiment outlined above?

...surface area

Concentrate now

You will find out:
- How concentration affects reaction rate
- How to carry out experiments to see the effect of changing the concentration on rate of reaction
- How to interpret graphs showing rates of reaction involving concentration changes

Increasing concentration can speed up reactions

Since the gargoyle in figure 1 was carved, the concentration of acid in rain has increased, causing the rate at which it weathers to increase.

Look at figure 2. You can probably work out that the flask on the right contains more concentrated acid. When the concentration is high, the reaction will be faster as there are more particles in the same volume, so collisions are more frequent.

FIGURE 1: Weathering caused by acid rain.

What about gases?

Increasing the pressure on a gas pushes the particles closer together. For a reaction that involves gases, we would expect the rate of reaction to increase if the pressure is increased. Since there will be more particles in the same volume, collisions between them will occur more frequently.

The reaction between sulfuric acid and zinc

$$\text{zinc} + \text{sulfuric acid} \longrightarrow \text{zinc sulfate} + \text{hydrogen}$$
$$Zn_{(s)} + H_2SO_{4(aq)} \longrightarrow ZnSO_{4(aq)} + H_{2(g)}$$

In this reaction hydrogen gas is made. We could look at how fast this happens to measure the rate of reaction. Hydrogen is very insoluble in water so can be collected by displacement of water (see figure 3).

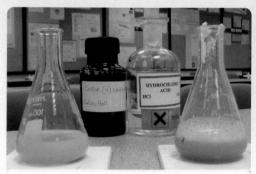
FIGURE 2: These two flasks both contain hydrochloric acid. Some powdered copper carbonate has been added to both.

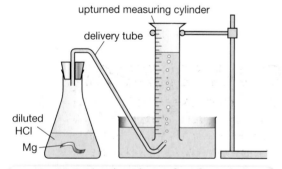
FIGURE 3: Measuring the volume of gas formed when zinc reacts with different concentrations of acid.

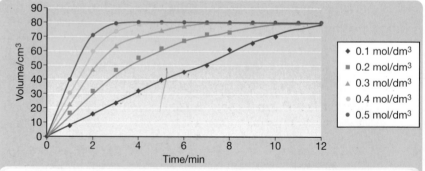
FIGURE 4: Graph to show the volume of hydrogen formed with five different concentrations of sulfuric acid.

QUESTIONS

Use figure 4 to help you answer the following questions.

1. How much gas is made in the first minute at each concentration?
2. What is the rate of reaction in cm³/min in the first minute at each concentration?
3. What is the effect on the rate of doubling the concentration?
4. Explain your answer to Q3 using ideas about collisions.

Remember:

$$\text{Rate of reaction} = \frac{\text{volume of gas made in cm}^3}{\text{time in seconds}}$$

...excess

Planning the experiment

Do a trial experiment first to find a good mass of magnesium and a good volume and concentration of hydrochloric acid to use. As you will want to try about five concentrations and repeat the experiments at least once, each experiment should last no more than five minutes.

You want to change the concentration of the acid but you must keep the actual amount of acid and its temperature the same. You would also need to keep the mass and surface area of the magnesium the same throughout.

Remember that if the HCl is in **excess**, all of the Mg will react in each experiment.

Procedure for the experiment

- Measure out 0.08 g of magnesium ribbon.
- Measure out 20 cm^3 of 1.0 mol/ dm^3 hydrochloric acid into a conical flask. This is a large excess.
- Fill a measuring cylinder with water and upend this into the trough of water and clamp it in position.
- Make sure the end of the delivery tube is under the upturned measuring cylinder.
- As you add the magnesium ribbon to the flask, place the bung into the mouth of the flask and start timing.
- Measure the volume of gas at 30 seconds and thereafter every 30 seconds until the reaction is complete.
- Repeat the experiment keeping everything the same but using different concentrations of acid.
- For each experiment, plot a graph of volume of gas against time.

What else does the graph tell us?

- Figure 4 shows that the more concentrated the acid, the faster it reacts.
- If we measure the volume of gas formed in the first minute from the graph for each experiment, we can calculate the **initial rate of reaction** for each experiment.
- We can also see that the slope of the graph is steepest at the beginning for all graphs, showing that the rate of reaction is greatest at the beginning of each experiment. As the experiment proceeds, the slope gets less steep, telling us that the rate of reaction slows down.

Can you explain the results?

A reaction can only occur when particles collide. Increasing the concentration of the solution increases the number of particles in a given volume so there are more collisions in the same amount of time. Doubling the concentration of acid doubles the number of effective collisions in a given time so the rate of reaction doubles.

The total amount of gas is the same in all experiments because the amount of each reactant is the same.

The reaction is fastest at the beginning of the experiment because the acid concentration is highest then. As the reaction proceeds, the magnesium is used up, so the rate of reaction decreases until it is all gone.

EXAM HINTS AND TIPS

Remember: 1 mol/dm^3 hydrochloric acid has twice as many particles in the same volume of acid as 0.5 mol/dm^3 acid.

EXAM HINTS AND TIPS

Do not just say that a more concentrated solution has more particles in it. You must say there are more **particles in the same volume**.

QUESTIONS

5   One problem with this experiment is that, when you try to put the bung in, some gas escapes. Find a way of improving the experiment to avoid this. (An internet search for 'divided flask' might help.)

6   Explain why the same amount of gas is formed in each experiment.

7   An excess of acid is used. Why is this important?

8   Look again at figure 1. Why has the concentration of acid in the atmosphere increased?

Catalysts

You will find out:
- What a catalyst does and some examples of catalysts
- Why catalysts are useful
- How a gas syringe can be used to follow a reaction

Sweeping up platinum dust

Our cities are paved with platinum, worth about £17 a gram in 2006! Where does it come from? The exhausts of modern cars!

Cars have catalytic converters to make sure harmful gases do not come out of the exhaust. The metals in the catalytic converter are platinum, rhodium and palladium. And that is how these metals end up on our streets.

FIGURE 1: Before catalytic converters, this exhaust would have poured toxic and irritant gases into the atmosphere.

How catalytic converters work

In a car engine, carbon dioxide and water vapour are produced. So are some other rather nasty gases – poisonous carbon monoxide and oxides of nitrogen (that contribute to the formation of **acid rain**). Catalysts in the catalytic converter make these gases react with each other to make less harmful gases.

carbon monoxide + nitrogen dioxide ⟶ carbon dioxide + nitrogen

This reaction could not happen without the catalysts.

An experiment with a catalyst

Hydrogen peroxide (H_2O_2) breaks down slowly into water and oxygen. Add a catalyst like manganese (IV) oxide and it decomposes very quickly.

hydrogen peroxide ⟶ water + oxygen

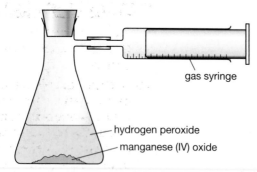

gas syringe

hydrogen peroxide

manganese (IV) oxide

FIGURE 2: The decomposition of hydrogen peroxide can be followed by measuring the amount of oxygen that forms.

WANT TO KNOW MORE?

Look up the work of Hazel Pritchard on the internet. Type in her name and the word **platinum** and see what you come up with.

QUESTIONS

1. Which metals are found in a car's catalytic converter?
2. Which gases are removed from exhaust fumes using a catalytic converter?
3. Write a word equation for the decomposition of hydrogen peroxide.
4. Name a catalyst that will break down hydrogen peroxide.

EXAM HINTS AND TIPS

All of the catalysts on this spread contain transition metals. Transition metals and their compounds make good catalysts.

...acid rain ...adsorbing ...ammonia

Manganese (IV) oxide (MnO$_2$)

Catalysts speed up chemical reactions without being used up themselves. We can show this by adding manganese (IV) oxide to hydrogen peroxide.

- Weigh out 5 g of manganese (IV) oxide (MnO$_2$) (a black solid).
- Weigh a piece of filter paper.
- Carry out the reaction, then filter to get the MnO$_2$ back from the mixture.
- Dry the filter paper and the black solid that is on it, and reweigh it.
- Subtract the mass of the filter paper. The mass of MnO$_2$ remaining should still be 5 g.

Comparing catalysts

To compare catalysts for the decomposition of hydrogen peroxide, use the apparatus in figure 2. Try out 5 g of various other transition metals or their compounds and see which produce 100 cm^3 of oxygen most quickly. To make the test fair, keep the volume and concentration of the hydrogen peroxide and the temperature the same.

Why use catalysts?

Catalysts can be used to make a reaction happen that would not occur under normal conditions or to speed up a slow reaction.

FIGURE 3: The chemical industry keeps its costs down by using catalysts.

INHIBITORS

Inhibitors slow down reactions. Some paints contain corrosion inhibitors and many foods have antioxidants to slow down oxidation of fats in them.

Different reactions need different catalysts

Here are some examples of reactions that use catalysts to speed them up.

The **Haber process** uses an iron catalyst to change nitrogen and hydrogen gas into **ammonia** gas. The **Contact process** uses a vanadium (V) oxide (V$_2$O$_5$) catalyst to convert sulfur dioxide to sulfur trioxide so that can be turned into sulfuric acid. Nickel is used as a catalyst in converting vegetable oils into margarine.

QUESTIONS

5   Make a table of all the catalysts named in this topic and what each does.

6   What are the **two** ways in which catalysts help industry?

7   Why do catalysts save industry money?

8   In an experiment to show that a catalyst is not used up, the mass of MnO$_2$ seemed to have gone up. How could you explain this?

Poisoning catalysts

When you start driving, make sure you use unleaded petrol if your car has a catalytic converter. If you put leaded petrol in, you may have to buy a new catalytic converter. The lead in the petrol poisons the catalyst by irreversibly coating the active metal.

FIGURE 4: Oops ... must check the pump first next time!

Biological catalysts

Enzymes are biological catalysts and you meet these on pages 58–65 of this book. They too make slow reactions faster and difficult reactions possible.

Action of catalysts

Many catalysts work by first **adsorbing** gases onto their surface. This weakens the bonds in the reactants and makes it easier for them to react. It also increases the concentration of reactants at the surface. After the reaction has occurred, the products are **desorbed** from the surface.

QUESTIONS

9   What is a catalyst poison? Give an example in your answer.

10   Catalysts are often added to central heating systems to prevent corrosion inside the radiator. What do we call a substance that slows reactions down? Give another example.

11   Arrange these words in the right order to describe how a catalyst works:

desorbtion, bonds weakened, reaction, adsorption.

12   Write a symbol equation for the reaction of nitrogen oxide and carbon monoxide in the catalytic converter.

Energy changes

You will find out:

- That some chemical reactions are exothermic and give out energy
- That some chemical reactions are endothermic and take in energy
- About a reversible reaction

Feel the warmth or cool it

Have you ever used one of those hand warmers that you can take away camping or on a fishing trip? You might have wondered how they work. When the plastic cover is taken off, the pouch lets oxygen through to the contents inside it. When the oxygen reacts with iron inside the pouch, heat is given out. And guess what, to make the reaction happen quickly, the iron is powdered.

FIGURE 1: An exothermic reaction.

Exothermic reactions

The fire in figure 1 shows **combustion** occurring. All combustion reactions are exothermic. Most **oxidation** reactions are also exothermic; for example, the reaction that occurs when magnesium is oxidised.
Neutralisation reactions are also exothermic; for example, the reaction between hydrochloric acid and sodium hydroxide:

$$HCl_{(aq)} + NaOH_{(aq)} \longrightarrow NaCl_{(aq)} + H_2O_{(l)}.$$

FIGURE 2: Exothermic reactions give out energy.

Endothermic reactions

The plants in figure 3 are taking in energy in the form of sunlight. Photosynthesis is an endothermic reaction. **Thermal decompositions** are always endothermic; for example, when calcium carbonate is heated to decompose it:

calcium carbonate ⟶ calcium oxide + carbon dioxide.

FIGURE 3: An endothermic reaction.

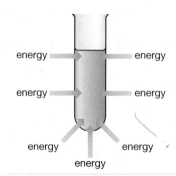

FIGURE 4: Endothermic reactions take in energy.

QUESTIONS

1. Give **two** examples of exothermic reactions.
2. Give **two** examples of endothermic reactions.
3. Write a word equation for the neutralisation reaction above.
4. If you touched the tube in figure 4, would it feel hot or cold?

EXAM HINTS AND TIPS

Exit means the way OUT and Exothermic reactions give OUT energy. Endothermic is the opposite.

...anhydrous   ...combustion   ...hydrated   ...neutralisation

A blue and white reaction

Sejal takes some crystals of copper sulfate. The label on the container says the crystals are **hydrated**.

She heats them in a crucible. The crystals are turning white and a steamy-looking gas is forming.

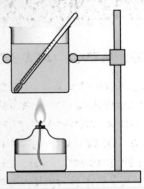

FIGURE 5: The crystals are blue.

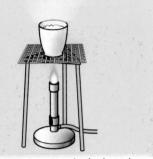

FIGURE 6: Heating the hydrated copper sulfate crystals.

Sejal leaves the apparatus to cool down. She wonders if the steamy gas was water vapour and wants to know what would happen if she put a few drops of water on the white powder in the crucible.

She tries it and the white powder turns blue again and gets very hot. Some of the water turns to steam.

This is a **reversible reaction**. If Sejal reheated the blue crystals at the end of the experiment they would give off water and form white powder again. This white powder is known as **anhydrous** copper sulfate.

FIGURE 7: Adding water to the white powder in the crucible.

We can write an equation for this reaction.

hydrated copper sulfate ⇌ anhydrous copper sulfate + water

Energy changes in reversible reactions

When the copper sulfate was heated, energy was taken in and the water was driven off from the crystals. When the water was added to the white powder at the end, energy was given back out again as heat and the blue hydrated copper sulfate formed again.

WOW FACTOR!

Anhydrous copper sulfate can be used to test for water. If water is added, it turns from white to blue.

QUESTIONS

5   Is the reaction to make anhydrous copper sulfate from blue hydrated copper sulfate exothermic or endothermic?

6   Is the reaction to make hydrated copper sulfate crystals from the white powder exothermic or endothermic?

7   If 500 J of energy were needed to drive off the water, how much energy would be given out when the water was added back again?

8   When magnesium burns, is this a reversible reaction?

How exothermic?

Iain carried out an experiment to see which of two fuels gave out most energy.

FIGURE 8: The apparatus used in Iain's experiment.

- First he heated 100 g of water using 1 g of ethanol. The temperature rose by 50 °C.

- Next he heated 100 g of water using 1.2 g of propanol. The temperature rose by 67 °C.

- In a textbook he found that the amount of energy needed to raise the temperature of 1 g of water by 1 °C is 4.2 J.

- In the experiment, ethanol raised the temperature of 100 g of water by 50 °C, so to find the energy given out per g of fuel he did this calculation:

  Energy = (100 x 50 x 4.2) J

- He found that the 1 g of ethanol gave out 21 000 J of energy.

QUESTIONS

9   Use the same method to calculate the energy given out by 1.2 g of propanol.

10 Calculate the energy given out by 1 g of propanol.

11 According to the experiment, which is the best fuel in terms of energy per g?

12 When Iain checked the data on the internet, he found other experiments gave more energy/gram for both fuels. What improvements to the method could be made to get a better answer?

...oxidation   ...reversible reaction   ...thermal decomposition

Equilibrium

You will find out:
- That in reversible reactions the forward and reverse reactions keep happening
- That equilibrium is reached when both reactions happen at equal rates
- That changing the conditions will affect the position of equilibrium

Back and forth, back and forth

Not all chemical reactions are like the one in figure 1. If you heat calcium carbonate in a closed metal box, it starts to decompose into calcium oxide and carbon dioxide. Unless the temperature is extremely high, it does not decompose completely. Instead, as fast as the calcium carbonate decomposes, calcium oxide and carbon dioxide join together again to make calcium carbonate.

calcium carbonate $\rightleftharpoons$ calcium oxide + carbon dioxide

$$CaCO_{3(s)} \rightleftharpoons CaO_{(s)} + CO_{2(g)}$$

FIGURE 1: When magnesium burns, it reacts completely to make magnesium oxide.

Reaching a balance point

At first the forward reaction happens faster than the reverse reaction. Then the amount of carbon dioxide and calcium oxide starts building up and the reverse reaction starts to speed up.

After a while the rate of the forward reaction is equal to the rate of the reverse reaction. We say that this **reversible reaction** has reached **equilibrium**. At equilibrium all three chemicals will be in the box. As the forward and reverse reactions are both still happening we call this a dynamic equilibrium.

Making the box hotter

If the calcium carbonate is made hotter, more $CaCO_3$ **decomposes** and less of the CaO and CO_2 are present. Changing the conditions has affected the position of the equilibrium.

Let's open the box

If we open the box, then we no longer have a **closed system**. Carbon dioxide can now escape from the box so cannot recombine with the calcium oxide. More calcium carbonate will decompose and more carbon dioxide will escape. The calcium carbonate will now decompose completely.

QUESTIONS

1. What forms when calcium carbonate is decomposed?
2. What forms when calcium oxide and carbon dioxide react?
3. What can we say about the rates of the forward and reverse reactions at equilibrium?
4. What would happen to the equilibrium if we stopped heating the box so strongly?

Watch Out The reactants are the chemicals that react together in a chemical reaction. The products are the new substances that are made.

...activation energy ...closed system ...decompose

Closed systems

In a closed system, no products or reactants can enter or leave the system. In the calcium carbonate example, the chemical system was only closed when the box remained shut.

What if the system is not closed?

Adding more reactants

If we add more reactants, the forward reaction (in which $CaCO_3$ is decomposed) gets faster and more CaO and CO_2 are made. After a while, the forward and reverse rates will balance again and a new point of equilibrium will be reached.

Removing the products

If we remove some of the products, the forward reaction will speed up to make more products. After a while, the forward and reverse rates will balance again and a new point of equilibrium will be reached.

Adding more reactants or removing a product as it forms would both be good ways of getting as much of the product as possible.

Changing the conditions in a closed system

Temperature and pressure both have an effect on systems in equilibrium. Changing these conditions can affect the **yield** (amount of products) of the reaction. If we make more products, the yield has been increased.

Effect of increasing temperature

If the forward reaction is endothermic, raising the temperature always increases the yield. If the forward reaction is exothermic, increasing the temperature always decreases the yield.

Effect of increasing pressure

In a gaseous reaction (one involving gases), increasing the pressure always makes the reaction go in the direction that makes the smallest number of molecules. For example, in the reaction $N_{2(g)} + 3H_{2(g)} \rightleftharpoons 2NH_{3(g)}$, there are four molecules of reactant gases and only two molecules in the products, so increasing the pressure would make the equilibrium go forwards. This would have the effect of increasing the yield of ammonia.

Catalysts

We know catalysts speed up reactions, but do they affect the yield? A catalyst provides a way of lowering the **activation energy** for the reaction. This is shown in figure 2.

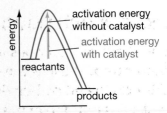

FIGURE 2: Activation energy, with or without a catalyst, for the forward reaction.

The activation energy for the forward reaction is lower with a catalyst.

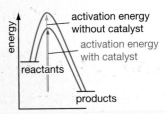

FIGURE 3: Activation energy, with or without a catalyst, for the reverse reaction.

The activation energy for the reverse reaction is also lower with a catalyst.

It is easier for both the forward and reverse reactions to occur when a catalyst is used. This means that both the forward rate and the reverse rate will be faster and by the same amount.

▒▒▒▒ QUESTIONS ▒▒▒▒

9   If both the forward and reverse reactions are speeded up with a catalyst, what happens to the yield of the reaction?

10 What happens to the time it takes for a reaction to reach equilibrium if a catalyst is used?

11 In the decomposition of calcium carbonate, how many molecules of gas are on each side of the equation?

12 The decomposition of calcium carbonate is endothermic. What conditions of temperature and pressure would give the best yield in this reaction?

▒▒▒▒ QUESTIONS ▒▒▒▒

Another equilibrium is: $2SO_2 + O_{2(g)} \rightleftharpoons 2SO_3$. The forward reaction is exothermic.

5   What would happen to the yield of SO_3 if you increased the pressure?

6   What would happen to the yield of SO_3 if you increased the temperature?

7   In another reaction, the yield of product went up when the temperature was raised. Was this reaction exothermic or endothermic?

8   If you wanted the best possible yield of ammonia, would you use a high or low pressure?

...equilibrium   ...reversible reaction   ...yield

The dead cat

SELF-CHECK ACTIVITY

Ellie's college friend Dave has a car. Not a great car but a car nevertheless, and still worth having, Dave reckons.

Until it comes to the annual MOT test, that is. Dave dropped Ellie off at the stables (she was off riding her horse, Whisper) and took the car to the garage. He watched as it was driven into the test bay and the mechanic tested various things. He even stuck a tube up the exhaust pipe and ran the engine. Dave was too far away to see what was being written on the report sheet, but it didn't look good.

"Well young man," said the mechanic. "I hope you've been saving up your money. I think you've got a dead cat."

Later that day Dave tried to explain the problem to Ellie. He hadn't been looking forward to this – he didn't know much about how cars worked.

"We-ell, " he started, "it's a catalytic converter, and it, well, it converts..." His voice trailed off but Ellie's friend Georgina cut in. She was doing Chemistry at AS level.

"It converts pollutant gases into harmless substances" she said, "such as using oxygen to turn carbon monoxide into carbon dioxide."

"Since when was carbon dioxide harmless?" Ellie retorted.

"Well, OK" said Georgina, "but not as dangerous. And it converts nitrous oxide to nitrogen and oxygen."

"Correction" came a disgruntled male voice, "it used to convert. Its converting days are over."

"Does that mean," said Ellie, "that if your catalytic converter thing uses oxygen and gives off carbon dioxide it's doing the same as Whisper? She uses oxygen and gives off carbon dioxide – especially when I'm working her hard!"

Georgina looked at Dave and rolled her eyes, but Dave didn't notice. He was too busy trying to work out how to pay for a new catalytic converter.

CHALLENGE

STEP 1

Why did the mechanic put a tube up the exhaust pipe of Dave's car? Why do many cars have catalytic converters? What is special about a catalyst?

What is particularly unpleasant about carbon monoxide? Write down a word equation to show what happens to the carbon monoxide in the catalytic converter. Now write this equation using chemical formulae.

STEP 3

Why did Ellie query Georgina about carbon dioxide being harmless?

STEP 4

Write down a word equation to show what happens to nitrous oxide in the catalytic converter. Now write this equation using chemical formulae.

In fact, nitrous oxide has two different forms. Find out what they both are and write a chemical equation for the other one.

STEP 5

Ellie suggested that both a horse and a catalytic converter use oxygen and release carbon dioxide. Is she right? Does this mean that the same chemical reaction is taking place in both of them?

STEP 6

Georgina then asked Dave if it was a three way converter.

Find out what else a three way converter does as well as deal with nitrous oxide and carbon monoxide. Devise an effective diagrammatic way of summarising this information.

Maximise your grade

These sentences show what you need to include in your work to achieve each grade. Use them to improve your work and be more successful.

Grade	Answer includes...
F	State that in a chemical reaction there are reactants and products.
	State that the rate of a reaction can be increased or decreased.
	Explain that one way of altering the rate of a reaction is by using a catalyst, but that the catalyst isn't a reactant.
	Explain that a catalytic converter uses a catalyst to reduce the emission of dangerous gases from cars.
C	Explain that although carbon dioxide is less of a problem than carbon monoxide it is still a cause for concern.
	Use word equations to summarise reactions with carbon monoxide and with nitrogen oxide.
	Find out about the two different forms of nitrogen oxide and how the catalytic converter deals with them.
A	Use formulae and balanced chemical equations to summarise the reactions.
	Compare the chemical reactions in respiration and in a catalytic converter to summarise the similarities and differences between these two processes.

Industrial processes

You will find out:
- What the Haber process is
- What the best conditions are for carrying out industrial processes including the Haber process
- Why knowing about equilibrium is important in industrial processes

Making the most of our resources

For thousands of years, humans have been adding organic waste like that for sale in figure 1 to their fields to replace nutrients removed when crops are grown. It is a source of the nitrates that plants need.

Nowadays we cannot rely on natural fertilisers alone. An artificial source of the soluble nitrogen compounds provided by manure is used to produce the crops to feed our population.

FIGURE 1: Why would anyone want to buy 'Pony poo'?

The Haber process

To make **nitrates**, we must first make ammonia (NH_3). This is made from nitrogen (from the air) and hydrogen (obtained from methane (CH_4)).

The equation for the equilibrium reaction is: $N_{2(g)} + 3H_{2(g)} \rightleftharpoons 2NH_{3(g)}$.

The conditions used for this process are: a temperature of 450 °C, a pressure of 200 atmospheres and an iron catalyst. Under these conditions, the yield of ammonia is about 30 per cent.

Why settle for 30 per cent?

These are the **optimum conditions**. The yield is not high but the ammonia is made at a reasonable rate and costs are kept low. This is important as less energy is used and less released into the environment which helps **sustainable development**.

> **WOW FACTOR!**
>
> A pressure of 200 atm could squash 1 litre of gas down to a volume not much bigger than your thumb.

> **WOW FACTOR!**
>
> Fritz Haber received the Nobel prize in 1908 for his work on manufacturing ammonia.

FIGURE 2: Fritz Haber, a German chemist, came up with a solution.

QUESTIONS

1. What is the most important element in ammonia that plants need?
2. What is the word equation for the formation of ammonia?
3. What **three** conditions are used in the Haber process?
4. What is the purpose of the iron catalyst in this process?

...activation energy ...Contact process ...exothermic ...nitrate

Electrolysis of copper sulfate

We have seen that copper forms at the negative electrode in figure 2. Can you remember what the positive electrode is for?

Copper from the impure positive electrode is transferring to the negative electrode. It does this because this **half equation** is happening at the positive electrode:

$$Cu_{(s)} \longrightarrow Cu^{2+}_{(aq)} + 2e^-$$

Copper atoms are losing their electrons and forming copper ions which enter the solution. The copper ions are then attracted to the negatively charged electrode and when they reach it, this half equation happens:

$$Cu^{2+}_{(aq)} + 2e^- \longrightarrow Cu_{(s)}$$

Copper ions collect two electrons and become copper atoms which form on the surface of the electrode.

More reactive **impurities** like zinc go into the solution as ions but cannot get their electrons back as easily as copper ions, so they stay in the solution. Metals less reactive than copper, such as gold, do not go into the solution as ions but stay as metal atoms and drop to the bottom of the tank.

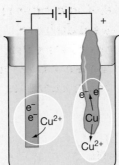

FIGURE 4: Copper transfers from the positive to the negative electrode. Reactive impurities stay in the solution. Unreactive impurities collect as sludge.

The products of sodium chloride electrolysis

From just one chemical – salt – we can make three new substances using electrolysis. Each of these has many important uses in the chemical industry, as shown below.

Chlorine	Hydrogen	Sodium hydroxide
Making bleaches	As a fuel	Soap making
Making chlorinated solvents	Making ammonia	Making detergents
Making chloroethene for PVC production	Changing vegetable oils to margarine	Paper making
Extracting bromine from sea water	In weather balloons	Purifying bauxite, the ore of aluminium

Electrolysis of water

Pure water is a bad conductor of electricity but it will conduct if a little dilute sulfuric acid is added.

Water produces $H^+_{(aq)}$ ions and $OH^-_{(aq)}$ ions. The sulfuric acid produces $H^+_{(aq)}$ ions and $SO_4^{2-}_{(aq)}$ ions.

The $H^+_{(aq)}$ ions are attracted to the negative electrode. Two $H^+_{(aq)}$ ions collect an electron each and the two atoms of hydrogen made combine to form a molecule of hydrogen gas.

$$2H^+_{(aq)} + 2e^- \longrightarrow H_{2(g)}$$

Both $OH^-_{(aq)}$ and $SO_4^{2-}_{(aq)}$ ions are attracted to the positive electrode. The $OH^-_{(aq)}$ ion is most easily oxidised (it loses its electron more easily than the sulfate ion).

This reaction occurs at the positive electrode:

$$4OH^-_{(aq)} \longrightarrow 2H_2O_{(l)} + O_{2(g)}$$

In effect, the reaction is:

$$2H_2O_{(l)} \longrightarrow 2H_{2(g)} + O_{2(g)}$$

Water is being split into oxygen and hydrogen gas.

Acids and metals

You will find out:
- How to make a soluble salt by reacting an acid with a metal
- Which metals can be used to make salts in this way
- How to choose the right acid to make a salt

Hubble bubble, let's make ... salts

Figure 1 shows the reaction between sulfuric acid and magnesium. We can see that a gas forms. When we put a lighted splint near the gas, it gives a squeaky pop.

Sulfuric acid has the formula H_2SO_4. Magnesium is more reactive than hydrogen so it pushes the hydrogen out of the acid and takes its place. We have made a salt, magnesium sulfate.

FIGURE 1: When we put a lighted splint near the gas formed in this reaction, it gives a squeaky pop. What is it?

Do all metals react with acids?

Any metal higher than hydrogen in the **reactivity series** can react with an acid to make a **salt** and hydrogen.

Some metals are just too reactive though. You would not try to react potassium or sodium with an acid as this would be too dangerous.

Metals lower than hydrogen are not reactive enough to displace hydrogen. Copper and silver will not react with dilute sulfuric acid.

> **EXAM HINTS AND TIPS**
>
> If you are asked whether a metal reacts with acids, look at the reactivity series.

> **WOW FACTOR!**
>
> Jabir Ibn Hayyan an alchemist who lived from 720–813 AD, first made aqua regia, a mixture of sulfuric and nitric acids that can dissolve even gold and platinum.

Different types of salts

The type of salt you make depends upon two things: the metal used and the acid used. Sulfuric acid makes salts called sulfates. Nitric acid makes salts called nitrates. Hydrochloric acid makes salts called chlorides.

> **QUESTIONS**
>
> 1 What is the name of the salt forming in figure 1?
> 2 Can zinc react with nitric acid? Explain your answer.
> 3 Can gold react with hydrochloric acid? Explain your answer.
> 4 Write a word equation for the reaction of magnesium and sulfuric acid.

...ammonium ...excess ...reactivity series

Choosing your reagents

A **reagent** is a substance used in a chemical reaction. If we want to make a particular salt using a metal and an acid, we need to work out which reagents to use. So to make a sample of zinc sulfate we would need to react zinc with sulfuric acid:

$$\text{zinc} + \text{sulfuric acid} \longrightarrow \text{zinc sulfate} + \text{hydrogen}$$

$$Zn_{(s)} + H_2SO_{4(aq)} \longrightarrow ZnSO_{4(aq)} + H_{2(g)}$$

Carrying out the reaction

Powdered zinc is used as it has a high surface area, so the reaction happens quickly.

FIGURE 2: Powdered zinc is added to 25 cm³ of dilute sulfuric acid in a beaker.

FIGURE 3: All of the zinc has reacted. But has all of the acid been used up?

FIGURE 4: More zinc is added. This is continued until no more will react.

Some zinc remains unreacted. We say the zinc is in **excess**. This is done to make sure that all the acid has reacted. The mixture is then filtered to obtain zinc sulfate solution.

To obtain zinc sulfate from the solution, we need to evaporate the water so that the salt crystallises.

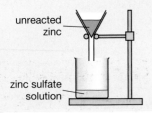

unreacted zinc

zinc sulfate solution

FIGURE 5: The mixture is filtered to separate the unreacted zinc from the salt solution.

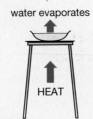

water evaporates

HEAT

FIGURE 6: After heating we are left with pure zinc sulfate.

What is a salt?

A salt is formed when the hydrogen of an acid is replaced by a metal or an **ammonium** ion. Examples of salts that can be made by reacting an acid with a metal are: magnesium nitrate, iron (II) sulfate and zinc chloride.

QUESTIONS

5 When zinc is reacted with sulfuric acid, why is an excess of zinc needed?

6 What reagents would be needed to make iron (II) chloride?

7 Could the following salts be made in this way?

   a copper (II) chloride   b magnesium nitrate   c sodium nitrate

8 Put these processes for making zinc sulfate in the correct order:

   filter, crystallise, react an excess of zinc with sulfuric acid.

Insoluble salts

Insoluble salts cannot be made this way. If we react lead with sulfuric acid, the reaction happens at the surface of the metal and insoluble lead sulfate then forms, coating the metal. The acid can no longer reach the metal and so the reaction stops.

Even if lead sulfate was a soluble salt, this would probably be a poor way of making it as lead is close to hydrogen in the reactivity series so would react extremely slowly.

Balanced equations

To write a balanced equation, first remember the general equation.

METAL + ACID → SALT + HYDROGEN

Then write a word equation for the particular reaction.

**magnesium + hydrochloric acid →
magnesium chloride + hydrogen**

Now work out the formula of the salt. Use the exam data sheet to help.

The formula is therefore $MgCl_2$

Write the symbol equation (NB The formula for hydrogen is H_2.)

$$Mg + HCl \longrightarrow MgCl_2 + H_2$$

Finally, balance the equation and add state symbols.

$$Mg_{(s)} + 2HCl_{(aq)} \longrightarrow MgCl_{2(aq)} + H_{2(g)}$$

QUESTIONS

9 Write balanced equations to show the following salts forming when an acid and a metal react:

   a making iron (II) sulfate

   b reacting aluminium with hydrochloric acid

   c making calcium nitrate.

Making salts from bases

You will find out:
- What a base is and what an alkali is
- How insoluble bases react with acids
- How to make a salt using an acid and a base

Eye of newt, toe of frog, pinch of base, drop of alkali

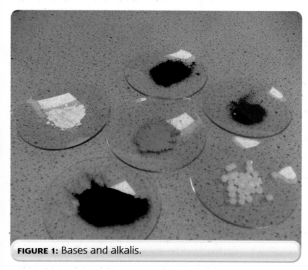

FIGURE 1: Bases and alkalis.

All of the substances here are bases. They are all the oxides or hydroxides of metals. But which ones are alkalis?

To find out we could try to dissolve them in water: only the alkalis will dissolve.

An alkali is a soluble base. Most bases are insoluble metal oxides or hydroxides.

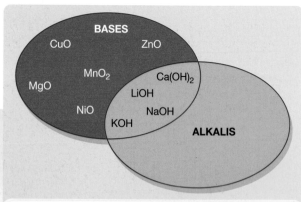

FIGURE 2: All the substances are bases but only some are alkalis.

Pinch of base with drop of acid

When a small amount of an insoluble **base** such as zinc oxide is placed in warm acid, it reacts and forms a **salt** solution. The other product is water.

BASE + ACID ⟶ SALT + WATER

The salt made depends upon which acid is used. If hydrochloric acid is reacted, the salt is zinc chloride and the equation is:

zinc oxide + hydrochloric acid ⟶ zinc chloride + water

$$ZnO_{(s)} + 2HCl_{(aq)} \longrightarrow ZnCl_{2(aq)} + H_2O_{(l)}$$

This is another way of preparing salts and is particularly useful for low reactivity metals like copper when the metal itself would not react with acid.

QUESTIONS

1. Give the formulae of **three** bases.
2. Give the formulae and names of **three** alkalis.
3. Give the formulae and names of **three** insoluble bases.
4. What **two** new substances always form when an acid reacts with a base?

...base ...excess

Choosing your reagents

To make a particular salt using an insoluble base and an acid, we need to work out which reagents to use. If we want to make magnesium chloride, we would need to react magnesium oxide or hydroxide with hydrochloric acid.

magnesium oxide + hydrochloric acid ⟶ magnesium chloride + water

$$MgO_{(s)} + 2HCl_{(aq)} \longrightarrow MgCl_{2(aq)} + H_2O_{(l)}$$

Carrying out the reaction

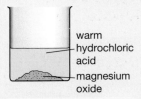

warm hydrochloric acid

magnesium oxide

FIGURE 3: Some hydro-chloric acid is warmed and a spatula of magnesium oxide is added.

FIGURE 4: All of the magnesium oxide has reacted. But has all of the acid been used up?

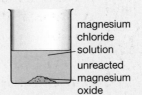

magnesium chloride solution

unreacted magnesium oxide

FIGURE 5: More magnesium oxide is added. This is continued until no more will react.

Some magnesium oxide remains unreacted. It is in **excess**. This is done to make sure that all the hydrochloric acid has reacted. How do we obtain magnesium chloride from the solution?

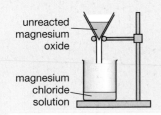

unreacted magnesium oxide

magnesium chloride solution

FIGURE 6: The mixture is filtered to separate the unreacted magnesium oxide from the magnesium chloride solution.

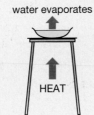

water evaporates

HEAT

FIGURE 7: Evaporation of the water leaves behind solid magnesium chloride.

Obtaining crystals of the salt

When you evaporate all of the water, as shown in figure 7, you are left with a powder. If you want to obtain crystals you need to just reduce the volume of the solution. This concentrates the solution. When the volume has been reduced by half, remove the evaporating basin from the heat and place a filter paper over it. Allow the water to evaporate slowly so that large crystals form.

Naming salts

The salt always starts its name with the metal and the second part of its name is taken from the acid.

If the salt contains only two elements then its name will always end in –ide. So KCl = potassium chloride; NaI = sodium iodide.

If a salt contains more than two elements and oxygen is present then it ends in –ate. So $CaSO_4$ = calcium sulfate; Na_3PO_4 = sodium phosphate.

Formula of a salt

An ionic salt will have the right number of each ion to make their charges cancel out.

Metal ions	Non-metal ions
Na^+, K^+, Li^+,	Cl^-, Br^-, I^-,
Ca^{2+}, Mg^{2+}, Zn^{2+}	SO_4^{2-}
Cu^{2+}, Fe^{2+} (iron II)	NO_3^-
Al^{3+} Fe^{3+} (iron III)	PO_4^{3-}

Check the formulae of the salts above the table to see how this works. Now check:

- sodium nitrate = $NaNO_3$
- zinc chloride = $ZnCl_2$
- aluminium phosphate = $AlPO_4$
- calcium phosphate = $Ca_3(PO_4)_2$

Cleaning tarnished copper

The surface of a copper coin slowly oxidises forming copper oxide. You can clean tarnished copper using the acid in lemons, citric acid, which reacts with the copper oxide exposing shiny new copper. Try it!

Acids and alkalis

You will find out:

- How indicators are used to see when an acid has neutralised an alkali
- How to make a salt from an acid and an alkali
- That ammonia is an alkali and it can be neutralised to make fertilisers

Pass the salt please

Look at the caption to figure 1. To find out when just enough of the alkali, sodium hydroxide, has been added, we use an **indicator**. We add just enough alkali to make the indicator show a pH of 7 which is neutral.

pH 14		pH 1			pH 7		
sodium hydroxide	+	hydrochloric acid	$\longrightarrow$	sodium chloride	+	water	
$NaOH_{(aq)}$	+	$HCl_{(aq)}$		$NaCl_{(aq)}$	+	$H_2O_{(l)}$	

FIGURE 1: If we add just the right amount of sodium hydroxide to hydrochloric acid we make some salt.

Making salt

Make salt by pouring sodium hydroxide into a flask with universal indicator. The indicator will be deep blue/purple at first. Next add hydrochloric acid, swirling the flask to mix the reactants. The colour of the indicator starts to change as some of the alkali is **neutralised**. When the universal indicator turns green, stop adding the acid. You have made some rather impure salt solution!

Making fertilisers

We don't have to make sodium chloride in this way as we can extract rock salt, containing sodium chloride, from rocks underground or from the sea.

Some salts must be made in factories, however, and two examples are ammonium sulfate and ammonium nitrate. These are made by neutralising sulfuric acid and nitric acid with an alkali called ammonia.

Ammonium salts need to be manufactured as they are used to make artificial fertilisers.

WOW FACTOR!

Farmers worldwide need about 80 million tonnes of fertiliser per year. That means a lot of ammonia has to be neutralised.

QUESTIONS

1. Name **one** salt that we do not need to make by neutralisation.
2. Name **two** salts that must be made by neutralisation.
3. What **two** substances are needed to make the salt ammonium nitrate?
4. What **two** substances are needed to make the salt ammonium sulfate?

...burette   ... eutrophication   ...indicator

Making pure sodium chloride

To do this, the acid has to completely neutralise the alkali. It is difficult to see when you have the exact shade of green for neutral using universal indicator. A better indicator – phenolphthalein – can be used in such experiments.

Phenolphthalein is pink in alkali but colourless in neutral and acidic solutions. All the time a solution is alkaline the phenolphthalein is pink, but the moment the exact volume of hydrochloric acid needed to neutralise the alkali is added, the indicator becomes colourless.

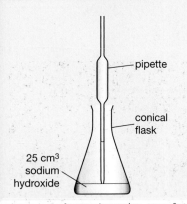

FIGURE 2: A **pipette** is used to transfer exactly 25 cm³ of 2 mol/dm³ hydrochloric acid into a conical flask.

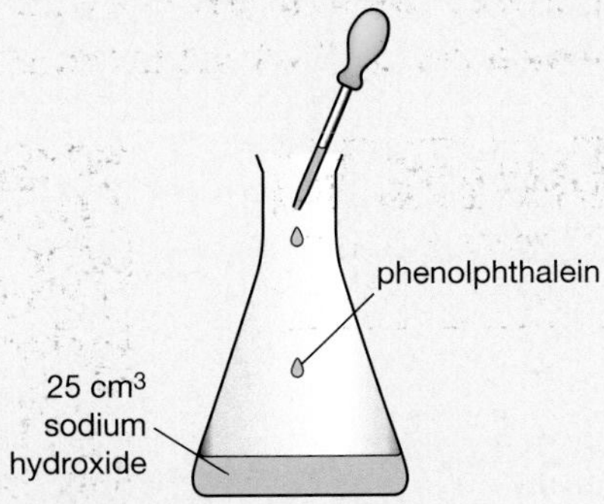

FIGURE 3: Two or three drops of phenolphthalein indicator are added to the flask. As the solution is alkaline it goes pink.

A **burette** is filled with hydrochloric acid and a volume reading is taken.

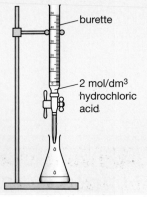

FIGURE 4: Hydrochloric acid is added until one drop of the hydrochloric acid turns the indicator colourless.

The solution is now neutral but the sodium chloride solution is not pure. The (toxic) indicator is still in the flask. A note is made of the new volume reading on the burette and the total volume of acid needed is recorded.

The experiment is repeated using this exact volume of acid with 25 cm³ of alkali but without the indicator.

All that remains is to evaporate the water and you have pure sodium chloride crystals.

Ammonia NH₃

The bonding in ammonia is covalent and it forms simple molecules. Ammonia is a pungent gas which is very soluble in water and forms alkaline solutions. You may smell this gas if you clean out stables or a hamster cage that has needed doing for a while! You may also have smelt it in some household cleaners as it is good at dissolving grease.

Ammonia itself would not make a good fertiliser as it is volatile and would make the soil alkaline. This is a problem, as the ammonia would not stay in the soil and because most crops grow best in soils with a pH of 6–7.5.

This is why ammonia is reacted with acids. This converts them to ionic compounds which are not volatile, still dissolve in water and are not alkaline. They contain the NH_4^+ ion. For example:

$$\text{ammonia} + \text{sulfuric acid} \longrightarrow \text{ammonium sulfate}$$

$$NH_{3(aq)} + H_2SO_{4(aq)} \longrightarrow (NH_4)_2SO_{4(aq)}$$

Problems with using artificial fertilisers

Nitrates from fertilisers get washed from the soil into streams and rivers where they cause **eutrophication**. They may also enter our water supply and, as their salts are so soluble, they are difficult to remove. Although there has been much debate about the harmful effects of such nitrates, there is no reliable evidence to suggest they cause any real damage.

WOW FACTOR!

In East Anglia, where nitrate levels in drinking water are at their highest in Britain, stomach cancers are lower than average for Britain.

QUESTIONS

5 If at the beginning of the experiment above, the reading on the burette was 5.15 cm³ and after it was 24.50 cm³, what volume of acid was added to neutralise the alkali?

6 Why will this method be able to make pure sodium chloride?

7 How could you obtain large crystals of sodium chloride?

8 Could potassium sulfate be made using this method?

QUESTIONS

9 Draw a table to compare the properties of ammonia and ammonium compounds.

10 Why do you think the level of nitrates in East Anglia's water is so high?

Neutralisation

You will find out:
- Which ions make a solution acidic or alkaline
- About the pH scale
- What happens during neutralisation

I've been stung ... but what by?

Wasp stings can be treated with vinegar, a weak acid. Bee stings can be treated with sodium hydrogencarbonate, a weak alkali. The reason both these treatments work is that neutralisation is happening. We use a weak acid or alkali to treat the stings as strong acids and alkalis would damage our skin and cause more pain than the sting!

FIGURE 1: Is it a wasp or a bee?

What exactly is in acids and alkalis?

Look at the formulae of the common acids and alkalis in the table. What do you notice?

Acid	Formula	Alkali	Formula
Sulfuric	H_2SO_4	Sodium hydroxide	NaOH
Nitric	HNO_3	Potassium hydroxide	KOH
Hydrochloric	HCl	Lithium hydroxide	LiOH

The acids all contain hydrogen. When acids dissolve in water they release this as hydrogen ions, $H^+_{(aq)}$. The alkalis all contain hydroxide and this is released as $OH^-_{(aq)}$ when they dissolve.

The difference between a weak and a strong acid

A strong acid makes lots of $H^+_{(aq)}$ when it dissolves in water and a weak acid makes far less $H^+_{(aq)}$. This is related to the pH scale. A piece of **universal indicator** paper dipped into a strong acid goes red and shows a pH of 1. Dipped into vinegar (ethanoic acid), it goes orange and shows a pH of 3.

1	2	3	4	5	6	7	8	9	10	11	12	13	14

strong acid · weak acid · neutral · weak alkali · strong alkali

← increasingly acidic   increasingly alkaline →

FIGURE 2: The pH scale shows how strong an acid or alkali is.

Neutralisation

During **neutralisation**, the $H^+_{(aq)}$ from the acid react with the $OH^-_{(aq)}$ from alkalis to make water.

QUESTIONS

1 Would you treat a bee sting with sodium hydrogencarbonate (baking powder) or vinegar?
2 Are bee stings acidic or alkaline?
3 What would be the pH of sulfuric acid?
4 What would be the pH of a substance that releases lots of $OH^-_{(aq)}$ when it dissolves in water?

EXAM HINTS AND TIPS

Acids are substances that contain $H^+_{(aq)}$.
Alkalis are substances that contain $OH^-_{(aq)}$.

...ionic equation   ...litmus

pH all around us!

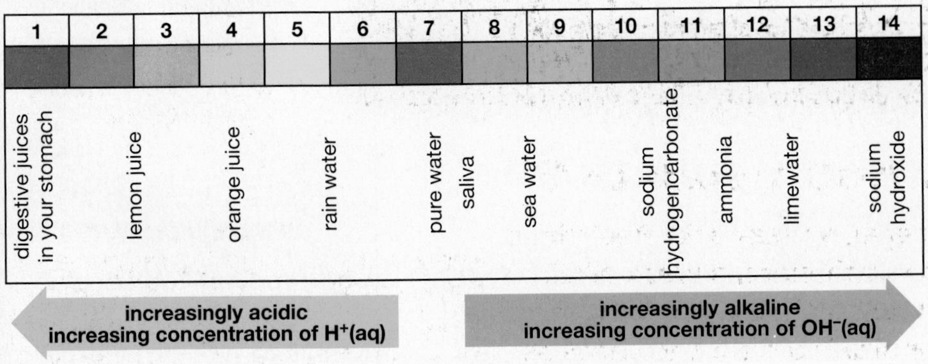

1
2
3
4
5
6
7
8
9
10
11
12
13
14
digestive juices in your stomach
lemon juice
orange juice
rain water
pure water
saliva
sea water
sodium hydrogencarbonate
ammonia
limewater
sodium hydroxide
increasingly acidic
increasing concentration of H⁺(aq)
increasingly alkaline
increasing concentration of OH⁻(aq)

FIGURE 3: Most solutions around us are not neutral.

WOW FACTOR!

Universal indicator is a mixture of different indicators. Each indicator has its own colour change which occurs over a particular pH range.

Equations for neutralisation reactions

When a strong acid such as hydrochloric acid dissolves in water it splits completely into its ions.

$$HCl_{(aq)} \longrightarrow H^+_{(aq)} + Cl^-_{(aq)}$$

When a strong alkali such as sodium hydroxide dissolves in water it splits completely into its ions.

$$NaOH_{(aq)} \longrightarrow Na^+_{(aq)} + OH^-_{(aq)}$$

When hydrochloric acid and sodium hydroxide are mixed they react with each other.

$$HCl_{(aq)} + NaOH_{(aq)} \longrightarrow NaCl_{(aq)} + H_2O_{(l)}$$

This last equation shows that the NaCl is dissolved in water so really it is split into its ions. If we show all of the ions being mixed we can write this equation:

$$H^+_{(aq)} + Cl^-_{(aq)} + Na^+_{(aq)} + OH^-_{(aq)} \longrightarrow Na^+_{(aq)} + Cl^-_{(aq)} + H_2O_{(l)}$$

As you can see, the $Cl^-_{(aq)}$ and $Na^+_{(aq)}$ ions have not changed at all. In fact the only change that has occurred is:

$$H^+_{(aq)} + OH^-_{(aq)} \longrightarrow H_2O_{(l)}$$

This is called an **ionic equation** and it can be used to show what always happens when any acid and any alkali react.

Neutralisation always produces a salt

Acid + metal ⟶ metal salt + hydrogen

Acid + insoluble base ⟶ metal salt + water

Acid + soluble base ⟶ metal salt + water

Acid + ammonia ⟶ ammonium salt

Useful neutralisations

Acid indigestion can be cured by neutralising the excess acid with magnesium hydroxide.

Acid soils can be treated by neutralising with quicklime (calcium oxide) or slaked lime (calcium hydroxide).

Acidic effluent from factories is treated by neutralising with slaked lime.

LITMUS

Litmus is an indicator which will tell us if a substance is an acid or an alkali but it does not tell us how acidic or alkaline it is.

QUESTIONS

5 What is the ionic equation for neutralisation?

6 In the equations above, the $Cl^-_{(aq)}$ and $Na^+_{(aq)}$ ions are sometimes called spectator ions. Why?

7 What pH would you suggest for the pH of magnesium hydroxide? Explain your answer.

8 Using figure 3, can you suggest another treatment for excess acidity?

Precipitation

You will find out:
- That insoluble salts can be made by mixing the right solutions together
- What we call a solid that forms when two solutions are mixed
- Some uses for this type of reaction

FIGURE 1: The yellow colour in these lines comes from lead chromate.

Chemistry keeps the traffic moving

Lead chromate is an insoluble salt. It can be made by mixing together two soluble salts.

Both lead nitrate and potassium chromate form clear solutions when mixed with water. When they are mixed together, they immediately form lead chromate, a yellow solid. Lead chromate is an insoluble salt which does not dissolve in water.

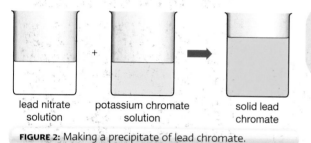

lead nitrate solution + potassium chromate solution → solid lead chromate

FIGURE 2: Making a precipitate of lead chromate.

lead nitrate + potassium chromate → potassium nitrate + lead chromate

$$Pb(NO_3)_{2(aq)} + K_2CrO_{4(aq)} \longrightarrow 2KNO_{3(aq)} + PbCrO_{4(s)}$$

When we mix two solutions together like this and a solid forms, we call the solid a **precipitate**.

Hard water

In some areas of Britain, the water is said to be hard. Hard water is not good for getting soaps to lather.

Hard water contains dissolved calcium and magnesium ions. We can remove these ions by making them precipitate out of the solution. All we need is another solution which contains ions that would combine with the calcium ions and magnesium ions to form a solid. We usually use sodium carbonate.

calcium ions + carbonate ions → calcium carbonate
(from hard water) (from sodium carbonate) (a solid precipitate)

WOW FACTOR!

The calcium ions present in water are good for your health. They are needed for making teeth and bones and some people believe that they prevent heart disease.

QUESTIONS

1 What compound is used to make the yellow lines on our roads?
2 What do we call a solid that forms when two solutions are mixed?
3 What **two** ions make water hard?
4 What is added to remove the hardness from water?

...insoluble ...ionic equation

Making insoluble salts

To make an **insoluble** salt you need to mix together two salts that are **soluble**. You filter to obtain the insoluble salt, then wash the salt with distilled water to remove any solution from it. The table below gives three examples.

Insoluble salt needed	Mix solution A ...	... with solution B
Lead sulfate	Lead nitrate	Sodium sulfate
Silver bromide	Silver nitrate	Sodium bromide
Calcium carbonate	Calcium nitrate	Potassium carbonate

Water and effluent treatment

Two common pollutants in water supplies are nitrate ions (from fertilisers) and phosphate ions (from washing powders). Nitrate ions are very soluble and cannot be removed by precipitation but phosphates can be removed in this way.

Phosphate ions can be precipitated using calcium, iron or aluminium ions.

calcium ion + phosphate ion ⟶ calcium phosphate

(in solution)   (in water supply)   (precipitates out)

Figure 3 shows the effluent being released from a chemical works. Before release, the metal ions that were in solution were removed by precipitation reactions. The carbonates of heavy metals are usually insoluble, so one way of doing this is to add sodium carbonate which provides the carbonate ions, to cause precipitation. The sludge that forms during this process can often be sold on to companies that extract the metals from them for profit.

FIGURE 3: Before the effluent is released, heavy metal ions must be removed.

Testing for metal ions

You can detect the presence of many metal ions in solution because their hydroxides are insoluble. Simply add some sodium hydroxide solution to the solution you are testing and from the colour of the precipitate you can say what metal is present in it.

Soap and hard water

Soap is sodium stearate and contains sodium ions and stearate ions. It is the stearate ions (which can be shown as $St^-_{(aq)}$), that cause the lather. With hard water, the Ca^{2+} ions in the water combine with the stearate ions to make calcium stearate which is a solid, so they are not available to make lather.

$$Ca^{2+}_{(aq)} + 2St^-_{(aq)} \longrightarrow CaSt_{2(s)}$$

This is another precipitation reaction. We normally call the precipitate of sodium stearate 'scum'. This type of equation is called an **ionic equation** as it only shows the ions that react.

Testing for halide ions

FIGURE 4: Adding silver nitrate to solutions of halides.

Silver halides are insoluble so when we add a solution of silver nitrate to a solution containing a chloride, bromide or iodide, a precipitate forms. For example:

$$AgNO_{3(aq)} + NaCl_{(aq)} \longrightarrow$$
$$AgCl_{(s)} + NaNO_{3(aq)}$$

AgCl is white, AgBr is cream and AgI is yellow.

QUESTIONS

9 What is the name of the chemical substance in soap?

10 What is the chemical name for scum?

11 If sodium carbonate provides $CO_3^{2-}_{(aq)}$ ions, write an ionic equation to show how washing soda removes water hardness.

12 When lead nitrate and sodium iodide are mixed, a bright yellow solid is formed. Suggest a name for this precipitate.

QUESTIONS

5 What **two** solutions would you mix to make barium sulfate?

6 What precipitate would form if you mixed calcium nitrate and sodium carbonate?

7 Name an ion that needs to be removed from our water supply using precipitation.

8 What colour are the following precipitates:

   a iron (II) hydroxide b iron (III) hydroxide.

Unit summary

Concept map

Rates of reaction

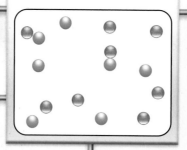

To gauge the speed of a reaction, measure how fast a product appears or a reactant is used up.

A reaction can be speeded up by increasing the temperature; concentration of a solution; pressure of a gas; surface area of a solid, or by using a catalyst.

Collision theory: particles must collide with each other and with sufficient energy in order to react.

The minimum energy needed for a successful collision is the activation energy.

A catalyst speeds up a chemical reaction by lowering the activation energy.

Types of reaction

Exothermic reactions give OUT energy; endothermic reactions take IN energy.

Reversible reactions go forwards and backwards, e.g.

hydrated copper sulfate $\rightleftharpoons$ anhydrous copper sulfate + water.

When a reversible reaction occurs in a closed system, an equilibrium is reached.

Factors affecting equilibrium:

increasing pressure favours the side with the smallest number of molecules; increasing temperature favours the endothermic side of the reaction.

Ions

When molten or dissolved in water, the ions in ionic solids are free to move.

Electrolysis of salt solution makes hydrogen, chlorine and sodium hydroxide. Copper can be purified by electrolysis.

If ions are free to move, passing an electric current through an ionic substance breaks it down into its elements. This is called electrolysis.

During electrolysis, non-metal ions lose electrons and form atoms and molecules; positive metal ions gain electrons and form atoms.

OILRIG: **o**xidation **is** **l**oss of electrons, **r**eduction **is** **g**ain.

Making salts

Insoluble salts can be made as precipitates when two solutions are mixed together.

sulfuric acid $\rightarrow$ sulfates
nitric acid $\rightarrow$ nitrates
hydrochloric acid $\rightarrow$ chlorides

Some metals can be reacted with acids to make salts.

Metal oxides and hydroxides are bases and react with acids to make salts.

Soluble bases are alkalis and these react with acids to make salts

Best conditions for the Haber process

Let us look at the equation again: $N_{2(g)} + 3H_{2(g)} \rightleftharpoons 2NH_{3(g)}$. The forward reaction is **exothermic**.

For a fast reaction, we need the particles to collide as frequently and energetically as possible. We also want the **activation energy** to be as low as possible so that a higher proportion of molecules have sufficient energy to overcome it, meaning more successful collisions.

	Temperature	Pressure	Catalyst
For a fast rate	High	High	Yes

To achieve a high yield we need a high pressure, as there are four molecules of gas on the reactant side and only two on the product side. The forward reaction is exothermic, so a low temperature is needed for a good yield.

	Temperature	Pressure	Catalyst
For a high yield	Low	High	No effect

The optimum conditions   (H)

A high temperature gives a high rate of reaction but a low temperature is needed for a good yield. A compromise is used: a moderate temperature which gives a moderate yield at a reasonable rate.

A catalyst is used to allow the use of a reasonably low temperature, but still have an acceptable rate of reaction.

A high pressure gives both a good rate and a good yield but in fact very high pressures are not used as this needs expensive equipment and a lot of energy.

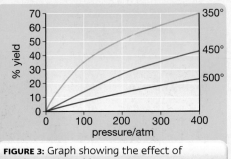

FIGURE 3: Graph showing the effect of conditions on yield.

EXAM HINTS AND TIPS

When explaining the conditions used in an industrial process, stick to the format used here.
1st: conditions for a good yield
2nd: conditions for a good rate
3rd: explain the actual conditions in terms of a compromise.

QUESTIONS

5 figure 3, what is the optimum temperature for a good yield?
   From figure 3, what is the optimum pressure for a good yield?
   Explain how the use of a pressure of 200 atm saves money.
8 Copy and complete this table.

	Temperature	Pressure	Catalyst
Optimum conditions			

Making hydrogen and nitrogen react

Nitrogen is a very unreactive gas.

$$N \equiv N$$

FIGURE 4: The strong triple bond in nitrogen is hard to break.

The bond holding the nitrogen molecule together is strong. It requires a great deal of energy to break the nitrogen–nitrogen bond. So the reaction has a high activation energy. Therefore, a catalyst and high temperature are needed to get a good rate of reaction.

Making the fertiliser

Ammonia itself is not a good fertiliser as it is too alkaline and **volatile**. It is reacted with acids to make **ammonium** salts which are neutral, not volatile and very soluble in water (necessary for uptake by plant roots to occur).

The Contact process

The second step in the **Contact process** for making sulfuric acid is another equilibrium reaction:

$$2SO_{2(g)} + O_{2(g)} \rightleftharpoons 2SO_{3(g)}$$

The reaction is exothermic. Optimum conditions for this process are: 450 °C, 2–3 atm pressure and a V_2O_5 catalyst.

QUESTIONS

9 In the Contact process, what conditions are needed for a high yield?

10 In the Contact process, what conditions are needed for a high rate?

11 Explain why the catalyst speeds up the reaction but does not affect the yield.

12 Explain the optimum conditions used in the process.

Free ions

You will find out:
- What happens when things dissolve
- What state symbols are
- How electrolysis works

The solution is clear

In ionic solids, the ions are held tightly together and even in the tiniest grain, there are billions of ions. Because there are so many ions close together, we can see the grain of solid (see figure 3).

When a solid dissolves completely in water, all the particles separate from each other and are now too tiny to see. If the solid was an ionic solid, the particles are ions. The solution is clear (see figure 4).

FIGURE 1: How many times have you heard your teacher say, "It's not clear, it's colourless"? ...

FIGURE 2: ...Then they pick up the nearest coloured solution they can find and say, "This is clear too, but it's not colourless"!

Another way of separating the ions in a solid

Melting a solid also frees the **ions** from their fixed positions in the **giant lattice**.

When solid lead bromide is heated it melts. Lead ions and bromide ions become free to move. This can be shown using an equation:

$$PbBr_{2(s)} \longrightarrow PbBr_{2(l)}$$

In other words, the solid (s) melts to form a liquid (l) when heated. $PbBr_{2(l)}$ is made up of Pb^{2+} and Br^- which are free to move.

State symbols used in chemical equations: s, l and g stand for solid, liquid and gas respectively. When a substance is dissolved in water it is shown as (aq).

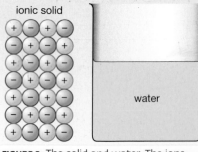

FIGURE 3: The solid and water. The ions are fixed in position.

Electrolysing molten lead bromide

An electric current splits molten lead bromide into its elements:

$$PbBr_{2(l)} \longrightarrow Pb_{(l)} + Br_{2(g)} \text{ (if the crucible is still hot)}$$

The lead is a liquid and the bromine a gas because the temperature is high. The process is called **electrolysis**.

FIGURE 4: The solid has dissolved. The ions are free to move.

QUESTIONS

1 What does $NaCl_{(aq)}$ mean in words?
2 If a beaker contains a cloudy liquid, has the solid dissolved completely?
3 What two elements form when a current is passed through lead bromide?
4 What will form when a current is passed through molten sodium chloride?

...*decomposes* ...*electrodes* ...*electrolysis*

Electrolysis in the laboratory

The ions must be free to move. There are two ways you can do this:

- Two **electrodes** are put into the melt or the solution.
- A battery or the D.C. output from a power pack is connected.

The electrodes are often made of carbon because it is unreactive and conducts electricity.

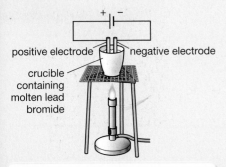

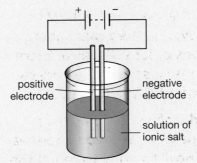

FIGURE 5: If a solid is electrolysed, we must first melt it, and then keep it molten for electrolysis to occur.

FIGURE 6: Electrolysis of sodium chloride solution.

Why does electrolysis happen?

Ionic compounds are always made of metal ions and non-metal ions. Metal ions are positively charged. Non-metal ions are negatively charged.

If we try to pass a current through an ionic solid it does not conduct but when the compound is melted or dissolved in water, the ions become free to move and it can then conduct.

Opposite charges always attract, so the positively charged metal ions are attracted to the negative electrode. Here they collect electrons and form metal atoms.

The negatively charged non-metal ions are attracted to the positive electrode. Here they lose electrons and form non-metal atoms or molecules.

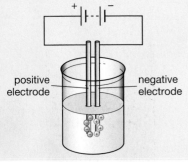

FIGURE 7: The ions move to the electrode with a charge opposite to theirs.

> ### EXAM HINTS AND TIPS
>
> When a metal and non-metal react together they form an ionic solid which is made of positive and negative ions held tightly together forming a giant lattice.

> ### QUESTIONS
>
> 5   Explain why solid sodium chloride does not conduct electricity.
> 6   Explain why pure water does not conduct electricity.
> 7   During the electrolysis of molten sodium bromide (NaBr), what would you expect to form at the: **a** positive electrode? **b** negative electrode?
> 8   Why does a solution of sugar ($C_{12}H_{22}O_{11}$) not conduct electricity?

Why don't we make sodium when we electrolyse $NaCl_{(aq)}$?

When we electrolyse molten sodium chloride it **decomposes** into its elements. Sodium forms at the negative electrode and chlorine at the positive.

When we electrolyse sodium chloride solution we make chlorine at the positive electrode but we do not make sodium at the negative electrode. Instead we make hydrogen.

Where has the hydrogen come from? The only other substance in the beaker is the water, so the hydrogen must have come from there.

Water has the formula H_2O. To simplify, we can think of it as splitting into H^+ ions and OH^- ions. The beaker would then contain the following ions:

$$Na^+_{(aq)}, Cl^-_{(aq)}, H^+_{(aq)} \& OH^-_{(aq)}$$

So during electrolysis of sodium chloride solution, the positive ions ($Na^+_{(aq)}$ and $H^+_{(aq)}$) both go to the negative electrode but only the hydrogen is given off there.

At the positive electrode both of the negative ions ($Cl^-_{(aq)}$ and $OH^-_{(aq)}$) gather but only chlorine gas is produced.

> ### QUESTIONS
>
> 9   During electrolysis of $NaCl_{(aq)}$:
>   a Which ion is not released at the negative electrode?
>   b Which ion is not released at the positive electrode?
>   c What new substance will start to accumulate in the beaker during electrolysis?
> 10 What **three** new substances can be made by the electrolysis of aqueous potassium bromide?

Electrolysis equations

You will find out:
- What the battery does during electrolysis
- That special equations can be written for the reactions that happen during electrolysis
- About oxidation and reduction during electrolysis

Positives and negatives of electrolysis

What happens next?

- The positive metal ions gain electrons and make metal atoms.
- The negative non-metal ions lose electrons and form atoms.
- Electrons produced by the non-metal ions at the positive electrode move into the wire. At the negative electrode, positive ions take electrons from the wire.

The battery acts as a pump, pushing the electrons continuously around the circuit.

FIGURE 1: During electrolysis, positive ions move to the negative electrode and negative ions move to the positive electrode.

Electrolysis of molten sodium chloride

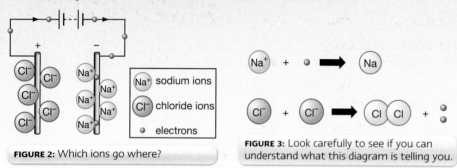

FIGURE 2: Which ions go where?

Na$^+$ sodium ions
Cl$^-$ chloride ions
● electrons

FIGURE 3: Look carefully to see if you can understand what this diagram is telling you.

OPPOSITES ATTRACT

Opposite charges attract each other. That is why positive ions are attracted to the negative electrode.

Figure 3 shows that: one positively charged sodium ion gets one electron and makes one neutral sodium atom; and two negatively charged chloride ions both lose their electrons and make a chlorine molecule. We can also write a symbol equation to describe this reaction. Electrons are shown as e$^-$.

$$Na^+ + e^- \longrightarrow Na \qquad 2Cl^- \longrightarrow Cl_2 + 2e^-$$

These are called **half equations**.

Reduction and oxidation

When positive ions gain electrons we call this **reduction**. When negative ions lose their electrons we call this **oxidation**.

EXAM HINTS AND TIPS

OILRIG
Oxidation is loss (of electrons).
Reduction is gain (of electrons).

QUESTIONS

1 What charge do metal ions always have?
2 Which electrode do metal ions always travel to?
3 What do metal ions collect at this electrode?
4 Which **two** elements form when molten sodium chloride is electrolysed?

...half equations ...oxidation

A revealing exercise on electrolysis

Work through this sequence of questions and answers. Try to answer each question before checking the answers below to see if you were right.

Lead bromide has the formula $PbBr_2$.

Q1 In this formula, how many lead ions and how many bromide ions are there?

Q2 If a bromide ion is Br^-, then what is the charge on a lead ion?

Q3 Which electrode will the lead ion be attracted to?

Q4 What will the Pb^{2+} ion do when it reaches the negative electrode?

Q5 Write a half equation to show this.

Q6 Has the lead been oxidised or reduced?

Q7 Which electrode will the bromide ions go to?

Q8 Write an equation to show what happens there.

Q9 Is this reduction or oxidation?

A1 There is one lead ion and there are two bromide ions.

A2 There are two Br^- ions for every one lead ion. To balance the two negative charges that the bromides have, the lead must have a 2^+ charge.

A3 As it is positive, it will be attracted to the negative electrode.

A4 It will gain two electrons to form a neutral lead atom.

A5 $Pb^{2+} + 2e^- \longrightarrow Pb$

A6 As it has gained electrons it has been reduced.

A7 As they are negatively charged, they will be attracted to the positive electrode.

A8 $2Br^- \longrightarrow Br_2 + 2e^-$. Two bromide ions lose an electron each and the two neutral atoms join to form a molecule of bromine.

A9 As there is loss of electrons, this is oxidation.

QUESTIONS

5   What ions would be present in molten aluminium oxide and what charges are on them?

6   Write the half equations for the reactions at the positive and negative electrodes.

7   State and explain what process is happening at each electrode.

8   These reactions are called **redox** reactions. Can you think why?

Uses for electrolysis

You will find out:
- How copper can be purified by electrolysis
- That if there is a mixture of ions, then the products of electrolysis depend on the reactivity of the elements present
- What forms when sodium chloride is electrolysed

All wired up

FIGURE 1: Highly pure copper is mostly used for wiring.

About 17 million tonnes of copper are used every year in Britain and about three-quarters of this has to be in a highly pure state. This pure copper is produced by electrolysis of solutions containing copper ions with electrodes made from copper. The copper ions come from the positive electrode which is made from impure copper.

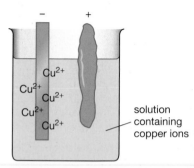

FIGURE 2: The Cu^{2+} ions are attracted to the negatively charged electrode where they collect two electrons forming copper atoms

Electrolysis of sodium chloride solution

The ions from sodium chloride are Na^+ and Cl^-. There are also H^+ and OH^- ions from the water. Both positive ions are attracted to the negative electrode but only the H^+ ions get their electrons back. The Na^+ ions stay in the solution. This always happens if the metal is more reactive than hydrogen in the reactivity series.

At the positive electrode, the Cl^- ions lose their electrons more easily than the OH^- (hydroxide) ions. This means the hydroxide ions stay in the solution too.

So there are three **products** when we electrolyse sodium chloride solution. Chlorine, hydrogen and sodium hydroxide from the ions which remain in the solution.

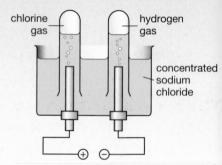

FIGURE 3: Passing a current through sodium chloride (salt) solution does not give us sodium and chlorine.

WOW FACTOR!

Copper is extracted from its ore, malachite, by heating with carbon. The copper made is 99% pure. For the electrical industry this purity must be increased to 99.99%.

QUESTIONS

1 What forms at the negative electrode during the electrolysis of copper sulfate solution?

2 What will happen to the size of the negative electrode during the electrolysis of copper sulfate solution?

3 What is the common name for sodium chloride?

4 What forms at the negative electrode when sodium chloride solution is electrolysed?

...half equation ...impurities

Unit quiz

1 Which of the following will not speed a reaction up?

increase temperature   increase pressure
add a catalyst   decrease concentration

2 What is the minimum energy needed for a successful collision?

heat energy   acidification energy
activity energy   activation energy

3 Solid sodium chloride will only conduct when ...

molten   heated   dissolved in water
molten or dissolved in water

4 Which of the following equations show reduction?

$Cu^{2+} + 2e^- \rightarrow Cu$
$Cu \rightarrow Cu^{2+} + 2e^-$
$2Cl^- \rightarrow Cl_2 + 2e^-$
$4OH^- \rightarrow O_2 + H_2O + 4e^-$

5 Which of the following is not an exothermic reaction?

combustion   neutralisation
photosynthesis   respiration

6 Which of the following would increase the yield of NH_3 in this exothermic reaction?

$N_{2(g)} + 3H_{2(g)} \rightleftharpoons 2NH_{3(g)}$

increase temperature   decrease pressure
decrease temperature   use a catalyst

7 Which of the following is not formed during electrolysis of salt solution?

sodium   sodium hydroxide
chlorine   hydrogen

8 Which metal cannot be reacted with sulfuric acid to make a salt?

zinc   iron   copper   magnesium

9 What salt will form when hydrochloric acid reacts with copper oxide?

copper hydrochloride   it won't react
copper oxychloride   copper chloride

10 When nitric acid reacts with sodium hydroxide, sodium nitrate and what else forms?

salt   water   hydrogen   oxygen

11 An alkali is ...

a soluble base   an insoluble base
a basic salt   a type of salt

12 When sodium iodide and lead nitrate are mixed solid lead iodide forms. This is called ....

precipitation   neutralisation
filtration   oxidation

Literacy activity

Electrolysis of salt

Salt, or sodium chloride, can be obtained from underground deposits or by evaporating sea water. The salt in this picture has been made in a salt pan in Portugal by evaporating the water using heat from the sun. The salt itself has many uses, including food preservation and flavouring, but much salt is electrolysed in order to obtain other useful products.

QUESTIONS   Imagine you are a chloride ion in the middle of the pile of salt. Tell the story of how you end up in a boiling tube full of chlorine gas in your school laboratory. Illustrate your work with diagrams to help explain your journey. Your account MUST include all of the following words (you can use each one more than once).

atoms	beaker	boiling tube	dissolve	electrode	electrolysis
electron	evaporate	free	gain	ionic	ions
laboratory	lose	molecule	negative	Portugal	positive
power pack	school	sea water	ship	solid	sun
van	water	wires			

Exam practice

1 Some magnesium ribbon is reacted with 1.0 mol/dm^3 hydrochloric acid and this makes a salt and hydrogen gas.

a What is the name of the salt formed? [1]

b Explain why increasing the temperature of the acid speeds the reaction up. [2]

c Another way of speeding up reactions is to use a catalyst. Why is it so important to use a catalyst in industrial processes? [1]

d Give two other ways of speeding the reaction up. [2]

2 **a** Reactions can be described as being either 'exothermic' or 'endothermic'. Explain what is meant by these two terms and give an example of each one. [4]

b When blue crystals of hydrated copper sulfate are heated, the following reaction occurs:

Hydrated copper sulfate (blue) $\xrightleftharpoons[\text{exothermic}]{\text{endothermic}}$ Anhydrous copper sulfate (white) + water

State two things that could be observed if a few drops of water were added to anhydrous copper sulfate. [2]

3 In the Haber process the following reaction occurs:

$$N_{2(g)} + 3H_{2(g)} \rightleftharpoons 2NH_{3(g)}$$

a Complete the following sentences using the words below. (Each word may be used **more than once** or **not at all**.) [4]

In order to achieve a high rate of reaction, the temperature should be .... and the pressure should be .... To obtain the best possible yield of ammonia, the temperature should be low because this reaction is .... and the pressure should be .... as there are fewer molecules in the products than the reactants.

| exothermic | endothermic | low | high |

b Explain why the following conditions are used in the Haber process.
  i A temperature of 450 °C.
  ii An iron catalyst.

4 The diagram shows the electrolysis of sodium chloride solution.

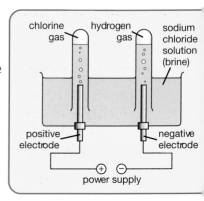

a Complete the following ionic equations which show the reactions occurring at the electrodes.

  i At the positive: $Cl^-_{(aq)} \rightarrow Cl_{2(g)} + e^-$

  ii At the negative: $H^+_{(aq)} + \rightarrow H_{2(g)}$

b Explain what is meant by '(aq)' and '(g)'.

c Is the production of chlorine at the positive electrode an example of oxidation or reduction?

5 Using one word only, state what is being described the following descriptions.
  A Metal oxides and hydroxides.
  B Soluble hydroxides.
  C A solution that makes $H^+_{(aq)}$.
  D $H^+_{(aq)} + OH^-_{(aq)} \rightarrow H_2O_{(l)}$.
  E A scale that is a measure of the acidity or alkalinity.

6 A class of students are asked to plan an experiment to make some salts.

a **i** Lianne and Becky have to make sodium chloride. Lianne suggests adding some sodium to hydrochloric acid. Explain why Becky thinks this is a bad idea.

  ii Anil and Heeral have to make copper sulfate. Heeral says they should put copper into sulfuric acid. Explain Anil's reasons for thinking this will not work.

b Explain how Anil and Heeral could make some copper sulfate solution.

7 Insoluble salts can be made by mixing appropriate solutions of ions so that a precipitate forms.

a Copy and complete the following **word** equation to show what two solutions must be added to make lead iodide:

.... + ... ➡ lead iodide + potassium nitrate   [2]

b Precipitation reactions can also be used to remove unwanted ions. Describe an example of when this might be useful.   [1]

(Total 42 marks)

Worked example

Ammonia and its salts are important industrial chemicals and have many uses.

a i Ammonia is made in the Haber process by reacting nitrogen and hydrogen. Write a balanced symbol equation for this reaction.   [2]
  ii When ammonia dissolves in water the pH becomes 12. Is ammonia solution an acid or an alkali?   [1]
  iii A student wants to make some ammonium sulfate. What acid should he react with the ammonia?   [1]
  iv If an ammonium ion is written NH_4^+, what is the formula for ammonium sulfate?   [1]

b The reaction can be carried out using the apparatus shown opposite. Explain how some pure crystals of ammonium nitrate could be prepared.   [4]

c Write an ionic equation for this neutralisation reaction.   [1]

d Why are ammonium salts important?   [1]

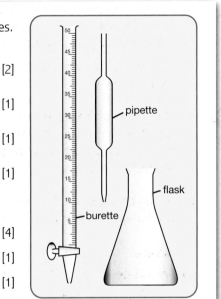
pipette
flask
burette

Gases like nitrogen and hydrogen are diatomic. This should be N_2 + $3H_2$ ➡ $2NH_3$. Parts **ii** and **iii** are correct. In **iv**, The sulfate ion is SO_4^{2-}. This means that two NH_4^+ ions are needed for each SO_4^{2-} and so the formula should be $(NH_4)_2SO_4$.

This answer is correct.

a i N + 3H ➡ NH_3
  ii Ammonia is an alkali.
  iii Sulfuric acid.
  iv NH_4SO

b 1. Measure out some of the alkali into the flask.
   2. Add the acid until it is all neutral.
   3. Heat the solution to evaporate the water.

c $H^+_{(aq)}$ + $OH^-_{(aq)}$ ➡ $H_2O_{(l)}$

d Ammonia is used for removing grease.

The student has not said how they know when it becomes neutral. You have to add an indicator to the alkali and stop adding the acid when the indicator shows that it is neutral. The experiment then needs to be repeated without the indicator but using the same volumes of acid and alkali. Finally, they would need to heat gently to evaporate the water in order to obtain crystals.

Overall Grade: C

How to get an A

All the common gases that react are diatomic. Their formulae are written H_2, O_2, N_2, Cl_2. The student needs to recap on the section of the textbook that explains how to write formulae and practise writing them. They should make sure that they use the information given on the Data Sheet provided by AQA to help them

Yes it is, but that is not what the question asked! Ammonium salts are important as artificial fertilisers. The student needs to be clear about the difference between 'ammonia', a gas that dissolves in water to make alkalis, and 'ammonium salts', the salts made by neutralising ammonia.

DISCOVER FORCES!

Even a good crash helmet couldn't protect your brain from this force – and the results could be fatal.

This bike is stopping in a distance of about one metre. Even if the bike was only travelling at a speed of 30 mph, the rider would still feel an acceleration equal to more than twice the maximum G-force experienced by fighter pilots. This could cause unconsciousness or death.

Energy and energy changes affect everything we do. When there are energy changes, there are usually forces involved. Forces affect the speeds we can travel at, the work we can do, the seriousness of accidents we might have and even 'play' activities such as sticking balloons to ceilings or making someone's hair stand on end!

Sensors allow scientists to measure the forces on different parts of the dummy. They can then use this information to design features to try to make accidents safer, although of course no accident is ever completely safe.

CONTENTS

See how it moves!

You will find out:
- How to represent high speed and low speed movement on a distance-time graph
- Why the slope of a distance-time graph represents speed
- How to construct distance-time graphs

Who will win?

A bicycle can travel faster than a runner and a car can go faster still. But in a race between a car, a bicycle and a runner, the runner might win! What is going on? Distance-time graphs can help us solve problems like these. They can show us that the runner reaches top speed much sooner than the car or the bicycle, so the runner will win very short races.

FIGURE 1: Who will win this race?

Distance-time graphs

You already know that we can use **distance-time graphs** to help us 'picture' journeys. A 'journey story' tells us how something moves, such as the following journey story for a trip to school:

'At first I travelled very slowly because I was walking to the bus stop. Then I stopped and waited for the bus. The bus travelled quickly, but it slowed down when it got near to school. Then it stopped and I got off.'

Look at figure 2, which shows the distance-time graph for the same journey. Can you see these features?

- The very shallow **slope** that represents the person walking. A very shallow slope means the **speed** is very slow. In each unit of **time**, the person doesn't move very far, so the **distance** doesn't increase very much.

- The two places where the person has stopped. The graph is a horizontal line because the person is **stationary**, so even though the time is changing the distance isn't.

- A steep slope represents the bus travelling quickly. It travels a long way in each unit of time, so the distance increases a lot.

- The part of the graph that represents the bus travelling slowly. Can you explain why the slope for this part of the graph is steeper than when the person was walking and shallower than when the bus was travelling fast?

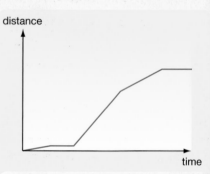

FIGURE 2: How would this distance-time graph change if the bus went more slowly all the way to school?

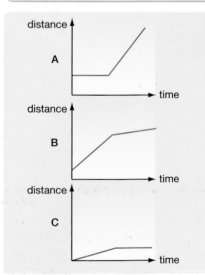

FIGURE 3: Match each of these distance-time graphs to the correct journey story.

▌▌ QUESTIONS ▐▐

Look at the three distance-time graphs, labelled A, B and C in figure 3.

1. Which distance-time graph represents an object that travels fast then slower?

2. Which distance-time graph represents an object that goes slowly, then stops?

3. Describe what the third distance-time graph shows.

...average speed   ...distance   ...distance-time graph   ...slope

Making distance–time graphs

You can construct your own distance-time graphs to show how you move, using a **ticker-timer** or **ultrasonic motion sensor**.

A ticker-timer is a machine that makes 50 dots on a tape every second. If you walk away from the ticker-timer, pulling the tape through the machine as you go, you can use the tape to plot a distance-time graph of how you move. After one second you have travelled the distance between the start line and the fiftieth dot on the tape. After two seconds you have travelled the distance between the start line and the hundredth dot and so on. But that's a lot of tape! So usually people plot the distance travelled after each one-fifth of a second – that's just 10 dots.

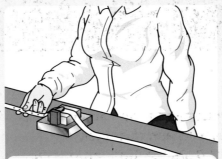

FIGURE 4: Describe how you could construct a distance-time graph from ticker tape like this.

An ultrasonic motion sensor, connected to a computer, uses an ultrasound beam to measure the distance for you, and may even plot the graph.

Speed and average speed

We can find the **average speed** of an object using the equation:

average speed = total distance travelled
────────────────────────
total time taken

If a distance-time graph has figures on it, we can use them to find out the average speed of the object.

A distance-time graph can tell us much more than just the average speed. The slope of the graph can show us how the actual speed changed, so we may be able to see why a driver got a speeding ticket, even though his average speed for a journey was less than the speed limit!

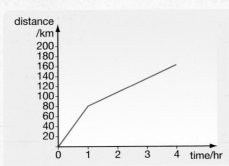

FIGURE 5: What is the average speed of this car? The speed limit was 50 kph; can you explain why the driver got a speeding ticket?

Calculating speed   (H)

The gradient of a distance-time graph at any point gives the speed of the object at that point. In real life speeds don't often change suddenly, so many real life distance-time graphs have curved, not straight lines. This distance-time graph shows an object that is speeding up gradually; the gradient of the graph is gradually increasing.

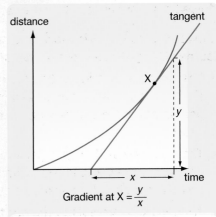

Gradient at X = $\frac{y}{x}$

FIGURE 6: Why are many real life distance–time graphs curved?

The speed of the object at any point can still be found by drawing the tangent to the curve at that point and then calculating the gradient of the tangent.

QUESTIONS

4   Draw the distance-time graph an ultrasonic motion sensor would give if you ran away from it then walked back towards it.

5   Look again at the introductory paragraph, then write a comparison of the distance-time graphs for the runner and the car, at the beginning of a long race and at the end.

QUESTIONS

6   Draw a distance-time graph for a car that speeds up gradually to a maximum speed, then brakes hard before crashing into a tree.

Speed isn't everything

You will find out:
- The difference between speed and velocity
- The definition of acceleration

Look where you're going!

Scientists use space shuttles like this one to take astronauts into space and to launch probes to explore the planets in our solar system. The shuttle moves fast to get away from the Earth and the Earth's gravity, but just high speed is not enough. What else do scientists have to think about if a spacecraft is to reach Venus, for example?

FIGURE 1: What else matters for this space shuttle, besides speed?

Direction matters

You can probably think of lots of examples where it isn't enough to know just the **speed** of something. For instance, when a footballer kicks the ball, the speed alone won't tell you whether or not he will score a goal! Often we need to know more. Look at this example:

Asad   The lion

Asad and the lion both have the same top speed. Will the lion catch and eat Asad? We don't know; we need to know more.

The lion will never catch Asad (unless Asad gets tired first and slows down).

Asad will probably get eaten!

We can't tell if Asad will get caught. We need to know where both he and the lion started from, and the **direction** they are both heading.

Velocity

The **velocity** of an object tells us its speed and its direction. We use the letter 'v' for an object's velocity. In this example, all the velocities are measured upwards, away from the ground.

v = 12 000 m/s

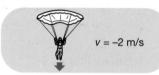

v = −2 m/s

v = 0 m/s

The **positive velocity** of the rocket tells us that it is moving at 12 000 m/s upwards, away from the ground.

The parachute has a **negative velocity**, because it is travelling *towards* the ground and velocity is measured *away from* the ground.

The aeroplane might have a very high speed, but its velocity *away from the ground* is 0 m/s. It is not moving towards the ground or away from the ground.

QUESTIONS

1. What **two** things does the velocity of an object tell us?
2. Two runners both have the same velocity. What can you say about the direction they are moving in?
3. A ball is dropped. It hits the ground with a velocity of 5 m/s and bounces back up with a speed of 3 m/s. What will its velocity be?

...acceleration   ...direction   ...negative velocity

Acceleration

You may have learned that '**acceleration**' is the scientific word for 'speeding up'. You may have heard 'slowing down' called 'deceleration' or 'negative acceleration'. These are simple definitions that work well when things do not change direction, but now you need to know a more accurate definition of acceleration, that works even when things change direction. We can work out the acceleration of an object using the equation:

$$\text{acceleration (in m/s}^2) = \frac{\text{change in velocity (in m/s)}}{\text{time taken for change (in s)}}$$

Acceleration has to have a direction, as well as a size, because velocity has a direction.

Finding the direction of the acceleration

When something has an acceleration, it tries to move in the direction the acceleration is acting in. We can use this to help us decide the direction of the acceleration.

When this archer lets go of the arrow, it will shoot straight forward. This tells us that the acceleration acts straight forward, in the direction shown on the diagram.

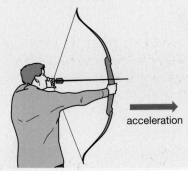

acceleration

FIGURE 2: In which direction will this arrow move?

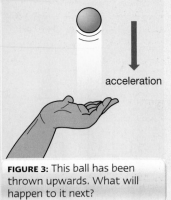

acceleration

FIGURE 3: This ball has been thrown upwards. What will happen to it next?

This ball is moving upwards at the moment, but it is slowing down and trying to move downwards. This tells us that the acceleration is acting downwards, towards the ground.

EXAM HINTS AND TIPS

If a question doesn't tell you which way velocity acts, you can choose which way is positive, but keep it the same for the whole question.

QUESTIONS

4   Which way does the acceleration act when a car is braking?

5   Use the idea of acceleration to explain why an arrow falls downwards, as well as flying forwards.

Circular motion

When an object moves round in a circle with constant speed, its velocity is constantly changing, because its direction is constantly changing. This means it must be accelerating, even though its speed is constant. The object acts as though there is a force constantly pulling it towards the centre of the circle (and stopping it travelling off in a straight line), so this is the direction the acceleration must be in, towards the centre of the circle.

For planets orbiting the Sun, gravity provides the acceleration towards the centre of the circle. For cars, or other vehicles, travelling around bends, the frictional force between the tyres and the road provides the acceleration.

FIGURE 4: Which way does this bung accelerate? What provides the acceleration?

QUESTIONS

6   What is the average velocity of an object moving in a circle?

7   Use friction and acceleration to explain why cars can't turn such tight corners at higher speeds.

Velocity–time graphs

You will find out:

- How to draw and interpret velocity-time graphs
- What a velocity-time graph shows about the acceleration
- What a velocity-time graph shows about the distance travelled

How fast?

Good roller coaster rides are exciting, but they don't have to be long. The velocity and the acceleration are much more important than the distance it travels. Designers of fighter aircraft care more about velocity and acceleration than about distance, too. If the plane accelerates too quickly the pilot will become unconscious. Velocity-time graphs help us see how velocity is changing and help us work out the acceleration.

What are velocity–time graphs?

Velocity-time graphs tell us how the **velocity** of something changes with time. Look at figure 2, which shows the velocity-time graph for a cyclist. The velocity is measured along the road in the direction the cyclist is travelling.

- At A the cyclist is speeding up steadily from stationary.
- At B the cyclist is travelling at a high **constant velocity**. Perhaps she is pedalling hard along a flat road.
- At C the cyclist is slowing down. Perhaps she has reached a hill.
- At D the cyclist is travelling at a low constant velocity. Perhaps she is walking and pushing the bicycle.

Making velocity–time graphs

You can construct your own velocity-time graphs using a **ticker-timer** machine and ticker tape (see figure 3). As you pull the ticker tape through the machine, the machine puts 50 dots on the tape every second. The velocity of the tape, in metres per second, is the **distance** that the tape travels in each second. So the velocity in the first second is shown by the distance from the starting line on the tape to the fiftieth dot. The velocity in the second second is shown by the distance from the fiftieth dot to the hundredth dot and so on. You can make the velocity-time graph by cutting the tape into 50 dot sections, and sticking them side-by-side, to make a graph.

FIGURE 1: These riders don't really care how far the roller coaster travels. What do they care about?

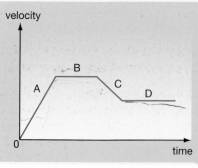

FIGURE 2: What does this velocity-time graph tell us?

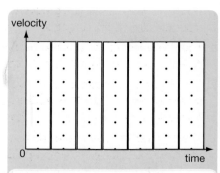

FIGURE 3: What would this velocity-time graph look like if the tape were speeding up?

▪▪ QUESTIONS ▪▪

1   With a partner, think of a different story to explain the way the cyclist's velocity changes.
2   Sketch a velocity-time graph for an object that is speeding up.
3   Sketch a velocity-time graph for an object that is slowing down.
4   How could you use velocity-time graphs to tell which of two runners was faster?

...acceleration   ...constant velocity   ...distance   ...distance-time graph

Interpreting velocity–time graphs

When an object speeds up quickly the velocity-time graph shows a steep slope (a large **gradient**). When an object speeds up its velocity is changing, so it is accelerating. The more the velocity changes in unit time, the steeper the gradient and the larger the object's **acceleration**. A positive gradient means a positive acceleration and a negative gradient means a negative acceleration.

If an object travels at 10 m/s, then after one second it will have travelled 10 m, after two seconds it will have travelled 10 m + 10 m = 20 m, after three seconds it will have travelled 30 m and so on. Look at the velocity-time graph for the object travelling at 10 m/s. Can you see how the area under the graph shows us the distance the object has travelled? An object travelling at 15 m/s will travel further than an object at 10 m/s, and you can see that it has a larger area under its velocity-time graph.

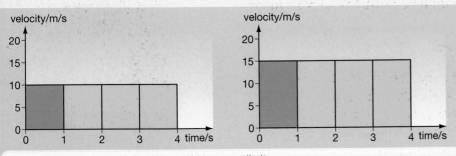

FIGURE 4: How far have each of these objects travelled?

Comparing velocity–time graphs and distance–time graphs

Look at figure 5, which shows the velocity-time graph and **distance-time graph** for a falling skydiver. Velocity is measured towards the ground. The distance is the height above the ground. Can you see the features described below?

- The skydiver has just left the aeroplane. His velocity is increasing. The gradient of the distance-time graph is getting steeper.
- The skydiver is falling at maximum velocity. The distance-time graph is a straight line.
- The skydiver has opened his parachute. He is slowing down rapidly. The gradient of the distance-time graph is getting shallower.
- The skydiver has reached a constant, lower velocity. The distance-time graph is a straight line again.
- The skydiver has landed. His velocity and height above the ground are zero.

FIGURE 5: At which point has the skydiver opened his parachute?

QUESTIONS

5 For a cyclist travelling along a straight road, explain what 'positive acceleration' and 'negative acceleration' mean.

6 Explain to a partner why the gradient of the distance-time graph changes when the velocity increases or decreases.

EXAM HINTS AND TIPS

The slope (gradient) of a velocity-time graph shows the acceleration.

Calculations again

The gradient of a graph is found from:

gradient = change in y ÷ change in x

So the gradient of a velocity-time graph is change in velocity ÷ time taken, which is acceleration. So the acceleration of an object can be calculated from the gradient of its velocity-time graph. If the graph is a curve, the gradient at any point is the gradient of the tangent to the curve at that point.

The distance travelled by an object can be calculated from:

distance travelled = velocity × time

This is the area underneath the object's velocity-time graph. If the velocity is changing then the area can be calculated by splitting it up into triangles and rectangles and using the fact that:

area of a triangle = ½ base × height

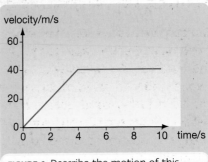

FIGURE 6: Describe the motion of this object falling under gravity.

QUESTIONS

7 Calculate the acceleration while the object is accelerating at a constant rate.

8 Calculate the average acceleration.

9 Calculate the distance fallen during the 10 seconds.

Let's force it!

You will find out:

- How the resultant force affects the way an object moves
- How to find the size of the resultant force
- How to resolve forces

Forces everywhere

It would be very unusual to find a situation where only one force was acting. Usually objects have lots of forces acting on them, all having different effects. Some of the forces act together, making the effect larger; some forces act against each other, making the effect smaller. Fortunately there is a way to find out the overall effect of lots of forces acting together – we can find the resultant force.

FIGURE 1: What forces are acting here?

Adding up, cancelling out

You already know that lots of things have more than one **force** acting on them.

To find out how the object moves, we can imagine all the forces acting on the object being replaced by a single **resultant force**.

> **The resultant force on an object is the single force that would have the same effect as all the forces acting on the object.**

- Forces that act in the same direction as each other add up.

  So the total force backwards on the car is

  air resistance + **friction** = 400 N + 400 N = 800 N

- Forces that act in opposite directions try to cancel out. We take them away. So the total forwards force on the car in figure 2

  = forward force from engine – backward force

  = 1000 N – 800 N = 200 N

We say there is a resultant force of 200 N acting forwards on the car.

FIGURE 2: What is the overall effect of these different forces?

How things move

If the resultant force on an object is zero:

- **stationary** objects stay stationary
- moving objects stay moving at the same **speed** and in the same **direction**.

If the resultant force on an object is not zero:

- stationary objects start to **accelerate** (speed up) in the direction of the resultant force
- moving objects start to accelerate (speed up) in the direction of the resultant force.

QUESTIONS

1 Describe **two** forces that might act on the person abseiling in figure 1.
2 Describe what a 'resultant force' is.
3 How do you find the resultant force when two forces act in the same direction?
4 What happens to an object when the resultant force on it is not zero?

EXAM HINTS AND TIPS

Remember: an object always accelerates in the direction of the resultant force – unless the resultant force is zero.

...accelerate ...air resistance ...component ...direction ...force ...friction

Drawing resultant forces

Often we can't just add together or cancel out the forces on a body because they don't act in the same or opposite directions. Then we can use drawing to find the resultant force.

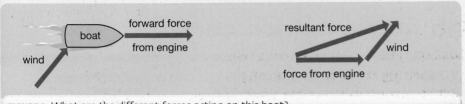

FIGURE 3: What are the different forces acting on this boat?

This boat has two forces on it: the forward force from the engine and a force from the wind. We can draw a **triangle of forces** to find the resultant force. The first two sides of the triangle represent the two forces on the boat. The length of each side is proportional to the size of each force. The direction of the third side of the triangle shows the direction of the resultant force. Its length is proportional to the size of the resultant force.

Resolving forces

Will this skier speed up as she slides down the slope? We need to know the size of the forward force making her move down the slope. This is not the same size as the gravity, because gravity is acting straight downwards, but it is a **component** of gravity.

We can imagine the force of gravity split into two separate forces, one acting down the slope, and one acting at right angles to the slope. This is called **resolving** the gravity force.

If the length of the arrow we draw to represent gravity is proportional to the size of the gravity force, then the length of the other arrows will show the size of the components of gravity in each direction. If the component of gravity acting down the slope is bigger than the resistance the skier will speed up; if it is smaller than the resistance she will slow down.

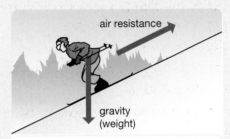

FIGURE 4: Can you suggest a reason why friction has been ignored in this example?

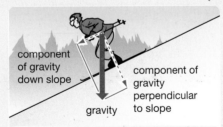

FIGURE 5: How does this diagram help to resolve the gravity force?

Resolving without drawing

Forces can be resolved using trigonometry instead of drawing. This is particularly useful for calculating the total horizontal or vertical force; for example, when an object is being acted on by several forces. For the skier, the gravity force would usually be resolved into a component acting down the slope and a component acting at right angles to the slope.

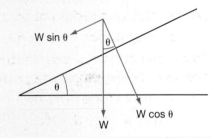

FIGURE 6: This diagram uses trigonometry to show the forces acting on the skier.

Trigonometry using triangles shows that the component acting down the slope is $W \sin \theta$ where θ is the angle the slope makes with the horizontal, and the component acting at right angles to the slope is $W \cos \theta$.

QUESTIONS

7 Look at the person abseiling in figure 1. In which directions would you resolve forces to find out how the abseiler moves? Which forces would you need to resolve?

QUESTIONS

5 For the skier, draw diagrams to show that the component of gravity acting down the slope gets larger as the slope gets steeper.

6 Look at the diagram of the boat in figure 3. Draw a triangle of forces to show the resultant force on it if the wind blows from the opposite direction.

Force and acceleration

You will find out:

- The factors affecting the acceleration of an object
- How to investigate how the acceleration of an object changes
- The relationship between acceleration, force and mass

FIGURE 1: How would you design a car so it could accelerate quickly?

High performance cars

People looking for high performance cars usually want to know how quickly the car can accelerate from 0 to 60 mph (or 0 to 100 kph). High performance 'sporty' cars may do so in four seconds or less, small 'family' cars may take more than 10 seconds. So what do car designers do to high performance cars to make them accelerate so quickly?

Unbalanced forces

When the forces on an object are not balanced, we say there is a **resultant force**. And you know that a resultant force changes the way something moves.

This car is travelling at a constant speed along a straight road. We know the resultant force is zero because the car is not speeding up or slowing down. The forward force from the engine must be exactly the same size as the **air resistance** and the **friction** added together.

- When the driver presses the accelerator, the forward force from the engine gets bigger. There is a resultant force forwards and the car speeds up. There is an **acceleration** in the direction of the resultant force.

- When the driver presses the brake, the friction force increases. There is a resultant force backwards and the car slows down. There is an acceleration in the direction of the resultant force.

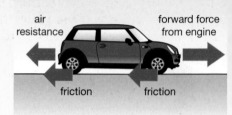

FIGURE 2: What is the resultant force on this car?

How big is the acceleration?

The bigger the acceleration, the more quickly something speeds up or slows down.

You know that the man is going to get to the sale first. He can push his trolley much harder, and it will speed up much more quickly.

- Using a bigger force makes the acceleration bigger.

You also know that this Pet Push Race is going to be won by the twin with the rabbit. It will take ages to make the trolley with the dog in it speed up!

- The acceleration is less if the **mass** is bigger.

FIGURE 3: Who will get into the sale first when the doors open?

FIGURE 4: Which twin will win this Pet Push Race?

QUESTIONS

1. How can you tell if the resultant force on a car is zero?
2. Use forces to describe why the car speeds up when the driver presses the accelerator.
3. What is the connection between mass and acceleration?
4. How can you tell which direction an object will accelerate in?

...acceleration ...air resistance ...directly proportional ...force meter ...friction

Investigating acceleration

We know that acceleration increases when force increases, and acceleration increases when mass decreases. But that is not very precise. How does it increase? Does it double when force doubles? Does it increase up to a maximum value, and then stop? Or something else? We can use trolleys and ticker tape to find out.

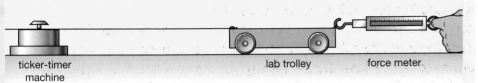

ticker-timer machine   lab trolley   force meter

FIGURE 5: How can you use this apparatus to investigate how acceleration changes?

Attach a **force meter** (newton meter) to a laboratory trolley and pull the trolley along the bench. The force meter will tell you what force you are using. Keep the force the same for the whole length of the bench. Attach ticker tape to the trolley so that the ticker tape goes through a **ticker-timer** as the trolley moves. Use the tape to make a **velocity-time graph**. The slope of the velocity-time graph shows you the acceleration. Using different forces, and plotting a graph of acceleration against force used, shows that:

- acceleration is **directly proportional** to force, $a \propto F$.

Changing the mass of the trolley, but keeping the force constant shows that:

- acceleration is **inversely proportional** to mass, $a \propto 1/m$.

Your teacher may show you how to do this investigation using a motion sensor and a computer instead of a ticker-timer and trolleys.

The newton

You have learned that $a \propto F$ and $a \propto 1/m$. Putting these together gives $a \propto F/m$, which we can rearrange as:

$$F \propto ma$$

The unit used to measure force, the **newton**, has been defined as 'the force needed to make a mass of 1 kg accelerate at a rate of 1 m/s^2. This means that we can write the connection between force, mass and acceleration as:

$$F = ma$$

where force is measured in newtons, mass in kilograms and acceleration in metres per second squared.

Acceleration is always in the direction of the resultant force

Mass in space

FIGURE 6: This Mars explorer is analysing rocks on Mars. What things do you think scientists want to find out?

Imagine scientists want to use a remote controlled robot in space to find the mass of some dust, so they can calculate its density to tell what it is made from. Usually mass is found by measuring the pull of gravity on an object (its weight), but that doesn't work in space because weight changes when gravity changes. Instead scientists use a force of a known size to push the object, and measure its acceleration. They then use the equation $F = ma$ to calculate the mass. By pushing the object backwards and forwards they can get readings for acceleration in two different directions, so they can cancel out the effect of any other forces that might be affecting the object.

QUESTIONS

5   Describe to a partner an example of your own to show that acceleration decreases when mass increases.

6   What graph would you plot to show $a \propto 1/m$? What would you expect the graph to look like?

QUESTIONS

7   Discuss how scientists could measure the size of gravity in space. Is it possible to do so without carrying known masses from Earth?

Balanced forces

You will find out:
- What equal and opposite forces are
- How Newton's Third Law applies to stationary and moving objects
- How Newton's Third Law affects objects that start moving

Where are the forces?

The ice skater in figure 1 is obviously a good skater and has no problems skating where he wants to. But learner ice skaters often get towed out to the middle of the ice rink by their friends and left there! They find it very hard to get back to the edge! Can you work out why? Think about the forces acting on them.

FIGURE 1: What forces are acting here?

Balanced forces

Look at figure 2. Which of these two tug-of-war teams is pulling harder? You know that if they are not moving anywhere Team A and Team B must be pulling exactly as hard as each other. You can show this is true using two **force meters**, joined together so they pull on each other. Hold one force meter still and pull on the other one. The readings on both force meters are always the same, no matter how hard or how gently you pull.

Finding pairs of forces

Newton said that for objects that are joined together, or in contact with each other, both objects exert exactly the same size force on each other. This is his Third Law and it is usually written as:

For every force there is an equal and opposite force.

FIGURE 2: Which team is pulling harder?

An **equal and opposite force** is a force that is the same size, but acting in the opposite direction. We can find these balanced forces in lots of different situations:

- When you sit on a chair, your weight pushes down on the chair seat, but the chair seat pushes up on you just as hard. That's why you don't sink through the chair!

- The chair legs push down on the floor, but the floor pushes up on the chair legs as well.

When you push down on a floating tray, as in figure 3, you can feel the **upthrust** of the water pushing back. The harder you push, the harder the water pushes back.

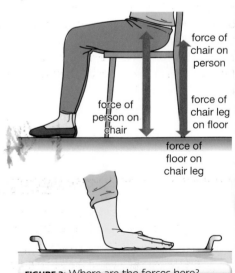

force of chair on person

force of person on chair

force of chair leg on floor

force of floor on chair leg

FIGURE 3: Where are the forces here?

QUESTIONS

1. If two tug-of-war teams are not moving, what does that tell you about the forces?
2. Explain in your own words what 'equal and opposite forces' are.
3. The force of a person down on the ground is 500 N. What other force acts, and what size is it?
4. Draw a situation of your own where a pair of balanced forces act. Label the forces.

...*acceleration* ...*air resistance* ...*constant velocity* ...*equal and opposite force*

Forces on moving objects

Newton's Third Law works for objects moving at **constant velocity**, as well as for **stationary** objects. So when a parachutist is falling at a constant velocity the **weight** of the parachutist acting downwards is exactly the same size as the **air resistance** acting upwards.

Sometimes we have to think really carefully about how the objects are moving. When a car pulls a caravan along the road, the force of the car forwards on the caravan is exactly the same size as the force of the caravan backwards on the car. This is always true, even when the car and caravan are speeding up or slowing down, because the car and caravan are always travelling at the same speed as each other.

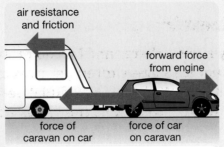

FIGURE 4: Which forces are the same sizes? Which forces are different sizes?

Starting moving

This cartoon seems a bit unlikely! But guns do 'kick' or recoil when they are fired. The exploding gunpowder makes hot gases rush down the barrel, carrying the bullet out. The forward force of the moving gases is balanced by an equal and opposite force acting backwards on the gun. So the gun moves in the opposite direction to the bullet.

FIGURE 5: Could this really happen?

We can use F = ma to show why the bullet hurtles off at high speed, but the gun only moves slowly. The forces on the bullet and on the gun are the same size, but the **mass** of the gun is much bigger than the mass of the bullet, so the bullet has a much higher **acceleration** than the gun (and quickly reaches a very high speed). Modern guns are designed to allow some gases to escape backwards, making the recoil of the gun less.

Watch Out Equal and opposite forces are two forces that are the same size but acting in opposite directions to each other.

That lifting feeling

FIGURE 6: Is this correct?

When a lift starts accelerating upwards, the floor pushes harder than usual on the people inside, making them accelerate upwards too. The larger-than-usual force of the floor on them causes them to push down on the floor with a larger-than-usual reaction force, so they feel heavier than usual. When the lift slows down, the floor pushes less hard than usual on their feet. The smaller-than-usual force of the floor causes a smaller-than-usual reaction force and so the people feel lighter than usual, as the lift slows down.

QUESTIONS

5 Explain to a partner why allowing some gases to escape backwards from a gun makes the recoil of the gun less.

6 Use Newton's Third Law to explain why a blown-up balloon flies around the room when you let go of it so the air can come out.

QUESTIONS

7 Explain what the people inside a lift would feel as the lift started to accelerate downwards, and then stopped.

...force meter   ...mass   ...stationary   ...upthrust   ...weight

Terminal velocity

You will find out:

- Why accelerating objects reach a terminal velocity
- The connection between mass and weight
- How to draw and interpret velocity-time graphs involving terminal velocity

Why bother with a parachute?

Skydivers enjoy the feeling of free fall, when they are falling downwards without a parachute, but they all open their parachutes before they land. If they didn't, they would hit the ground at about 200 kph, which would be fatal. So how does using a parachute enable them to land safely? Can you use forces to explain?

FIGURE 1: Would you enjoy this? Would you want a parachute?

Faster, faster!

You would be surprised if your bike just kept getting faster and faster as you pedalled it. However hard you pedal you always reach a top speed, where you can't get any faster. Your bike has three main forces acting on it; the forward force of you pedalling, and the backward forces of **friction** and **air resistance**.

- To begin with, the air resistance is very small, so there is a **resultant force** forwards and the bike speeds up.
- As you get faster the air resistance gets bigger, because you have to push more air particles out of the way each second.
- Eventually the air resistance and the friction added together are the same size as the forward force of you pedalling. Then there is no resultant force on the bike and it can't speed up any more.

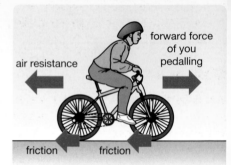

FIGURE 2: How could you change the size of any of these forces?

Falling objects

Falling objects reach a top speed too, called their **terminal velocity**. The force acting downwards is their **weight**. We can calculate their weight using the equation:

$$\text{weight} = \text{mass} \times \text{gravitational field strength}$$
$$\text{(in newtons, N)} \quad \text{(in kilograms, kg)} \quad \text{(in newton/kilogram, N/kg)}$$

On Earth the value of **gravitational field strength** is 9.8 N/kg, but we usually round it to 10 N/kg for calculations.

The force acting upwards on falling objects is the air resistance. The air resistance gets bigger as they fall faster and faster. They stop **accelerating** when the air resistance is the same size as their weight. Then they are falling at their terminal velocity.

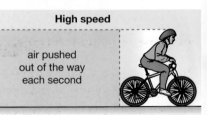

FIGURE 3: What else, other than speed, would change the air resistance?

QUESTIONS

1. Racing cyclists wear streamlined clothing to make their air resistance less. Discuss with a partner how this will affect their top speed.
2. Either mass or weight changes on the Moon. Discuss with a partner which one changes. Do you know why?

...accelerating ...air resistance ...friction ...gravitational field strength

Graphs to show terminal velocity

The **velocity-time graph** in figure 4 shows how the velocity towards the ground changes for a skydiver before and after the parachute opens. So why do these changes happen?

- At A, the weight is bigger than the air resistance. There is a resultant force towards the ground so the skydiver accelerates. But as he accelerates his air resistance increases.

- At B, weight and air resistance are equal. There is no resultant force. He travels at terminal velocity.

- At C, the parachute is open. The air resistance has increased, so it is much bigger than the weight. There is a resultant force upwards, so the skydiver slows down. As he slows down his air resistance decreases.

- At D, air resistance and weight are again equal. The skydiver is again travelling at terminal velocity.

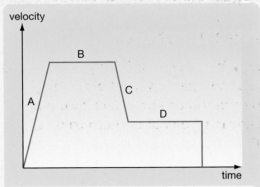

FIGURE 4: When does the skydiver have equal and opposite forces acting on him?

Falling objects reach a top speed, called their terminal velocity

Size matters

You have already seen that the area of something affects its terminal velocity. A skydiver with a parachute open has a smaller terminal velocity than a skydiver without. His air resistance is greater at any particular speed, so it will be big enough to balance the weight when he is travelling at a lower speed.

Does weight affect the terminal velocity too? We can see that it does if we imagine two skydivers each with the same size parachute, but one skydiver much, much heavier than the other. Both skydivers have the same air resistance at the same speed, but when they reach a speed where the air resistance and the weight balance for the light skydiver, the heavy skydiver still has a resultant downward force, because his weight is still much greater than the air resistance, so he is still speeding up.

Watch Out Air resistance increases as speed increases – the object has to push more air particles out of the way.

WOW FACTOR!

Space shuttles falling from above the Earth's atmosphere do not have a terminal velocity as there is no air resistance.

Birdmen

FIGURE 5: Is this really flying?

For hundreds or thousands of years people have dreamed of being able to fly like birds. Between 1930 and 1961, 75 'birdmen' tried to build wing suits to do so – 72 of them died. But now, modern materials have made this dream almost possible. The modern wing suit has parachute material, strengthened with struts, stretched between the legs, and between the arms and legs to create a mini parachute. It is not real flying; the birdman can only go downwards, but the terminal velocity can be as low as 40 kph. A skilled birdman jumping from a plane at 13 500 feet can glide for over 8 km.

QUESTIONS

3   Copy the velocity-time graph for the skydiver and add an extra line to show what you would expect to see if his parachute was much bigger.

4   A spider does not fall like you would but floats gently downwards. Use forces and terminal velocity to explain why.

QUESTIONS

5   Discuss how birdmen might be able to adjust their wing suits to change direction. Discuss the forces involved.

Stop!

You will find out:

- The factors affecting the distance a moving car takes to stop
- The difference between thinking distance, braking distance and stopping distance

Accidents don't just happen

Police and motoring organisations tell us that traffic like this can be very dangerous. If one car brakes suddenly, the car behind may not be able to stop soon enough to avoid an accident. So how can drivers tell what is a safe distance to leave between them and the car in front? It certainly helps to know how far your car will travel while you're trying to stop.

FIGURE 1: When is traffic like this dangerous? Why?

Force it to stop!

You know that when a car travels at a constant speed, the forward force of the engine and the backward forces of air resistance and friction are balanced. There is no **resultant force** on the car. When the driver brakes, friction between the brakes and the wheels increases the backwards force. There is a resultant force backwards on the car and the car slows down.

Imagine a cat runs out in front of the car. A car that is going faster has to brake much harder. The faster car has much more **kinetic energy** to get rid of, so needs a bigger force to make it stop before it hits the cat.

FIGURE 2: What is the link between this damage and the kinetic energy?

Stopping distance

The **stopping distance** tells us how far a car travels before it stops. Imagine a driver sees a hazard ahead. We can split the stopping distance into two parts: the **thinking distance** and the **braking distance**.

- The thinking distance is the distance the car travels while messages race from the driver's eyes to her brain and from her brain to her foot on the brake pedal.
- The braking distance is the distance the car travels while it is slowing down, after the brake pedal has been pressed.

So the stopping distance is given by:

Stopping distance = thinking distance + braking distance

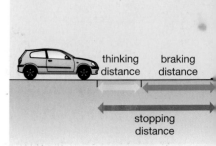

FIGURE 3: What might make the thinking distance or braking distance change?

▥ QUESTIONS ▥

1 Discuss, with a partner, why braking harder makes the car slow down more quickly. Can you decide what forces change and how they affect the way the car moves?

2 Discuss why accidents at high speeds do much more damage to the car and the passengers. Think about how much kinetic energy there is and what happens to it.

...braking distance   ...directly proportional   ...kinetic energy   ...reaction time

Thinking distance and reaction time

The distance a car travels after the driver has spotted the hazard but before he brakes depends on the car's speed. It also depends on the driver's **reaction time**. This is because a faster car travels further in each tenth of a second and a slower reaction time means the car has more time to travel in. We can find the thinking distance using the equation:

Thinking distance = speed x reaction time

A driver's reaction time will be slower than usual if he or she has taken alcohol or drugs, including many prescription drugs, and if he or she is tired. So tiredness, alcohol and drugs all make accidents more likely.

Braking distance

Speed/mph	Thinking distance/m	Braking distance/m	Stopping distance/m
20	6	6	12
30	9	14	23
40	12	24	36
50	15	38	53
60	18	55	73
70	21	75	96

TABLE 1: The relationship between speed, thinking distance, braking distance and stopping distance.

The braking distance of a car depends on its speed. The table shows that the braking distance is not **directly proportional** to the speed. Doubling the speed makes the braking distance increase by four times. The braking distance also depends on the mass of the car. Heavier cars travel further before they stop because they have more kinetic energy to lose.

The braking distance also increases if the size of the friction force decreases. Badly worn brakes or tyres make the friction force less – that is why brakes are tested in an MOT test and why tyres are illegal if they have too little tread. Wet or icy road surfaces make the friction force less too. On a wet road the braking distance can be doubled; on an icy or snowy road it can be up to 10 times as far as on a dry road.

Watch Out Tiredness, taking alcohol or drugs, worn tyres or brakes, wet or icy road surfaces all make accidents more likely.

Aquaplaning

Badly worn tyres are illegal, which may seem odd because a badly worn or bald tyre actually has more tyre in contact with the road and more friction! Bald tyres do actually make stopping distances shorter on a dry road.

On a wet road, tyre treads channel water out from between the tyre and the road. Bald tyres allow a thin layer of water to stay between the tyre and the road, reducing the friction almost to zero and making the car aquaplane, or slide across the surface of the water. That's why racing cars change their tyres when it is wet. Ordinary drivers wouldn't want to change their tyres every time the weather is damp, though!

FIGURE 4: Both these types of tyre have their advantages. What are they?

QUESTIONS

3 Look at table 1. Is the thinking distance directly proportional to speed?

4 Draw a graph of stopping distance against speed.

5 Which, out of thinking distance or braking distance, has most effect on the total stopping distance **a** at low speed, and **b** at high speed?

QUESTIONS

6 Discuss what difference you would expect to see between the tyres on a high performance car and on a family car.

...*resultant force* ...*stopping distance* ...*thinking distance*

Moving through fluids

You will find out:
- Why fluids resist the movement of objects through them
- The factors that affect the size of the resistance of a fluid

Bog snorkelling

The World Bog Snorkelling Championships are held every year in Wales. For some people, it is the perfect leisure activity. It's tough going to complete the course, and even the winners are not going to break any cycling speed records! Can you use forces to explain why they don't go very fast and why they end up very, very fit?

FIGURE 1: This isn't the fastest way to get around on a bike! Do you know why?

What is a fluid?

A **fluid** is anything that flows. Water, and all other liquids, are fluids. Air is a fluid too and so are other gases. You can feel air flowing every time the wind blows, and air also flows around the objects that move through it, such as cars or aeroplanes. A fluid always slows down an object moving through it. It does this in two ways:

- the moving object has to push the fluid particles out of the way
- the moving object rubs against the fluid particles.

When we talk about **air resistance** or **drag** (water resistance), we usually mean the total force of the fluid slowing something down, because of both pushing particles out of the way and rubbing against them.

Forces in fluids

As the **speed** of the object gets faster, the resistance gets bigger as the moving object has to push more particles out of the way each second. The **friction** part of the resistance gets bigger too, because the object rubs against more fluid particles. As the fluid gets **denser**, the resistance gets bigger too, because each bit of the fluid is heavier and so harder to push out of the way.

A body falling through a liquid will initially accelerate due to the force of **gravity**. Eventually, it will reach a **terminal velocity**, when the forward force (its weight) and the resistance (often called the **upthrust**) are the same size as each other.

FIGURE 2: Which of these two will find it easier to run with their card? Discuss why.

▌▌ QUESTIONS ▌▌

1 What is a fluid? Write down **two** examples of fluids.
2 Describe **two** ways in which a fluid slows an object moving through it.
3 Describe why the resistance gets bigger when a fluid gets denser.
4 Draw a labelled diagram to show the forces acting on a body falling at its terminal velocity.

...air resistance ...denser ...drag ...fluid ...friction

Land and water speeds

Boats are usually much slower than cars or aeroplanes. It takes hours to fly to America, but days to go by boat. It is much harder to push water out of the way, than to push air out of the way, so water resistance slows objects down much more than air resistance does. Fast boats, such as hydrofoils or jet skis, are able to go faster than most boats because they lift out of the water at higher speeds to reduce their water resistance.

FIGURE 3: Discuss what makes this faster than a normal boat.

Streamlining

Think about the range of animal shapes. Animals that move through water are much more likely to have a **streamlined** shape than animals that move through air. It takes much more energy to move through water than through air, because the resistance is greater, so a streamlined shape is much more important for an animal that lives in water. Objects that move at very high speed through air, and so have a high air resistance, such as bullets or rockets, also have a streamlined shape.

The Bermuda triangle

The Bermuda triangle is a vast triangle of the Atlantic Ocean off the east coast of America where ships are reported to have vanished without trace. Now scientists have used moving through fluids to attempt to explain the disappearances. Normally a ship floats because the upthrust of the water is equal to the ship's weight. Some scientists have suggested that landslides on the seabed could release bubbles of methane that make the seawater much less dense than usual, so its upthrust is much less, and no longer enough to balance the weight of a ship, which sinks and is covered with mud from the landslide.

FIGURE 4: Can you find any other explanations for why boats sink in the Bermuda triangle?

Ships are reported to have vanished without trace in the Bermuda triangle

Viscosity

Why is it easier to move through water than through oil, even though oil is less dense than water (oil floats on water)?

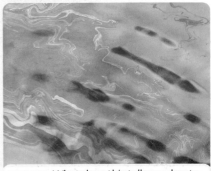

FIGURE 5: What does this tell you about oil and water?

Density is not the only factor that affects the resistance of a fluid. The bonding of the fluid particles is also important. Oil has a higher viscosity than water, which is why it flows more slowly than water. The particles in oil are much more tightly bonded to each other than the particles in water. This means that they are harder to push apart and therefore it is harder for an object to move between them.

QUESTIONS

5 Why is it much easier to swim through water than it is to wade?

6 Racing boats have very narrow hulls. Discuss how this affects their movement through the water and their maximum speed.

7 Do some research to find out more about the Bermuda triangle.

QUESTIONS

8 Work together to devise an experiment to compare the viscosity of two fluids. What factors might cause errors or inaccuracies?

Energy to move

You will find out:
- Examples of energy transformations involving kinetic energy
- What happens to the kinetic energy when objects stop moving
- How kinetic energy, frictional forces and heating are related

Exciting energy

This quad bike clearly has lots of kinetic (movement) energy – most of our exciting sports do! Imagine yourself on the bike. Think about all the types of energy you notice. What are they? Where are they coming from? What energy changes are taking place? Do you know where the kinetic energy of the quad bike comes from originally?

FIGURE 1: What types of energy are there here?

What is kinetic energy?

Kinetic energy is the scientific name for movement energy. Everything that is moving has kinetic energy. The Law of Conservation of Energy tells us that energy cannot be created or destroyed. It cannot just appear or disappear. Kinetic energy can come from many different types of energy:

- our kinetic energy comes from chemical energy in the food we eat
- the kinetic energy of a car comes from chemical energy in the petrol
- the kinetic energy of an electric motor comes from electrical energy transferred in the wires
- the kinetic energy of water from a solar fountain comes from light energy from the Sun.

Kinetic energy can be **transformed** into other types of energy too:

- when a car crashes, its kinetic energy is transformed into **work done** to damage the car
- if you rub your hands together very hard, the kinetic energy is transformed into heat energy in your hands
- the kinetic energy of a loudspeaker moving is transformed into sound energy.

Energy transfer diagrams

An **energy transfer diagram** shows how energy is transferred or transformed by different devices. They can be single stage, like the energy transfer diagram for the bicycle dynamo, or they can have more than one stage, like the energy transfer diagram for the toy car.

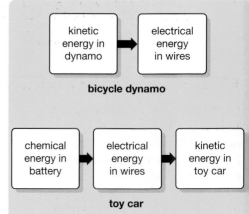

FIGURE 2: What do these energy transfer diagrams show?

॥ QUESTIONS ॥

1   What are the main energy changes that take place when you kick a ball?

2   What energy changes take place when you use an elastic band to fire a paper pellet?

3   Draw an energy transfer diagram to show what happens when you rub your hands together very hard.

4   Draw an energy transfer diagram of your own, involving kinetic energy. Say what device it is for.

...energy transfer diagram   ...frictional forces   ...kinetic energy

Friction and heating

It takes energy to keep a car moving because the car's kinetic energy is continually transformed into work to overcome **frictional forces** (friction). Most of the work done against the frictional forces is transformed into heat.

- Tyres get warm. The air inside tries to expand and the tyre pressure increases, which is why you should always check car tyre pressures after the car has been driven for a while.
- When the car brakes, friction makes the brakes hot. This sometimes caused brakes on early cars to stop working whilst going down long, steep hills!

Some objects, such as spacecraft or meteors, move so quickly through the air that friction against the air particles makes them heat up. Shooting stars are meteors that are glowing white hot because of friction. The material on the inside of non-stick saucepans was originally invented as a super-smooth coating to reduce the friction of spacecraft re-entering Earth's atmosphere, to stop them heating up so much they melted. Passenger aircraft can be up to 20 cm longer in the air than they are on the ground because the heating due to friction makes them expand.

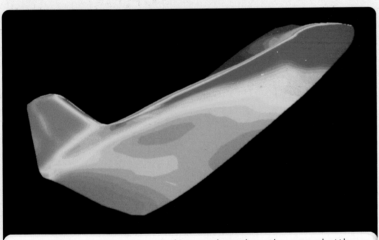

FIGURE 3: This computer-generated image shows how the space shuttle heats up as it re-enters the Earth's atmosphere.

Kinetic energy and potential energy

A swing continually gains height and loses speed, then loses height and gains speed. So the energy keeps changing from kinetic energy to **potential energy** and back again. But at each swing, some of the swing's energy is transformed into work done against friction and air resistance. That is why a swing eventually slows down and stops.

WHAT DOES IT MEAN?

'Kinetic' comes from a Greek word meaning 'to move'. So does 'cinema' – a place with moving pictures.

QUESTIONS

5 High speed aircraft tend to fly at high altitude, where the air is thinner. Suggest some reasons why.

6 When you drop a bouncy ball it never bounces as high as the point from which you dropped it. Use energy transformations to explain why.

WOW FACTOR!

A satellite 1000 km high can orbit Earth for thousands of years. There is no air resistance or friction to slow it down.

Storing kinetic energy

Unlike chemical energy, kinetic energy cannot be stored permanently. On Earth, frictional forces and air resistance ensure that all moving objects slow down and stop eventually. A flywheel, a heavy, spinning wheel, can be used to store kinetic energy for short periods. Flywheels are heavy because a heavy wheel has the same air resistance as a lighter wheel of the same size, so a smaller proportion of the wheel's energy is lost overcoming air resistance. The flywheel spins as fast as possible without breaking the bearings or the axle, because a faster spinning wheel stores more kinetic energy than a slower one.

FIGURE 4: Where does the kinetic energy stored by this flywheel come from? Why is it useful to be able to store it?

QUESTIONS

7 What other types of energy can be stored? How?

8 Discuss situations where it might be useful to store kinetic energy.

Surf's up!

SELF-CHECK ACTIVITY

CONTEXT

Will is 15 and keen on surfing. It's too cold to do much in the winter but as soon as spring comes, he and his friends get their boards out and head for the beach. This usually means a car ride as the rail links don't go near the best beaches and the buses don't take surfboards. Their parents usually take it in turns: this time it's Will's dad's turn. This means four passengers in the car and three short boards strapped to the roof (one of Will's friends rents his board), and this adds to the weight.

People who are into surfing are often into music too and Will usually persuades his dad to put something decent on the car stereo. He sneaks the volume up a bit as well. On the road down to the beach the wind has been blowing the sand around and some has been left on the road surface.

The road doesn't have any pavements and the ground on either side rises quite steeply, so pedestrians are on the road as well as cars. No one's in too much of a hurry, but a couple of lads are play fighting and one is suddenly pushed further out into the narrow road. Will's dad brakes hard and the car slows and then slides. It comes to a rest about a metre from the lad in the road, who gives a sheepish smile and jogs off. A couple of Will's mates swear. They all know it was a bit close that time.

CHALLENGE

STEP 1

Will's dad does a lot of driving, though mostly for work, with just him in the car. He's reluctant to admit it but he was a bit surprised by how far the car travelled before it came to a halt. He wasn't travelling at any great speed because of the narrow road and pedestrians. Why did it take longer?

STEP 2

One of the ways in which we can explain the greater braking distance is by using the concept of kinetic energy. How does this help?

STEP 3

We can also explain the greater stopping distance with reference to friction. How might we do this?

STEP 4

Will's dad's car is fitted with ABS (anti-lock braking system). Find out how ABS works. What difference did ABS make to the braking distance in this case?

STEP 5

The stopping distance of the car is made up of thinking distance and braking distance. How might the thinking distance have been greater in this case?

Maximise your grade

These sentences show what you need to include in your work to achieve each grade. Use them to improve your work and be more successful.

Grade	Answer includes...
F	State that stopping distance is the distance a car travels before coming to rest.
	Suggest factors that will affect the stopping distance of a car from this context.
	Explain how friction affects stopping distance with reference to this context.
	Explain what would cause a car to have more or less kinetic energy.
C	Distinguish between factors affecting thinking distance and those affecting braking distance.
	Find out and explain how ABS works.
A	Suggest what contribution ABS made to the situation described.
	Evaluate the hazards and safety factors of the situation described.

Working hard

You will find out:
- How work and energy are related to each other
- The factors that affect the amount of work done by a force
- How to calculate the work done or the energy transferred by a force

Floating around

Whenever canals go up or down hills, they have locks to lift the boats up or down. It is easy for one person to pull a canal boat into the lock using ropes, but it would certainly be impossible for one person to lift the canal boat without using the lock. Do you know why? And do you know where the energy to lift the boat in the lock comes from?

FIGURE 1: Locks lift boats to a higher level. Do you know how?

Work and energy

Work and **energy** are closely linked to each other. You know that if you do lots of work lifting or moving things, you feel tired and hungry. You have 'used up' lots of energy, and eating food is your body's way of replacing the energy that you have used. It is not really scientific to say the energy has been 'used up'. There is still the same amount of energy, but it has been **transferred** from you to somewhere else, such as to the objects that you move or lift. The more work you have to do to move or lift the objects, the more energy you are transferring. We can say:

Work done = energy transferred

Pushing, pulling and lifting

Every time you use a **force** to make something move, you are doing work, and transferring energy.

- The person with the umbrella is doing work against **air resistance**. His force is transferring energy to the air particles to make them move out of the way of the umbrella.

- The gardener is doing work against **friction**. Most of the energy she transfers will be **transformed** to heat energy, but there will probably be some sound energy too.

- The pet owner is doing work against **gravity**. The energy is being transformed from his muscles into **potential energy** in the dog. The dog has much more potential energy when it is on the table because it is higher.

FIGURE 2: Can you explain how these people are doing work?

■ **QUESTIONS** ■

1. Describe **two** examples of your own to a partner: one example where you do a lot of work and one example where you do a little work.
2. Describe in your own words the connection between using a force and transferring energy.
3. Describe how you are doing work when you climb a ladder.

...*air resistance* ...*distance* ...*energy* ...*force* ...*friction*

How much work?

Who would do more work, a person pushing a bus for 10 metres or a person pushing a bicycle for 10 metres? Who would do more work, a person lifting a box of books into a shopping trolley or a person lifting a box of packets of crisps into a shopping trolley?

■ The amount of work done depends on the force used. Using a large force transfers a lot of energy and does a lot of work.

Who would do more work, a person who carried a rucksack upstairs or a person who carried a rucksack up a mountain?

■ The amount of work done depends on the **distance** the force moves an object.

Calculating the work done

We can combine the two factors affecting the work done in this equation:

work done = force × distance moved in the direction of the force

The force is measured in newtons, the distance in metres, and the work is measured in joules, because the work done is also equal to the energy transferred.

FIGURE 3: Who is doing the most work?

It is very important to measure the distance moved *in the direction of the force*. Gravity acts vertically, and these two people both move their block the same distance vertically, so they both do the same amount of work against gravity, giving their blocks the same amount of extra potential energy. But the person using the ramp does more work in total, because he also does some work against friction as the block slides up the ramp. This work is transferred into heat energy.

Watch Out A force does work whenever it makes something move. Doing work transfers energy.

HOW MUCH?

You would use about 1 joule of energy to lift a medium sized apple from the floor onto a table.

The clock's stopped!

FIGURE 4: Why did this clock stop at this time?

Battery-powered clocks almost always stop with the minute or second hand at the 'quarter to' position when the battery goes flat. This can be explained by considering the energy transferred by the battery and the forces and distances involved. The clock stops when the battery is too flat to supply enough energy to lift the clock hand against gravity. The force needed to lift the hand a given distance does not change as the hand goes round; it depends on the mass of the hand. But the vertical distance the hand has to be lifted against gravity each time it moves, changes as the hand goes round. It is greatest at the 'quarter to' position, so this is where the clock stops.

QUESTIONS

4 Calculate the work done when a force of 40 N moves a block 2 m.

5 Estimate the energy transferred when you climb one flight of stairs. (Your weight is probably in the range 500 N to 750 N.)

6 Discuss why astronauts are able to jump higher on the Moon than on Earth.

QUESTIONS

7 Use your knowledge of forces and energy transferred to explain why steep hills are harder to climb than shallower hills.

...gravity ...potential energy ...transformed ...transferred ...work

How much energy?

You will find out:

- The factors that affect an object's kinetic energy
- Where potential energy and elastic potential energy come from
- How to compare the elastic potential energy of different elastic bands

Archery

When Henry VIII's warship, the Mary Rose, was lifted from the seabed, the bows and arrows were so well preserved that archaeologists were able to work out that the archers must have used a force of 800 N to pull back the bow to fire arrows. They could tell which skeletons had been archers because the arm bones had become thicker and stronger than normal to support the muscles needed to pull this hard.

FIGURE 1: How can this archer make sure her arrow goes as far as possible?

How much kinetic energy?

You know that everything that is moving has **kinetic energy**. But how can you decide how much kinetic energy something has? What factors affect the amount of kinetic energy a moving object has? You can find out by imagining how different moving objects would affect you if they **transferred** all of their kinetic energy to you! The more kinetic energy a moving object transfers to you, the more damage it will do and the more it will hurt!

Imagine a table tennis ball and a golf ball were thrown at you. The golf ball would hurt most. So:

- the kinetic energy of an object increases when its **mass** increases.

Imagine a bullet was thrown at you, and then fired at high speed from a gun. The first might hurt, but the second would kill you. So:

- the kinetic energy of an object increases when its **speed** increases.

Kinetic energy and stopping distance

Do you remember that the **stopping distance** for a car is greater when it is travelling faster? This is because the brakes on a faster car have to do more work, to transfer more kinetic energy away from the car. The maximum friction force of the brakes is always the same size, so if the car is going faster the brakes have to do work for a bigger distance, to transfer the extra kinetic energy away from the car.

Safety: Don't try any of these at home. That would be really stupid and dangerous.

FIGURE 2: Who do you agree with? Why?

Kinetic energy increases when mass or speed increase

QUESTIONS

1. Write down the **two** factors that affect how much kinetic energy an object has.
2. Give **one** example of an object with a high kinetic energy and **one** example of an object with a low kinetic energy.
3. Describe the connection between kinetic energy and stopping distance.

...elastic potential energy   ...kinetic energy   ...mass   ...potential energy   ...speed

Potential energy and elastic potential energy

How could you make a model vehicle that moved by itself? If you didn't have an electric motor, you might just let it roll down a steep ramp, or you might use stretched elastic bands or a blown-up balloon.

- For the ramp, the **potential energy** at the top of the ramp is being **transformed** into kinetic energy at the bottom of the ramp.
- For the elastic band, the **work done** to stretch the band is stored as **elastic potential energy** in the stretched band, and then transformed into kinetic energy.
- For the balloon, the work done to blow up the balloon is stored as elastic potential energy in the inflated balloon, and then transformed into kinetic energy.

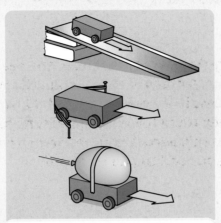

FIGURE 3: Where does the energy to move these vehicles come from?

Investigating the elastic potential energy

We cannot measure elastic potential energy directly, but we can compare the elastic potential energy of stretched elastic bands, for example, by measuring what the stretched bands can do. We can use a stretched elastic band to fire a ball vertically upwards, transforming the elastic potential energy of the band into potential energy of the ball. The more elastic potential energy the stretched band has, the higher the ball will rise.

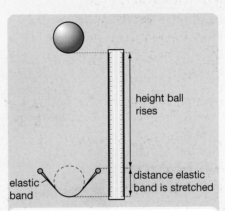

height ball rises

elastic band

distance elastic band is stretched

FIGURE 4: Discuss other ways you could use elastic bands to compare elastic potential energies.

We can calculate the maximum potential energy of the ball using the equation:

maximum potential energy = weight × maximum height

= mass × 10 × maximum height.

The units are joules for energy, kilograms for mass and metres for height.

This is not a direct measurement of the elastic potential energy, because not all of the elastic potential energy of the elastic band will be transformed into potential energy of the ball.

Calculating kinetic energy (H)

The kinetic energy of an object can be calculated from:

kinetic energy = $\frac{1}{2} mv^2$

where m = mass and v = speed.

Suppose a force, F, is used to make a stationary object accelerate steadily up to a speed of v m/s. The kinetic energy gained by the object is the same as the work done by the force. So:

kinetic energy = work done
= force × distance moved

But:

force = mass × acceleration

F = mass × [change in speed ÷ time]

F = m × [(v − 0) ÷ t] = m × v/t

distance moved = average speed × time

d = [(v + 0) ÷ 2] × t = $\frac{1}{2}$ v × t

Putting these together gives:

kinetic energy = F × d
= m × v/t × $\frac{1}{2}$ v × t
= $\frac{1}{2} mv^2$

▨▨▨ QUESTIONS ▨▨▨

6 A mass of 4 kg has a speed of 4 m/s. What is its kinetic energy?

7 A mass of 6 kg has a kinetic energy of 75 J. What is its speed?

Momentum

You will find out:

- What momentum is and the factors affecting it
- The difference between momentum and kinetic energy
- How to investigate the momentum of colliding objects

Playing pool

If you have ever played pool or snooker, you will know it is not as easy as the professionals make it look! Often the balls just do not seem to go in the direction you thought they would. Knowing about their kinetic energy does not help, but there is something that can help predict where the balls will go when you hit them. Scientists call it **momentum**.

FIGURE 1: How could a pool player use science to help improve his or her play?

What is momentum?

Momentum is something you are only likely to hear about in science, though it affects lots of everyday things. Only moving objects have momentum. Momentum tells you about how hard it would be to stop a moving object. An object with a high momentum would be harder to stop than an object with a lower momentum. The momentum of an object can be found from the equation:

momentum = mass × velocity

From this you can see that the momentum increases if the mass increases, and momentum increases if the velocity increases. You know this is true, because heavy objects are harder to stop than lighter objects and fast moving objects are harder to stop than slow moving objects.

FIGURE 2: Explain why the train has high momentum and the bird has low momentum.

Momentum and kinetic energy

At first it sounds like momentum and **kinetic energy** are the same things, but they are not. Kinetic energy is a **scalar** quantity – it has **size** only, not **direction**. You can't have negative energy, and a moving object has the same kinetic energy whatever direction it is moving in.

Momentum is a **vector** quantity. This means momentum has a direction as well as a size, just as velocity does. If two identical objects are moving in opposite directions, one will have a positive velocity and positive momentum and the other will have a negative velocity and a negative momentum.

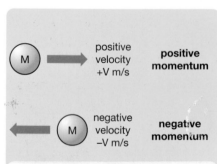

FIGURE 3: Do you know any other vector quantities?

QUESTIONS

1. What types of objects have momentum?
2. Write down the equation for momentum.
3. What happens to the momentum when mass increases?
4. Describe the difference between momentum and kinetic energy.

...conservation of momentum ...direction ...elastic collision ...inelastic collision

Investigating momentum

We can use laboratory trolleys and ticker-timer machines to investigate what happens to the momentum when two objects collide. We use a ticker-timer machine and ticker tape attached to each trolley to find out the velocity of each trolley immediately before the collision, and then again immediately after the collision. Multiplying by the mass of each trolley gives the momentum of each trolley immediately before and after impact. Using a short stretch of ticker tape, such as five or ten dots, gives the velocity in the one tenth or one fifth of a second just before and after impact, which gives more accurate results if the velocity of the trolleys is changing.

There are two types of collision to investigate:

- **Elastic collisions** are where two objects collide and bounce apart. A moving trolley hitting a stationary trolley and both trolleys moving off separately would be an elastic collision.
- **Inelastic collisions** are where two objects collide and stick together. Attaching a pin to a stationary trolley and a cork to a moving trolley ensures they remain stuck together after collision.

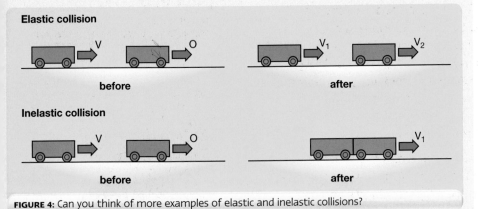

FIGURE 4: Can you think of more examples of elastic and inelastic collisions?

The Law of Conservation of Momentum

Newton showed that when two objects collide and exert a force on each other, the total momentum before the collision is the same as the total momentum after the collision, provided that there are no other forces acting on the two objects. This is called the Law of **Conservation of Momentum** and it is usually written as:

total momentum before collision = total momentum after collision

Therefore, if a 1 kg mass travelling at 10 m/s collides with a stationary 4 kg mass and they move off together, we can find the velocity after the collision using:

$$\textbf{momentum} = \textbf{mass} \times \textbf{velocity}$$
$$(1 \times 10) + (4 \times 0) = (1 \times 4) \times v$$
$$10 + 0 = 5\,v$$
$$v = \frac{10}{5} = 2 \text{ m/s}$$

EXAM HINTS AND TIPS

Remember: kinetic energy is a scalar quantity; momentum is a vector quantity.

Angular momentum

FIGURE 5: How can this skater spin faster?

Momentum tells us how hard it would be to stop a moving object. Angular momentum tells us how hard it would be to stop an object spinning. The angular momentum of an object depends on the mass of the object, the speed it is spinning at, and also the distance of the centre of mass from the centre of rotation. This explains how ice skaters, spinning with outstretched arms, are able to spin much faster by pulling their arms in close to their bodies. As they pull their arms in, the distance from their centre of mass to the centre of rotation decreases. The angular momentum is conserved, and their mass can't change, so the speed they are spinning at must increase.

QUESTIONS

7 Explain the difference between the 'speed an object is spinning at' and the 'velocity of a spinning object'.

QUESTIONS

5 Describe what is meant by an 'inelastic collision'.

6 If two identical trolleys, travelling in opposite directions at equal speeds, collide with each other then bounce apart, discuss the total momentum and how the momentum of each trolley changes.

...kinetic energy   ...mass   ...momentum   ...scalar   ...size   ...vector   ...velocity

Off with a bang!

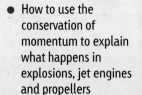

You will find out:

- How to use the conservation of momentum to explain what happens in explosions, jet engines and propellers

FIGURE 1: Can you explain why fire hoses sometimes need two people to hold them?

The hose is alive!

Have you ever dropped a garden hosepipe and seen it flip round soaking everyone nearby? It's more likely to happen if the tap is on full. Fire hoses, with very high-pressure water coming from them, sometimes need two firemen to hold them steady and point them in the right direction. Thinking about the conservation of momentum can tell us why.

Explosions

The Law of **Conservation of Momentum** tells us that when two moving objects collide, the total momentum before the collision is the same as the total momentum after the collision, provided that there are no other forces acting on the objects.

The Law of Conservation of Momentum is also true for explosions. The momentum before the explosion is zero, because nothing is moving. The momentum after the explosion is still zero because one object moves in one **direction** with **positive momentum**, and the other object moves in the opposite direction with **negative momentum**.

If we were able to measure the mass and the velocity of each of the pieces from a real explosion we would find that whatever direction we looked in, the total momentum in that direction was zero. Adding up all the positive momentum would give the same size answer as adding up all the negative momentum.

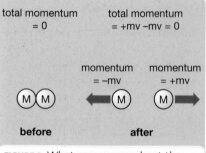

FIGURE 2: What can you say about the velocity of each of these objects?

Balloons and jet engines

It can be fun to blow up a balloon then let it go, and watch it zoom around the room. But why does it do this? The balloon has zero momentum to begin with, when it isn't moving. When you let go, the air rushes out of the neck of the balloon, with a positive momentum. The balloon has to move in the opposite direction, with a negative momentum, so that the total momentum is still zero. Aeroplane jet engines work in the same way. Hot gas rushing from the back of the engine makes the plane move forwards.

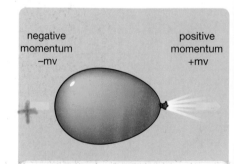

FIGURE 3: Can you explain why the balloon slows down when the air comes out more slowly?

QUESTIONS

1. Write your own version of the Law of Conservation of Momentum to describe what happens to the momentum in an explosion.
2. How does the velocity differ for objects with positive momentum and negative momentum?
3. For the balloon, what happens to the total momentum if the balloon goes faster?

...conservation of momentum ...direction ...mass

Newton's cradle

The Newton's cradle is a popular executive toy that is relatively easy to make using thread and heavy beads. If you lift one bead and let go, one bead will bounce out from the other end of the line. Lifting two beads makes two bounce out from the other end, and so on. All the beads have the same **mass**; so one bead hitting the others transfers just enough momentum through the toy to make one bead move from the other end. Two beads transfer enough momentum for two beads to move from the other end and so on.

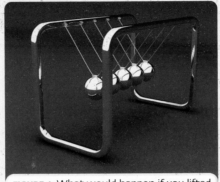

FIGURE 4: What would happen if you lifted three beads and let go?

Using momentum

You have already seen how aircraft engines use momentum. Propellers on boats work in a similar way. The turning propeller pushes the water backwards. The mass of the water being pushed backwards is much smaller than the mass of the boat, but they both have the same momentum. So the **velocity** of the boat is much smaller than the velocity of the water passing through the propeller.

Recoiling guns

When a gun is fired, an explosion inside the gun propels the bullet out of the muzzle of the gun. The gun itself recoils in the opposite direction, or 'kicks'. The gun moves much more slowly than the bullet. Its much larger mass means it has to have a much smaller velocity, to have the same size momentum. Modern guns are designed to allow some of the hot gases from the explosion to leave the gun backwards, balancing some of the bullet's momentum and making the recoil of the gun itself as small as possible.

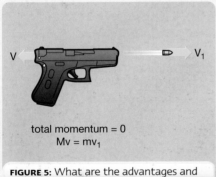

total momentum = 0
$Mv = mv_1$

FIGURE 5: What are the advantages and disadvantages of making the gun lighter?

Steering submarines

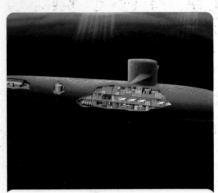

FIGURE 6: Is it possible to steer this submarine using any method other than fins?

Traditionally submarines are steered by moving fins on the outside of the submarine. This does not work well at low speeds and makes the submarine less streamlined, so slower. In 2002 scientists began experimenting with a method already used to steer spacecraft. Three wheels are placed inside the submarine, all at right angles to each other. When the submarine needs to turn, a motor is used to spin one of the wheels. Because angular momentum is conserved, and because the original angular momentum was zero, this tends to make the submarine spin in the opposite direction. Because all the wheels are inside the submarine, it is much more streamlined.

QUESTIONS

7 Discuss how you would solve this problem:

   An ice skater is somehow stuck, stationary, in the centre of a completely friction-free ice rink. How can she reach the edge?

QUESTIONS

4 Use momentum to explain why a boat moves through the water faster when the propeller turns faster.

5 What would happen to the kick of a gun if the bullet had more mass?

6 Use momentum to explain why fire hoses are harder to hold than garden hoses.

Keep it safe

You will find out:

- How a force affects the momentum of a moving object
- The importance of the rate of change of momentum
- How momentum is involved in a range of safety features

A soft landing

Pole-vaulters jump over bars more than 4 m high; the men's world record jump is over 6 m. They land on a soft, bouncy mat and you can easily imagine what it would be like if they landed on sand or on a concrete floor. But why does landing on a soft mat make any difference? See if you know why, when you have finished reading this page.

FIGURE 1: Why is there a soft mat to land on?

Using force

You know that **momentum** is only conserved when no **forces** act on colliding or exploding objects. A force makes the momentum change because a force makes an object:

- speed up or slow down; the **velocity** changes so the momentum changes
- change **direction**; the velocity changes because the direction changes, so the momentum changes.

We can work out how big the change in momentum will be by thinking about the effect that a force has on a moving object. The harder you push or pull something, the more it speeds up or slows down, so the more its momentum changes.

- The change in momentum depends on the size of the force.

The longer you push or pull something for, the more it speeds up or slows down, so the more its momentum changes.

- The change in momentum depends on the **time** for which the force acts.

FIGURE 2: Which sledge will have the bigger momentum change? Can you explain why?

Does the rate of change matter?

When we think about the effect that changing momentum has, we need to think about how quickly the momentum changes, as well as about the amount that the momentum changes. Imagine a car slowing down and stopping.

- If the car slows down gradually, the momentum changes slowly and no harm is done.
- If the car stops really suddenly, the momentum changes very quickly. It takes a very big force to make the momentum change very quickly, and a very big force does lots of damage.

FIGURE 3: What are the forces that stopped these cars? How did the momentum change?

▌▌ QUESTIONS ▌▌

1. List **three** effects that a force can have on a moving object.
2. Describe in your own words why a force makes the momentum change.
3. State the **two** things that affect the size of the change in momentum.
4. Why does a big change in momentum cause a lot of damage?

...direction ...directly proportional ...force ...kinetic energy

Momentum and safety

The change in momentum of a moving object is **directly proportional** to:

- the force acting on the object
- the time for which the force acts.

So increasing the time for which a force acts to stop a moving object means that the force used can be smaller. This is very important in lots of safety features.

- Car seat belts 'give' a little in accidents, allowing a passenger to move forward slightly before the safety belt stops them. Their momentum change is slightly slower, the force on them is slightly less, and so they are slightly less likely to be injured.

- Cars have 'crumple zones', parts of the car bodywork that are designed to crumple on impact. The momentum change is spread out over a slightly longer time, resulting in a smaller force on the car passengers. The damage to the car also absorbs some of the car's **kinetic energy**, leaving less energy to be **transferred** to people.

- High jumpers and pole-vaulters land on padded mats. The mat 'gives' when they land on it, slowing down the rate of change of their momentum and reducing the force on them.

Ow, that hurts!

Kicking a football doesn't hurt, but stubbing your toe on a stone does, even if the stone and the football have the same mass! When you kick a stone, the stone does not change shape. All the change in momentum happens in a very short time. The force is large and hurts your foot. When you kick a football, it changes shape slightly, spreading the change in momentum over a longer time and making the force on your foot smaller.

FIGURE 4: Can you use momentum to explain why kicking the stone hurts?

> *A force on a moving object makes the momentum change*

Momentum and acceleration (H)

Large forces are associated with rapid changes in momentum, because large forces cause large accelerations. Force and acceleration are connected by the equation:

force = mass × acceleration

But **acceleration = velocity change/time**

So **force = (mass × velocity change)/time**

So **force = change in momentum/time**

The units are:

- newtons for force
- kilogram metres/second for momentum
- seconds for time.

Bulletproof vests

Even safety features such as bulletproof vests work by spreading the change in momentum over a longer time, and so decreasing the acceleration and the force. The bulletproof vest is made of many layers of tough material, each of which stretches slightly, slowing down the bullet's rate of change of momentum, and also absorbing some of the bullet's energy.

QUESTIONS

5 Describe **two** ways in which 'crumple zones' reduce injury to car passengers in an accident.

6 Suggest why the rope used by bungee jumpers is designed to stretch.

7 Write a word equation connecting momentum, force and time.

QUESTIONS

8 Suppose a raw egg breaks when the force on it reaches 250 N. If a raw egg of mass 0.05 kg is travelling at a speed of 10 m/s, what is the shortest time you can stop it in, without it breaking?

...momentum ...time ...transferred ...velocity

Static electricity

You will find out:

● Where we might experience static electricity

● How materials gain a static electric charge

● The different types of electric charge and how they affect each other

Lightning

A flash of lightning is a spark of electricity moving between Earth and the clouds. You know that to fly a kite in a storm is extremely dangerous, but early scientists experimenting with electricity didn't – and several of them were killed. Benjamin Franklin worked out that lightning was connected to electric current by flying a kite early in a storm and watching the sparks from a metal key threaded on the kite string!

FIGURE 1: You should NOT do this in a thunder-storm. Do you know what you should do?

Static electricity

Have you ever rubbed balloons on your jumper and then stuck them to walls or the ceiling? Rubbing the balloon gives it **static electricity** and the static electricity makes it stick to the ceiling. There are other places where you can see static electricity too.

■ If you rub a plastic ruler hard with a duster then hold the ruler near a trickle of water from a tap, the water changes direction. Rubbing the ruler puts static electricity on the ruler and the static electricity makes the water move.

■ If you rub a plastic ruler or comb hard with a duster you can use it to make tiny pieces of paper or polystyrene beads jump about. Rubbing the ruler or comb gives it static electricity and the static electricity makes the paper or beads move.

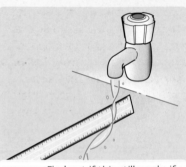

FIGURE 2: Find out if this still works if the water touches the ruler.

What is going on?

You know that all **atoms** have tiny, **electrically charged particles** called **electrons**. When you rub some materials together, some of the electrons are transferred from one material to the other. This makes the materials **attract** or **repel** each other and can make electricity flow between them. That is why you sometimes feel a small electric shock when you touch a car door. Your clothing has rubbed on the car seats and when you touch the car door a tiny spark of electricity flows between you and the car.

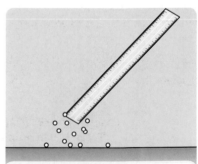

FIGURE 3: Discuss why this does not work with large pieces of paper or heavy beads.

QUESTIONS

1   How could you put static electricity on a plastic ruler?
2   Describe **one** effect the static electricity could have on the ruler.
3   What are electrons?
4   What can happen to the electrons when you rub some materials together?

OUCH!

US Park Ranger Roy Sullivan has survived being struck by lightning a record seven times. Is that very lucky or very unlucky?

...atoms ...attract ...electrical insulators ...electrically charged particles ...electrons

Electric charge

Do you remember that atoms are made from even smaller particles? Some of these particles, called **protons**, have a **positive electric charge** and some, called electrons, have a **negative electric charge**. Rubbing **electrical insulators** together can make electrons move from one material to the other.

- The material that gains electrons ends up with a negative electric charge.
- The material that loses electrons ends up with a positive electric charge.

Whether a material gains or loses electrons depends on what atoms the material is made from. Some types of atoms lose electrons more easily than others.

Investigating charges

We can test different materials to see how different charges affect each other. Figure 4 shows a cellulose acetate strip that has been rubbed to give it an electric charge. We can then hold near it, in turn, another rubbed cellulose acetate strip and a rubbed polythene strip.

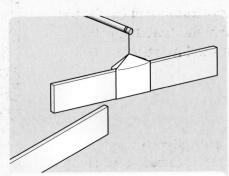

FIGURE 4: What would happen if you held your cellulose acetate rod near the opposite end of the hanging cellulose acetate rod?

The two cellulose acetate strips move apart. They must have the same type of electric charge, because they are the same type of material. The cellulose acetate strip and the polythene strip move together. Polythene and cellulose acetate must have different electric charges, because they behave differently from the two cellulose acetate strips. This tells us that:

- like (similar) charges repel
- unlike (opposite) charges attract.

Scientists found out what type of charge each material had by connecting the charged strips to a very sensitive ammeter and comparing the way the needle moved with the way it moved when a cell was connected to the ammeter. They found that:

- cellulose acetate has a positive electric charge
- polythene has a negative electric charge.

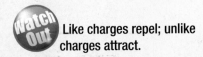 Like charges repel; unlike charges attract.

WHAT'S IN A WORD?

'Electricity' and 'electron' come from the Greek word 'elektros' meaning amber. The Greeks first discovered static electricity by rubbing amber.

Leyden jar

In about 1746 the Dutch physicist Pieter van Musschenbroek was trying to electrify water. He filled a glass jar with water, dipped in a wire and held the wire near a friction machine generating sparks of static electricity. When apparently nothing happened, he moved the jar away and tried to take out the wire – and received an electric shock that made him write in a letter to a friend 'In a word, I believed that I was done for.' A huge electric charge had built up on the inside of the jar and had been unable to flow away through the insulating glass. He had invented the first Leyden jar, a way to store electric charge, which led eventually to the development of batteries and capacitors.

FIGURE 5: The metal round the inside of this Leyden jar means it can store more electric charge.

QUESTIONS

5. Name the **two** types of charged particles in atoms.
6. Describe how rubbing an electrical insulator can give it an electric charge.
7. What would happen if you held two charged polythene strips close together?
8. Two charged strips repel. Suggest how they might behave if you rubbed each one for longer.

QUESTIONS

9. Use the Internet, CD-ROMs or books to find out more about early discoveries about static electricity and electric cells or batteries.

Charge

You will find out:
- The connection between electric charge and electric current
- How to use a gold leaf electroscope to measure and identify electric charges
- What electrostatic induction is, and how it works

Dust that screen!

Unless you have a flat screen television, you will have noticed how quickly the television screen gets dusty. It is as though it attracts dust! The television works by a beam of charged particles hitting the back of the screen and making parts of the screen light up. When you have read this section you will be able to explain why that makes the screen attract dust.

FIGURE 1: Can you explain why this screen gets so dusty?

Charges and force

You have seen how we can use a ruler with a **static electricity charge** to make other objects move. If two strips both have a static electricity charge they try to move together or move apart. They **attract** or **repel** each other. We can say that:

- electric charges exert a force on each other
- like charges (both positive or both negative) repel each other
- unlike charges (one positive and one negative) attract each other.

Electric charges always move closer together or further apart if they can. That is why you cannot put a static electricity charge on a metal strip. The metal is an **electrical conductor**, so electricity can flow easily through it. As fast as your rubbing transfers **electrons** on to, or off, the metal, they flow away to earth through the metal and your hand. So the metal never charges up. The flow of electrons (electric charge) is called an **electric current**.

Measuring charge

We can use a **gold leaf electroscope** to find out if an object has an electric charge.

The gold leaf electroscope is **uncharged**. It has equal numbers of **positive** and **negative** charges all over it.

The negative electric charge on the strip repels the negative electric charges on the electroscope. They move as far away as they can.

The metal rod and the gold leaf both get a negative electric charge. They move away from each other. The gold leaf rises.

The more electric charge the strip has, the more the gold leaf rises.

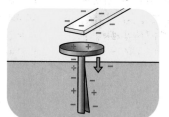 

▌QUESTIONS▐

1 How do 'like charges' affect each other?
2 Describe what an electric current is.
3 What do we mean when we say a gold leaf electroscope is 'uncharged'?
4 Discuss why the gold leaf goes up more when the strip has more electric charge.

WOW FACTOR!

Put your ear close to a television screen after it has been on. You will feel and hear the electrostatic charge.

...attract   ...electric current   ...electrical conductor   ...electrons   ...electrostatic induction

Identifying charges

You have seen how we can use a gold leaf electroscope to find out if an object has an electric charge. We can also use it to find out what type of charge, positive or negative, an object has.

Wipe a charged polythene strip across the cap of the electroscope. The negative charges try to get as far apart as possible, so some of them will move down onto the electroscope.

Remove the polythene strip. The electroscope now has a negative electric charge. The gold leaf stays up.

Holding a negatively charged object near the electroscope repels more negative charges down the metal rod of the electroscope. The gold leaf rises more.

Holding a positively charged object near the electroscope attracts negative charges up to the cap. The gold leaf falls.

Electrostatic induction

Why does rubbing a balloon make it stick to the ceiling? Rubbing the balloon on a woollen jumper gives the balloon a negative electric charge. When the charged balloon is held near the ceiling, the negative charges on the balloon repel the negative charges on the ceiling, leaving the surface of the ceiling with a positive electric charge. The negatively charged balloon and the positively charged ceiling attract each other and the balloon sticks. This is called **electrostatic induction**.

It is much easier to stick balloons to ceilings on dry days than on damp days. Water is a very good conductor of electricity; on damp days the static electricity charge you put on the balloon rapidly flows away through moisture in the air. The balloon does not stay charged long enough to stick.

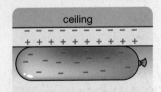

FIGURE 2: Why does rubbing the balloon harder make it more likely to stick?

A flow of electric charge is an electric current

Safe pest control?

Houseflies tend to become positively charged as they walk across carpets and other insulating materials. In 2002 scientists from the University of Southampton used this to make an 'environmentally friendly' fly killer. Pheromones attracted the flies to walk across a walkway that gave them a positive charge, then into a container of negatively charged fly-killing fungal spores. They hope to develop this into a safe way to control a range of insect pests, using natural diseases rather than insecticides that harm the environment.

QUESTIONS

5   How could you put a positive electric charge on a gold leaf electroscope?

6   What would happen to a negatively charged electroscope if you touched the cap with your finger?

7   Use electrostatic induction to explain why television screens get dusty.

QUESTIONS

8   In what conditions will the electrostatic fly killer work best, and worst? Does this matter?

...gold leaf electroscope   ...negative   ...positive   ...repel   ...static electricity charge   ...uncharged

Van der Graaff generator

You will find out:

- What a Van der Graaff generator is and how it works
- How to use moving charges to explain the effects of a Van der Graaff generator

FIGURE 1: Is this as hair-raising as it looks?

The Van der Graaff generator

The Van der Graaff generator is an exciting way to demonstrate some of the effects of static electricity. It can give off sparks several centimetres long; it can make a person's hair stand on end, and many other things. But how does it work? And is it really as dangerous as it looks?

How does a Van der Graaff generator work?

Figure 2 shows how a **Van der Graaff generator** works. The motor turns a roller and a belt, both made from electrical insulators. As the belt moves over the roller, a static electricity charge builds up on the roller and the opposite static electricity charge builds up on the belt. The belt carries the static electricity charge up to the dome at the top of the Van der Graaff generator.

If you stand on an insulating mat and touch the dome of the Van der Graaff generator, your hair will stand on end. Some of the electric charge from the dome spreads out over you. All your hairs get the same type of electric charge, so they all repel each other.

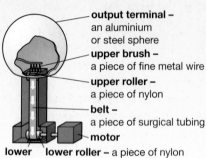

- **output terminal –** an aluminium or steel sphere
- **upper brush –** a piece of fine metal wire
- **upper roller –** a piece of nylon
- **belt –** a piece of surgical tubing
- **motor**
- **lower brush**
- **lower roller –** a piece of nylon covered with silicon tape

FIGURE 2: The belt and the rollers of a Van der Graaff generator are made from electrical insulators. Do you know why?

Making sparks

As you move an electrical conductor, connected to **earth**, towards the dome of the Van der Graaff generator, sparks start jumping from the dome to the conductor. Because the dome has so much electric charge on it, there is a very high **potential difference (voltage)**, between the dome and earth. When the conductor is close enough, some of the charge jumps across the gap and flows away to earth through the conductor. This is the spark of electricity that you see. The Van der Graaff generator is safe to use because, even though it has a very high voltage, the spark only transfers a tiny **electric current**, and not much energy.

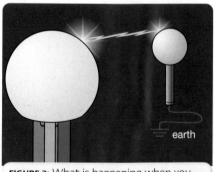

earth

FIGURE 3: What is happening when you see this spark?

QUESTIONS

1. What do you think is meant by an 'insulating mat'?
2. Why are the belt and rollers of the Van der Graaff generator made from electrical insulators?
3. Why is there a very high potential difference between the dome and earth?
4. Describe in your own words what the spark of electricity is.

...*earth* ...*electric current* ...*electrons* ...*induce* ...*ionised*

Moving charges

If you blow soap bubbles near the dome of a Van der Graaff generator, they are attracted to the dome. When they touch – if they don't pop – they are suddenly repelled. Light, polystyrene balls show the same effect. The high static electricity charge on the dome **induces** an opposite charge on the nearer side of the bubble, which is then attracted. If it touches, some of the charge from the dome spreads onto the bubble. The dome and the bubble then have the same charge, so they repel each other.

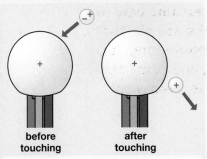

before touching   after touching

FIGURE 4: What do we mean by an 'induced charge'?

FIGURE 5: Can you use moving charges to explain what is happening here?

Can you use a pin to blow out a candle flame? Charges always concentrate at a point. The sharper the point, the more charge it will have. So the pin has a very high static electricity charge. The air nearby is **ionised**; it is split into **electrons** and **positive ions** (atoms with electrons missing). A stream of electrons flows towards the pin, and a stream of positive ions flows the other way, trapping more air particles and carrying them along too. It is this stream of positive ions that blows the candle flame over.

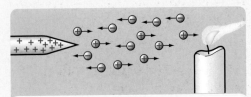

FIGURE 6: What is causing the candle flame to blow over?

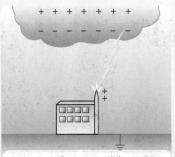

FIGURE 7: What material would you make a lightning conductor from? Why?

Lightning conductors use a sharp point to attract lightning. The static electricity charge on the thunderclouds induces a high charge on the point of the lightning conductor. This makes a spark of electricity (the lightning) more likely to jump to this point, where the current can be conducted safely to earth through the lightning conductor. The noise of the thunder and the crackle of smaller sparks is the sound of the air heating up and expanding very rapidly.

ELECTRIC MONKS!

In the 1740s a French abbot formed a circle of monks, 1 km in circumference, joined together by holding iron rods. When he touched one monk with an early static electricity generator, all the monks shrieked and leapt in the air!

Solar wind

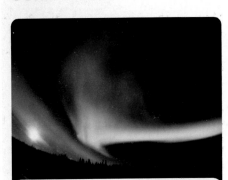

FIGURE 8: The Northern Lights are caused by charged particles from the Sun.

As well as giving out light and heat, the Sun also emits charged particles, called the solar wind. The solar wind contains roughly equal numbers of protons and electrons that travel towards us at an average speed of 400 km/s – that's almost one million miles per hour. The Earth's magnetic field attracts these particles down into the Earth's atmosphere above the poles. The Northern and Southern Lights are caused by these charged particles interacting with gases in the Earth's atmosphere.

QUESTIONS

5 Describe why soap bubbles are attracted to the Van der Graaff generator.

6 It is possible to light a Bunsen burner by putting one hand on a Van der Graaff generator dome and pointing a finger of the other hand at the Bunsen burner. Discuss how this works. (SAFETY: Don't try this – it burns your finger!)

QUESTIONS

7 Discuss whether or not it would be accurate to describe the solar wind as an electric current.

...positive ions   ...potential difference   ...Van der Graaff generator   ...voltage

Sparks will fly!

The Hindenburg disaster

In the 1990s, sixty years after the Hindenburg caught fire, scientists suggested that static electricity was to blame. A static electricity charge had built up on the airship in bad weather. When the damp mooring rope was dropped, some charge flowed to earth, but some of the frame remained charged. A spark jumped, igniting the covering material, which had been stiffened and waterproofed with chemicals used today as rocket fuel.

FIGURE 1: On May 6th 1937 the Hindenburg disaster killed 35 of the 97 passengers on board.

Danger!

You have seen how some of the charge on the dome of a Van der Graaff generator jumps to an **earthed conductor** nearby, making a spark. The same thing can happen with other objects that get a **static electricity charge** on them.

In operating theatres, static electricity charges can build up on **insulating** materials such as plastic mattresses or pillow covers, or medical staff's clothing. Many of the liquids and gases used in operating theatres are flammable and could catch fire or explode if there was a spark. So the floor of the operating theatre is made from an electrical conductor and the air is kept damp.

Aircraft often refuel in mid-air. A 'tanker aircraft' pumps fuel through a long hose to the refuelling aircraft. But aircraft fuel is flammable and aircraft can build up a static electricity charge, especially if they have flown through clouds. So a conducting wire is connected between the aircraft before refuelling starts, to make sure that any charge spreads out evenly over both aircraft.

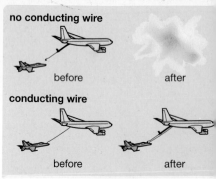

FIGURE 2: Can you explain why the conducting wire is necessary?

Paint spraying

Static electricity can be very useful too. Car manufacturers know that as paint is sprayed from a spray gun, the paint droplets get a static electricity charge. Giving the car bodywork the opposite charge makes more of the paint droplets stick to the car bodywork, so the car gets a more even coat of paint and less paint is wasted.

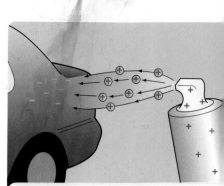

FIGURE 3: What would happen if the car bodywork were positively charged?

QUESTIONS

1. Describe what is happening when you see a spark from a Van der Graaff generator dome.
2. What does the conducting wire between refuelling aircraft do?
3. How does keeping the air in an operating theatre damp help stop a build up of static electricity?
4. Give **two** benefits of using static electricity in painting cars.

...earthed conductor   ...high voltage   ...induce   ...insulating   ...ionise

Cleaning oil tanks

Oil tankers and large oil storage tanks are cleaned using high-pressure water hoses. The nozzles of the hoses are always made from metal and always connected to earth, so that charge cannot build up on them. If friction caused a build up of charge on the nozzle or the water jet, a spark could cause oil vapour in the tank to explode.

Cleaning up pollution

Power stations and other industries often use a device called a smoke precipitator to trap smoke particles in their chimneys, reducing pollution. **High voltage** wires in the centre of the chimney **ionise** the air. The ionised air particles **induce** a charge on smoke particles, and stick to them. The charged smoke particles then stick to earthed metal plates at the edges of the chimney.

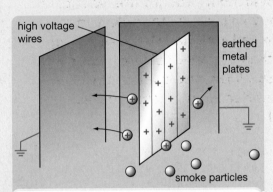

FIGURE 4: Suggest a reason why the charged smoke particles stick to the earthed metal plates.

Photocopying

Photocopiers use static electricity. Inside is a drum that is **photoconductive** – it conducts electricity when light shines on it, but not when it is dark.

- The drum is given a **positive charge**.
- A bright light reflects from the white parts of the document you are copying onto the drum below, but not from the dark parts. The positive charge flows away from the parts of the drum the light hits.
- **Negatively charged** black toner pigment is spread onto the drum, but only sticks where the drum is positively charged.
- A positively charged sheet of paper passes over the drum, attracting the toner away from the drum.
- The sheet of paper is heated to make the toner stay permanently stuck to the paper.

Charge cannot build up on earthed conductors

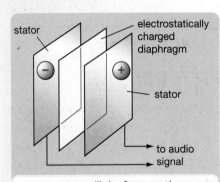

QUESTIONS

5 Why are the nozzles of hoses used to clean oil tankers earthed?

6 What does 'ionised' mean?

7 In a photocopier, discuss which has the larger positive charge: the drum or the paper.

8 Use the Internet or other sources to find out more about the Hindenburg airship.

Electrostatic speakers

Static electricity is used in very high quality loud speakers. In a traditional speaker a cone vibrates back and forth, moved by an electromagnet. The cone is heavy and slow to move, so poor at reproducing high frequency sounds. An electrostatic speaker has a very thin, plastic diaphragm, with a static electricity charge on it, suspended between two conducting plates called stators. The music signals are split into two high voltages of equal size but one positive and one negative. One voltage signal goes to each stator. The charge on the movable diaphragm means that it is pushed by one stator and pulled by the other. Because the moving diaphragm is so light, it can respond very quickly to changing frequencies and so produces a very high quality sound.

FIGURE 5: How will the force on the diaphragm change as the voltage on the stators changes?

QUESTIONS

9 Discuss the disadvantages an electrostatic speaker has compared with a traditional speaker.

Unit summary

Concept map

Distance-time graphs help us to 'picture' how something moves – the slope of the graph shows the speed.

Every moving object has momentum that depends on its mass and its velocity. Momentum has a direction as well as a size and is conserved in collisions and explosions. The bigger the force on a moving object, the larger its rate of change of momentum.

The velocity of something tells us its speed and direction. Acceleration is the rate of change of velocity. Velocity-time graphs show how the velocity changes – the gradient shows the acceleration; the area under the graph shows the distance travelled.

Motion and forces

Using a force to do work on an object gives it energy. The bigger the force and the bigger the distance it moves through, the more work is done and the more energy the object gains.

Every moving object has kinetic energy that can be transformed into other forms. The faster the object, the more kinetic energy it has.

Forces can add up or cancel out to give a resultant force. Whenever there is a resultant force, an object accelerates. The acceleration is bigger if the force is bigger, and smaller if the mass is bigger.

Objects moving through fluids are slowed down by drag; this gets larger when the fluid gets denser.

When objects are in contact, they exert equal and opposite forces on each other.

A falling or moving object reaches terminal velocity when the forces on it are balanced.

The stopping distance of a car is the thinking distance plus the braking distance. This increases as the speed increases.

Rubbing electrical insulators together can give them a static electricity charge, because electrons transfer from one material to the other.

Static electricity

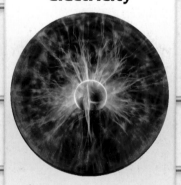

Static electricity can be dangerous if sparks cause flammable materials nearby to ignite or explode; but it can be useful in devices such as paint sprayers, smoke precipitators and photocopiers.

If an object gains electrons it has a negative charge; if it loses electrons it has a positive charge.

A charged object will discharge to an earthed conductor nearby – this is seen as a spark.

Similar charges repel each other. Opposite charges attract each other.

A gold leaf electroscope shows the size and type of charge.

Unit quiz

1. How would a distance-time graph show a slow speed?

2. Explain the difference between speed and velocity.

3. What does the area under a velocity-time graph show?

4. Which of the following does the acceleration of an object depend on?

   its mass   its speed   force

5. Describe what is meant by terminal velocity and explain when an object would reach terminal velocity.

6. What factors affect the thinking distance travelled by a car before stopping?

7. Describe two things that would increase the terminal velocity of an object moving through a fluid.

8. Calculate how much work is done by a force of 600 N moving an object a distance of 15 m.

9. Describe the energy changes that occur when a swing moves to and fro.

10. Which of the following three terms is the odd one out? Explain why.

    velocity   speed   momentum

11. Explain how the 'crumple zones' on a car help reduce injury to passengers in an accident.

12. Rubbing a particular electrical insulator makes it positively charged. Explain what happens to the electrons.

13. A gold leaf electroscope has a negative charge. Bringing a charged object near the cap of the electroscope makes the gold leaf fall. What is the charge on the object? How do you know?

14. Describe a situation where static electricity could be dangerous. What could be done to make it safe?

Numeracy activity

The distance-time graph opposite depicts an inelastic collision between two trolleys. The first part of the graph shows trolley A of mass 200 g travelling on its own. The second part shows what happens after trolley A hits trolley B and they move off together.

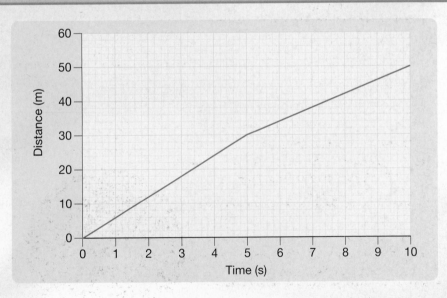

QUESTIONS

1. Calculate the velocity of trolley A when it is travelling on its own.
2. What is the velocity of trolley A and trolley B when they are moving together?
3. Calculate the momentum of trolley A before the collision.
4. Using the conservation of momentum in an inelastic collision, calculate the mass of trolley B.

Exam practice

Exam practice questions

1 The diagram shows an experiment to measure the time taken for a ball to fall through a liquid.

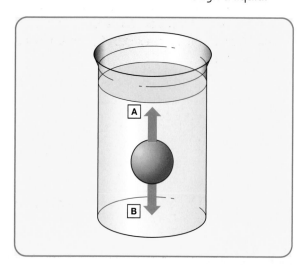

a Name force A and force B. [2]

b Initially the ball accelerates, then reaches a steady speed. What is the name given to this steady speed? [1]

c Explain why the resultant force changes as the ball accelerates. [2]

d Explain, in terms of forces, why the ball eventually falls at a steady speed. [1]

2 **a** Calculate the acceleration of a tennis ball that reaches a speed of 35 m/s after 0.1 s. [3]

b What force is needed to cause this acceleration? (The mass of the tennis ball is 0.2 kg) [3]

3 The diagram shows two supermarket trolleys being pushed towards each other.

a Calculate the momentum of each trolley. [4]

b The two trolleys collide and join up. Explain which direction the two trolleys will travel in after the collision. [2]

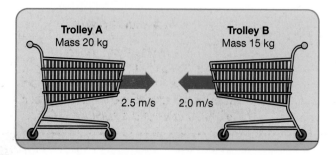

Trolley A
Mass 20 kg
2.5 m/s

Trolley B
Mass 15 kg
2.0 m/s

4 **a** A girl rubs a balloon against her sleeve. Explain, in terms of movement of charged particles how the balloon can become negatively charged. [2]

b Copy the diagrams below and draw arrows to show the direction of the force that the balloons feel when they are placed near each other. [2]

i

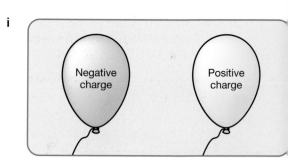

Negative charge   Positive charge

ii

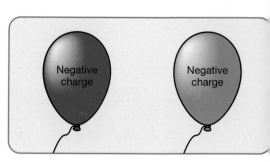

Negative charge   Negative charge

A boiler manufacturer uses powdered paint to spray onto metal surfaces before they are heated. When the powder melts, a strong paint surface is created.

c When the powder is sprayed, the particles are given the same electrostatic charge. Explain why this ensures a thin, even coverage. [2]

d The metal surface is given an opposite charge to the powder. Explain why this ensures little wastage of paint. [2]

5 The table gives information about the speed of a lift.

Time (s)	Speed (m/s)
0	0
1	0.9
2	1.8
3	1.8
4	1.2
5	0.6
6	0

a Plot a velocity-time graph for this trip. [4]

b Label the section of the graph where the lift was accelerating as A, and where it was travelling at a steady speed as B. [2]

c Use your graph to calculate the distance travelled by the lift [4]

6 A lump of rock has a mass of 2.5 kg and was taken from the moon back to Earth. Gravity on the moon is 1.67 N/kg

a Calculate the weight of the rock on the moon. [3]

b The astronaut lifts the rock and holds it steady while still on the moon. State the size and direction of the force exerted by the astronaut on the rock. [2]

(Total 41 marks)

Worked example

A child runs out into the road in front of a car. The distance it takes the car to stop depends on the thinking time and the braking time.

a How does an increase in the driver's thinking time affect the stopping distance? [1]

b State two factors that affect the braking distance. [2]

c State how the braking force must change for the car to stop in the same distance if it is travelling faster initially, and explain, in terms of work done, why this is the case. [4]

This is not enough for the mark – the stopping distance will increase.

a It changes it.

The pupil gets one mark for this answer but has totally forgotten the explanation.
Work done = kinetic energy transferred by the braking force
= force × distance moved.
The car has more kinetic energy to begin with, so more work is done by the brakes. The distance is the same so the force must increase.

b The condition of the road and whether the driver has been drinking or not.

Two marks as both points are correct. Also the weather conditions, lighting conditions, any distractions in or out of the car will have an effect.

c The braking force is harder.

Overall Grade: D

How to get an A

Although the question looks simple, the examiner wanted detailed explanations. Take care to read questions carefully so your answers contain all the information that is needed.

DISCOVER NUCLEAR FUSION!

Nuclear fusion is the joining of two hydrogen molecules to form helium and an enormous release of energy. This process is how stars fuel their core energy.

In a star, gravity pulls together molecules of hydrogen gas. As more molecules come together mass increases and so does the force of gravity.

Eventually gravity is so strong that it compresses the hydrogen until the temperature gets high enough for it to spontaneously fuse.

Nuclear fusion is the energy source of the future. There is plenty of hydrogen and it is clean, with none of the radiation problems associated with fission. But it does require a temperature of 15 million Kelvin and we do not currently have the technology to control the reaction.

CONTENTS

Circuit diagrams

You will find out:
- How to interpret and draw circuit diagrams using standard symbols
- About series and parallel circuits

The professor and the physicist

The first 'electric battery' was invented by an Italian professor, Count Alessandro Volta in 1800. In deference to his work, the driving force which pushes current around a circuit was called the 'Volt'. Just a few years later, in 1820, the French physicist André Ampère brought the two concepts of electricity and magnetism together and developed a way of measuring current. The unit of current is named after him: the 'Ampere'.

Symbols

As the science of electricity developed, electrical circuits and components became more numerous and complex. A short-hand method of writing down these circuits was invented so that other scientists could reproduce the circuits. A new language of symbols and circuit diagrams was born.

WOW FACTOR!

Electricity is the flow of electrons around a circuit.

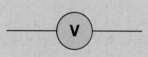

open switch

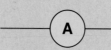

closed switch used to make and break electrical circuits

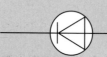

cell a single unit producing electricity

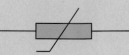

battery several cells connected together

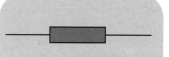

resistor a component which slows down the flow of current in a circuit

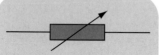

variable resistor a component in which the resistance can be varied

lamp a device which gives out light

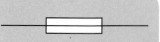

fuse a component which protects equipment from electrical surges

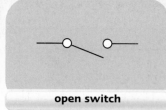

voltmeter an instrument which measures the potential difference across a component

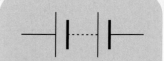

ammeter an instrument which measures the current flowing in a circuit

diode a component that makes sure that current flows only in one direction

thermistor a component whose resistance is affected by temperature

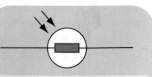

LDR (light dependent resistor) a component whose resistance is affected by the amount of light shining onto it

QUESTIONS

1. Make a list of electrical components and draw the correct symbol beside each one.
2. What is the difference between a cell and a battery?
3. Which are the **two** instruments which measure electricity?
4. Name the **two** components whose resistance is affected by temperature and light.

...ammeter ...battery ...cell ...closed switch ...diode ...fuse ...in parallel ...in series

Circuits

Series circuit

Figure 1 shows a circuit with two lamps connected **in series**. The switch is closed so the circuit is complete. The ammeter measures the current flowing 'in' the circuit (ammeters are always connected 'in' to the circuit). The voltmeter measures the potential difference (p.d.) 'across' the lamp (voltmeters are connected 'across' a component). In a series circuit, the current flowing is the same at any point in the circuit.

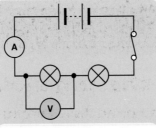

FIGURE 1: Series circuit.

Parallel circuit

Figure 2 shows a circuit with two lamps connected **in parallel**. Current behaves differently in a parallel circuit. When current comes to a junction it splits. The sum of the splits must always equal the amount going into the junction.

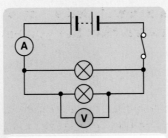

FIGURE 2: Parallel circuit.

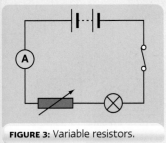

FIGURE 3: Variable resistors.

Variable resistors

Figure 3 shows a circuit with a lamp and a variable resistor. Moving the slider up and down varies the resistance in the circuit. The higher the resistance the more difficult it is for current to flow through the circuit. The lower the resistance the easier it is for current to flow.

Fuses

Figure 4 shows a circuit with a lamp and a fuse. If too much current flows through the circuit, the lamp will burn out. But with a high current, the fuse gets hot and melts. This breaks the circuit and protects the lamp from damage.

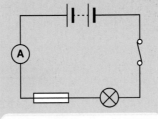

FIGURE 4: Fuses.

Energy givers – energy takers

The principle of conservation of energy works in circuits. The cell or battery is the 'energy giver'. The lamp is the 'energy taker'. The amount of energy given by the cell must equal the energy taken by the lamps.

In the series circuit, the sum of the voltages (p.d.) across each lamp must equal the voltage (p.d.) provided by the cell. The current remains the same at all points in the circuit.

In the parallel circuit, the voltage (p.d.) across each lamp is the same as that of the cell. The sum of the currents flowing through each lamp must equal the current given by the cell.

QUESTIONS

9   In figure 1, the battery provides a p.d. of 12 volts. Assuming the two lamps are identical, what is the p.d. across each lamp?

10 In a parallel circuit (figure 2), what is the p.d. across each lamp?

11 In figure 3, imagine you had a voltmeter across the lamp. Can you work out what would happen to the p.d. across the lamp as you altered the variable resistance?

QUESTIONS

5   In figure 1, how could you get the lamp to give a brighter light? Explain your answer. How will this affect the current flowing in the circuit?

6   In figure 2, the ammeter reads 3 amps. If the two lamps are identical, how much current will flow through each lamp? Explain your answer. What happens to the current on the other side of the lamps where the junctions join back together?

7   In figure 3, what will happen to the brightness of the lamp as the variable resistance increases? Explain your answer.

8   In figure 4, the fuse is fitted in series with the lamp. What would happen if the fuse were fitted in parallel with the lamp? Explain your answer.

Resistance 1

You will find out:
- About the concept of electrical resistance
- What insulators, semi-conductors and super-conductors are

Energy carriers

Electricity is our most common source of energy. Almost every utensil, appliance and convenience is powered by electricity, including lights, radio, TV, telephone, kettle, hairdryer, washing machine and lawn mower. And it's all done by tiny electrons moving along copper wires. Each electron carries a little charge. The charge is given up to the appliance and that is how a kettle gets the energy to heat water for a cup of tea. Millions of electrons continually carry tiny amounts of charge from the energy giver to the energy taker.

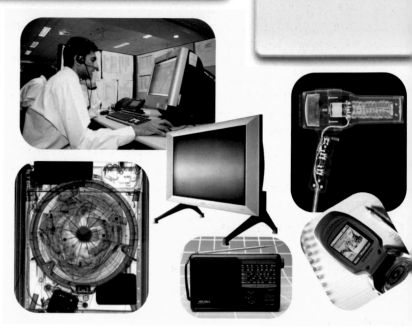

Electrons on the move

You will recall that electricity is the flow of **electrons** around a circuit. This means that the electrons must be moving through the solid copper wires that connect the components of the circuit. How can this be? You will also remember that the wire is made from copper atoms and that atoms are mostly empty space. Electrons travel through the spaces between the atoms of the wire.

The problem is that the electrons do not have a clear run through the wire. As they move along, they 'bump' into atoms of copper. Every time they **collide** with an atom they slow down. The more bumps or collisions, the more the flow of electrons slows down. The slower the flow of electrons, the smaller the current will be. This slowing down effect on electrons is called **resistance**.

A wire with high resistance will reduce the current flowing through it because electrons are experiencing lots of collisions with the atoms in the wire. A wire with low resistance will allow a large current to flow through it because electrons have few collisions and move along with little disturbance.

FIGURE 1: Electrons travel through the spaces between the atoms of the copper wire.

QUESTIONS

1. How can electrons move through a solid metal wire?
2. What obstacles do the electrons experience as they try to move through the wire?
3. Explain, in your own words, the idea of resistance.
4. Which has the lower resistance: a long wire or a short wire? Explain your answer.

...collide   ...electrons   ...force of repulsion   ...nucleus

Resistance

Let's have a closer look at what is going on inside the wire.

- When a potential difference (**voltage**) is applied across the wire, it creates an electric field. Within this field all electrons experience a force which pushes them along the wire.

- You will recall that electrons carry a negative charge. You will also remember that all atoms have shells of electrons surrounding the **nucleus**. As the electron begins to approach the outer electron shells of an atom, the two sets of negative charges begin to repel each other.

- This **force of repulsion** deflects the electron and slows it down. As more electrons are slowed down, the average speed of the electron flow decreases. This results in a reduction in current flowing through the wire.

- This effect of slowing down the flow of electrons is called resistance.

- The higher the resistance of a wire, the more constrained the current flowing. The lower the resistance in a wire, the easier it is for current to flow.

Resistance in metals

Metals consist of a lattice of atoms where some of the outer shell electrons are free to move around. This is why metals are good conductors with low resistances.

Insulators

These are materials where the atoms bind in such a way that there are no free electrons to carry electric charge. This is why insulators are poor conductors and have very high resistances.

Semi-conductors

These are special materials that have properties part way between those of conductors and insulators.

Super-conductors

These are certain metals and ceramic materials which have almost zero resistance when they are cooled down to very low temperatures.

> ### PERPETUAL MOTION?
>
> Once a current is set in motion through a superconductor it will flow forever. This is the closest thing to perpetual motion in nature.

Relationship between p.d. and current

- You might visualise that, as the potential difference increases, there is more push to drive electrons round the circuit, so current increases. Equally, if the resistance increases, it chokes the current flowing. If the resistance is high enough, all current will stop flowing.

- There is a relationship between the potential difference which pushes electrons around a circuit, the current flowing and the resistance of the wire. They are related by the equation:

potential difference = current × resistance
(volt, V)   (ampere, A) (ohm, Ω)

or **V=IR**

This is known as **Ohm's Law**.

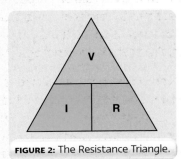

FIGURE 2: The Resistance Triangle.

QUESTIONS

9 What potential difference is needed to push a current of 3 A through a 4 Ω resistor?

10 A resistor of value 12 Ω has a potential difference of 6 V across it. What is the current flowing?

11 A resistor has a potential difference of 12 V across it and a current of 2 A flowing through it. What is the value of the resistor?

QUESTIONS

5 When a potential difference is placed across a conductor, what is created and what effect does this have on electrons?

6 Explain why electrons slow down as they move through a wire.

7 Explain the idea of resistance.

8 Do you think wires made from different materials have the same resistance? Explain your reasoning.

Resistance 2

Michael Faraday

Michael Faraday (1791–1867) was born into a poor family and only learned to read when he was apprenticed to a book binder. He was self-taught and went on to develop all the first modern ideas about electricity. He built the first electric transformer and generator and coined words like electrode, anode, cathode, ion and electrolyte. Faraday also worked on the theory of electric induction and static electricity.

FIGURE 1: Michael Faraday.

The long and the thin of it?

You will recall from the previous chapter that resistance has to do with the number of collisions electrons have as they pass along a wire. We are going to apply this principle to a number of practical applications.

Long wire – short wire

Imagine an electron moving through a long copper wire. As it moves along, the chances are that it will encounter many 'bumps' and collisions with the big atoms of copper. The more collisions, the more the electron will slow down. You would see this as a greater **resistance**.

The longer the wire, the greater the resistance.

The opposite also holds true. An electron moving through a short wire will still experience collisions, but not so many.

The shorter the wire, the lower the resistance.

Thick wire – thin wire

Imagine the electron moving through a thick wire. You might think a thick wire will have more atoms so more collisions. However, a thick wire does have more atoms but it also has more spaces between the atoms. The electron will find it easier to get through.

The thicker the wire, the lower the resistance.

The opposite holds true for a thin wire. A thin wire has fewer spaces for the electron to pass through. This increases the chances of 'bumps' and collisions with copper atoms.

The thinner the wire, the greater the resistance.

QUESTIONS

1. What happens to the resistance in a wire as the wire gets longer?
2. Explain the physics behind your answer.
3. What happens to the resistance in a wire as the wire gets thinner?
4. Explain the physics behind your answer.

...*accelerated* ...*deflections* ...*kinetic energy* ...*repulsions*

Other factors affecting resistance

Temperature

Electrons moving through a copper wire are deflected and slow down as they approach the copper atoms in the wire. If the wire is heated, the atoms gain in **kinetic energy** and begin to **vibrate** more. How would this affect the electrons? Would there be more or less interactions between an electron and copper atoms?

With the copper atoms moving about more, the chances of a collision would increase. The electron would encounter more **repulsions** and **deflections** and a greater slowing down.

> *As a wire gets hotter the resistance increases.*

Material

Different materials will have different atomic structures. The atoms may be larger or smaller than copper. They may be closer or further apart. A material with larger atoms closer together may offer more resistance to the electron moving through it. A material with smaller atoms further apart may offer less resistance to the electron.

> *Different materials will have different resistances.*

Specialist materials

Almost all electric cable is made from copper. Wire that carries electricity needs to have as small a resistance as possible to allow an easy path for the electrons. High resistance would slow down the flow of electricity and much energy would be wasted as heat.

FIGURE 2: Wire that carries electricity is usually made from copper. High voltage wires are made from aluminium.

The wire that is used in light bulbs and electric bar heaters has quite the opposite characteristics. In this case we want the wire to get hot and give off heat and light. So we choose a wire that has a very high resistance.

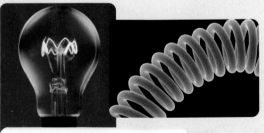

FIGURE 3: The wire in light bulbs is made from tungsten.

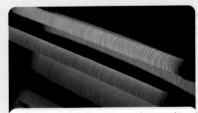

FIGURE 4: Nichrome is used to make electric bar heaters.

Why does a wire get hot?

When electrons move through a wire and experience repeated repulsions, the kinetic energy of the moving electron is absorbed by the atom. This **transfer of energy** leaves the electron moving more slowly and the atom gradually increasing its level of vibration.

Because the wire is surrounded by an electric field created by the potential difference across the wire, the electron is once again **accelerated** forward and gains in speed, until the next collision.

This continuing process of acceleration and energy transfer increases the kinetic energy (and vibration) of the atoms which we see and experience as the wire getting hotter.

QUESTIONS

5　How does heat affect the atoms inside a material?

6　Describe how heating a metal wire would influence how an electron moves along the wire.

7　Explain how different metal wires might have different resistances.

8　Explain why copper wire is used to carry electricity and tungsten is used in light bulbs.

QUESTIONS

9　Explain why the temperature of a wire increases as current flows through it.

10　Can you suggest which factors might affect the rate of temperature increase?

Ohm's Law

You will find out:
- That the resistance in a wire is proportional to the potential difference and the current flowing

Georg Simon Ohm

Georg Simon Ohm (1789-1854), was a German physicist born in Erlangen. His most important work exerted an important influence on the development of the theory and applications of electric current. Ohm's name has been incorporated in the terminology of electrical science in Ohm's Law and adopted as the SI unit of resistance, the ohm (symbol Ω).

FIGURE 1: Georg Simon Ohm.

Resistance

Georg Ohm worked out the relationship between **potential difference** and the **current** flowing in a wire. He set up a simple electric circuit and carried out a series of measurements.

Connecting up the circuit as in figure 2, Ohm adjusted the **variable resistor** until there was zero voltage across the resistor. He noted the values of **voltage** and current on a table of results.

He adjusted the variable resistor again until he got a small voltage across the resistor and noted readings of voltage and current. This sequence was repeated to obtain a series of at least five or six pairs of readings.

The values of voltage and current were plotted on a graph (figure 3).

Ohm found that the graph was a straight line. As voltage increases, so does the current. The straight line showed that the resistance of the resistor was constant.

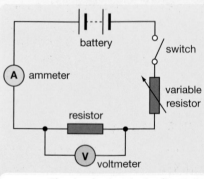

FIGURE 2: The simple electric circuit set up by Georg Ohm.

The value of the resistance can be calculated by using the formula:

$$\frac{\text{voltage}}{\text{current}} = \text{resistance}$$

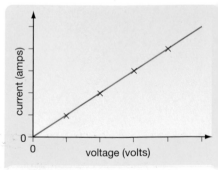

FIGURE 3: Ohm's graph to show the values of voltage and current.

▌▌ QUESTIONS ▌▌

1 When setting up and carrying out an experiment with electric circuits, what should you do between each set of readings? Can you explain why?

2 How many readings should you take when doing an investigation experiment?

3 Write down the formula for Ohm's Law. If a resistor has a potential of 10 V across it and it is carrying a current of 2 A, what is the value of its resistance?

4 If a bulb operates at a p.d. of 3.0 V and carries a current of 0.5 A, what is the resistance of the bulb?

...current ...diode ...Georg Ohm ...lamp

The lamp

Set up the circuit (figure 2) but replace the resistor with a lamp. Repeat the same sequence of adjustments and readings as with the resistor experiment and note the pairs of values for potential difference and current. Plotting the graph of voltage against current gives quite a different shape of graph (figure 4). It is a curve which shows current beginning to level off as voltage increases.

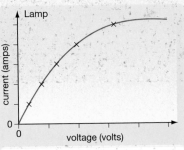

FIGURE 4: Current begins to level off as voltage increases.

The diode

This is a specialised component which allows electricity to flow only in one direction. If you look at the symbol, the arrowhead shape shows the direction of current flow and the vertical line symbolises a wall which stops current flowing backwards. In the backwards direction the diode has a very high resistance. Set up as before (figure 2) and repeat the procedure to obtain a table of paired readings. Plot the values of voltage against current. The graph (figure 5) has quite a unique shape. The line runs along the voltage axis and then moves off as a straight line, rather like the resistor.

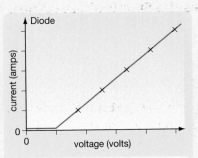

FIGURE 5: The line runs along the voltage axis then moves off as a straight line.

Why the differences?

- **Resistor**: The resistor always behaves in the same way as long as its temperature remains constant. It has the same resistance irrespective of the combination of voltage and current. The main thing is not to allow the resistor to heat up, so always switch off the current when not taking readings.

- **Lamp**: As the lamp filament heats up, the atoms begin to vibrate more vigorously. The moving atoms increase the chances of a collision for the electrons; hence an increase in resistance. The hotter the filament, the higher the resistance. This is why the graph shows current flattening out.

- **Diode**: The diode is a semi-conductor which will allow current to flow in one direction only. When the voltage is negative, the current is zero. It requires an initial activation voltage, usually about 0.6 V, before it allows electricity to flow. You can see this in the shape of the graph. After the activation voltage, the diode behaves just like a normal resistor.

Three graphs

We have drawn the graphs with positive potential difference and current. But they can also be negative. The three diagrams below show the full graphs of each electrical component.

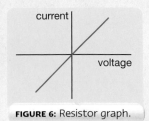

FIGURE 6: Resistor graph.

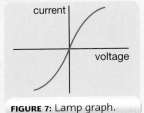

FIGURE 7: Lamp graph.

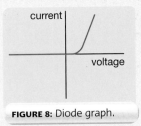

FIGURE 8: Diode graph.

QUESTIONS

5 Sketch out the electrical circuit that you would use to investigate the resistance of a lamp. Draw the full graph of voltage against current. Take care to note which axis is voltage and which is current.

6 Describe in words the shape of the graph. What happens to the current as voltage increases?

7 Can you explain what is happening to the resistance of the lamp as you increase the voltage?

8 Compare the graphs of a straight resistor and the diode. In what way do they differ? In what way are they similar?

QUESTIONS

9 Given the graph of current against p.d. for a resistor, how could you calculate the value of the resistance?

10 Explain why the resistance of a bulb is not constant, but increases with p.d. and current.

11 Describe how a diode works.

More components

You will find out:
- The characteristics of the thermistor and the light dependent resistor
- How we use thermistors and light dependent resistors

Superconductors

Superconductors are metal alloys or compounds which lose their resistance when they are super-cooled down to temperatures of 4 K. This is done by using liquid helium. If a material has zero resistance, current can flow through it without causing any heating effect and loss of energy. Superconducting technology is used in Magnetic Resonance Imaging (MRI) scanners in medicine. It is also used in Maglev trains which have no wheels but float on strong magnetic fields.

FIGURE 1: A Maglev train floats on magnetic fields.

Thermistors and LDRs

Two more components are used extensively in the electronics industry: **thermistors** and **Light Dependent Resistors** (**LDRs**). You will find them in many domestic and industrial circuits, particularly in security and safety equipment.

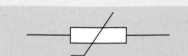
FIGURE 2: Symbol for a thermistor.

- Thermistor: when you heat a thermistor the resistance decreases. In a circuit, when the resistance decreases, it allows more current to flow.

Connect the circuit as in figure 3. Set the variable resistor to obtain a small current flowing through the milli-ammeter. Using a hairdryer, begin to heat up the thermistor. What effect do you see?

As the thermistor heats up, the current begins to increase.

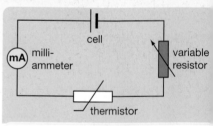
FIGURE 3: Connect this circuit.

- Light Dependent Resistor (LDR): when you allow light to shine onto a LDR, the resistance decreases. When resistance in a circuit decreases, it allows more current to flow.

Connect the circuit as in figure 5. Set the variable resistor to give a small current flowing through the circuit. Shine a bright light onto the LDR. What happens?

As the light on the LDR increases, the current begins to increase.

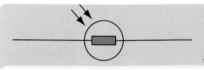
FIGURE 4: Symbol for a LDR.

QUESTIONS

1. Draw out the circuit used to test a thermistor. Clearly label the thermistor.
2. Describe how the experiment was carried out. What did it show about how a thermistor works?
3. Draw out the circuit used to test a LDR. Clearly label the LDR.
4. Describe how the experiment was carried out. What can you say about how a LDR works?

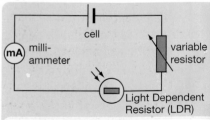
FIGURE 5: Connect this circuit.

...cadmium sulfide   ...Light Dependent Resistor (LDR)

So how do they work?

Both the thermistor and the LDR are made from special materials called **semi-conductors**. Substances like germanium and silicon are semi-conductors; they are neither conductors nor insulators. Semi-conductors can be used in their 'pure' state to make thermistors and LDRs. But they can also be doped with trace impurities. This changes the way they work. This type of impure semi-conductor material is used to make diodes, thermistors and transistors.

Thermistor

In the experiment where you heated the thermistor, you found that as it got hotter the resistance decreased and the current increased. Can you suggest why this should happen?

> *The heating effect causes more free electrons to be released, which allows more electrons to flow round the circuit.*

Thermistors are mostly used as electronic thermometers. They are also used in heat-sensitive protection devices like fire alarms or to protect data projector lamps from overheating.

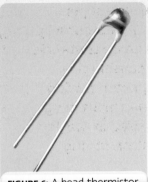

FIGURE 6: A bead thermistor.

LDR

FIGURE 7: LDR.

When you shine a light on the LDR, again the resistance decreases and the current increases. The LDR is made from a semi-conductor called **cadmium sulfide**. When light strikes the surface of the cadmium sulfide, it has enough energy to free an electron from its outer shell. More free electrons carry more current round the circuit.

LDRs are used in smoke detectors, automatic light controls and burglar alarm systems.

Thermistors and LDRs working at home

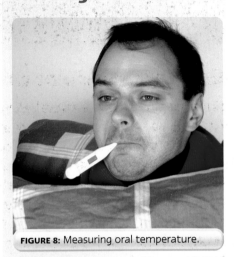

FIGURE 8: Measuring oral temperature.

- These days, the old-fashioned glass clinical thermometers are being replaced by digital thermometers. They are much more responsive and a lot safer to use, especially with young children.

- The working part of the thermometer is a thermistor. As it warms up, current flow increases, which is then displayed on a calibrated digital readout.

- Automatic light controls are an integral part of office space design. It is important for office staff to have consistent levels of lighting throughout the working day. LDRs are positioned inside the offices.

- Too much sunlight and the LDR circuits sense an increase in current. This will trigger a signal to dim the lights or even draw shades over the windows. If the sky gets cloudy or it begins to grow dark, current in the LDR circuit reduces. This will trigger lights to come on automatically.

QUESTIONS

9 Why are digital thermometers replacing glass thermometers?

10 Can you describe how a thermistor will act to protect the lamp in a digital projector?

11 Can you explain how a LDR will work inside a smoke detector?

QUESTIONS

5 What special substances are thermistors and LDRs made from? What can you tell about these materials?

6 Explain why the resistance of a thermistor decreases when it is heated up and how this affects the current flowing.

7 Describe the physics behind how the LDR works. Explain why current increases with increased levels of light.

8 Make a list of devices which use thermistors. Make a list for LDRs.

Components in series

You will find out:

- How components behave when connected in series

Christmas tree lights

It happens every year – you dig the Christmas tree lights out, decorate your beautiful tree, hit the switch ... only to find that one bulb has blown so none of the lights work. This is because the lights are connected in series. If one bulb fails, the circuit is broken and all the lights go out.

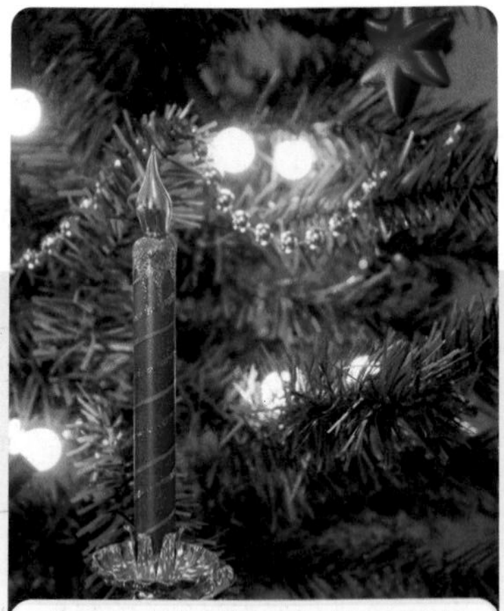

FIGURE 1: Why if one bulb goes do none of them work?

Lamps connected in series

Figure 2 shows three lamps connected in **series**, following on, one after the other. It is a single **continuous circuit** without any splits or breaks.

Start to build the circuit one lamp at a time. Connect the first lamp, switch on and note the brightness. Add the second lamp, switch on and note the brightness. Repeat for the third lamp.
What can you say about the brightness of the bulb at each stage?

In a series circuit, the brightness of the bulbs gets dimmer as more lamps are connected.

Current in a series circuit

Set up the circuit as in figure 2. Connect the ammeter in series at position 1, switch on and note the current flowing. Switch off. Disconnect the ammeter and reconnect it into the circuit at position 2.
What do you think the current will be in this new position, a little further along the circuit?

With the circuit complete, switch on and note the current. How does it compare with your first reading?

Repeat the experiment for positions 3 and 4. What conclusion can you make?

For a circuit connected in series, the current is the same at any point in the circuit.

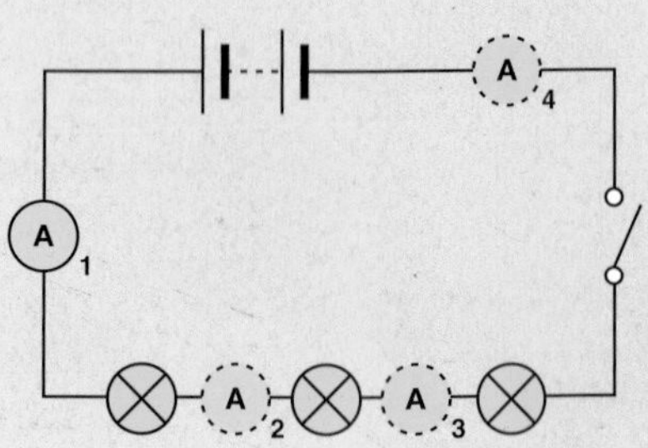

FIGURE 2: Three lamps connected in series.

QUESTIONS

1. Explain what is meant by a series circuit. Draw a diagram to illustrate.
2. Describe what happens to the brightness as more bulbs are connected in a series circuit. Can you explain why this happens?
3. What can you say about the current flowing anywhere in a series circuit?

...battery ...components ...continuous circuit ...net potential

Resistance in a series circuit

Figure 3 has three bulbs connected in series. Set up the circuit. Connect a voltmeter across the first bulb. Note the voltage and current. Repeat the procedure for each bulb in turn, noting the voltage and current for each.

Now set the voltmeter across all three bulbs and again note the voltage and current readings.

You will recall Ohm's Law which allows you to calculate the value of **resistance** for each bulb using its voltage and current readings.

$$\text{Resistance} = \frac{\text{potential difference}}{\text{current}}$$

Use this formula to calculate the resistance of each bulb and then the resistance of the three bulbs together. Look at your tabulated results. What can you say about resistances in series?

In a series circuit, the total resistance is equal to the sum of the resistances of each of the **components**.

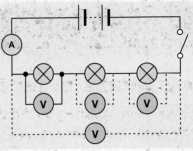

FIGURE 3: Three bulbs connected in series.

Cells in series

A **battery** is a number of cells connected in series. When cells are connected in series the total potential difference across the battery is equal to the sum of the individual potential differences from each cell. So, looking at figure 4, each cell has a potential difference of 1.5 volts. The total potential from the battery is 4.5 volts.

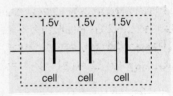

FIGURE 4: What is the total potential from this battery?

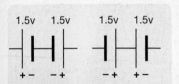

FIGURE 5: If cells are connected 'minus' to 'minus' or 'plus' to 'plus' they cancel each other out.

But you have to be careful how you connect the cells. Cells should always be connected 'plus' to 'minus'. If you connect them 'plus' to 'plus' or 'minus' to 'minus', the potential of each cell pushes against the other and so they cancel each other out.

Look at figure 5. Three 1.5 v cells are connected in series. What is the **net potential** of this battery?

Answer: only 1.5 v. Two cells are connected 'minus' to 'minus', so they cancel each other out. This leaves only the third cell to give a potential of 1.5 v to the circuit.

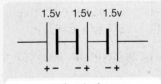

FIGURE 5: What is the net potential of this battery?

▦ QUESTIONS ▦

4 What is the formula used to calculate resistance? Whose law is this?

5 What can you say about resistances connected in series?

6 What is the difference between a cell and a battery?

7 When you connect cells together to make a battery, what do you have to watch out for? What will happen if you make this mistake?

...potential difference ...resistance ...series

Components in parallel

You will find out:
- How components behave when connected in parallel
- How the law of Conservation of Energy applies to circuits

How many science teachers does it take...

... to change a light bulb? It depends on whether or not the lighting system is wired on a parallel circuit. If it is, then when one light bulb fails, the rest will continue to work and at least they will be able to see what they are doing!

Current in parallel circuits

Components connected in **parallel** behave in quite a different way from series connections. Parallel circuits have **junctions** or **splits** in them, so current flowing round the circuit has to divide itself when it comes to a junction.

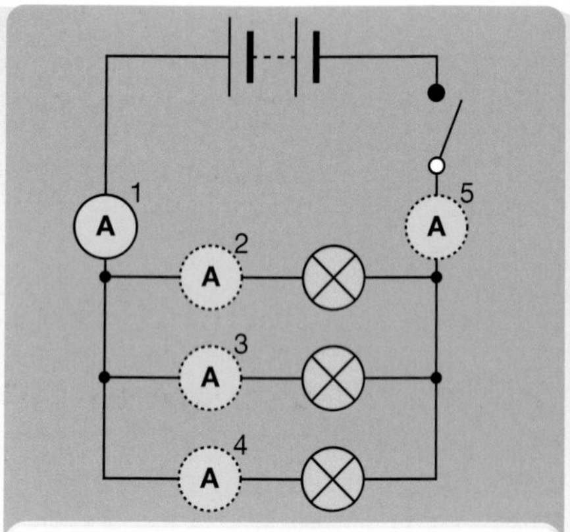

Figure 1 shows three lamps connected in parallel.

- Begin to set up the circuit, one lamp at a time.
- Connect the first lamp, switch on and note the brightness.
- Add the second lamp, switch on and note the brightness.
- Repeat for the third lamp.
- What can you say about the brightness of the bulb at each stage?

    In a parallel circuit, the brightness of the bulbs is always the same.

- Complete setting up the circuit by connecting the ammeter at position 1.
- Measure the current flowing at this point in the circuit. This is the **current** flowing before it arrives at the first junction.
- Note it down in your table of results.
- Disconnect the ammeter and re-connect it into the circuit at position 2. This is the current flowing through the first lamp.
- Note the value.
- Repeat for positions 3 and 4.
- What is the relationship between the four ammeter readings?   **A1 = A2 + A3 + A4**

If you placed the ammeter in position A5, can you predict the value?

    The total current through the whole circuit is the sum of the currents through the separate components.

FIGURE 1: Three lamps connected in parallel.

WOW FACTOR!

Domestic lighting is always wired in parallel circuit. When one lamp fails, the remainder will continue to work.

⬛ QUESTIONS ⬛

1 Explain what is meant by a parallel circuit. Draw a diagram to illustrate.
2 As you connect more lamps in parallel, what happens to the brightness of the bulbs?
3 Describe how current flows through a parallel circuit.
4 What is the relationship between the current from the battery (position 1) and the currents in all the other parts of the parallel circuit?

EXAM HINTS AND TIPS

Current is the flow of electrons.
Unit of current = amp (A)
Symbol for current = I

...current   ...energy giver   ...energy takers   ...junctions

Potential difference in parallel

We have looked at the current flowing through a parallel circuit. Let's investigate what is happening with the **potential differences**.

- Go back to the parallel circuit in figure 1. This time instead of measuring current we are going to measure potential difference. Using a voltmeter, measure the potential difference across the battery and note the voltage. Measure the potential difference across each lamp and note the voltages. What can you deduce?

  The potential difference across each lamp is the same.

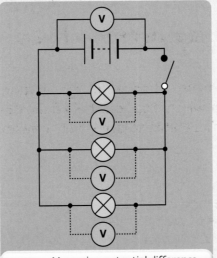

FIGURE 2: Measuring potential difference.

Summary of findings about parallel circuits

- The total current is equal to the sum of the individual currents through each component.

  $$IT = I1 + I2 + I3$$

- The potential difference is the same across each component.

Comparing with series circuits

How does this compare with the series circuit? Summarising your findings from the last spread:

- The total potential difference of the battery is shared between each component.

  $$VT = V1 + V2 + V3$$

- The current is the same at any point in the circuit.

Energy in = energy out

You will recall the Law of Conservation of Energy: energy cannot be created nor destroyed. We can apply this law to our series and parallel circuits.

- The battery is always the **energy giver**. The components, be they lamps or resistors, are always the **energy takers**.

- Applying the conservation law: the energy given by the battery must equal the sum of all the energy taken by all the components.

- You can track the energy flow by calculating **power**. The formula is:

power = potential difference × current

P (watts) = V (voltage) × I (current)

- Go back to your potential difference and current readings for both the series and parallel circuits. Calculate the values of power for the battery and compare these to the sum of power values for the components.

QUESTIONS

8 How does the Law of Conservation of Energy apply to series and parallel circuits?

9 How can you track the energy flow in an electric circuit?

10 What did your calculations show?

11 Were there any energy flow differences between the series and parallel circuits?

QUESTIONS

5 In a parallel circuit, what can you say about the potential difference across each component?

6 In a parallel circuit, what can you say about the currents flowing through the different parts of the circuit?

7 How do the two statements above compare with p.d. and current in a series circuit?

The three-pin plug

You will find out:
- How to wire a three-pin plug
- What double insulation is

Connecting to mains electricity

The three-pin plug is used to connect an electrical appliance to the mains socket. In earlier times, appliances came without plugs attached; just the three bare wires on the end of the electric lead. Everyone had to buy a new plug and wire it up themselves. Today, all electrical appliances must come with the three-pin plug already attached.

Can you think of a reason why it is now a legal requirement for all electrical appliances to have three-pin plugs fully wired in?

The three-pin plug

Nevertheless, there will still be times when you have to wire up a plug yourself. You might have to replace the **fuse**, or the plug itself may become damaged.

It is absolutely vital that everyone is familiar with the inside of a plug and knows how to wire it up correctly. The simplest mistake could result in someone getting seriously injured by electric shock.

- Figure 1 shows a picture of the inside of a **three-pin plug**. The three wires are colour-coded. This is to help you connect the right wires to the right pins in the plug. The **brown** wire is the live. The **blue** wire is the **neutral**. The yellow and **green** is the **earth**.

- The **live/brown** wire is connected to the right pin. The **neutral/blue** wire is connected to the left pin. The **earth/yellow-green** striped wire is connected to the top pin.

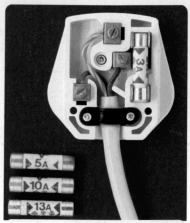

FIGURE 1: Wiring up a three-pin plug.

▐▌ QUESTIONS ▐▌

1. Why is it important for everyone to be able to wire a 13 amp plug?
2. How would you recognise the live and neutral wires?
3. Draw a diagram showing where each of the three wires is correctly connected.
4. This 13 amp, three-pin plug has been wired up to be connected to an electric kettle. Is this plug correctly wired? Can you spot the mistakes? Suggest how these mistakes could be rectified.

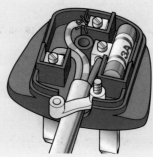

...cable ...cable grip ...case ...double insulation ...earth ...fuse

More about electric cables and plugs

- Electric **cable** is used to connect appliances to power sockets. The cable is constructed in a way which provides optimum safety to consumers. Cables generally carry three wires: live, neutral and earth. This is usually referred to as '**twin** and **earth**'. Each wire is covered by a coloured plastic coating. The three coated wires are wrapped in an outer plastic sheath. The sheath and wire coating are made from plastic which is a good insulator.

  In some cases, the cable only has two wires: live and neutral. Again, each wire has a coloured plastic coating. **Twin-core cable** is used for appliances which are **double-insulated**.

- The **case** of the plug is usually made from plastic or rubber because these materials are good insulators.

- The fuse is always connected in series with the live/brown wire. When the fuse blows, it isolates the live wire and stops the flow of current.

- The **cable grip** should always secure the whole cable and not just the three wires. This is to ensure that if the cable is accidentally pulled or jerked, the wires will not be pulled out of their connections.

- When you secure the ends of the wires, make sure there are no strands of wire sticking out from under the brass connectors.

- When you finally replace the back of the plug make sure that none of the wires are nipped or crushed.

- Now take a three-pin plug and cable and practise wiring it up correctly. Make sure you avoid all the pitfalls of faulty wiring to ensure a safe and secure electrical appliance.

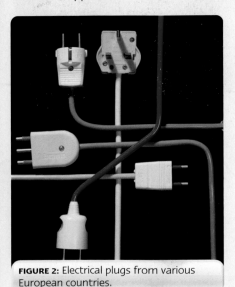

FIGURE 2: Electrical plugs from various European countries.

Double insulation

All power cables have three wires: live, neutral and earth. But with appliances that have a plastic outer casing, you can use twin-core cable: live and neutral only.

This is because the plastic casing acts as an insulator. If a fault developed in the wiring and there was a short circuit, electricity would not be able to flow through the person holding the appliance.

Today there are many appliances with plastic casings: hairdryers, electric drills, fan heaters, lawn mowers. They do still need to have fuses, just in case the electric wires become damaged.

Appliances with double insulation are labelled with the following symbol:

QUESTIONS

9 What is twin-core cable? In what way is it different from the standard twin and earth cable?

10 Why is it safe to use twin-core cable?

11 Name **three** appliances which are safe to use twin-core cable.

12 In which circumstances would it be dangerous to use twin-core cable?

QUESTIONS

5 Why are electric wires sheathed in coloured plastic?

6 The fuse must always be connected in series with which wire? Can you explain why?

7 Explain the function of the cable grip. Why is it so important?

8 Why should all the strands of wire be neatly tucked into the brass connectors?

Domestic electricity

You will find out:
- About domestic, mains electricity
- About the cathode ray oscilloscope

Money versus Science?

Mains electricity is not the same across the world. In the United States, the mains voltage is 110 volts (60 Hz); in Europe it is 230 volts (50 Hz). In the 1900s Thomas Edison, the famous US inventor, installed 110 V d.c. mains power to the big US cities. At around the same time, Nicola Tesla, a brilliant scientist in Europe, proved that 230 V a.c. mains power was a more efficient way of transmitting electric energy.

FIGURE 1: Small equipment such as Walkmans are powered by low voltage d.c.

Direct current–alternating current

Electricity can be produced as **direct current** (d.c.) or **alternating current** (a.c.). All cells and batteries are d.c. They have a positive and a negative terminal and supply current which always passes in the same direction. Most batteries give a potential difference of 1.5 volts, with some stronger batteries being rated at 9 volts. Low voltage d.c. is used to power small equipment like torches and cameras.

■ All our domestic electricity is a.c. This means the current is constantly changing direction. Look at the diagram of a.c. power supply. You can see that the voltage is continually changing from plus to minus to plus; hence the name 'alternating'.

Domestic electricity delivers an average potential difference of 230 volts. This is because it has to power larger appliances like hairdryers and kettles.

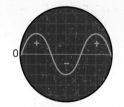

FIGURE 2A: Oscilloscope trace of alternating current.

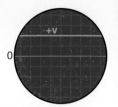

FIGURE 2B: Oscilloscope trace of direct current.

The number of times per second the voltage changes from plus to minus back to plus again is called the frequency. The frequency of UK and European electricity is 50 Hz. This means it oscillates plus/minus 50 times per second. Because domestic electricity carries such a high potential difference (230 V), there is always a real danger of serious accident leading to shock, severe burns or even death.

FIGURE 3: All our domestic electricity is a.c. This microwave is powered by mains electricity: 230 v 50 Hz.

QUESTIONS

1   What is the mains electricity in the UK and Europe? How does this compare to mains electricity in the United States?
2   What do the abbreviations d.c. and a.c. stand for? Give **one** example of each type of electricity.
3   What is the frequency of electricity in the UK and Europe? What are the units of frequency?
4   Why is domestic electricity potentially dangerous? How do we protect against serious accidents?

More about alternating current

- Electricity can be difficult to get to grips with. We certainly know it's flowing through the wires as it powers our television or runs the tumble dryer, but if you look inside the cable, you cannot see anything.
- There are instruments, however, that show us what the electricity is doing. You will recall that a voltmeter measures the potential difference across a component, and an ammeter tells you the amount of current flowing. There is another type of instrument which can show you a picture of the electricity in a circuit.

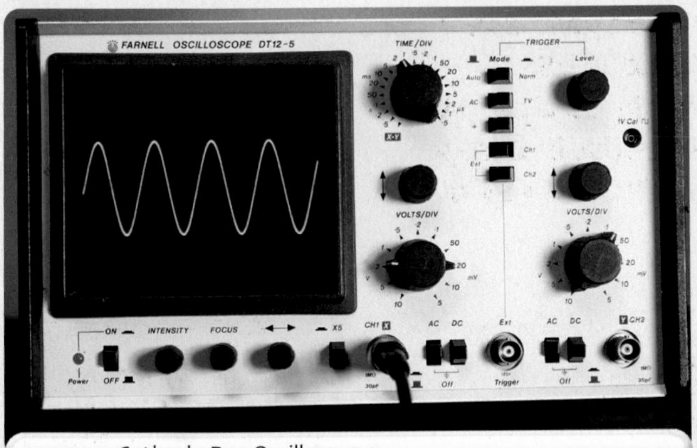

FIGURE 4: Cathode Ray Oscilloscope.

The **cathode ray oscilloscope** (CRO) has a screen with a grid. It shows you an image of the electricity flowing through a circuit.

- Figure 2B shows the picture of direct current (d.c.).

Along the middle of the screen is the zero line. Above the line the potential is positive; below the line it's negative. For direct current, the potential difference (voltage) remains constant. The wave trace on the oscilloscope is a continuous straight line.

- Figure 5 shows the representation of alternating current (a.c.). You can see immediately how the trace makes an 'S' wave. Above the zero line the voltage is positive and, below, it is negative. The height of the wave gives the peak voltage, V_0.
- The x-axis is the time base. From the trace you can work out the time for one oscillation.

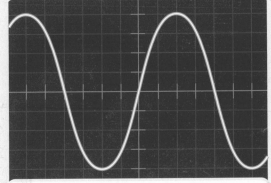

FIGURE 5: Picture of alternating current.

Watch Out

In the UK and Europe the mains frequency is 50 Hz. In the US and Canada the mains frequency is 60 Hz.

Using the CRO trace to measure voltage and frequency (H)

It is possible to take direct measurements from the trace using the screen grid. But first you need to check the scales set on the oscilloscope. Let's say that the vertical scale is 1 division = 2 volts and the horizontal scale is 1 division = 10 milliseconds.

- The peak voltage is 4 divisions = 8 V
- The period for one cycle is 8 divisions
  = 8 X 10 milliseconds
  = 80 milliseconds = 0.08 seconds
- So, frequency = 1/time = 1/0.08 = 12.5 Hz

QUESTIONS

8 An oscilloscope is calibrated to vertical scale 1 division = 5 volts and time base scale 1 division = 100 milliseconds. If the peak voltage is 4 divisions and the period for one cycle is 5 divisions, what is the value of peak voltage V_0 and what is the frequency?

9 An oscilloscope is calibrated to vertical scale 1 division = 2.5 volts and time base scale 1 division = 10 milliseconds. If the peak voltage is 3.5 divisions and the period for one cycle is 2 divisions, what is the value of peak voltage V_0 and what is the frequency?

QUESTIONS

5 Which instrument can show you an image of the electricity flowing through a circuit?

6 Draw a trace of both d.c. and a.c. electricity.

7 On the oscilloscope there are vertical (y-axis) and horizontal (x-axis) grid lines. What can you measure off the vertical grid? What can you measure off the horizontal grid?

Making the sparks fly

SELF-CHECK ACTIVITY

CONTEXT

Gemma is 16 and wants to earn some money. Her neighbours have a large garden and don't really have the time to look after it properly. They agree to pay her to mow their lawn and do a bit of weeding.

The first time she goes round she gets out the mower. It is an electric one and has a flex to connect it to the electricity supply in the house. The lawn is quite long and she needs to use two extension leads to get to the far end. The leads are bright red and have a two pin connector at each end.

She thinks about this and wonders why there isn't a third pin in the connector, which she knows is there for safety. The mower has a metal handle which is attached to the plastic body.

She mows the lawn, clears away and goes home. That evening her father asks her how it went and she tells him about the extension leads. He says he doesn't think this sounds very safe and that next time she goes he'll lend her a safety device to use. He tells her she needs to plug this into the mains and then plug the mower into the safety device.

The next time Gemma goes she takes the safety device. It is marked "earth trip device". She uses it as she is told and the mower works just as it did before. She doesn't see how it can make a difference if the lead doesn't have a third pin but thinks that perhaps as it has an earth pin it does the job of an earth lead.

As she is mowing the lawn the flex gets caught around something, tightens, and pulls the connection in the extension lead apart. The ends fall to the ground and land in the soil. The end that is connected to the mains supply has soil in the holes of the socket and she knows that if she pushes the two ends together the soil will get ground in and stop it from connecting properly. She has to get the soil out, but what with? She goes into the tool shed and finds a small screwdriver. Perfect! She is about to put the blade in the end when a neighbour who is working in his garden shouts "Stop!". Gemma is so surprised she drops the lead and the screwdriver.

"That was a lucky escape!" says the neighbour. Gemma smiles weakly and mumbles some words of thanks. "Surely it wasn't dangerous" she thinks to herself. "If I had put the blade in there it would only have made contact with one terminal – it wouldn't have completed the circuit. Anyway, the screwdriver had a plastic handle and that's an insulator."

Why do some electrical appliances need an earth lead and others don't? Should this mower have had an earth lead?

STEP 2

Did the earth trip device make the mower safer? Explain your answer.

STEP 3

Gemma would quite possibly have been electrocuted if she had put the screwdriver blade into one of the holes in the end of the mains lead. Why is this, even though she would only have made contact with one of the terminals? Where is the complete circuit?

The plastic handle of the screwdriver might not have saved her. Why not?

Maximise your grade

These sentences show what you need to include in your work to achieve each grade. Use them to improve your work and be more successful.

Grade	Answer includes...
F	State that mains voltage is dangerous and can be fatal.
	State that a metal casing on an appliance can conduct electricity into a person if it becomes live.
	Explain that an earth lead will conduct electricity away from the metal casing of an appliance.
	Explain how an earth trip device works.
C	Explain what use the earth trip device is in this situation.
	Explain the risks from inserting a screwdriver blade in the connector.
A	Suggest a better way than the earth trip device of making the mower safer.
	Produce an overall summary of the hazards and remedial steps relating to Gemma's activities in the article.

STEP 4

Design a plan to make use of the mower much safer. Your plan should include a number of bullet points to make clear each change and an explanation of each of the changes that should be made.

Safety at home

You will find out:
- How fuses and earth wires keep us safe
- About other safety devices

Zero potential

Our planet Earth is electrically *neutral*, which means that it has an electric potential of zero. The earth wire of a mains plug is connected to the actual Earth by being fixed to the copper pipe of the domestic mains water supply. Because the Earth is so big, any charge is just absorbed into itself. This is the reason why many items have their outer casing wired to the Earth. It means that if a fault develops inside the equipment, the charge is absorbed by the Earth and you should not get an electric shock from touching the outside of the appliance!

FIGURE 1: Our neutral Earth.

Fuses and earth wires

A **fuse** is a thin wire placed in series in a circuit. When too high current flows through the circuit, the fuse wire heats up and melts. When the fuse 'blows', the circuit is broken and current stops flowing.

Fuses are used to protect your electrical appliances or equipment. Sometimes when parts of a circuit become faulty, this causes an increase or surge of current flowing through the circuit. If this surge of high current is allowed to flow through your appliance, it will burn out and damage all the sensitive operating mechanisms. The fuse is designed to blow as soon as there is an increase in current. The electrical circuit is broken and your equipment is safe. The cost of replacing a television or music centre is hundreds of pounds. The cost of a fuse is £0.20.

FIGURE 2: Standard fuses are available in 3 A, 5 A, and 13 A ratings.

All electrical appliances with metal casings must be connected to an **earth wire**. If a fault develops in an appliance and the live wire touches the outside casing, a large current flows from the live wire to the earth wire. This blows the fuse, current stops flowing and everything is safe until you repair the fault and replace the fuse. The earth wire also protects people from getting an electric shock.

QUESTIONS

1. What is a fuse? What are the commonly available sizes of fuse?
2. How does a fuse work? What would be the danger if there was no fuse in your expensive music system?
3. How does the earth wire protect your appliance?
4. How does the earth wire protect you?

EXAM HINTS AND TIPS

Remember: the fuse and earth wire together protect the appliance and the user.

...earth wire   ...fuse

More about fuses

FIGURE 3: Switch-operated miniature circuit breaker.

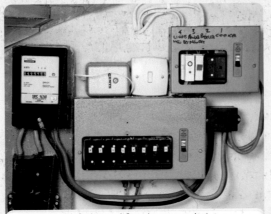

FIGURE 4: Old-fashioned fuse boxes are being replaced by miniature circuit breakers.

- **Miniature Circuit Breakers** (**mcb**). Modern consumer units (fuse boxes) use mcb rather than old-fashioned fuse wires. The mcb uses an electromagnet or electronic mechanism and is very sensitive to small fluctuations in current. The slightest increase in current triggers the mcb, which immediately breaks the circuit. Once the fault is fixed, the mcb can be reset with no need to rewire blown fuses.

- **Residual Current Device** (**RCD**). This is a fast-acting circuit breaker. It is designed to stop current flowing in less than 0.05 seconds. It works by detecting any difference between current in the live and neutral wires. RCDs should be used when using appliances like lawn mowers and hedge trimmers.

FIGURE 5: Residual current device.

Which fuse should I use?

Fitting the correct fuse is very important. Too high a value and the appliance will burn out before the fuse does. Too low a rating and the fuse will keep blowing every time you switch on.

QUESTIONS

5   Where would you more commonly find a Miniature Circuit Breaker (mcb)?

6   Why are they gradually replacing the old-fashioned fuse box?

7   What is so special about a Residual Current Device (RCD)?

8   Where are RCDs mostly used? Can you think why?

More about mains a.c. (H)

- It is the live terminal which carries the alternating voltage.

- The neutral terminal remains more or less at a potential close to earth (zero).

- The voltage in the live wire alternates between +230 V and −230 V.

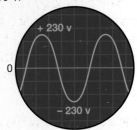

oscilloscope trace of alternating voltage

FIGURE 6: Representation of alternating current.

QUESTIONS

9   Which wire carries the alternating voltage? Between what voltages does the potential oscillate in Europe?

10   What is the voltage of the neutral wire?

11   Knowing this, can you say where a fuse should be placed for maximum safety? Explain why.

Which fuse?

You will find out:
- How to calculate the correct fuse rating
- How to calculate power

What are the dangers?

If electrical items in your home are unsafe, you could be at risk of:
- electric shocks – severe electric shocks can cause heart failure
- electrical burns – these can require major surgery and can be permanently damaging
- fire – every year, 12 500 fires are caused in UK homes by electrical faults.

What are the danger signs?

You can check for possible danger signs yourself. These include:
- plugs or wall sockets which are overheating or are scorched or cracked
- cables or wires which are loose, exposed or fraying
- a burning smell when appliances are switched on
- fuses which blow frequently.

FIGURE 1: Selection of fuses.

Calculating the correct fuse rating

Every appliance has a power rating (in watts) printed on a silver label attached to the casing. This label also gives information about the manufacturer, the model number, the serial number, mains voltage, frequency and power rating.

Uk mains voltage is 230 V. Using the equation: **watts = p.d. × current** allows you to calculate the current that your appliance will draw when switched on.

Using the power triangle, rearrange the equation: **current = watts / p.d**

Once you calculate the current you can choose the appropriate fuse.

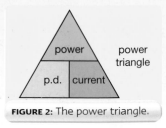

FIGURE 2: The power triangle.

Worked example

An appliance label shows a rating of 1000 watts, what fuse should you use?

Use the equation: current = watts / p.d.

      current = 1000 watts / 230 V = 4.3 amps

The correct fuse to use would be a 5 A fuse. If you used a 3 A fuse, it would blow every time you switched on the appliance. If you used a 13 A fuse, there is a good chance that the appliance would be damaged well before the current got high enough to blow the 13 A fuse.

QUESTIONS

1. How would you find out what power rating an appliance has?
2. An electric kettle is rated at 2.8 kW (2800 watts). What fuse is needed?
3. A hairdryer is rated at 500 watts. What fuse should you fit?
4. A lawn mower is fitted with a 5 A fuse. What is the approximate power rating for the mower?

...coulomb ...current ...joule

Understanding power

You will recall that electricity is the flow of electrons. But the electrons are only the charge carriers. Each electron carries a charge. So really we can say that electricity is a flow of charge. The unit of electric charge is called the **coulomb**.

The rate at which charge flows in a wire is called the current. The faster the charges flow the greater the current.

This can be written as: **current = charge × time**

You will also recall that when electric charge moves through a resistor, like a wire or a lamp, electrical energy is transformed into kinetic energy, which we feel as heat.

The rate at which energy is transformed in a device is called the **power**.

The unit of power is the **watt** (W) and the unit of energy is the **joule** (J).

power = the energy transferred / the time taken in seconds
(watts (W)) **(joule (J))** **(seconds (s))**

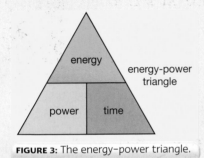

FIGURE 3: The energy–power triangle.

If a light bulb is rated at 100 W, it means that it is converting electricity to light and heat at a rate of 100 joules/second.

There is a second equation which links power, potential difference and current:

power = potential difference × current
watt (W) **volt (V)** **amp (A)**

This is the equation you used to calculate the size of fuse required for an appliance.

Energy transformation

In Physics, energy is always measured in joules (J). The rate at which an appliance uses energy is called power. Power is measured in joules/second, also known as watts (W).

- The energy transformed in a circuit is related to the amount of push (potential difference) and the charge being pushed along.

  energy = p.d. × charge
  (joule, J) (volt, V) (coulomb, C)

- The amount of electric charge that flows is related to current and time by the equation:

  charge = current × time
  (coulomb, C) (amp, A) (second, s)

- If we substitute for charge:

  energy = p.d. × current × time
  and divide by time:

  energy/time = p.d. × current

  it brings us to the original power equation:

  power = p.d. × current

QUESTIONS

5 When a current of 4 A passes through an appliance for 10 minutes, 30 000 J of heat energy are produced. What is the power rating of the appliance? What is the operating voltage of this appliance? What would be an appropriate fuse to fit? Explain why.

6 An electric heater transforms electrical energy at a rate of 3.6 MJ every hour. What is its power rating? Assuming this is a mains voltage appliance, what current does it draw and what size of fuse should you fit?

7 How much energy does a 2 kW electric fire transform if it is switched on for 45 minutes? What current will the fire draw and what fuse should be fitted in the plug?

QUESTIONS

8 Work through the equations above, particularly the substitution and dividing the whole equation by time.

9 A current of 5 A flows for 30 minutes. How much charge has passed through the circuit?

10 A 100 W lamp which runs off mains electricity (230 V) is switched on for 1.5 hours. How much electric charge is transformed during this time?

Radioactivity

You will find out:
- About the structure of an atom
- What makes certain substances radioactive

Pioneers in radioactivity

Marie Curie and her husband Pierre won the Nobel Prize for Physics in 1903 for their work on radioactivity. After the death of her husband in 1906, Marie was appointed the first woman lecturer at the Sorbonne in Paris where she continued to research ways of using radium as a cure for cancer. In 1911 she received a second Nobel Prize. She died in 1934 from leukaemia due to overexposure to radiation.

FIGURE 1: Marie Curie.

Structure of an atom

You will remember that all things are made from atoms. For a long time scientists thought atoms could not be broken down into anything smaller. But now we know atoms are made up of smaller particles. Nowadays we picture the atom as a small central **nucleus** made up of **protons** and **neutrons**, surrounded by **electrons**.

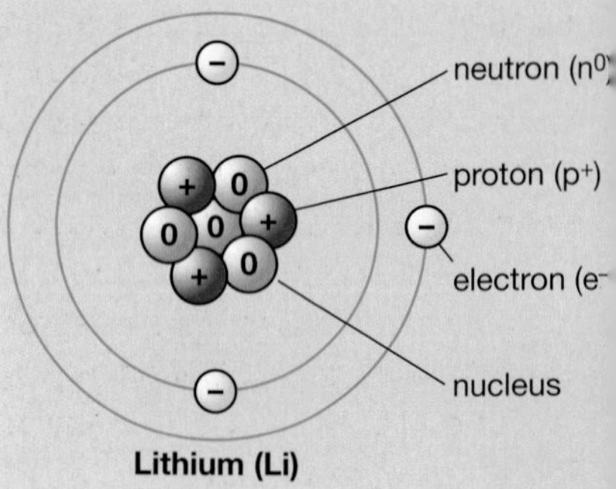

Protons, neutrons and electrons

Each of these particles has its own characteristics. Each has a certain mass and electric charge. The table summarises these characteristics.

All atoms have no net electrical charge; they are neutral. This means that the number of protons must always equal the number of electrons.

Particle	Relative mass	Charge
Proton	+1	+1
Neutron	+1	0
Electron	0	−1

Lithium (Li)

FIGURE 2: An atom of lithium.

Ions

You will recall that the nucleus of an atom is surrounded by shells of electrons. On occasions, it is possible for an outer electron to be knocked out of its shell and away from the atom. When an atom loses an electron it loses a negative (−1) charge. From being neutral, it becomes one positive (+1). The atom is now called an ion (with a positive charge of +1).

Atoms can lose or gain electrons. So ions can be either positive or negative.

QUESTIONS

1. Name the different particles of an atom.
2. Sketch the picture of an atom of lithium. Show the numbers of each of the particles.
3. What does it mean when we say that an atom is neutral?
4. How does an atom become an ion?

WOW FACTOR!

Henri Becquerel discovered radio-activity by accident when he was experimenting with uranium ore. The Becquerel (Bq) is a unit of radiation.

...*atomic number* ...*disintegration* ...*electrons* ...*isotopes* ...*mass number* ...*neutron*

More about atoms

The number of protons in an atom is called the **atomic number**. The number of protons plus the number of neutrons is called the **mass number**. Scientists have developed a shorthand notation to make it easier to write. For example, lithium has 3 protons plus 4 neutrons.

This can be written as

$_3^7\text{Li}$ — mass number — atomic number

Table 1 shows the first six elements in the Periodic Table.

Element	Atomic No.	Notation
Hydrogen	1	$_1^1\text{H}$
Helium	2	$_2^4\text{He}$
Lithium	3	$_3^7\text{Li}$
Beryllium	4	$_4^9\text{Be}$
Boron	5	$_5^{11}\text{B}$
Carbon	6	$_6^{12}\text{C}$

TABLE 1: First six elements in the Periodic Table.

Isotopes

Atoms of the same element always have the same number of protons and neutrons. That's how you know they are atoms of that element. Atoms of different elements have different numbers of protons. But some atoms of the element have a different number of neutrons. Atoms with the same number of protons but different numbers of neutrons are called **isotopes**. Because isotopes have different numbers of neutrons, they are unstable and begin to break down. As the isotope breaks down, it releases a lot of energy. The energy is carried out of the nucleus by particles and rays. This is called **radiation**.

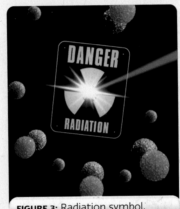

FIGURE 3: Radiation symbol.

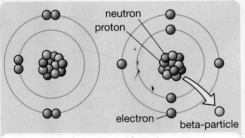

FIGURE 4: a Carbon-12 and **b** Carbon-14 emitting a beta particle.

Carbon is a good example. A normal carbon atom has 6 protons + 6 neutrons in the nucleus. This is called Carbon-12. But carbon also has an isotope called Carbon-14. It has 6 protons + 8 neutrons in the nucleus. Carbon-14 is **radioactive** because it is an isotope and gives out radiation to get rid of the extra weight inside its nucleus.

Radiation

Being an isotope with all these extra neutrons makes the atom **unstable**. The atom wants to come down to a more balanced state and begins to break down. This process is called **disintegration**.

As the nucleus begins to disintegrate, a great deal of nuclear energy is released and carried out of the nucleus by sub-atomic particles. The emission of these sub-atomic particles is called radiation. A substance which is an isotope and is in the process of disintegrating is radioactive.

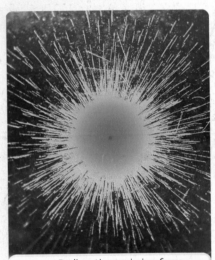

FIGURE 5: Radioactive emission from radium.

Most elements have one or more isotopes which are unstable. As the nucleus breaks down into smaller parts it emits alpha particles, beta particles and gamma rays. This is called **radioactive decay**.

QUESTIONS

5   What do you understand by atomic number and mass number?

6   Look at the Periodic Table. What is the shorthand notation for oxygen and also sodium?

7   In what way is an isotope different from its stable element relative?

8   $_{53}^{123}\text{I}$, $_{53}^{124}\text{I}$, $_{53}^{127}\text{I}$, $_{53}^{129}\text{I}$, $_{53}^{131}\text{I}$ are all atoms of iodine. Which are isotopes and which is the stable element? (Check out your Periodic Table.)

QUESTIONS

9   Describe what you understand by radiation and radioactive decay.

10 How is excess energy carried out of an isotope as it begins to disintegrate?

Alpha, beta and gamma rays

You will find out:
- That there are three main types of nuclear radiation
- What the three main types of radiation look like and how they behave

Good guys ... bad guys?

Most of us have heard of radiation. It often comes up as the doomsday scenario in film fiction where the 'bad guys' hijack a nuclear bomb and the hero has to save the world. But Three Mile Island (1979) and Chernobyl (1986) were not fiction. These disasters really happened. Both nuclear reactors went into partial meltdown. Fallout from Chernobyl even reached the UK; Welsh farmers could not sell lamb for three years because the hillsides had been contaminated. Nuclear radiation can be both dangerous and beneficial. It depends how we choose to use it.

FIGURE 1: Chernobyl, scene of one of the world's worst nuclear accidents.

The three radiations

You will know that some isotopes of elements are radioactive. They are unstable and give out nuclear radiation as they break down. Scientists have discovered three different types of radiation.

Alpha (∝) radiation: These are particles. They are helium nuclei that move about quite slowly. Although they are large, they do not have much penetrating power. They can be stopped by a single sheet of paper.

Beta (β) radiation: These are particles. They are electrons and beta radiation is a flow of electrons. They are small, light and move around very fast. Beta particles have good penetrating power. It takes about 3 mm of aluminium sheet to stop them.

Gamma (γ) radiation: These are not particles but waves (think about electromagnetic radiation, that you have learned about). The waves travel at the speed of light and carry a lot of energy. Gamma rays can penetrate almost everything. Even a thick sheet of lead only slows them down but doesn't stop them completely.

MEASURING RADIATION

The Geiger-Muller tube is used to measure radiation. When radiation enters the tube, it creates a small electrical pulse which is counted as a click.

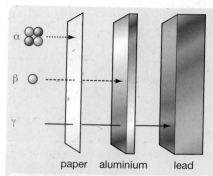

FIGURE 2: Three radiations and their penetrating properties.

RANDOM RADIATION

When an atom disintegrates, radiation is emitted randomly. The Geiger counter counts the pulses and gives an average count per second.

QUESTIONS

1. What are the **three** types of nuclear radiation that can come from inside an unstable isotope?
2. Which radiation is big and heavy? How would you describe it to someone?
3. Which radiation is almost unstoppable? Write down its characteristics.
4. Which radiation needs about 3 mm of aluminium to stop it? Describe it as best you can.

Alpha, beta and gamma rays

Ionisation

If something collides with an atom hard enough, it can knock out one or two of the atom's outer electrons. With some of its electrons missing, the atom now becomes an **ion** with a positive charge. This process is called **ionisation**.

Alpha ($\propto$) particles are helium nuclei $_2^4\text{He}$ and carry a positive (+) charge. They move at about one tenth the speed of light. Because of its size, the alpha particle collides with lots of the atoms around it. Because of its mass, the alpha particle knocks electrons from an atom's outer shell. This makes alpha particles good ionisers. The problem with all this colliding and ionising is that the alpha particle quickly loses its energy. That's why it has poor penetrating power and is stopped by a sheet of paper or a few centimetres of air. Americium-241 is a source of $\propto$-particles.

Beta (β) particles are electrons and carry a negative (−) charge. They are 1/7000 the size of the alpha and move at about half the speed of light. Because of their small size, they frequently miss hitting atoms. But occasionally they will collide and ionise the atom. They are weak ionisers. Beta particles are stopped by 3 mm of aluminium. Strontium-90 is a source of β-particles.

Gamma (γ) rays are waves. As electromagnetic waves, they have no charge: they are neutral. They have very short wavelengths, travel at the speed of light and carry a lot of energy. Gamma rays have excellent penetration. They just pass straight through everything so there is not much chance of knocking out electrons. Gamma particles are poor ionisers. Cobalt-60 is a source of γ-rays.

Properties	Alpha particle ($\propto$)	Beta particle (β)	Gamma ray (γ)
Nature	Positive helium nucleus $_2^4\text{He}$ about 7000 times the mass of an electron	Negative charge electron e^-	Electromagnetic waves, very short wavelength and high energy
Charge	Positive (+)	Negative (−)	Neutral
Penetration	Stopped by sheet of paper or skin, or 6 cm of air	Stopped by 3 mm aluminium	Slowed down but not stopped by lead
Ionisation	Strong	Weak	Very weak
Speed	One tenth the speed of light	Half the speed of light	Speed of light
Dangerous	Yes	Yes	Yes

TABLE 1: Properties of the three types of radiation.

Alpha and beta decay

When an isotope disintegrates, the nucleus begins to throw out particles. As the particles pass out of the atom, the nucleus rearranges itself into a new element.

Alpha decay

Radium $_{88}^{228}$ decays by ejecting an alpha particle ($_2^4\text{He}$). When Radium $_{88}^{228}$ loses 2 protons and 2 neutrons it becomes Radium $_{86}^{228}$.

Beta decay

Polonium $_{84}^{218}$ decays by ejecting a beta particle ($_{-1}^{0}\text{e}$). When Polonium $_{84}^{218}$ loses an electron it becomes Astatine $_{85}^{218}$. The electron is not one of the electrons orbiting the nucleus. The electron (beta particle) comes from inside the neutron itself. The neutron ejects an electron to become a proton.

QUESTIONS

9   How can radioactive decay cause a new element to be formed?

10 Describe an example of alpha decay.

11 Describe an example of beta decay.

12 From where does the beta particle originate? What is the consequence of such decay?

QUESTIONS

5   What do you understand by ionisation?

6   What makes alpha particles particularly strong ionisers?

7   Beta particles carry a lot of energy, but they are not strong ionisers. Can you explain why?

8   Why are gamma rays so different from the other two radiations?

Background radiation

You will find out:
- About background radiation
- About the various sources of background radiation

Protecting the planet

In the early days of our planet, the Earth had no atmosphere. There was no protection from cosmic and solar radiation. The levels were so high that no living things could survive in the open. Gradually, over millions of years, the atmosphere developed and offered a shield against the deadly radiation. Only then was it possible for life on Earth to move from the sea onto the land. The atmosphere does not offer 100 per cent protection; some radiation still gets through but at very low levels. We need to look after our atmosphere; it is the only natural protection that we have got!

Geiger counters

You know that:

- a radioactive isotope emits radiation
- we use a **Geiger counter** to detect and count the particles and rays.

Switch on a Geiger counter in the laboratory with all radioactive sources safely put away. You will hear a low level of clicks from the counter. Go into the street or into the countryside with the counter. You would still hear the low level of clicks.

The Geiger counter tells you that there is a small amount of radiation all around us all the time. It's called **background radiation**. Background radiation comes from various sources. Some of it comes from the soil and rocks of the Earth. Some of it comes from space. Some of it is man-made. Fortunately the amount of radiation is quite small and it does not harm our bodies.

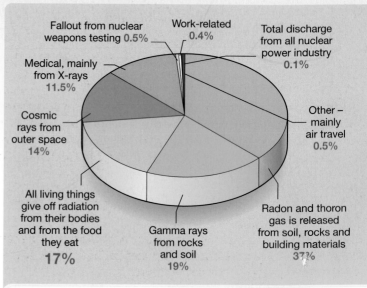

FIGURE 1: Sources of background radiation.

Where does it come from?

Look at the pie chart in figure 1 for a detailed breakdown of where background radiation comes from.

QUESTIONS

1 What is background radiation?
2 Why does this radiation not harm us?
3 Which of the sources in figure 1 surprised you most? Why?

WOW FACTOR!

Pilots and air crew wear radiation badges. If they get too much exposure to cosmic radiation, they are grounded until their levels return to normal.

Sources of background radiation

Humans and all other living things have evolved and adapted to background radiation so it does not harm us. The amount of background radiation varies depending on where you are. In the UK for example, areas of Cornwall and Scotland give off much higher radiation than in London or East Anglia.

Granite rock emits gamma rays. Some rocks and soil give off **radon gas**. In some villages, radon gas crept into people's houses and caused mysterious illnesses. Once doctors and scientists discovered the cause, special vents were cut into the foundations to allow the radon gas to be cleared away.

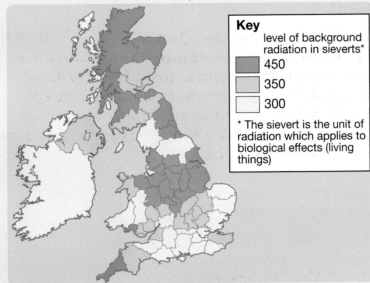

Key

level of background radiation in sieverts*

- 450
- 350
- 300

* The sievert is the unit of radiation which applies to biological effects (living things)

FIGURE 2: How high is background radiation in your area?

The Earth is constantly bombarded by **cosmic rays** from outer space. Fortunately the atmosphere absorbs much of this radiation. Pilots and air crew who fly long-haul journeys are exposed to higher doses of cosmic radiation. Modern aircraft fly 'seven miles high'. At that altitude the atmosphere is very thin and offers little protection.

Many of you will have had an X-ray. Radiographers use small doses to make sure we are not harmed.

There is much controversy about nuclear power stations and the testing of nuclear weapons. Many people believe we are contaminating our environment. Check out the pie chart in figure 1 – what do you think?

All living things produce tiny amounts of radioactive material. The food we eat is radioactive, as are our own bones. Later on we shall learn how scientists can use this phenomenon to date the age of fossil remains.

Everyone who works with or near radioactive materials has to wear a 'radiation badge'. The badge is used to measure the amount of radiation to which workers have been exposed.

QUESTIONS

4 What do you understand by the term background radiation?

5 Is it harmful to humans? Explain your answer.

6 State two sources of background radiation and give some information about each.

7 What is your opinion about the use and testing of nuclear power and its effect on our environment?

Taking into account?

Background radiation is always there. So when you are doing an experiment with a radioactive source, the Geiger counter will read the activity of the source plus the background radiation.

The correct experimental technique is always to measure background radiation before you begin your experiment. Then once your experimental results are tabulated, you must remember to subtract the average background reading from each reading.

FIGURE 3: Radiation monitoring in London.

Averaging out

Radioactive decay is random, which means that radiation does not emit as a steady stream of particles or rays. You might, for example, get three or four pulses almost together, then one on its own.

The right technique to measure the rate of radioactive decay is to use a stop clock, count the number of pulses for 10 seconds and then average per second. Repeat several times. You will find that you begin to get a consistent average for the rate of decay.

QUESTIONS

8 During experimental work, why should you take background radiation into account? How would you do this?

9 Why is it important to use the word 'average' when measuring or discussing rates of radioactive decay?

Inside the atom

You will find out:
- How the Thompson scattering experiment revealed the true structure of the atom
- About the electrical and the strong nuclear force

The structure of the atom

It was the Greeks who first used the word 'atom' to express the idea of an indivisible particle. But it was John Dalton, an English chemist and physicist, who developed the first scientific theory (1810) of atomic structure. In 1897, JJ Thompson discovered the existence of a much smaller particle than the atom: the electron. Recognising that electrons had a negative charge and that atoms were neutral, he put forward the idea (1904) that atoms were like a blob of positive matter studded inside with a number of negative electrons. This was nicknamed the **'plum pudding' model** of an atom.

But it was Ernest Rutherford, working at Manchester University with Hans Geiger and Ernest Marsden (1911), who carried out the famous scattering experiment which truly revealed the structure of the atom.

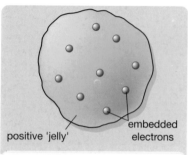

FIGURE 1: Thompson's 'plum pudding' model.

positive 'jelly'

embedded electrons

FIGURE 2: The physicists JJ Thompson and Ernest Rutherford.

The scattering experiment

The three scientists set up an experiment where a thin beam of alpha particles was fired at a very thin foil of gold leaf. Bearing in mind Thompson's 'plum pudding' model, they expected the alpha particles to pass straight through the gold leaf. Instead they discovered that the alpha particles were scattered like the reflecting light beams of a torch.

They found that:
- most particles did indeed pass straight through the foil
- a few were deflected back, some through quite wide angles
- a very few bounced straight back towards the source.

These results were quite unexpected so Rutherford had to get down to working out what it all meant.

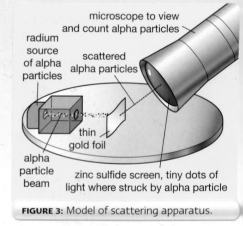

microscope to view and count alpha particles

radium source of alpha particles

scattered alpha particles

thin gold foil

alpha particle beam

zinc sulfide screen, tiny dots of light where struck by alpha particle

FIGURE 3: Model of scattering apparatus.

QUESTIONS

1. Describe the basic set-up of the scattering experiment, or draw a diagram.
2. What did the scientists expect to see happen? Why?
3. What did they actually observe?
4. Who were the three scientists involved in the famous scattering experiment?

...electrical force ...plum pudding model

So what did it all mean?

Rutherford now took each of the experimental observations and tried to work out the meaning and implications. This is a good example of science at work. No one could see into an atom, but looking at the experimental evidence, the scientists were able to apply their Physics knowledge and understanding and deduce what it all meant.

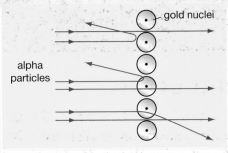

FIGURE 4: Diagram showing particle tracks.

■ The alpha particles which passed straight through the gold foil were unaffected by the atoms. This implied that they had passed through empty space.

Conclusion: the atoms in the gold foil contained a lot of empty space.

■ The positively charged alpha particles were deflected by the force of a repulsion. This could only happen if there was a central part of the atom which was positively charged.

Conclusion: the atom contains a positively charged core, the nucleus.

■ Very few alpha particles bounced straight back. They must have collided with something quite small but very heavy (relatively).

Conclusion: this nucleus must be very small but very dense.

■ What about all the electrons? They did not appear to influence the passage of particles.

Conclusion: electrons are not part of the inner atom (nucleus) but orbit in the empty space around the nucleus.

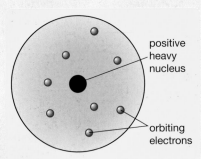

FIGURE 5: Rutherford's model of the atom.

■ Rutherford's model of the atom was accepted by the scientific community in 1911. Niels Bohr used the model to work out how electrons were able to orbit the nucleus without falling into it and went on to become the 'father of atomic theory', thanks to the original work of Rutherford, Geiger and Marsden.

QUESTIONS

5 Taking each of the observations from the scattering experiment:
  a Describe the observation.
  b State the implications.
  c What conclusion about the structure of the atom was reached by Rutherford and his fellow scientists?

Electrical vs strong nuclear force

■ Each nucleus contains a number of positively charged protons. Positive charges repel each other. This force of repulsion is called the **electrical force**. It is very strong because of the close proximity of protons to each other.

So what's stopping all the protons from flying apart?

■ There is another force, stronger than the electrical repulsion force which attracts the protons and neutrons and keeps the nucleus together. This force is called the **strong nuclear force**. This force is about 100 times stronger than the electrical repulsion force.

QUESTIONS

6 What would you expect to happen to a bunch of protons all bundled together? Why?

7 Why does this not happen?

8 What else can you say about the two forces?

Nuclear fission

You will find out:
- How the energy contained within an atom can be released
- What is meant by critical mass

The quest for energy

The world's need for energy is unquenchable. Industrialised nations in Europe and North America have well-established industrial and manufacturing bases and enjoy high standards of living. Developing nations like China, India and Brazil are fast catching up. It is the availability of cheap energy which underpins this growth and development.

Yet everyone is also aware of the problems caused by burning fossil fuels, our traditional cheap and easy-to-use energy sources. Soon fossil fuels will run out and, in the meantime, we are contaminating our Earth with carbon emissions and poisonous gases. So what is the way forward?

$E = mc^2$

This is Einstein's most famous equation. E = energy, m = mass and c = the speed of electromagnetic radiation (speed of light). The equation shows that mass and energy are interchangeable. Mass can be converted to energy and energy can be converted back to mass. C is just a constant (a number), but it is rather a large number: 300 000 000 m/s. So looking at the equation $E = mc^2$, we can see that a small amount of mass will produce huge quantities of energy.

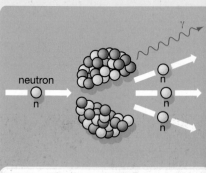

FIGURE 1: Single atom splitting.

Splitting the atom

One way of releasing the energy inside an atom is to split it. Large isotopes like uranium-235 and plutonium-239 are best suited to this purpose. A slow-moving neutron is fired into the nucleus of a uranium-235 atom. The large nucleus splits into two almost equal parts, releasing huge amounts of energy plus a few extra neutrons. This is called **nuclear fission**.

These extra neutrons move on and split more U-235 nuclei, releasing even more energy plus more neutrons. The increasing number of neutrons splits more and more nuclei so the reaction gets faster and faster. This is called a **chain reaction**.

The amount of nuclear energy released is prodigious. 1 kg of plutonium-239 can produce enough energy in it to keep a small town in electricity for a whole year, or produce an explosion equivalent to 20 000 tonnes of TNT.

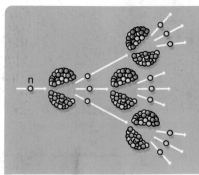

FIGURE 2: Chain reaction.

QUESTIONS

1. What is Einstein's famous equation? Write the equation and explain what each letter stands for.
2. What do you understand by nuclear fission?
3. Explain how splitting an atom of uranium can lead to a chain reaction.
4. Why is so much energy released from a small amount of uranium?

...chain reaction ...critical mass

Nuclear fission

Nuclear fission is the splitting of a large radioactive isotope like U-235 or P-239. Every time the U-235 atom splits it releases huge amounts of energy plus three extra neutrons. The three neutrons can then find three new atoms of U-235. When these three atoms split, you will have nine neutrons, and so on. It is like an avalanche, beginning slowly then getting faster and faster until it becomes unstoppable. This is why it is called a chain reaction.

■ **Critical mass**: If the initial size of uranium is smaller than a tennis ball, some of the neutrons will escape from the mass without hitting and splitting an atom. If this happens, the reaction cannot sustain itself and will stop.

If the size of uranium is larger than a tennis ball, all the neutrons will impact a U-235 atom and the chain reaction will take place.

The minimum amount of uranium required for the chain reaction to be sustained is called the critical mass.

■ The atomic bomb is an example of nuclear fission as an uncontrolled chain reaction. The avalanche of neutrons becomes so great, the number of atoms being split so large, that it results in a huge release of uncontrolled and destructive energy: the atomic bomb.

FIGURE 3: An atomic bomb detonation.

FIGURE 4: A nuclear power station.

■ But it is possible to control and tame this chain reaction. By checking the numbers of neutrons, scientists can control the rate of the chain reaction and therefore the rate at which energy is released. This technology is used to our benefit in nuclear power stations.

Nuclear equations

Fission reactions can be represented in the form of an equation. This shows the original atom of uranium and the incoming neutron leading to the formation of the two new products, the three neutrons and the release of energy.

■ The superscript number is the atomic mass, which equals the sum of protons and neutrons.

■ The subscript number is the atomic number, which equals the number of protons.

$$^{235}_{92}U + ^{1}_{0}n \longrightarrow$$
$$^{90}_{36}Kr + ^{143}_{56}Ba + ^{1}_{0}n + ^{1}_{0}n + ^{1}_{0}n + \text{energy}$$

QUESTIONS

9 How many protons and neutrons does an atom of U-235 contain?

10 What does the notation $^{1}_{0}n$ indicate?

11 What are the **two** new elements formed from the split uranium atom?

12 Mass is always conserved. Check out the superscript and subscript numbers from both sides of the equation.

QUESTIONS

5 Why can a fission reaction become unstoppable?

6 Why do we need a critical mass of uranium to ensure the reaction gets going? What will happen if there is less than the critical mass of uranium?

7 What is the result if a nuclear fission reaction becomes unstoppable? Explain your answer.

8 What must scientists do to harness this energy safely?

Nuclear power station

The nuclear power station

All power stations generate electricity in the same way. High pressure steam is jetted onto high speed turbine blades; the turbine spins and drives a generator which in turn produces electricity. Step-up transformers lift the potential to very high voltages, link into the National Grid which delivers to each city and town in the country.

The differences lie in the way that the steam is produced. Coal, oil and gas-fired power stations burn fossil fuels to heat water in a huge boiler to produce the super-heated steam which drives the turbine. A nuclear power station uses nuclear energy to heat water to become super-heated steam.

The nuclear reactor

In a nuclear reactor, energy is generated by long thin fuel rods which are inserted into the **core** of the reactor. The core is surrounded by pressurised water (sometimes gas) which is pumped through the core to carry away the heat energy. The pressurised hot water is passed through a **heat exchanger** where a separate water supply is boiled to super-heated steam. The most common type of nuclear reactor is the pressurised water reactor (PWR).

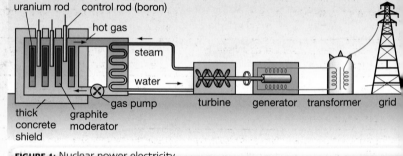

FIGURE 1: Nuclear power electricity.

The speed of the nuclear reaction is controlled in two ways: the use of a **moderator** and **control rods**.

- Moderator: The neutrons released when a U-235 atom is split have a high velocity. At such high speeds neutrons cannot easily penetrate a nucleus; they bounce off. They need to be slowed down. This is done either by graphite rods or the cooling water surrounding the core.

- Control rods: Once the nuclear reaction starts, the speed of reaction is controlled by the number of neutrons available. Control rods made of boron or cadmium absorb neutrons.

Raising or lowering the rods from the core controls the number of free neutrons and hence the speed of the nuclear reaction.

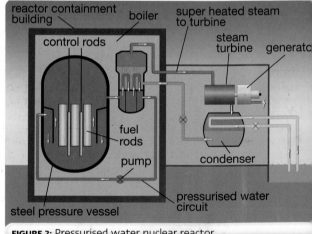

FIGURE 2: Pressurised water nuclear reactor.

QUESTIONS

1. In the UK we have fossil-fuel and nuclear power stations. In what ways are they similar and in what ways are they different from each other?

2. How is the heat energy of the nuclear reaction used to make super-heated steam?

3. Once the chain reaction starts we should get an uncontrolled nuclear explosion. Why does this not happen in a nuclear reactor in a power station?

...control rods ...core ...heat exchanger ...moderator

The nuclear debate

The nuclear debate is a hot issue. Everyone knows that burning fossil fuels causes the greenhouse effect and acid rain. But they are cheap and convenient.

Nuclear power is 'clean' but what if something goes wrong? The consequences can be disastrous (Chernobyl, 1994). And what do we do with the long-term **radioactive waste**?

Renewable energy seems a good alternative. But the technology is inefficient and not well developed. At the moment, it cannot supply energy cheaply enough in the quantities required to satisfy the world's demand.

It is a complex issue with no obvious answer. But it does stir deep passions in people on both sides of the debate.

What is your opinion?

For	Against
We need more nuclear power stations to satisfy our energy requirements in order to maintain our standard of living.	We should become more energy efficient. We should save energy and insulate our homes to ensure that demand for energy does not keep rising.
Nuclear power can replace fossil fuels which will soon run out.	Renewable energy (solar, wave, wind, tidal etc) does less damage to the environment.
Nuclear power is 'clean'. It does not produce CO_2 and SO_2 so will reduce the greenhouse effect and acid rain.	Nuclear power leaves waste material which will be radioactive for thousands of years.
The amount of nuclear waste is relatively small. It can be safely disposed of by encasing it in glass and burying it deep underground.	Leaving such dangerous waste is irresponsible with regards to future generations. What if it begins to leak out and contaminate the land?
Only a tiny fraction (0.1%) of background radiation is due to the nuclear industry.	No level of radioactivity is acceptable. Children living near nuclear power stations have an increased chance of leukaemia.
The technology of nuclear power stations is well developed and very safe.	The Chernobyl disaster was due to human error. Its effects were felt throughout most of Europe. Many people locally died. We cannot take such risks.
The risks to people due to the nuclear industry are minimal compared to other possible areas of concern, e.g. cancer, heart disease, road accidents.	Comparing this to other risks is not appropriate. All it takes is one mistake, one disaster and we might destroy our world for future generations.

Nuclear fuel

Uranium is the fuel for nuclear reactors. U-238 is the most common radioactive element found in the Earth's crust but it has to be enriched before it can be used as a nuclear fuel. The enriched uranium, U-235 and U-238, is pressed into pellets and placed into stainless steel tubes to become the fuel rods for the reactor. As the uranium fuel is used up it changes into **plutonium**, which has to be disposed of safely.

The spent fuel can be reprocessed to recover useable uranium which is then re-enriched and recycled back into the reactor. Sellafield in Cumbria is such a reprocessing plant. The spent fuel can also be set into solid glass and stored deep underground.

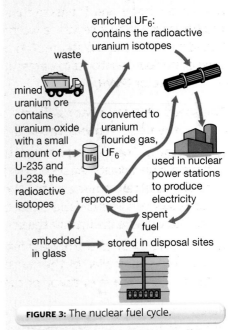

FIGURE 3: The nuclear fuel cycle.

QUESTIONS

4   Working in groups of four, discuss the issues regarding nuclear energy.

5   Write down your own thoughts and feelings.

6   Give your reasons for your standpoint.

7   Can you argue the points made against your point of view?

QUESTIONS

8   Look at each step of the nuclear fuel cycle. Discuss in small groups. What are your impressions?

9   Would you like to live close to the Sellafield reprocessing plant in Cumbria? Why?

...*plutonium*   ...*radioactive waste*   ...*uranium*

Nuclear fusion

You will find out:
- How energy can be released through the fusion of two small atoms

Nuclear fusion

You have studied how energy can be released by splitting the large nuclei of uranium and plutonium. But there is another way to get energy from inside the nucleus. The Sun and stars get their energy from the opposite process to nuclear fission. Small light nuclei join and fuse together. This forms a larger nucleus and a huge amount of energy is released. This is called **nuclear fusion**.

Einstein's equation $E = mc^2$ comes into play again. Some of the mass of the two light nuclei is lost and converted to energy. This is the process by which stars use hydrogen as a fuel to ignite and power the nuclear fusion reaction in their core.

A star is born

Space isn't as empty and void as you might think. It is full of gas – mostly hydrogen – and dust and particles all floating about in huge clouds called **nebula**. Even the tiniest particle has mass, so the force of gravity gradually begins to attract molecules of gas and dust together. With time, the cloud pulls itself together into a ball of matter.

As the size of the ball grows, the pressure inside the core increases and the centre becomes solid and very dense. As the particles are pulled into the mass, their potential energy is changed into kinetic energy. Molecules begin to vibrate more and the temperature in the core begins to rise. This is the first beginnings of a star coming to life. It would look like a huge dull red glow hanging in space. At this stage it is called a **protostar**.

FIGURE 1: A star is born.

With time, more matter is pulled in, the size increases and the core becomes hotter and hotter. At about 15 million Kelvin, hydrogen molecules fuse spontaneously and a nuclear fusion reaction ignites within the core of the protostar. It explodes brilliant white, and a star is born.

The word equation for this nuclear fusion is:

$$\text{Hydrogen} \xrightarrow{\text{nuclear fusion}} \text{Helium} + \text{Energy}$$

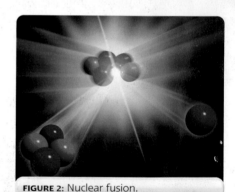
FIGURE 2: Nuclear fusion.

QUESTIONS

1. What are the **two** ways that energy can be released from inside a nucleus?
2. Describe each type of reaction and show how they are different from each other.
3. Describe how a cloud of hydrogen gas can become a star.
4. Write the equation which shows how energy is released by nuclear fusion.

...nebula   ...nuclear fusion

15 million Kelvin

Nuclear fusion requires huge temperatures to initiate the reaction. Two hydrogen protons will naturally repel each other. The temperature must be high enough to give the protons enough kinetic energy to overcome this force of repulsion. They must be travelling at very high speeds to get close enough to each other for the nuclei to fuse together.

Proton–proton reaction

The fusion of hydrogen to produce helium is a three-stage process. This is called the proton–proton chain.

1. proton + proton = hydrogen 2 + electron + neutrino

2. hydrogen 2 + proton = helium 3 + photon

3. helium 3 + helium 3 = helium 4 + proton + proton

You can see that the sequence begins with two protons colliding and ends with helium and two more protons. These two protons work their way back into the beginning of the next reaction cycle. And so the fusion reaction becomes a self-perpetuating chain.

FIGURE 3: Birth of a star.

WOW FACTOR!

Nuclear fusion is a very effective way of releasing energy. Our Sun will have a life of 10 billion years. It's just about halfway through its life cycle.

QUESTIONS

5   Explain why the temperature for the fusion of hydrogen nuclei has to be so high.

6   Write out the proton–proton chain reaction.

7   Can you suggest why this reaction allows a star to carry on its nuclear fusion reaction for millions of years?

Fusion energy?

■ So can we harness this fusion energy for our own use? This is a very clean and efficient way of producing energy. All we need is hydrogen, which is plentiful, cheap and easy to obtain. Just at the moment, the answer is: 'not yet... but we're working on it'.

■ Getting nuclei up to a temperature of 15 million K is problematic.

■ The reaction has to be contained in an electromagnetic field, because any container will have vaporised.

■ And how do you control the reaction? There are no control rods or moderators like you have in a nuclear fission reactor. Nuclear fusion reactions have been initiated, but only as an uncontrolled explosion: the hydrogen bomb.

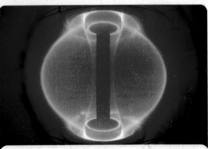

FIGURE 4: Fusion research.

FIGURE 5: A hydrogen bomb explosion.

QUESTIONS

8   Why is nuclear fusion energy a particularly good option to pursue?

9   Why has this technology been particularly difficult to develop?

10 Has there been any successful example of nuclear fusion?

Unit summary

Concept map

Ohm's Law states that: potential difference = current $\times$ resistance.

A diode allows current to flow in one direction only.

The resistance of a filament lamp increases as the temperature of the filament increases.

The resistance of a light dependent resistor (LDR) decreases as light intensity increases.

Resistance

The resistance of a thermistor decreases as the temperature increases.

Components can be connected in series and in parallel.

In the UK, mains electricity is 230 V a.c. 50 Hz and is extremely dangerous.

Power supplies can be both d.c. and a.c.

An oscilloscope shows the voltage and the frequency of electricity.

The current through an appliance and the size of fuse required can be calculated by using:
power = current $\times$ potential difference.

Mains electricity

Fuses protect appliances and earth wires protect the user. Three-pin plugs must be correctly wired and hold the correct fuse.

Electric current is the flow of charge. Electrical energy is transformed to heat energy when electric charge flows though a resistor.

The Rutherford-Marsden scattering experiment revealed the structure of the atom.

Radioactive substances

Atoms of the same element with the same number of protons, but a different number of neutrons are called isotopes.

An atom consists of a small dense nucleus of protons and neutrons surrounded by shells of fast-moving electrons.

Background radiation comes mainly from rocks, soil, cosmic rays, living things and medical X-rays.

Alpha particles are helium ions and beta particles are electrons.

Nuclear fission is the splitting of an atomic nucleus. It releases a great deal of energy and if the chain reaction gets out of control, a nuclear explosion can occur. U-235 and Pu-239 are fissionable elements in common use in nuclear reactors.

Nuclear fission and nuclear fusion

Nuclear fusion is the joining of two smaller nuclei to form a larger one. This is the process by which energy is released in stars.

1 Draw a circuit which has a battery, two bulbs, a switch and an ammeter connected in series.

2 State the Ohm's Law equation which links potential difference, current and resistance.

3 Draw the current–voltage graph for a filament bulb. Explain why it is this shape and not a straight line.

4 a) What can you say about the current flowing in a series circuit?

   b) How would you calculate the total resistance of such a circuit?

   c) Is the potential difference shared amongst the components or is it the same for each one?

5 a) How is current distributed throughout a parallel circuit?

   b) Is the potential difference shared amongst the components or is it the same for each one?

6 Name the colour of each wire in a three-pin plug and state the function of each one.

7 Why should all three-pin plugs be properly wired and fitted with the correctly rated fuse?

8 What is so important about the earth wire?

9 How is UK mains electricity described on an appliance ID label?

10 Describe the famous experiment carried out by Rutherford, Marsden and Geiger. Why was it so important?

11 What is an isotope?

12 Describe what you understand by nuclear fission.

13 Which two fissionable substances are most commonly used in a nuclear reactor?

14 What is a chain reaction and why is it so dangerous?

15 Describe what you understand by nuclear fusion.

Citizenship activity

Nuclear power: Salvation or judgement day?

The need for energy is unquenchable. In order to continue to sustain growth and development, the world needs infinite sources of cheap and convenient energy.

Fossil fuels are our traditional source of energy. But one day soon fossil fuels are going to run out and, in the meantime, we are contaminating and choking our Earth with carbon emissions and poisonous gases.

So what is the way forward? Should we just continue using fossil fuels and let the Earth take care of itself? Should we turn to renewable energy and go for wind farms, solar panels and water power? Should we go nuclear?

Renewable energy is clean, but at the moment the technology is expensive, inefficient and needs lots more development. It cannot provide the amounts of energy we currently require.

Nuclear energy is clean. There are almost limitless supplies of energy contained within the nucleus of every atom. But what if something goes wrong? The consequences can be disastrous – as they were in Chernobyl in 1994. What do we do with the long-term radioactive waste and what about the high cost of decommissioning?

QUESTIONS

1 What is the problem with the world's need for energy?

2 What options are open to us?

3 State some of the pros and cons for each option.

4 Is there an obvious way forward?

5 What would be your preferred option? Explain why.

Exam practice

Exam practice questions

1 The diagrams show 15 ohm resistors connected in two different circuits.

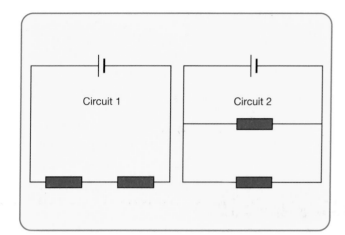

a Calculate the total resistance of Circuit 1. [2]

b Copy and complete the table to show how the potential difference varies in different circuits. [4]

	Series	Parallel
Current through each component is ...		
Potential difference across each component is ...		

2 A washing machine has a metal outer case. A radio has a plasic outer case.

a State one safety feature that will be included in the plug of both appliances, and explain how this feature works. [3]

b State one safety feature that is included in the plug of the washing machine but not the plug of the radio, and explain how this feature works [3]

3 **a** Copy and complete the table to show the mass and charge of atomic particles. [4]

	Mass	Charge
Proton	1	
Neutron		
Electron	negligible	

b Explain the difference between nuclear fission and nuclear fusion. [2]

c For each type of nuclear reaction, give an example of where these reactions occur.

d Carbon-12 and carbon-14 are examples of isotopes. State one difference and two similarities between an atom of each isotope.

e Some isotopes are radioactive and may decay by emitting beta particles. State how the mass and charge of a radioactive nucleus will change after undergoing beta decay.

f Rutherford and Marsden carried out an experiment by firing positively charged helium nuclei at thin gold foil.

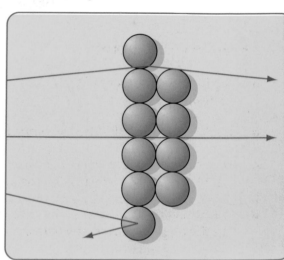

State why some nuclei passed through undeviated, while others changed direction. Explain how this provided evidence for the nuclear model of the atom. [3

4 This information was found on the base of a kettle:

> Power: 2300 W
> Voltage supply: 230 V a.c.

a Explain what is meant by the term: 230 V a.c [2

b Calculate the current flowing through the kettle. [3

c Explain which is the most suitable fuse rating for the kettle: 3 A, 10 A or 13 A [2

During an experiment, it was noticed that a sample gave off alpha radiation. The final measurements showed that the nuclei resulting from this nuclear reaction had an atomic mass number of 222 and charge of 86.

a How do the alpha particles given off by the sample affect nearby molecules in the air? [1]

b The initial measurements allowed for background radiation. State one source of background radiation in the laboratory. [1]

c What was the mass number and proton number of the original nuclei? [2]

(Total 39 marks)

Worked example

A radio is marked '6 V 0.4 A'.

a Calculate the resistance of the radio when it is working normally. [3]

b Calculate the charge flowing through the radio in 10 minutes. [3]

c Suggest a suitable component that could be used to control the volume on the radio and draw its symbol. [2]

d Explain how the resistance of the radio may change slightly after it has been on for a few hours. [2]

Full marks – remember to include units as appropriate.

a *resistance = volts/amps = 6/0.4 = 15 ohms*

The pupil loses one mark as they forgot to change minutes to seconds (by multiplying by 60).

b *charge = current × time = 0.4 × 10 = 4 coulombs*

Full marks – make sure you are familiar with the symbols used!

c *A variable resistor*

The student loses one mark – the resistance increases.

d *The circuit heats up and the resistance changes.*

Overall Grade: B

How to get an A

There is a lot of detail to get right in this topic. Learn the symbols thoroughly so you can recognise and draw components. Look out for tricks in equations – remember time should usually be converted into seconds and always show working and units!

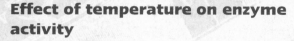
Effect of temperature on enzyme activity

Emma and David were asked to design and carry out an experiment to test the hypothesis that:

Amylase digests starch faster at higher temperatures.

This is what they did.

- They took four boiling tubes, all the same size.
- They measured 5 cm³ of starch solution into each boiling tube.
- They measured 5 cm³ of amylase solution into each boiling tube.
- They wrote a letter on each tube, and then put each one into a water bath at a different temperature. They drew a table like this, to remind them which tube was at which temperature.

tube	A	B	C	D
temperature / °C	0	20	40	60

- Every 2 minutes, they took a drop of liquid out of each tube, and tested it with iodine solution. They did this for 30 minutes.

These are the results that they found:

- The drops taken from tubes A and D were still turning the iodine solution blue-black at the end of their experiment.
- The drops from tube B turned the iodine blue-black up to 10 minutes, then after that the iodine stayed orange-brown.
- The drops from tube C turned the iodine blue-black up to 4 minutes, then after that the iodine stayed orange-brown.

Questions

1   What was the independent variable in Emma and David's investigation?

2   What was the dependent variable?

3   State **two** variables that they controlled in their investigation.

4   Copy Emma and David's table, and then extend it to show the results of their experiment.

5   Explain why the iodine solution sometimes went black, and sometimes stayed orange-brown.

6   Do Emma and David's results support their hypothesis? Use their results to explain your answer.

7   Their teacher was not impressed by their investigation. She said: "I don't think your results even prove that amylase digests starch at all."

(a) Explain why the teacher was right.

(b) Suggest what Emma and David should have done to avoid this problem with their experiment.

8   Suggest **two other** ways in which they could have improved the method of their investigation. For each one, explain why you think this would make it a better investigation.